Lincoln's Speeches
Reconsidered

LINCOLN'S SPEECHES

RECONSIDERED

John Channing Briggs

THE JOHNS HOPKINS UNIVERSITY PRESS

BALTIMORE & LONDON

Title page illustration: Chicago Historical Society.
Glass negative DN-0007097A, photographed
by *Chicago Daily News*

© 2005 The Johns Hopkins University Press
All rights reserved. Published 2005
Printed in the United States of America
on acid-free paper

2 4 6 8 9 7 5 3 1

The Johns Hopkins University Press
2715 North Charles Street
Baltimore, Maryland 21218-4363
www.press.jhu.edu

Library of Congress Cataloging-in-Publication Data
Briggs, John Channing, 1948–
Lincoln's speeches reconsidered / John Channing Briggs.
p. cm.
Includes bibliographical references and index.
ISBN 0-8018-8106-4 (hardcover : alk. paper)
1. Lincoln, Abraham, 1809–1865—Literary art. 2. Speeches,
addresses, etc., American—History and criticism. I. Title.
E457.2.B835 2005
973.7'092—dc22   2004021139

A catalog record for this book is available
from the British Library.

For my children

CONTENTS

ACKNOWLEDGMENTS

I am grateful for the sabbaticals and other research assistance afforded me over the years by the University of California. To the students and faculty in my department of English at the University of California, Riverside, I give my thanks for encouraging me to pursue a project I hoped would restore to the field of English a love of great nonfiction prose. To Scott Crider and the faculty of the University of Dallas, I owe a debt of gratitude for the opportunity to try out my ideas before lively, demanding audiences in Rome, Italy, and Dallas, Texas. My appreciation goes as well to Douglas L. Wilson, who read a primitive draft of chapter 9 with remarkable patience, and who should bear no responsibility for any defects in the final version. I would also like to thank the Johns Hopkins University Press for its early interest, and especially the anonymous senior historian who prepared many thoughtful suggestions for the final stage of revision. To my family, who were in my thoughts as I wrote these pages, I tender this book as a token of what is beyond words.

NOTE ON SOURCES

For the sake of standardization and ease of reference, all citations from Lincoln's works, unless otherwise specified, refer to volume and page number in Basler's edition: *The Collected Works of Abraham Lincoln,* edited by Roy P. Basler, 9 vols. (New Brunswick, N.J.: Rutgers University Press, 1953). All biblical references are taken from the ubiquitous King James Version. All citations of Shakespeare draw from *The Riverside Shakespeare,* edited by G. Blakemore Evans (Boston: Houghton Mifflin, 1997).

Lincoln's Speeches
Reconsidered

The Mind of the Persuader

It is plain that [Lincoln] was not innocent of the subtle arts of the public speaker. He cared more for his thought than for his style; but he cared so much for his thought that he studied with care the means of making it incisive and effective.

—Charles Smiley, "Lincoln and Gorgias"

Lincoln's power of speech served and elucidated his thought as he found his way into American history. In reconsidering his speeches, this book joins the work of historians and other scholars who, amid the riches of modern secondary scholarship, continue to be attracted to Lincoln's words. Concentrating on the best evidence we have of the motions of Lincoln's mind, these pages seek to complement historical research by directing attention to the interplay of form, substance, and context in the most primary records available. The prepresidential speeches, which tend to be overshadowed by the greatness of the presidential oratory, are the first subjects for investigation, for here Lincoln's art of oratory emerges to test itself against increasingly difficult challenges. When several of the great presidential speeches take our attention in the final chapters, we can approach them with the benefit of a gradual preparation in the woods and fields of Lincoln's earlier works.

Within an immensely promising, hazardous, and problematic environment, Lincoln achieved an oratorical distinction in the prepresidential years that may yet be underestimated. Confronting him were the seemingly intractable problem of slavery and the profound sectional and social fragmentation that followed the Era of Good Feeling. He began his rise toward oratorical prominence in a time when Jacksonian democracy and rapid expansion had put new demands on public rhetoric, simultaneously inflating and diminishing expectations for public speech. Any attempt to create an ed-

1

ifying eloquence for the new era—to compose and deliver oratory that would engage and raise the faculties of citizens in the growing republic—had to cope with newly emerging ideas of democratic citizenship, increasingly contentious debates over slavery, and the resultant sectional differences that seemed to be mollified (and yet were profoundly aggravated) by economic growth and the creation of new states.

In one sense, the situation rewarded silence and oratorical vacuity. It fostered a congressional gag rule, while encouraging a habit of issuing implicit threats. Jackson's Farewell Address and Martin Van Buren's First Inaugural both warned against raising issues, especially the slavery question, that would threaten the peace. The circumstances promoted legalism at the expense of deliberation and fostered irresponsible hopes for technological and territorial solutions to deeply human and political dilemmas. The conditions Lincoln referred to in his Lyceum Address of 1838 were the twin dangers of mob rule and political apathy. The very success of the American experiment, he believed, had begun to lure overconfident free men toward tyranny. Public rhetoric was under extraordinary pressure to subdue or inflate itself, to abandon its offices of genuine persuasion and edification.

The Lyceum Address drew attention to an additional danger: the ideas and aspirations that had so recently moved the country into its new circumstances were gradually losing their connection with the original (and most credible) actors in the drama of self-government. With suddenness and finality, the death of each Founder tolled the end of the republic's opening era and signaled the need for an untested generation to acknowledge these new circumstances and take up the responsibilities of self-government. For Lincoln, of course, the problem of perpetuating self-government was connected, from the earliest stages of his career, with the anomaly of slavery's presence in a self-governing republic. In all his speeches, early and late, these issues blended into one another.

To appreciate the significance of this process, we need to resist our modern impatience and read slowly. One way to retard the rush toward closure is to return to the chronological study of a variety of key speeches. As we submit to the discipline of reading Lincoln's sentences slowly and in order, without overactive hindsight, we are more likely to discover or rediscover the overtones, bass notes, and arching themes of his oratorical achievement.

Perhaps the greatest barriers to such a method of reading are preconceptions of Lincoln as saint or sinner. If we assume he could do no wrong, that his ends clearly justified all his words and actions, then the close study of his public language can hardly contribute to our understanding of his eloquence. If we think we already know, as many students in schools and universities have been led to believe, that Lincoln was a racist and so not worth reading except for the sake of diagnosing his defective condition, the effort to read him carefully and extensively must seem useless, even incorrect. Thus, we face the difficult task of reading Lincoln while resisting hagiography or, conversely, we risk flattening our expectations for political speech—unless we pursue the possibility that we are reading something that might be far more than an artifact of historical forces or a tool of personal ambition.[1] The very magnitude of Lincoln's presidential legacy tends to dull the desire to read the prepresidential works. Forrest McDonald has observed a similar phenomenon in the modern reception of the writings of the American Founders. Their oratorical accomplishments, he says, have come to seem "of pedantic and picayune consequence" in comparison with the "monumental proportions" of their achievements.[2] All these tendencies tempt us to take a moral position that is akin to laziness. We risk failing to preserve and pass on this living archive of great political speech.

Lincoln's oratorical texts are so interesting that the more one reads them with curiosity, the more they enlarge the field of analysis. They are themselves the best instruments for questioning interpreters' unimaginative and hagiographical reductions of his persuasive efforts. By reading a range of Lincoln's speeches in sequence, we enter a literary and political world that invites us to put aside disabling preconceptions. We are given a new opportunity to reassess Lincoln's preoccupations, to learn how he uses persuasive speech to do justice to his subject matter and to test and project his purposes. The great differences between Lincoln's prepresidential and presidential eloquence are less likely to distract us from important consistencies in his oratorical and political career. And we are more likely to appreciate the deeper significance of his presidential transformation.

Paradoxically, a close reading of Lincoln's speeches can contribute to our appreciation of his circumstances. Not only reflections of their time, the speeches are also encounters with (and discoveries of) the stresses and oratorical opportunities associated with the antebellum period and the Civil War. In his own way Lincoln aspired to a kind of eloquence that his circumstances called for and lacked. He contributed to an oratorical tradition that demonstrated its own insufficiencies even as it influenced him to create extraordinary examples of the oratorical art.

Many of the pressures working against eloquent speech in the 1830s were all the more powerful in the decade leading up to the Civil War. In an essay published in 1854, after the deaths of Webster, Calhoun, and Clay, and before Lincoln had achieved a national reputation, an anonymous author in the *United States Magazine and Democratic Review* lamented the decline of American oratory—its strange lack of great speakers despite the growth of the country and the surplus of false ones who "adopt too low a standard, and content themselves with a bare mediocrity" or drive out all caution with their overboldness. Viewed from one angle, the writer conceded, oratory was flourishing: "The People love to hear [speakers], and love to read their printed speeches whenever they get access to them. Hence, our public journals, which contain the speeches of our ablest orators, are sought with much eagerness and read with avidity. The efforts of our able speakers in Congress, will circulate in a few hours from end to end of our land, and be perused by thousands of eager readers, in their shops and countingrooms, and by their firesides and in their domestic circles." From another perspective, the vast opportunities awaiting the American orator seemed to distort him. His rhetoric hugged the earth or clawed the sky. What was needed, the *Review*'s writer asserted, was a hybrid oratorical power of "great boldness" as well as "vividness and force," a power that was not indifferent to "the modesty of nature [and] . . . strict philosophical accuracy," and yet of sufficient magnitude to "open the floodgates of the sensibility within us, and thus to bring into exercise our active powers for the promoting of good or the preventing of evil."[3]

Of course, the essayist conceded, the proposed cure might, if poorly understood, create new oratorical aberrations. Boldness and vividness might promote false views or appeal to the heart in misleading ways. Genuine oratory needed to work "through the understanding and the conscience," but even those mediating channels would be insufficient influences unless the orator appealed to the "American character." What distinguished the American audience, the essayist argued, was its yearning to be moved toward certain kinds of conviction that perfected its character. In this context, persuasion was assumed to be edification, which engaged the moral sense and the passions of the mind. The passions most worth cultivating were those capable of being "excited by any great subject of commanding interest to the mind." The mind could be "exceedingly delighted or exceedingly pained under a sense of the magnitude of the urgency" of the views it came to hold.[4]

These intriguing recommendations tell us something about the complexity of antebellum conceptions of oratorical persuasion. For the *Review* writer, the passions are causes of and responses to the mind's notions of significance. The mind is itself influenced by intellectual passions that arise from its contact with subjects of "commanding interest." Mind and passion may be proverbially at odds, as Lincoln argued insistently early in his career; but they are also potentially reciprocal. In the *Review* writer's world, they must both be substantially engaged if eloquence is to call the American character to better versions of itself.

As soon as we turn to Lincoln's speeches for guidance in these matters, we encounter a number of interpretive problems related to the difficulties Lincoln faced as he composed them. He was clearly interested in helping audiences rediscover and act upon principles of self-government, which were informed by a particular understanding of human nature and ideas such as those set out by the opening lines of the Declaration of Independence. Yet the ease with which one could lose one's grip on the principles of self-government, as Lincoln noted in his Lyceum Address, was not the simple result of moral failings or common ignorance, and so was not amenable to correction by oratory that was merely didactic or impassioned. If indeed the experience of the American founding was inevitably fading as the first American generation passed away, the uncoordinated power of memory, mind, and passion to hold that experience in the imagination was inadequate. The principles of the revolution had to be revivified and adapted under arduous circumstances that required new forms of speech.

Lincoln's position was doubly problematic because his thought was often intricate, layered, controversial, in many ways not in conformity with common opinion. His self-presentation was proverbially direct and simple, yet also in some ways awkward and strange. Anyone who reads the primary record in sequence runs into his paradoxical complexity. The friendliest audiences of Lincoln's prepresidential and presidential years were not likely to be receptive to the full range of his political views. Lincoln needed strategies to reach them and to make his points without distorting his ideas. He needed to be shrewd; but he could not consistently or predominantly rely on merely tactical maneuvers if he was to succeed by his own standards.

Testimony from Lincoln's friends and acquaintances indicates that he did not often reveal himself. His political wariness even in apparently free, informal conversation was a memorable attribute. Joshua Speed, probably his closest friend in his early Springfield years, recollected that in the late 1830s Lincoln had dominated the humorous nightly talks in Speed's store without discussing politics, the very thing that seems to have brought him to Springfield.[5] Henry Whitney, who traveled with Lincoln for many years on the Illinois circuit in the 1850s, insisted that his friend's straightforwardness was real, but that it did not transmit his intentions: Lincoln "never, at any time, did anything for dramatic effect, and his mental processes were furtive and secret."[6] Lincoln devoted himself to making good arguments that eschewed mere show; but he did not display his deeper purposes: "Mr. Lincoln could not talk for effect; he could not talk *to* nothing nor *about* nothing. He must be argumentative or nothing. He must have something to prove and somebody to convince."[7] Yet he "could far more effectively employ language to conceal his thought than Talleyrand . . . could do; and while guilty of no duplicity, could hide his thoughts and intentions more efficiently than any man with a historical record."[8]

The gist of the testimony we have from Lincoln's contemporaries indicates that he met the challenge of speaking publicly under these conditions by crafting oratorical forms of great simplicity and depth. Although he was proverbially direct in his political speech, he was also a calculating speaker, one who chose his words with great care. He carefully rationed even his expressions of humor according to his purposes. The general seriousness of most of his speeches was, according to Isaac Arnold (a friend for twenty years), the result of a conscious choice to limit his use of jokes and funny stories even though he knew they made him popular: "Sometimes when Lincoln's friends urged him to raise a storm of applause (which he could always do by his happy illustrations and amusing stories), he refused, saying the occasion was too serious, the issue 'too grave.' 'I do not seek applause,' said he, 'nor to amuse the people, I want to convince them.'"[9] In a similar vein, his law partner William Herndon noted a pattern of simplicity in Lincoln's bearing which, on the one hand, struck him as the opposite of art: "He never sawed the air nor rent space into tatters and rags as some orators do. He never acted for stage effect. He was cool, considerate, reflective—in time self-possessed and self-reliant. His style was clear, terse, and compact. In argument he was logical, demonstrative, and fair."[10] But Herndon observed as well that Lincoln developed a habit of delivery consisting of artful gesture, a habit all the more effective for being carefully rationed: "[Lincoln] did not gesticulate as much with his hands as with his head. He used the latter frequently, throwing it with vim this way and that."[11]

For some contemporary observers, of course, Lincoln's reputation for simplicity meant that he was not a leading orator. In 1861, the *Edinburgh Review* concluded, "[I]n a country where public speaking is one of the chief avenues to power, he [Lincoln] did not aspire to oratorical fame."[12] But Lincoln's simplicity in motion and speech was largely the result of arduous practice. According to Joseph Gillespie, a trusted friend for three decades, Lincoln's success on the stump stemmed from his habits of self-denial, constant labor, and reliance upon forms of logic that gave body and force to his arguments:

> If Mr Lincoln studied any one thing more than another and for effect it was to make himself understood by all classes[.] He had great natural clearness and simplicity of statement and this faculty he cultivated with marked assiduity[.] He despised everything like ornament or display & confined himself to a dry bold statement of his point and then worked away with sledge hammer logic at making out his case[.] I believe Mr Lincoln succeeded in his purpose for I think the great body of our People understood and appreciated him better than any man this Country ever produced[.][13]

Later interpreters remind us that his "sledge hammer logic" drew much of its strength from crafted tropes and occasional rhetorical flourishes. Pronunciation was important: Lincoln underlined key words for emphatic delivery so as to drive home his points. More important, he combined logic with rhetorical flourishes in such ways that, in the words of Charles Smiley, "the rhetorical forms that had been so severely censured as the marks of superficial sham and insincerity . . . somehow proved themselves capable of sincerity."[14]

The mere observation that Lincoln used rhetorical devices is misleading if we use it to explain away the paradoxical forms of Lincoln's speaking. Smiley, writing one hundred years ago, at a time when rhetorical training was still taken seriously, is careful not to reduce Lincoln's art to technique. Edward Pierce, a political friend during the war, recollected that Lincoln's simplicity was a convincing manifestation of what he most wanted to say. His "logical and reflective power," Pierce remembered, contrasted with an "absence of all attempt throughout his speech to produce a sensational effect."[15]

To understand more fully the eloquence that eschews eloquence in Lincoln's speeches, we need to take into account the subtler lineaments of his oratorical thought.

Lincoln's old friend Joshua Speed, who had no doubt about Lincoln's physical and moral courage, succinctly described the bravery in his ability to combine silence and frank statement. Lincoln "was cautious about expressing himself against public sentiment when it would do no good." Yet he was ready "when it became necessary" to express his views "with emphasis, earnestness, and force."[16] Speed detected a method in this alternation of concession and resolute insistence. In his friend's courtroom arguments, he saw an intriguing pattern of retreat, delay, and assertion: "He always resolved every question into its primary elements, and gave up every point on his own side that did not seem to be invulnerable. One would think to hear him present a case in the court, he was giving his case away. He would concede point after point to his adversary until it would seem his case was conceded entirely away. But he always reserved a point upon which he claimed a decision in his favor, and his concession magnified the strength of his claim."[17] Nicolay and Hay present a similar account of Lincoln's courtroom style, drawn from other witnesses.[18] Lincoln characteristically pared away his views, in seeming or genuine deference to his opponents' position, until he stood by a single decisive point. In the courtroom, he was well known for his habit of dispensing with the citation of legal authorities, even when they would have helped him, for the sake of winnowing the facts of the case until a basic principle or crucial observation could be brought to light.[19] This pattern of concession and resolute defense increased the chances for failure, and at the beginning of his career it may have been a way to cope with a lack of legal experience. Yet it persisted as a habit that tested and demonstrated the strength of his analysis, and of the principles that were central to his view. It tempered his discourse so that it became a rhetorical version of flexible steel.

Lincoln's habit of concession was in this sense an instrument of art. It was a form of indirection that focused attention, in the end, on what he did not concede. It should not shock us to recognize that it made him enemies as well as friends. Yet it was also a strategy that routinely created ethical tests for himself and his audiences. Having stripped his arguments of most of the usual appeals to authority, he ventured to offer himself to be proved wrong, *if* in the spare forms of his argumentation he proved insufficient. Surrounded by concessions to opposing views, the principles he did not concede took on additional force as the work of solitary resolve that others could identify in themselves—especially when Lincoln hit upon principles that disparate audiences, seeing that he understood their various points of disagreement, could discover they shared.

Again, the identification of a deep structure in Lincoln's prepresidential and presidential speeches is not, despite its usefulness, an adequate characterization of Lincoln's eloquence. The concessive-assertive trope had to take different forms in different speeches and had to be used appropriately and with proper timing in order to serve the full range of Lincoln's purposes. Implicit in these adjustments would have been Lincoln's grappling with the demands of necessity: the question of whether certain concessions had to be made because there seemed to be no alternative, or whether he needed to resist in order to honor a deeper necessity.

Of course, it is almost impossible to comment upon Lincoln's speeches without becoming involved in long-standing controversies over their silences, swerves, and declarations (especially those that concern slavery), the meaning of which often turns on the question of timing. Why in the early years as a speaker did he focus on the preservation of institutions and the encouragement of the Washingtonians' temperance movement? Why did he so vehemently oppose the Mexican War, perhaps at the expense of his congressional career, when it was popular in Illinois and had so little to do with issues with which he is now identified? Why, after a long period of quiescence, did he seem to force the slavery issue beginning in 1854? Why did he deliver the "House Divided" Speech in June 1858, using lines he had written but not delivered two years before? After losing the senatorial election to Douglas in 1858, why did he deliver academic lectures in Illinois and Wisconsin that seemed to have no connection with slavery? One question piles on another. If we examine some of the major speeches one by one, we can approach some of these issues from a familiar but novel direction—by taking into account many of the nuances of Lincoln's thought in the fabric of his public discourse. Without neglecting their political and historical contexts, we can observe how his speeches help to rearrange our retrospective speculations.

Lincoln not only had to "think hard," as Charnwood in his luminous 1917 biography noted few persons were able to do; he also had to be the sort of deep thinker who could "clothe" even some of his more difficult thoughts "in apt and simple words." He had to show himself able to do what "very,

very few" in that smaller group could do: "hold the attention of a miscella-neous and large crowd"[20] and do so in a way that held that audience in the presence of deep thoughts he did not and could not always communicate in full. Elucidation, far more than persuasion, was the stated goal; yet Lincoln would have had philosophical as well as practical reasons for relying on forms of persuasion that adumbrated—shadowed as well as clarified—the structure and substance of his thoughts. Separate reminiscences by Arnold and Herndon remark upon the effectiveness of the double action of thought-ful logic and careful persuasion that resulted from these preparations:

> It was often observed . . . that while Douglas was sometimes greeted with the loudest cheers, when Lincoln closed, the people seemed solemn and serious, and could be heard, all through the crowd, gravely and anxiously discussing the topics on which he had been speaking.[21]

> Douglas may have electrified the crowds with his eloquence or charmed them with his majestic bearing and dexterity in debate, but as each man, after the meetings were over and the applause had died away, went to his home, his head rang with Lincoln's logic and appeal to manhood.[22]

A book about Lincoln's eloquence cannot rest on his strategies and tac-tics. In the end, his eloquence is not interpretable unless one wrestles with what is being said. The focus of rhetorical analysis must be the unfolding of Lincoln's meaning in the words he chose. A close reading therefore needs to be in some sense unmethodical and, hence, vulnerable to the charge that it is not sufficiently "theorized"—not presented from a systematically analyzed point of view. Under the circumstances, the impulse to organize our precon-ceptions of Lincoln's speaking threatens to be a damaging preconception. If we immerse ourselves in the primary record of Lincoln's thoughts, we stand a better chance of learning to read Lincoln by reading Lincoln, much as his contemporaries tried to do. He becomes the best authority on his own elo-quence when we begin to see how his works of oratory are not only effective rhetorical gestures but also commentaries on themselves—on the means and ends that Lincoln has chosen to make his case.

One more fairly obvious qualification is in order. In order to read Lincoln closely, we need to familiarize ourselves with more of the things he read, because his speeches gain much of their meaning from their imitation, par-ody, correction, and departure from other speeches and a variety of collateral texts. Hence much of the following analysis depends on comparisons between Lincoln's formulations and those of his possible sources. Of course, those comparisons, no matter how illuminating, are frequently conditioned by another qualification: our uncertainty as to the extent and precision of Lincoln's use of particular texts. Reading Lincoln, whose fame for his allusions is matched by his reputation for almost always speaking in his own words and for transforming and eliding what he read, requires us to accept such imprecision for the sake of developing a clearer idea of what Lincoln was doing in his speeches.

The following chapters each focus on one major text or a small group of related works, attempting to grasp their formative principles and significance. They look into the way each performance seems to be made, what it is made of, and the purposes to which it is dedicated, in light of circumstances influencing those purposes, including Lincoln's care for the written record and his unusual sensitivity to the judgment of posterity. Each chapter seeks to understand the speeches' claim on our memory, their reason for being. The book's collection of chapters will have succeeded if it makes at least some of the qualities of Lincoln's eloquence more available to a wider audience, and his speeches more likely to be seen with fresh eyes.

To attempt such things, one must make choices. I do not discuss the Lincoln-Douglas debates. Their magnitude, and the amount of scholarly work already done on them, would turn attention away, if included here, from lesser-known works. I do not discuss several important speeches closely related to the debates: the Dred Scott Speech of 1857 and the Chicago Speech of July 1858. The interesting Speech on the Sub-Treasury (1839) and the Address to the Scott Club (1852) are worthy of attention; but their specialized subject matters would have required commentaries distracting to the plan of the book. There is a point beyond which a coherent book, when it takes on too many commentaries, becomes a reference work that is not read in its entirety. I have tried to write a book for an audience of specialists and general readers interested in reading these pages through.

Rhetorical Contexts

To study Abraham Lincoln then, we must examine his words, and not only the words that he wrote but also those that he uttered, insofar as they are known. . . . Sound interpretation of any historical text begins with an effort to determine the author's intended meaning. That includes paying attention to context and circumstance, keeping a sharp eye out for irony and other kinds of indirection, discriminating between denotative and connotative meanings, and coming to terms with the fact that intentions may be overt, or deliberately concealed, or at work only beneath the surface of consciousness.

—Don E. Fehrenbacher, *Lincoln in Text and Context*

Abraham Lincoln measured his words. He was acutely aware of the printed record of his writings and utterances and its possible influence upon his present and future audiences. Because those audiences were complex, spanning many political persuasions and electoral seasons, his language needed to work on multiple levels in a variety of ways. Thus, his words were calculated, though calculation was not enough to make them successful. His subjects, methods, and purposes wove and shaped his arguments, as did his engagement of the ideas and predilections of his audiences. And in order to be convincing in the way he intended it to be, his language had to be more than the sum of its parts, certainly more than an exhibition of his intention to win over his public.

Because many great speakers and writers undergo these challenges, a consideration of such factors does little to define Lincoln's achievement as a speaker and writer. What is remarkable about Lincoln's language is the degree to which it resonates throughout his career. To read him well is to listen for the multiple meanings within his printed texts, attempting to place them within a broader interpretation of his purposes. This ongoing process can sometimes discover and draw upon what listeners derived from the original performances, but it depends most of all on close readings of the printed speeches.

Knowledge of the historical context of Lincoln's words is of course a vital part of this interpretive process, and what follows is not intended to supplant historical investigation with close textual analysis. Rather, this work proposes that the depth and form of Lincoln's writings and utterances, and their remarkable continuity during the transformation of his public views and political fortunes, continue to be worthy subjects of inquiry. In fact, the more we learn about Lincoln, the more we wish to read him for ourselves. That experience is crucial to our full appreciation of historians' findings and serves to test our understanding of the man against the best evidence we have of the motions of his mind.

In November 1860, in the vexing time between Lincoln's election to the presidency and his inauguration, when many Americans were alarmed at his victory, his public voice was almost silent. He stood by the printed record. In a letter to a newspaper publisher who had asked him for a new statement of policy, perhaps to indicate that his views had changed under new circumstances, Lincoln concisely summarized his position: "I could say nothing which I have not already said, and which is in print and accessible to the public." His reluctance to speak was a form of eloquence; it declared a resolve not to change a position he thought the election had endorsed. "I am not at liberty to shift my ground—that is out of the question," his letter continued (4.140). His silence spoke beyond itself in another way, by highlighting his advice to make the newspapers' voluminous record available to the public. Lincoln had assembled the record of his 1858 debates with Douglas and organized its printing. He had edited many of his other speeches for publication in local journals. Numerous reports of his words had found their way into print.

The record, Lincoln argued, was clear. Given the tensions of the period immediately after the election, his public repetition of parts of the record might easily have changed its apparent meaning. The wrong kind of emphasis, even upon its unshakableness, might have altered or contradicted its significance. Opponents might have seized upon a statement out of context or assumed the speaker had been frightened into shrill repetition. Lincoln's supporters might have wondered whether he was subtly shifting his ground. It was better to make the record as accessible as possible, he wrote, by printing it in "copious extracts" in unfriendly newspapers as well as in friendly ones. That way a wider audience, including partisans from both sides, would be able to read and consider it (4.139–140). The "cure" for the country's "uneasiness" before the inauguration, he argued, would be the public's pondering of his words.

To read one speech well, one must read many, not only Lincoln's but also his contemporaries'. The advice Lincoln gives to the newspaper publisher suggests that a faithful reading of his written words should be "copious." Antebellum audiences, with their access to rail-delivered newspapers from throughout the country, were capable of such a task. Their periodicals' columns were often packed with summaries and transcriptions of political oratory. Selective, biased, and enthusiastic reporting presented an oratorical record that begged for study, comparison, and discussion. It seems likely that the public's high rate of literacy, its familiarity with public speaking, and its practice of reading aloud in company must have encouraged a habit of rereading that strengthened all these engagements with political speech.

Given that Lincoln's reputation is now again on the rise, why do his prewar speeches, other than the debates, remain in relative obscurity? Recent anthologies have included some of the earlier works, but interpretive criticism has been remarkably limited. Harry Jaffa's path-finding *Crisis of the House Divided*, which appeared in 1959,[1] remains a rare book-length attempt to give a number of Lincoln's prewar speeches a close reading. The ephemeral nature of most public oratory may explain why only a few oratorical texts have been preserved in the public imagination, to be pored over in repeated readings, while so many others have slipped into the quotidian flow of yesterday's newspaper. Newspaper archives are burgeoning repositories of history; but almost no modern reader who is not a professional investigator lingers over them. This is not true of earlier eras. The fact that Andrew Jackson carefully bound his own archive of periodicals, which were filled with the texts of lengthy speeches, is an indication of the reading habits of an age that saved and returned to a rich body of oratorical texts as part of the record of its political life.

Many of the concerns that preoccupied Lincoln and his audiences now seem arcane, but in Lincoln's lifetime, the general use of the term *literature* to include rhetorical works indicates that they were in more general circulation than they are today. Poetry and rhetoric were not by definition isolated from the world of fact and science nor was scientific writing barred from entering the realms of visionary and persuasive literary expression. Persuasion, whether it resulted from demonstration or appeals to principle, to the passions, or to settled opinion, was more readily accepted as a legitimate and even necessary activity of civilized life. Emerson's power of mixing ordinary concerns with flights of the philosophical imagination was unusual. But sermons, speeches, and essays were in general assumed to be occasions for making, or at least aspiring to make, literature that would be shared and remembered by the public.

Darwin's works were thought to be literature. In collegiate reading lists of the second half of the nineteenth century, he joined the company of Daniel Webster, Tennyson, and Shakespeare. All were treated as makers of literature. *The Western Orator,* an oratory textbook of the time, claimed to exemplify "the departments of popular, parliamentary, forensic, and dramatic eloquence, dialogue, poetry, humor, and burlesque."[2] The works of public speakers found a readership in the schools and colleges not yet influenced by the specialized modern academy's segregation of fiction from nonfiction, a separation at least as presumptuous as the indiscriminate fusion of poetry and science. The literary culture of the day, however sparse it might have been on the frontier, was conducive to an appreciation of rhetorical controversy. Many of the writings that were prominently accessible to a literate public shared an impulse, in James Engell's words, "to persuade, to carry one point of view, or to explore contested intellectual terrain."[3] Engell observes that Lincoln's formative reading put him in contact with the plain and probing energies of eighteenth-century rhetorical style as practiced by such masters as Gibbon, Addison and Steele, Defoe, Pope, and Johnson. We know he pored over Paine and Volney as well as Byron, Bunyan, and the Bible. He steeped himself in sources that presented him with overlapping and competing views of human possibility.[4]

The study of mathematics also played a role in Lincoln's rhetorical universe; the logic of geometry, with its austere dedication to axioms and deductive proofs, provided him with a means of concentrating his persuasive purposes. We know he carried Euclid's *Elements* on the circuit in the late 1840s and early 1850s and explicitly incorporated what he found there into his debates with Stephen Douglas.[5] At the same time, his attachment to Robert Burns's richly argumentative poetry exercised and broadened his early love of satire and controversy as well as his attraction to poetical expression. Enriched by his long-standing habit of borrowing books and reading a variety of newspapers (including subscribers' papers awaiting pickup in his New Salem store), he was from his early adulthood immersed, despite the frontier's lack of reading materials, in persuasive discourse influenced by older prose and poetry and an appreciation of logic.

The ubiquity of the Bible in largely Protestant, antebellum American households undoubtedly influenced the discursive habits of the day. If we trust Tocqueville's observation of frontier reading habits, Lincoln's rough upbringing in the civilizing company of the Bible and Shakespeare was not in all ways unique.[6] The rhythms and stories of biblical language not only influenced the sound and tenor of much formal speech and writing. Habitual reading of the Bible, silently and aloud, enforced the tendency to see a lesson in a story, a story in a lesson. The reading of Scripture had a power to settle a pioneer's soul to strains of a high yet vernacular King's English. Allied with the experience of listening to long weekly sermons, routine exposure to Scripture strengthened the capacity to attend to a range of registers in political speech.

The schoolbooks of the time encouraged routine recitation. We are probably wrong to assume that such absorption amounted to passive or ignorant conformity. Even if one accepts that such lessons dimmed students' critical faculties, they could also enlarge their repertoire of topics for recognizing and making arguments. Memorization and performance were the chief means of interpretation in an age that still put stock in arts of oral delivery, not just the elaborate schemes of physical gestures we see in some of the day's rhetorical handbooks. The art of reading was still in many ways an art of pronunciation, which tested the performer's power to comprehend, project, and be moved by the meaning of the text.[7] The coincidence of this practice with uninstructed common experience is evident in Lincoln's industrious habit, as a boy, of writing passages on a board, then placing them where he would see them, pore over them, and perform them before replacing them with new material. His brief experience in the crude "ranting" schools of his frontier schoolmasters, as ineffective as it probably was, combined reading and recitation in ways that could very well have strengthened his habit of absorbing and using the passages from great writers he found in his common reader.

We know that the habit of reading aloud to commit to memory extended into Lincoln's adulthood, much to the distress of his more genteel law partner, William Herndon. Lincoln's prodigious memory for words was, in his friends' experience, unique; but it also reflected the era's productive interest in reading, hearing, and revisiting poetical and persuasive speech. That interest is evident in the way Shakespeare traveled to the frontier, typically in the performance of set speeches, some of which had been printed in elementary textbooks for the purpose of memorization and performance. Lincoln's ability to give lengthy recitations from Shakespeare as well as from the works of Burns, William Knox, Byron, and other poets showed an unusual facility that complemented the pastimes of his age.

The ubiquity of persuasive speech in Lincoln's environment, however, does not permit easy generalizations about its particular bearing on Lincoln's oratory. Whatever evidence we can gather about early nineteenth-century America's capacity to appreciate, recite, understand, and compose various kinds of public oratory, Tocqueville's observations about democratic distrust of rhetorical flourishes should give us pause. *Democracy in America* is full of evidence that early America's democratic audiences, despite an interest in rhetorical display, were highly suspicious of the appearance of pretense—oratorical and otherwise. Attracted to the opportunities of the new republic and honed by the experience of securing the best chance, audiences were especially wary of what seemed undemocratic or might hinder their liberty of thought and action.

The promising conditions for American literature—including oratory—that Tocqueville observed in the 1830s were strangely limited, he thought, by democratic habits and enthusiasms that undermined the effort to create great literature.[8] His analysis of these limitations, which run counter to his great expectations for American democracy, is one of our best sources of information about the challenges Lincoln faced as an orator.

The United States represented, in Tocqueville's estimation, the greatest opportunity for oratorical excellence the world had known. Yet he worried that some democratic virtues, which needed a thriving oratory for their own prosperity, actually threatened the prospects of American eloquence. This danger ran counter to expectation, for the achievement of the American Revolution and the impressive development of the independent republic had been matched by the rhetoric of the founders. The oratory of the struggling American democracy had stirred Europe with its power of generalization. Unlike their predecessors in aristocratic nations, the early speakers for the American democracy could appeal to the nation as a whole rather than the interests of a class. Their circumstances drove them to consider general truths that superseded the intricacies of legal precedents. Because those truths had to do with human nature rather than the particular privileges of individuals, America's situation seemed to ensure that its speakers would address posterity, providing later ages with speeches worth reading and rereading.

> This was due not only to particular and fortuitous circumstances, but to general and lasting causes.
>
> I see nothing more admirable or more powerful than a great orator discussing great affairs within a democratic assembly. As there is never a class that has charged its representatives with asserting its interests, it is always to the whole nation in the name of the whole nation that one speaks. That enlarges thought and elevates language.
>
> As precedents have little dominion; as there are no longer privileges attached to certain goods, nor rights inherent in certain bodies or certain men, the mind is obliged to go back to general verities drawn from human nature in order to treat the particular affair that occupies it. Hence in the political discussions of a democratic people, however small it is, a character of generality arises that often makes them attractive to the human race. All men are interested in them because it is a question of man, who is the same everywhere.[9]

Conditions in America were right, Tocqueville argued, for a development of politics and sciences that would test and deepen their practitioners' guiding principles. The new democracy was fostering the people's capacities to declare their own conclusions about most things, based "only on the individual effort of [their] reason."[10] The industrious character of the country was rewarding curiosity by putting a premium on communicating practical information quickly, though often so quickly it was superficial or defective.[11] Good communication required forms of rhetoric that conveyed information in the light of general principles, not merely according to what was convenient. It was natural to assume that political speech would develop along similar lines.

In Tocqueville's view, however, Americans were hobbling the prospects of their country's potential greatness because they were dangerously ambivalent toward political speech. This attitude filtered down into administrative habits that made officeholders ill-disposed to keep careful records or to communicate special administrative knowledge to their successors: "It is very difficult for American administrators to learn anything from one another. Thus they bring to the conducting of society the enlightenment that they find widespread within it, and not knowledge that is proper to them. Therefore democracy, pushed to its final limits, harms progress in the art of governing."[12] Despite—and because of—their political virtue as free citizens, Americans were extraordinarily impatient and yet credulous. The speaker who attempted to bring something new to the political stage or to consider the principles under which the country was governed was subject to skepticism or indifference—not necessarily because Americans were undisciplined or lazy but because, as free citizens, they were suffering the effects of a philosophical conundrum.

Tocqueville insisted that Americans, at liberty in a land animated by the principle of equality, thirsted for forms of learning that would enlarge their minds and turn their circumstances to advantage. Their enlarged faith in human perfectibility, he maintained, threw their attention toward what expanded their minds: "When there are no longer inherited wealth, class privileges, and prerogatives of birth, and each draws his force only from himself, it becomes visible that what makes the principal difference among the fortunes of men is intelligence. All that serves to fortify, enlarge, and adorn intelligence immediately brings a high price. The utility of knowledge is revealed with a very particular clarity even to the eyes of the crowd. Those who do not taste its charms prize its effects and make efforts to attain it."[13] The democratic revolution of expectations throws people back upon their own resources. They are keen to discover what provides results—what clearly aids their own rise—and so they favor useful knowledge rather than received wisdom that seems to have no ready application.

Working against the new hunger for learning, Tocqueville contended, were subversive forces that democracy's virtues indirectly stimulated. American democratic curiosity tended to be "at once insatiable and satisfied at little cost."[14] In their eagerness to expand geographical and intellectual frontiers, Americans paradoxically favored information that did not require labor to acquire or understand.[15] The rolling success of their acquisition of practical knowledge yielded, he wrote, a diminishing interest in meditation and calm.[16] Studying the foundations of practical knowledge was strangely difficult. The enterprising man who made his fortune, and thus secured for himself the occasion to enjoy leisure, was likely to find he had lost his capacity to thrive intellectually in repose. Despite or because of its extraordinary enterprise, modern democratic America was "afraid of going into depth," instead seeking "in the works of the mind only easy pleasures and instruction without work."[17] A growing "habit of inattention," fed by the very success of practical knowledge, threatened the understanding of the most important principles that had generated technological prowess. Observe, Tocqueville warned, the moribund, ritualistic, and ornamental science of China, which fell into such disuse because its practitioners no longer remembered the work of their scientific predecessors.[18]

Independence of mind compelled America's democratic men and women to seek their fortunes. But because they were independent and sought to become more so, they were trying to find answers they could implement with the unassisted intellect. They therefore risked closing the circle of their explorations within a narrow compass: "I discover that in most of the operations of the mind each American appeals only to the individual effort of his own understanding." In America, the "precepts of Descartes" were therefore "least studied and most applied." Descartes' philosophy of skepticism, which leads to the isolated thinker's reconstruction of a world of learning based on original principles, was what Americans rejected as received wisdom while they struggled to reinvent it for themselves.[19]

Numerous difficulties had emerged, Tocqueville contended, from this paradoxical practice. Americans' independent minds, which they used to enhance their own fortunes, were threatened by their uncritical acceptance of the public's beliefs, not because American minds were weak but because the more independent they became, the more isolated and vulnerable they were to the "enormous pressure" that a seemingly unified public opinion of equals exerted upon democratic life. Caught up in the industrious application of practical reasoning for highly beneficial and immediate effects, the individual citizen's isolated facility for distinguishing between general ideas tended to weaken. The energetic curiosity that served democratic citizens' practical advantage reduced what "little time remain[ed] to them for thinking." General ideas, if they were not rejected precisely because they were general, hence impractical, were too readily accepted without attention to their significance.[20] Under the promising circumstances of America's rise, this "habit of inattention" was "to be considered the greatest vice of the democratic mind," not merely a common human failing.[21]

As a consequence, Tocqueville continued, Americans' independent minds set them apart on the basis of their material attainments, while their persistent belief in the principle of equality, joined with a habit of indifference toward philosophical inquiry, led them to conclude that their neighbors shared similar general ideas. In the press of time, they therefore tended to accept others' ideas as their own—or reject them as unremarkable. The powerfully independent judgment of democratic citizens was increasingly in danger of giving way to "ready-made opinions."

Tocqueville concluded: "I see very clearly two tendencies in equality: one brings the mind of each man toward new thoughts, and the other would willingly induce it to give up thinking. And I perceive how, under the empire of certain laws, democracy would extinguish the intellectual freedom that the democratic social state favors, so that the human spirit, having broken all the shackles that classes or men formerly imposed on it, would be tightly chained to the general will of the greatest number."[22] The ideas that did sink in, he contended, were tenaciously held, and therefore extremely difficult for orators to work upon. The speed of practical innovation was leading to philosophical rigidity:

> Two things are astonishing in the United States: the great mobility of most human actions and the singular fixity of certain principles. Men move constantly, the human mind seems almost immobile.
>
> When once an opinion has extended over the American soil and has taken root, one would say that no power on earth is in a position to extirpate it. . . . It is true that when the majority of a democratic people changes its opinion, it can work strange and rapid revolutions at will in the world of the intellect; but it is very difficult to change its opinion and almost as difficult to ascertain that it has changed.[23]

Tocqueville observed these cross purposes in the federal Congress. The man who stood in the Capitol as an exemplar of representative government seemed to use public speaking to serve the fixed ideas of his constituency in ways that undermined the speaker's own effort to compose a record of memorable oratory. Freed from the old partisanships of class and the orthodoxies of privilege, supported by the new technologies of publication and mail delivery, the democratic representative was likely to turn his eyes toward local grievances and "great general truths" familiar to his constituents but not necessarily to his colleagues. It was no wonder that southerners and northerners shared general notions of equality but not of slavery. The "great general truths" did not in themselves sustain a consensus.

Writing ten years before the appearance of *Democracy in America*, Edward Everett anticipated some of Tocqueville's judgments. He contended that despite the greatness of Henry Clay as a congressional leader, "the congressional eloquence of America . . . is in no high repute." One would think that Everett, a man of eloquence who admired Clay sufficiently to become a Whig himself in later decades, would have something more positive to say about the fabled orator; but Everett makes a point of distinguishing Clay's political from his rhetorical abilities: Clay's promise had not been fulfilled in the making of political speech that would last. Part of this harsh judgment is no doubt the consequence of Everett's preference for an older, Ciceronian eloquence—the sort of rhetorical display he would famously exemplify (and unfavorably so, years later, in contrast to Lincoln's startling brevity at Gettysburg). But his philosophical distance from the new forms of political speaking provides us with some useful observations.

Everett saw that because more American speakers were better informed than the English, and because they were not held back by party discipline, more of them were ready to speak. The potential for oratorical greatness seemed to be rich. But in Everett's estimation, the words that filled the proceedings were diluted by the sheer volume of speech. The congressional halls were simply too large, he argued, to temper and perfect the rhetorical energies of the new democracy. The magnitude of architectural, geographical, and intellectual space, which would seem most fitting for the great business of self-government, somehow diminished what was said. In the British Parliament, everyone saw and heard the speaker just a few feet away. In Washington, the space for deliberation resembled the vast emptiness of the new continent now filling up with noisy settlers: "Strange as it may at first appear, the evil of excessive speaking is encouraged and increased by the difficulty of being heard in the hall. . . . The vast space to be filled also tempts to vociferation, to exaggerated gesture, to wary repetition, and a sort of desperate effort, on the part of the members, to produce by length, that effect which they cannot aim at in a shorter discourse, of which every sentence would tell."[24] Filling the void, he said, were extemporaneous speeches that ghostwriters often refashioned for the local presses, or hastily prepared speeches directed toward remote constituencies. Without the pressure exerted by numerous journalists taking down each word for interested audiences from diverse parts of the country (as was the case in England), American congressional speech was less well prepared, less carefully edited for complex audiences.[25] Whereas in Parliament members were arrayed on spare benches, in Congress they sat behind writing desks, distanced from debates by the liberties of the building's architecture and the technology of writing and publication that enabled them to communicate speedily with their own home districts. Participation was vehement yet remote, earnest yet disengaged. For Everett, American oratory was pushing toward the extremes of triviality and overgeneralization.

Tocqueville's assessment was more optimistic and urgent. The key oratorical task, he wrote, was "elevating souls and not completing their prostration." The American democratic audience should somehow be brought to question the idea that "the useful is never dishonest" and to wonder "how honesty can be useful." New rules of effective political speech would have to be discovered. Orators would need to find a new way to speak to their audiences' convictions and self-interest, somehow connecting them to higher versions of themselves. To do so, they would need to appeal to what Tocqueville called "self-interest well understood"—the widespread if unexamined belief that self-interest could reach beyond itself toward higher actions and principles: "I do not believe that the doctrine of self-interest such as it is preached in America is evident in all its parts; but it contains a great number of truths so evident that it is enough to enlighten men so that they see them. Enlighten them, therefore, at any price; for the century of blind devotions and instinctive virtues is already fleeing far from us, and I see the time approaching when freedom, public peace, and social order itself will not be able to do without enlightenment."[26]

Self-interest, according to Tocqueville's analysis of American democracy, was relentlessly displacing the old "blind" and "instinctive" virtues, and so could not be ignored. Recognizing that Americans were "complacently" in the habit of explaining that their self-interest was obviously an "enlightened love of themselves" that "constantly brings them to aid each other," Tocqueville concluded that the philosophical grounds for that belief were real but undeveloped.[27] The best hope lay in education (and, by implication, the oratory of political speakers as well as educators) to connect notions of interest with ideas about central principles, and so strengthen new generations' attachment to the best kinds of political speech.

* * *

Whatever were the defects of American orators and their audiences, the rhetorical literature of the antebellum period includes powerful speeches that aspire to teach the sort of virtue Tocqueville had in mind. One can get an idea of antebellum oratory's potential as an educating force by examining a florid and impressive passage from Daniel Webster's famous 1826 eulogy for John Adams and Thomas Jefferson, a text widely circulated in pamphlet form and well known to Lincoln. It is worth noting that Edward Everett liked his neighbor Webster, whom he called a composer of "modern literature" worthy of the company of Washington Irving and William Ellery Channing.[28] Webster's work can still show a modern audience something important about how a speech for a ceremonial occasion could serve as an educative instrument of great power.

Much of Webster's oratorical achievement depended upon amplification and hyperbole—forms of exaggeration that enabled him, in the long periods that held his thoughts hovering over his subject, to draw out the connected meanings of notable ideas and remarkable facts. He used high-minded exaggeration to appeal to self-interest. Confronted with the proverbial impatience, credulity, and immense potential of his democratic audiences, his method suspended judgment so as to deepen and redirect it. At his best, he was able to use exaggeration to help his audiences grasp elusive facts and to promote their sober judgment as an extension of self-interest:

> The striking attitude . . . in which we stand to the world around us, a topic to which, I fear, I advert too often, and dwell on too long, cannot be altogether omitted here. Neither individuals nor nations can perform their part well, until they understand and feel its importance, and comprehend and justly appreciate all the duties belonging to it. It is not to inflate national vanity, nor to swell a light and empty feeling of self-importance, but it is that we may judge justly of our situation, and of our own duties, that I earnestly urge upon you this consideration of our position and our character among the nations of the earth. It cannot be denied, but by those who would dispute against the sun, that with America, and in America, a new era commences in human affairs. This era is distinguished by free representative governments, by entire religious liberty, by improved systems of national intercourse, by a newly awakened and an unconquerable spirit of free inquiry, and by a diffusion of knowledge through the community, such as has been before altogether unknown and unheard of. America, America, our country, fellow-citizens, our own dear and native land, is inseparably connected, fast bound up, in fortune and by fate, with these great interests. If they fall, we fall with them; if they stand, it will be because we have maintained them. Let us contemplate, then, this con-

nection, which binds the prosperity of others to our own; and let us manfully discharge all the duties which it imposes. If we cherish the virtues and the principles of our fathers, Heaven will assist us to carry on the work of human liberty and human happiness. Auspicious omens cheer us. Great examples are before us. Our own firmament now shines brightly upon our path. WASHINGTON is in the clear, upper sky.[29]

We cannot adequately appreciate what Webster is doing without noticing the philosophical and sometimes quasi-religious function of his commemorative rhetoric. His subject—the legacy of Adams and of Jefferson—stimulates his call for contemplation, submission, devotion, and resolution. His sentences enact rhetorically what he urges upon his hearers: an almost prayerful yet active appropriation of the founding and the legacy of those who made it possible. What modern audiences are prone to reject as airy fustian is here a masterful rendition of the commemorative art.[30]

In the peroration's first lines, Webster seems to offer no proof of America's exceptional character except to say that it is self-evident. Yet the hyperbolic argumentation exploits the rich, seemingly intangible implications of common words. Rather than attempting to prove directly, his sentences are designed to evoke. If we notice Webster's list of America's self-evident qualities, we see that he is creating an interlocking series of conditions "bound up," as the country is, with "great interests" that lift ordinary self-interest beyond the self. In one sense, the argument is highly logical. In the core of the paragraph is the idea that "fortune and fate" have brought about America's intellectual, political, and economic prosperity. The equally important cause of that prosperity is the interdependence of many types of prosperity, through which, because the harmony of these spheres cannot be taken for granted, the American nation "imposes" duties on the living. These duties include obligations toward what is inherited: the legacy of the fathers. Yet the defenders of that legacy are encouraged by "auspicious omens," as heaven assists those who perform this work by acting upon their enlightened self-interest in politics, commerce, and the quest for knowledge. In this sense, the past and present preserve one another, each offering the other a practical benediction. Webster works the epideictic function of the commemorative speech so that it mingles devotion with self-help.

John C. Calhoun, an exemplar of the discipline of logic whose ability to present an issue without filigree Lincoln admired, questioned with chilling force the limitations of Webster's hyperbolic rhetoric. Speaking shortly before his death in 1850, he was probably thinking of Webster's second reply to Hayne when he criticized those in the North who, like Webster, praised the Union without adequately recognizing what Calhoun thought were the fundamental constitutional issues bearing on slavery. The Union "cannot be saved by eulogies on the Union, however splendid or numerous. The cry of 'Union, Union—the glorious Union!' can no more prevent disunion than the cry of 'Health, health—glorious health!' on the part of the physician, can save a patient lying dangerously ill."[31] Logic and principle, Calhoun argued, should determine the issue. Hyperbole was evasion.

This did not mean that Calhoun abjured all appeals to self-interest and imagination. In a tour de force of logic in one of his speeches during the Mexican War, he showed how a rigorously systematic analysis of the circumstances—past, present, and future—could emerge from a dialogue between a logician and an audience thinking in terms of enlightened self-interest. Amid calls in the Senate for conquests of more Mexican cities to secure a peace, his deductive method cut through the daunting military and diplomatic uncertainties to set forth facts that seemed to speak for themselves:

> How is peace to be obtained? It can only be by treaty; War may be made by one nation, but peace can only be made by two. The object then is to obtain a treaty; but what treaty? One that will suit Mexico? That can be obtained at any time. No, the treaty which is wanted is one that will suit us; but how can this be effected, but by compelling Mexico, by force of our arms, *and at our dictation,* to agree to such terms as we may dictate; and what could these terms be, but to secure all the objects for which the war was declared; that is, as has been shown, to establish the Rio del Norte as our western boundary, and to obtain ample territory as the only means of our indemnity?
>
> The intention, then, is to compel Mexico to acknowledge that to be ours which we now hold, and can, as I have already shown, easily hold, without her consent. This is all—more or less cannot be made of it. . . . Now, with this object in view, I ask the Senate, Is it worth while to pursue a vigorous war to compel Mexico to acknowledge that to be ours, which we hold, and can easily hold, against her consent?[32]

Calhoun's famous facility for logical compression did not displace his ability to use hyperbole when he appealed to higher self-interest. In an early speech on the danger of disunion, for example, he helped define the Union for the next generation by describing the republic as though it were an animate organism. For all practical purposes, he said, it had a heart and a vascular and nervous system that needed better communication for it to prosper:

> Those who understand the human heart best know how powerfully distance tends to break the sympathies of our nature. Nothing—not even dissimilarity of language—tends more to estrange man from man. Let us, then, bind the republic together with a perfect system of roads and canals. Let us conquer space. It is thus the most distant parts of the republic will be brought within a few days' travel of the center; it is thus that a citizen of the West will read the news of Boston still moist from the press. The mail and the press are the nerves of the body politic. By them, the slightest impression made on the most remote parts, is communicated to the whole system; and the more perfect the means of transportation, the more rapid and true the vibration.[33]

Here the analogy between sympathetic communication and the benefits of public works appeals to self-interested citizens who can imagine themselves more nobly as part of a single organism protected and strengthened by a familiar yet "more rapid and true vibration."

Although the manner and goals of Webster's logic and hyperbole are different from Calhoun's, they serve a similar end: supporting an American union whose persistence depends upon its being informed by a self-interest that has the potential to know itself—to know its higher powers as well as its limitations. If Webster's reference to Washington "in the clear, upper sky" does not reveal to modern readers a convincing heavenly presence, it is important to notice that the orator refers to Washington as part of "our own firmament." Washington is there because Americans in their new era have made—and have been made by—a heaven whose powers evidently assist them when their self-interested striving honors "the virtues and principles" of their fathers. Even if it were concluded that such auspicious omens had to be mere superstitions, Webster's point, brought to light by means of careful hyperbole, remains. The American experiment has impressively benefited from a rare harmony of chance and self-interest too complex and edifying to be confidently attributed to ambition and self-interest; devotion to the cause would therefore be an acknowledgment of a reasonable sympathy in tune with that experimental fact.

In his own way, Lincoln incorporated both argumentative styles—the hyperbolic and the logical—in order to appeal to enlightened self-interest.

Working toward that end, he did not abandon hyperbole for logic as he matured. Nor did he subordinate logic to airy hyperbole when he became president. Throughout his life he entwined them, in their changing forms, in order to inspire, enlighten, and temper a higher and more realistic understanding of the American founding and its promise. In their various qualities, his public speeches are hyperbolic in their reaching beyond the Founders to manifest what Lincoln believed they projected. At the same time, they are self-consciously and almost vehemently dependent upon reason, not only in making their arguments but also in insisting upon submission to law and precedent, the founding ideas, and the limits of ordinary understanding. The careful mingling of logic and hyperbole in these performances strains and tempers his political speech because he both respects and tests the limits of ordinary understanding, especially ordinary understandings of self-interest. As he looks two ways at once—back to the Revolution and the Constitution and forward to a more perfect realization of the Declaration's principles—he humbles, clarifies, challenges, and redefines self-interest so that it can be rightly understood.

2

The Lyceum Address

"On the Perpetuation of Our Political Institutions"

[The Founders'] ambition aspired to display before an admiring world, a practical demonstration of the truth of a proposition, which had hitherto been considered, at best no other, than problematical; *namely, the capability of a people to govern themselves.* ... They succeeded. The experiment is successful; and thousands have won their deathless names in making it so. But the game is caught; and I believe it is true, that with the catching, end the pleasures of the chase. The field of glory is harvested, and the crop is already appropriated. But new reapers will arise, and *they,* too, will seek a field. It is to deny, what the history of the world tells us is true, to suppose that men of ambition and talents will not continue to spring up amongst us. And, when they do, they will as naturally seek the gratification of their ruling passion, as others have done *so* before them. The question then, is, can that gratification be found in supporting and maintaining an edifice that has been erected by others? Most certainly it cannot. (1.113–114)

On January 27, 1838, less than a year after arriving in Springfield from New Salem, Lincoln accepted an invitation to speak before the members of the Young Men's Lyceum. He was twenty-nine. The long-standing battle over the location of the state capital, which he had helped steer toward Springfield, had been fought to a successful conclusion. Having won a second term in the state legislature in 1836 (the year he acquired his license to practice law), he was on his way to being nominated for the speakership of the House. His speech at the Lyceum, titled "On the Perpetuation of Our Political Institutions," was a wide-ranging inquiry into the state of the American polity and the prospects for its preservation.

Twelve years after the deaths of John Adams and Thomas Jefferson on July 4, 1826, and less than a year after President Jackson's retirement, the young Illinois legislator and novice lawyer identified what he claimed to be a fundamental threat to the Founders' achievement, a threat that lay hidden within the country's success. Despite (and, in a sense, because of) their triumph, the Founders could not fully secure the new polity for future generations. As the experience of the Revolution faded in memory and ambitious men surveyed their prospects in the established order, the rule of law would be subject to increasingly wayward passions. If mob rule were permitted to displace the law, the common citizen would despair of the prospects of free government. An extraordinary man of tyrannical ambition would then take advantage of that disillusionment, destroying the institutions and practice of self-government.

The audacity of Lincoln's thesis partly served his party's cause. The Whigs' rivals, the Jacksonian Democrats, had just succeeded in elevating Jackson's vice president, Martin Van Buren, to the presidency. Whig leaders were characterizing Van Buren's victory as a perpetuation of Democrats' anticonstitutional temperament. Jefferson had called Jackson the last of the Romans; the Whigs were attempting to fix upon him the name of Caesar for his defiance of congressional wishes to protect the National Bank, and for his alleged corruption of federal offices.

These partisan battles between Jacksonian Democrats and the Whigs led by Henry Clay and Daniel Webster were in many ways contests for advantage without consideration of principle. Michael Holt, the most assiduous scholar of the Whigs' history, has recently argued that there was much more political maneuvering in these conflicts than scholars have previously recognized. But Holt also observes that the Whigs' fears of what they considered to be Jacksonian tyranny in the late 1830s were based on more than a willingness to use theatrical tactics to win the next election. The assumption that the conflict between parties was a mere rivalry for power "utterly misses," Holt argues, "the central ideological foundation of the [Whig] party." We should recognize that "[o]pposition to Jackson was based on principle. Whigs saw themselves acting from the necessity, as Clay had put it, 'to rescue the Government and public liberty from the impending dangers, which Jacksonism has created.'" The Whigs defined themselves in terms that their British forebears would have recognized: they saw themselves as resistors of kingly abuses of natural and legislated laws protecting the people's "rights and immunities."[1]

Of course, the Democrats claimed to support constitutional principles too. As Jackson's political heir, Van Buren attributed anticonstitutional motives to Whigs who favored a larger role for the federal government.[2] But, unlike the Democrats, the Whigs were born out of a personalized opposition to a particular man as well as to the precedent and political movement he created. They believed Jackson had subverted the Constitution. Holt argues that "[o]nly a passionate devotion to the Revolutionary experiment in republican government and a common conviction that Jackson threatened it explain how men with such diverse views on other matters formed a united front against him."[3]

Knowledge of this context helps us read the Lyceum Address closely. But when we begin to do so, we see immediately that Lincoln does not take a narrowly partisan Whig line. He implicitly comments on recent prominent speeches by Jackson and Van Buren; but he looks beyond the immediate issues to what he considers to be a much broader, subtler pattern of deterioration in the fabric of American freedom. As it happens, Jackson's Farewell Address and Van Buren's Inaugural both give prominent attention to the danger of a breakdown in the rule of law, and both connect that danger to sectional disputes and agitation over slavery. Lincoln imitates, criticizes, and counters his rivals' major arguments in order to reassess the larger question of how to perpetuate the Founders' legacy. To understand what this means, we need to dwell upon the two speeches Lincoln answers. We need to immerse ourselves in the stream of argumentation he navigated.

Both Democrats' speeches were clearly on Lincoln's mind as he framed the Lyceum Address. Both had taken up the problem of preserving the Constitution and the laws, each speech mixing optimistic pronouncements with dire warnings about the damage that heedless citizens might do. Both had touched on the role of slavery and slavery agitation in stimulating lawbreaking behavior. Jackson had been generally optimistic and expressed confidence in the power of citizens' good intentions to secure the country for the next generation: "Never for a moment believe that the great body of citizens of any State or States can deliberately intend to do wrong." But Jackson was also pessimistic: for that optimism to be fulfilled, he said, the laws needed to be "faithfully executed in every part of the country" without exception, and citizens had to be ready to join with the authorities to suppress "every attempt at unlawful resistance."[4] The tenor of his Farewell, spoken by a president who had threatened to use federal troops against a secessionist movement in South Carolina, mixed firm resolve and self-congratulation with a somber warning. He was not afraid to broach the subject of civil war:

> If the Union is once severed, the line of separation will grow wider and wider, and the controversies which are now debated and settled in the halls of legislation will then be tried in fields of battle and determined by the sword. Neither should you deceive yourselves with the hope that the first line of separation would be the permanent one, and that nothing but harmony and concord would be found in the new associations formed upon the dissolution of this Union. Local interests would still be found there, and unchastened ambition. And if the recollection of common dangers, in which the people of these United States stood side by side against the common foe, the memory of victories won by their united valor, the prosperity and happiness they have enjoyed under the present Constitution, the proud name they bear as citizens of this great Republic—if all these recollections and proofs of common interest are not strong enough to bind us together as one people, what tie will hold united the new divisions of empire when these bonds have been broken and this Union dissevered? . . . [H]arassed with conflicts and humbled and debased in spirit, [citizens] would be ready to submit to the absolute dominion of any military adventurer and to surrender their liberty for the sake of repose. . . . [L]et the battle result as it may, there will be an end of the Union and with it an end to the hopes of freedom. The victory of the injured would not secure to them the blessings of liberty; it would avenge their wrongs, but they would themselves share in the common ruin.[5]

Lincoln would absorb and transform the specific terms and sentiments of Jackson's grave alarm, but he would do so in a way that also responded to the much blander optimism of Van Buren's Inaugural. Whereas Jackson's Farewell used his doubts about the country's future to strengthen his warning against sectional strife over slavery, Van Buren's Inaugural projected an almost anesthetic optimism. The new president agreed that mob rule and sectional strife were hazards. But these would be overcome, he assured his audience, if no one upset sectional sensitivities, and if citizens secured the peace by relying on the powerful influence of America's stable political institutions and the persistent fellow feeling of democratic citizens. He claimed that the controversy over slavery raised the specter of a disaster that was only "*supposed* to lurk in our political condition" (emphasis added). It had been created, he said, by those who did not understand the nature of things. The more the agitators tried to disrupt the republic, the more the republic would demonstrate its resistance to change. Indeed, peace would prevail through the republic's almost automatic resistance to disruption. Van Buren's effort to quiet his audience's anxieties made Jackson's misgivings seem almost groundless:

> If the agitation [regarding slavery] was intended to reach the stability of our institutions, enough has occurred to show that it has signally failed, and that in this as in every other instance the apprehensions of the timid and the hopes of the wicked for the destruction of our Government are again destined to be disappointed. Here and there, indeed, scenes of dangerous excitement have occurred, terrifying instances of local violence have been witnessed, and a reckless disregard for the consequences of their conduct has exposed individuals to popular indignation; but neither masses of the people nor sections of the country have been swerved from their devotion to the bond of union and the principles it has made sacred. It will be ever thus. Such attempts at dangerous agitation may periodically return, but with each the object will be better understood.[6]

Yet if the republic was invulnerable, for Van Buren it was also eminently fragile. If one citizen should be offended by the words of another, the entire edifice was in danger. Elaborating upon Jackson's distrust of abolitionists' "motives of philanthropy," Van Buren insisted that everyone "should studiously avoid everything calculated to wound the sensibility or offend the just pride of the people of other States."[7] There seemed to be no margin for error: "Have not recent events made it obvious to the slightest reflection that the least deviation from this spirit of forbearance is injurious to every interest, that of humanity included? Amidst the violence of excited passions this generous and fraternal feeling has been sometimes disregarded. . . . I can not refrain from anxiously invoking my fellow citizens never to be deaf to its dictates."[8] There seemed to be no means of deliberating or adjudicating volatile questions regarding slavery if "the least deviation" jeopardized even the cause of humanity. "Fraternal feeling" was, in effect, hostility toward differences of opinion. To enforce "forbearance," it would suppress all "excited passions," the goal being to enforce silence on the question of slavery.

In his attempt to reassure his inaugural audience, Van Buren thus invoked a reassuring yet contradictory doctrine. Although fraternal feelings were supposedly the dominant ordering forces of the regime, they were not strong enough to ignore or repel the slightest threat. They needed to be freed from the dangerous harassments of uncivil speech and ensuing threats of physical violence so that they could bring peace to the republic. But their need for unhindered expression exposed their weakness. As long as common sentiments were not accepted as universal, there would be debate—and thus the need to suppress debate—for a very long time to come. Van Buren saw the necessity of strengthening fraternal feelings to resist such threats; indeed, his Inaugural Address sought to build them up by focusing their resistance on antislavery dissent. But this approach appealed to no principle but the necessity of peace, and to no emotion but vague patriotism and the fear of disruption. Nothing in the speech explained how fellow feelings could and should be developed, how they could be fostered and maintained. Van Buren provided no means of cultivating and strengthening fraternal feelings so that they might resist other, perhaps more significant threats to the constitutional order. His Inaugural made them the problematical pillars of the republic: they would always stand—as long as citizens bit their tongues.

Jackson had at least carefully analyzed the conditions for perpetuating the peoples' "affection" for constitutional self-government. Rather than assuming that the common sentiment could be maintained by government fiat or regulated speech, he spoke of the connection between the peoples' "affection" for the Constitution and the "security" it afforded them. The "attachment" they felt to the Constitution "as members of one political family, mutually contributing to promote the happiness of each other," derived, he argued, from an interaction of law and affection. Fraternal feeling grew and prospered under the influence of the laws, which were in turn strengthened by fraternal activities. Jackson did not attempt to delineate in detail how the government and citizenry could foster this organic polity; what he saw was that it *had* to be fostered and maintained in relation to a constitutional order, not by mere speech codes and silence. This position Lincoln would take up and enlarge in reply to the sinister neutrality of Van Buren's address.

* * *

In his Lyceum Address, Lincoln shows that neither predecessor's position is adequate. He questions Van Buren's quietism by adapting Jackson's daring depiction of the dangers that await a self-governing people that is no longer vigilant. In doing so, he reintroduces the slavery question almost unobtrusively, though in a form that challenges both men's warnings, particularly Van Buren's, that constitutional self-government must suppress public controversy over slavery. With almost no direct discussion of slavery, and without advocating abolition, Lincoln connects the controversy to the more general problem of perpetuating self-government under unprecedented circumstances in which "the basic principles of our nature" are beginning to break loose from the old revolutionary memories, threatening the heritage of the Revolution. Slavery broadly understood—as a condition that might be undergone by free citizens if they are not wary—becomes the common denominator for an explanation of the potential weaknesses of self-government. The result is a probing, disturbing, hopeful analysis of the means by which fraternal feeling and the political institutions of self-government can be sustained:

> At what point then is the approach of danger to be expected? I answer, if it ever reach us, it must spring up amongst us. It cannot come from abroad. If destruction be our lot, we must ourselves be its author and finisher. As a nation of freemen, we must live through all time, or die by suicide. (1.109)

How substantial and compelling is Lincoln's case? Americans have inherited, he says, "a system of political institutions, conducing more essentially to the ends of civil and religious liberty, than any of which the history of former times tells us" (1.108). Yet, he argues, that legacy is peculiarly vulnerable, in need of perpetual vigilance. The first sentences of the speech invoke the ambivalent language and mood of Ecclesiastes, as though wisdom and folly were almost inextricable:

> In the great journal of things happening under the sun, we, the American People, find our account running, under date of the nineteenth century of the Christian era. . . . We, when mounting the stage of existence, found ourselves the legal inheritors of these fundamental blessings. We toiled not in the acquirement or establishment of them—they are a legacy bequeathed us, by a *once* hardy, brave, and patriotic, but *now* lamented and departed race of ancestors. (1.108)

Care must therefore be taken to preserve the "*attachment* of the People" to their institutions. More than a fraternal feeling, as Van Buren describes it, that attachment must bond citizens to the laws. Without it, "any Government, and particularly ... those constituted like ours, may effectually be broken down and destroyed" (1.111). The postrevolutionary generations are not only increasingly vulnerable, as Jackson warned, to violent passions of anger, revenge, and envy. Their peril cannot be overcome by force as Jackson assumed. According to Lincoln's analysis, something more is needed: "political religion."

The people's affection for the institutions of self-government suffers from the depredations of mob rule's defiance of deliberate, self-governing rule. Indeed, that violence alienates the law-abiding because they see that the system of laws cannot protect them. To meet the threat of mob violence, they must not only repress the mobs; they must strengthen and renew their dedication to "the constitution and the laws." In order to do that, they must hallow the heritage of the laws that the mob's freedom tempts them to abandon or destroy. To address this challenge, Lincoln gestures toward his goal with an overstatement of complex force: he points toward a remedy that he has already indicated must be more particular than the generalities of his hyperbole:

> Let reverence for the laws, be breathed by every American mother, to the lisping babe, that prattles on her lap—let it be taught in schools, in seminaries, and in colleges;—let it be written in Primmers, spelling books, and in Almanacs;—let it be preached from the pulpit, proclaimed in legislative halls, and enforced in courts of justice. And, in short, let it become the political religion of the nation; and let the old and the young, the rich and the poor, the grave and the gay, of all sexes and tongues, and colors and conditions, sacrifice unceasingly upon its altars. (1.112)

The rising incantation, "Let ... let ... let," entreats as much as directs. The intricacies of the address's larger argument are the deeper means of fostering a political religion that can save the fabric of freedom.

Reverence serves to maintain the political forms without assuming that they are in all ways eternal. Some laws are bad and need to be changed. But until they are voted down, "for the sake of example, they should be religiously observed" (1.112). A constitutional order stands above particular laws. Legislative changes should be made "with the least possible delay; but till then, let them if not too intolerable, be borne with" (1.113). Lincoln recognizes, in this last concession, the need to preserve something paradoxical in the legacy of the Founders: the fact that they created the constitutional order as revolutionaries who believed in the possibility of self-government.

Lincoln phrases the thought so that it is rhetorically subordinate to his more prominent idea that the law should prevail. Still he puts it in. Some laws might indeed be "too intolerable" to be "borne with": changes in the laws might at some point need to be revolutionary rather than constitutionally deliberate. Self-government by its nature might entail facing a circumstance in which even the constitutional forms were dangerously inadequate for the preservation of self-government. This prospect, in the double negative of Lincoln's syntax and in general concept, is remote, embedded in the larger argument about the precedence of the laws. Yet it is within the horizon of his thought, acknowledged as a possibility and indeed partly enacted in his argument that conformity to the law is not enough, that citizens must have reverence and the practical intelligence to see—and, in the process, to acknowledge the leadership of one who sees—the hidden dangers of a tyranny that can pervert that conformity into slavery.

In the latter stages of the speech, Lincoln will recall the names of history's greatest tyrants to argue that sooner or later a Napoleonic genius will rise to threaten a land "lately famed" (as Tocqueville had characterized it) "for love of law and order" by taking advantage of a breakdown in the rule of law and a desperate desire to restore security (1.110). Lincoln must first prepare his audience to appreciate the significance of this possibility in themselves as well. He must first show how isolated instances of mob violence—instances already known to his audience—infect the body politic by spreading contempt for the law, and how that contempt softens resistance to a tyrant within and without. And to do so, he must paradoxically show an intelligence, morality, and reverence that, in detecting and meeting that danger, demonstrate his capacity to lead others beyond a merely reflexive adherence to the law. In this sense, at least, he must see beyond the law in order to save it, and show others that such sight is worthy to be followed, that it is not like the false vision of the tyrants he seeks to repress.

Characteristically, Lincoln almost concedes Van Buren's point that tranquillity will prevail and that fraternal optimism and good sense will be enough to resist mob violence. But he questions the validity of appearances. He grants, in effect, the truth of Van Buren's optimism by questioning its basis: he hopes the disaster he warns about will never materialize, and so he gradually tempers his audience's hopes, unraveling its sense of invulnerability while building its confidence in its capacity to conceive of a danger it will not at first see.[9]

Such outbursts, Lincoln argues, are no longer isolated. Mob violence is becoming "common to the whole country," including "the land of steady habits" with its "order loving citizens." No region has been spared (1.109). The variety of places in which mobs have arisen, not necessarily the number and extent of their excesses, is his emphasis. The ubiquity of the mob, its power to infect all sections, West, North, and South, is beginning to inculcate a "mobocratic" spirit (1.111). Claiming to avoid sensational narration, Lincoln forcefully sets out with compact, gothic detail a series of horrific crimes committed by those overcome by that spirit:

> It would be tedious, as well as useless, to recount the horrors of all of them. Those happening in the State of Mississippi, and at St. Louis, are, perhaps, the most dangerous in example, and revolting to humanity. In the Mississippi case, they first commenced by hanging the regular gamblers: a set of men, certainly not following for a livelihood, a very useful, or very honest occupation; but on which, so far from being forbidden by the laws, was actually licensed by an act of the Legislature, passed but a single year before. Next, negroes, suspected of conspiring to raise an insurrection, were caught up and hanged in all parts of the State: then, white men, supposed to be leagued with the negroes, and finally, strangers, from neighboring States, going thither on business, were, in many instances, subjected to the same fate. Thus went on this process of hanging, from gamblers to negroes, from negroes to white citizens, and from these to strangers; till, dead men were seen literally dangling from the boughs of trees upon every road side; and in numbers almost sufficient, to rival the native Spanish moss of the country, as a drapery of the forest. (1.109–110)

Lincoln concedes that his lengthy description might seem to depart from his topic: "But you are, perhaps, ready to ask, 'What has this to do with the perpetuation of our political institutions?'" (1.110). The gamblers' deaths are richly relevant to his contentions that seemingly disparate events are contributing to the degradation of self-government and that all sections and persuasions, slavery advocates as well as abolitionists in "the land of steady habits," are caught up in that broader process of political degeneration (1.109).

Lincoln's rendition of the Vicksburg incident sets out the problem indirectly, though in plain terms. He avoids tales of innocent victims destroyed by wild mobs. He shows a mixed case, one that juxtaposes flawed victims and ordinary men who lose themselves to tyrannical or potentially tyrannical impulses. Other examples are related to slavery, but their intriguing displacement of the slavery question helps Lincoln focus on the larger issue: the fate of the laws and the frame of self-government under the enslaving influences of fear and unbounded outrage.

The gamblers are doubly interesting cases because their deaths provoke new outrages that are connected to fears of slave revolt and abolition. They are "worse than useless" citizens whose unsavory activities are protected by the law. In that very distinction, as we think about it, they resemble slave traders (whom Lincoln describes in later speeches as despised though legally sanctioned in the South, hated yet constitutionally tolerated by the North) and to some extent they are like the abolitionists (unpopular even in many regions of the North yet exercising constitutionally protected freedom of speech). Under the growing influence of mob rule, suspicion and rumor assume authority over laws that are unpopular yet deliberate and constitutional. The gamblers' fate converges with those of widely dispersed black men who are thought to be somehow in league with one another. Mere strangers, wholly unconnected to slavery or abolition, fall next. The sequence of deaths at the hands of fearful, crusading mobs threatens the rule of law, the very idea of rule by law, as the slaughter encompasses all who are not immediately familiar.

Lincoln's second example stresses, though with equal complexity, the horror of the transformation from a lawful order to mobocratic violence. Lincoln retells the story, well known to his hearers, of a man in St. Louis named McIntosh who soon after his arrest was killed by vigilantes:

> Turn, then, to that horror-striking scene at St. Louis. A single victim was only sacrificed there. His story is very short; and is, perhaps the most highly tragic, of any thing of its length, that has ever been witnessed in real life. A mulatto man, by the name of McIntosh, was seized in the street, dragged to the suburbs of the city, chained to a tree, and actually burned to death; and all within a single hour from the time he had been a freeman, attending to his own business, and at peace with the world. (1.110)

Here is another mixed case like the gamblers': a mulatto victim, free and yet treated as mere chattel, innocent and yet—as we read further—guilty himself of murder. In one sense, the story features the pitiable circumstance of a free man ripped from the protection of the laws. In another, it reveals the polity's weakness in living by the law that protects the freedman and the accused, even the guilty, with due process. Reminding his audience of the victim's ambiguous racial identity (as a mulatto with a Scottish name, a freeman in a slave state), Lincoln's information blurs the slavery question to focus on the profound threat to everyone's safety when mobs annihilate the law. All men on trial are condemned; everyone is in danger of being a stranger in someone else's jurisdiction. What is to become of them if mobs are allowed to enlarge their rule?

McIntosh, we read a few sentences later, was himself guilty of "an outrageous murder" and most probably would have died by the sentence of the law if the mob had not become his judge and executioner. Like the gamblers who were deeply flawed men protected by the law, McIntosh was entitled to protection even though he was not, in Lincoln's eyes or those of his audience, an innocent man. The point is that one hour before his violent death (and before he himself killed a man) he was "at peace with the world." In other words, the violence that ripped him from the rule of law and reason was within him as well as within the mob; but it was greater, on principle, in the hands of the mob because the lynching of McIntosh, as he was awaiting trial, did far more violence to the constitutional order.

By starting out with the assertion that McIntosh was attending to his own business and then by referring to his crime, Lincoln's rhetoric emphasizes the untried man's innocence before the law, even in a case in which no one disputed that he committed murder. The speech's reversal of the order of events also dampens any invitation to indulge in abolitionist outrage. The crime was a lynching. But even more important, it was a mob's criminal defiance of the law, not the result of a peculiar perversity of one section of the country. The first part of the example detaches the audience's sentiments from radical and doctrinaire views of slavery and abolition; the second part counters the suspicion that Lincoln makes a selective appeal to abolitionists.

Although his stories are in many ways ambiguous, Lincoln is not neutral with regard to slavery. As we move into his speech, it becomes a subtle yet daring presentation of citizenship as the achievement and preservation of self-government. It argues, by implication, indirection, and direct statements, that slavery is an impending danger for all free men if they misunderstand those tasks. Indeed, we get the strong impression that neither freedom nor slavery is an assured inheritance in a self-governing polity. Just as the former is convertible into the latter, so might the slave rise, if only in principle at first, in imitation of the self-governing citizen's struggle to renew and protect what would otherwise pass away.

Lincoln had taken a related a position the year before, when he and a colleague submitted a written "protest" to the Illinois House taking issue with the legislature's defense of a "sacred" right of property in slaves. In January 1837 Illinois Whigs had passed a resolution explicitly accommodating themselves to southern demands for continued legal protection of their institution, and for repudiation of abolitionists' activities. Lincoln's distinctive protest declared that "the institution of slavery is founded on both injustice and bad policy" (1.74–75). He criticized the abolitionists for their "promulgation" of those doctrines, the manner of which, he said, "tends rather to increase than to abate [slavery's] evils." He argued that slavery should not be interfered with where it existed, and he urged recognition of a congressional power to abolish slavery in the District of Columbia if the people of the District requested abolition (1.74–75). In these actions Lincoln was not condemning abolition itself, as the legislature had done. He was distinguishing between two methods of promulgation—two ways of resisting slavery: the abolitionists' counterproductive agitation, and the approach embodied in his dissenting resolution, which sought an incremental yet fundamental legislative change that would preserve and refocus constitutional law.

Although Lincoln's measure had no legislative impact, the cosigner of the 1837 protest, Dan Stone, was among those extending the invitation for him to speak at the Lyceum (1.108).[10] Lincoln's apparent neutrality in the 1838 address—his reluctance to refer to slavery by name, let alone treat it directly or to indicate that the murdered newspaper editor he refers to is the abolitionist Lovejoy—does not efface the lineaments of a deeper argument that is connected to his declaration in 1837. If we look at the address's one specific reference to abolitionism, we see that Lincoln frames it as an aggressively neutral, procedural point connected to a moral principle. If, as Lincoln argues, the people and their legislators were to eschew mob violence and gag laws so as to debate whether abolitionists should be allowed to propagate their views, they would be bound to take up the question of what was "right within itself":

> There is no grievance that is a fit object of redress by mob law. In any case that arises, as for instance the promulgation of abolitionism, one of two positions is necessarily true; that is, the thing is right within itself, and therefore

deserves the protection of all law and all good citizens; or, it is wrong, and therefore proper to be prohibited by legal enactments; and in neither case, is the interposition of mob law, either necessary, justifiable, or excusable. (1.113)

Lincoln does not say he favors or opposes that promulgation; he does not even make abolitionism his central topic: it is an example, he says, of a political issue that deserves discussion. By raising that issue in these terms, which bring it back to the basic operations of deliberative self-government, he creates a double-edged challenge that moves the moral issue of slavery closer to the center of discussion. Toward the South, which Jackson and Van Buren try to protect from scrutiny by enforcing a code of fraternal silence, he gestures in favor of free political expression among voters and legislators, not ruling out further legislative action by state legislatures or the federal government. Facing the abolitionists, especially those who disdain constitutional remedies, he indicates that a new law might go the other way, thus limiting their freedom to advocate their views. In either case, he challenges his audience to look beyond the mechanisms of deliberation and legislation in order to choose what is "right within itself." What looks like a procedural argument directs attention, in other words, toward principles that are more substantial than belief in procedure or even belief in debate. Debate and legislation will not merely reflect personal preference: they will encounter the question of what is right in itself, what is in a sense beyond debate.

Lincoln's argument with Douglas over the true nature of self-government begins to emerge in this period. How does one distinguish false self-government from true? Is the exercise of majority rule the sufficient condition for replacing bad laws with good ones? The deliberate way of changing them is, for Lincoln, not merely an exercise of majority rule but one of patience. More important, it is an exercise of deference, not only to the Constitution but also to what is good, to what is "right within itself." The precedence of law in a truly self-governing political union strengthens the patient pursuit of that goal: "If such [bad laws] arise, let proper legal provisions be made for them with the least possible delay" (1.112–113). The point is that living under the law is an ordeal of patience and aspiration. Contrary to Van Buren's assurances, free citizens of the republic are precariously balanced between liberty and slavery: their situation mirrors (reflects inversely) the bondman's plight and his desire to be free. The fate of free citizens is alarmingly and somewhat reassuringly circular: it rests upon their ability to secure those political institutions and ideas that make it possible for them to govern themselves. Douglas's faith in local government and majority rule, like Van Buren's faith in silence and fraternal affection, is insufficient.

Recent events in Alton, Illinois, posed a challenge to Lincoln's views. The shooting of the prominent abolitionist editor Owen Lovejoy on November 7, 1837, had stirred pro-and antiabolitionist sentiment. Even though Lincoln delivered his speech two months after Lovejoy's death and less than a hundred miles from the scene, he mentioned what had happened in Alton only in a few words, without mentioning Lovejoy by name. Some commentators have variously interpreted his silence as evidence that he was politically immature, morally obtuse, or cannily flexible. Basler and particularly Jaffa have taken a different view, Basler arguing that Lincoln did not need to be explicit on a matter everyone knew in detail (1.111),[11] and Jaffa contending that the Lyceum Address was consistent with Lincoln's emergent and profound understanding of the foundations of the slavery issue.[12] We can get a sense of what Lincoln is getting at when we examine his manner of presenting his ideas.

Lincoln places the destruction of Lovejoy's printing press, the violent end of his life, and the hanging and burning of McIntosh in the conclusion of a dramatically compact list of recent incidents of mob violence. Mobs have presumed, he says, to "burn churches, ravage and rob provision stores, throw printing presses into rivers, shoot editors, and hang and burn obnoxious persons at pleasure, and with impunity" (1.111). Lovejoy's story was, in other words, part of a larger fabric. The Alton case was so replete with implications for Lincoln's argument and for his views of slavery and the law that it could not be excluded from his address. It augmented what Lincoln was already saying. McIntosh's death and Lovejoy's were intertwined. According to a prominent witness (the abolitionist minister Edward Beecher), Lovejoy had delivered a final speech in which he referred to the lynchings "of the individuals of Vicksburg" (one of Lincoln's subjects a few months later) and asked whether he would be treated "as they did McIntosh at St. Louis."[13] Lovejoy had himself printed a description of the McIntosh lynching, which he wrote after viewing the body, in his St. Louis newspaper before fleeing to Alton. If Lincoln and his neighbors had not seen Lovejoy's account, they were likely to have read other narratives that drew from it.

Just what Lincoln wanted his audience to draw from that brief reference Basler does not say. Jaffa does not pursue the Lovejoy matter in any detail. William Lee Miller has recently argued that Lincoln's references to the Alton story were strategic, and closely linked to his antislavery position.[14] A closer look at some of the most important evidence confirms, extends, and qualifies Miller's view.

Among the early written accounts of Lovejoy's death, Edward Beecher's reconstruction, published in 1838, argues that the law-abiding citizens of Alton faced stark choices in the days leading up to the mob's attack. At least as much as abolitionism, the rule of law was on trial, for the Alton incident had culminated in armed confrontation. Before the fighting broke out, the town's citizens met in large deliberative assemblies to discuss what they should do. Would it be better to do nothing in the face of imminent mob violence or to arm themselves, against neighbors as well as strangers, to protect Lovejoy and his press for as long as the threat continued, even though most of them were not abolitionists?

Although Beecher's book was probably not published until after Lincoln's speech, it drew from information that was likely to have become available to Lincoln and his Springfield audience in the eight-week interval between the murder and Lincoln's address. The crisis had not emerged all at once. It was general knowledge that Lovejoy had just moved his newspaper upstream to Alton after being forced out of St. Louis. Several replacement presses had already been destroyed by mobs on the Alton side of the river. The arrival of a successor brought new threats of mob violence and indications that armed supporters would be needed to defend the machine and its operator from assault. According to Beecher's account, it was not clear at that point whether the Alton constabulary or the leaders of the town would be able or willing to raise a body of armed men to meet the threat if Lovejoy insisted upon holding his ground. In their public meetings, Alton citizens, including some who according to Beecher later joined the mob, debated the rule of law, freedom of inquiry, and other issues related to abolitionism and slavery. They took up various resolutions proposed by Beecher and by their own subcommittee as to what course of action should be taken. In the end, after discussing at length the importance of the rule of law and the freedom of the press, the gathering was able to pass only one resolution: a request for Lovejoy to leave town.[15]

Beecher believed that a show of force against Lovejoy's enemies would have ended the threat; but he also indicated that without the hope of such protection, he would have advised Lovejoy to leave.[16] Deliberation had failed, and the imminence of conflict was foreclosing the possibility of enforcing the law. When the abolitionist editor declared his refusal to go, the confrontation proceeded, and within a few days an armed mob attacked the building that housed his press. A man in the besieging mob was killed by Lovejoy's defenders, and Lovejoy was shot by the mob soon after.

In the Alton story, Lincoln would probably have seen, *in extremis,* a breakdown of the rule of law, a culmination of the more subtle deterioration he predicted would eventually weaken citizens' attachment to the laws and hence their resistance to a tyrant's offer to restore order. The confrontation between a radical abolitionist and ruthless defenders of slavery would have been a part, but only a part, of this larger pattern. The circumstances in Alton compressed the encounter in a few days of crisis, when last-minute attempts to avert confrontation could not avert the dissolution of the rule of law. A lethal pattern of incipient tyranny had manifested itself in mob action and civil war.

Lincoln was in fact closer to Lovejoy than modern readers might suspect, for Lovejoy, when he wrote the original, detailed story of McIntosh's murder, had stressed the importance of the rule of law, not the cause of abolition. Although Lovejoy was greatly interested in making the case for abolition, he chose to describe the crime in other terms. His account, published in his own *St. Louis Observer,* took pains to link the mob's treatment of McIntosh to mobocratic excesses in other circumstances:

> We have drawn the above gloomy and hideous picture, not for the purpose of holding it up as a fair representation of the moral condition of St. Louis—for we loudly protest against any such conclusion, and we call upon our fellow citizens to join us in such a protest—but that the immediate actors in the horrid tragedy may see the work of their hands, and shrink in horror from a repetition of it, and in humble patience seek forgiveness of that community whose laws they have so outraged, and of that GOD whose image they have, without his permission, wickedly defaced; and that they may all see, (and be warned in time) the legitimate results of the spirit of *mobism,* and whither, unless arrested in its first out-breakings, it is sure to carry us. In Charleston it burns a Convent over the heads of defenceless women; in Baltimore it dese-

crates the Sabbath, and works all that day in demolishing a private citizen's house; in Vicksburg it hangs up gamblers, three or four in a row; and in St. Louis it forces a man—a hardened wretch certainly, and one that deserved to die, but not *thus* to die—it forces him from beneath the aegis of our Constitution and laws, hurries him to the stake and burns him alive![17]

Lovejoy's restraint was no doubt partly tactical, a way of presenting the abolitionists' cause in terms that their enemies might respect. But like Lincoln after him, Lovejoy universalizes McIntosh's case, not ostensibly for the cause of abolition but for the sake of the rule of law (and reverence for its connection to divine law), which he also sees endangered by attacks on Catholics and the Vicksburg gamblers. Whether or not Lincoln used Lovejoy's account directly, it is apparent that both men accepted the law's demand that a murderer be subject to execution. More important, both presented the lynchings and other attacks primarily as depredations that violated existing law, not as expressions of support for, or antagonism toward, slavery or abolitionism. Lincoln was able to focus on the principle of law that Lovejoy himself sought to stress in his *Observer* article, redirecting its antislavery implications for his own antislavery ideas.

If, as Lincoln says in an earlier passage, America shall live forever or die by suicide, the fate of McIntosh mirrors the fate of America if it takes the sinister path. Lincoln concentrates, in relating the tale of McIntosh, on the "most highly tragic" story that could be "witnessed in real life": a story of a man's destruction by "the wild and furious passions" that do away with the law (1.110). It is not accidental that the address, having touched on this tragic theme, will later echo *Macbeth*. Here the most important threat to America's political institutions comes from within, from the violence of the mob that mirrors the violence of the tyrant. McIntosh's own capacity to commit what Lincoln calls "an outrageous murder" fittingly assigns him the double role of tyrant as well as enslaved victim (1.110). Each is slave to the passions; one is enslaved by the other. In this sense, slavery is the cause and effect of the tyranny that comes with the abandonment of the discipline of self-government. This interaction of tyranny and slavery, Lincoln argues, is capable of provoking collective suicide by pulling free and law-abiding citizens toward self-destruction—if they are not vigilant.

* * *

The structure and substance of the Lyceum Address show that Lincoln did not assume that well-meaning rhetorical appeals, or acts of will on the part of his audience, would be sufficient means to serve his ends. The problem was amenable to a solution, but both the problem and the solution were difficult to grasp. His strategy was inquisitive and persuasive at once: he publicly questioned his own evidence, anticipating increasingly fundamental objections, and then found in those objections a means of reaching the substratum of his argument. Even if mob violence were a growing danger, he conceded, the question might reasonably be asked whether American political institutions, which had withstood numerous dangers for fifty years, were in new and perhaps mortal danger (1.113). The problem, he argued, was precisely there, within that apparent yet slowly deteriorating stability. Even if Americans recovered and strengthened their devotion to the laws, it would in time be severely tested by a tyrannical genius who would rise to exploit their imperfect vigilance:

> This field of glory is harvested, and the crop is already appropriated. But new reapers will arise, and *they,* too, will seek a field. It is to deny, what the history of the world tells us is true, to suppose that men of ambition and talents will not continue to spring up amongst us. And, when they do, they will as naturally seek the gratification of their ruling passion, as others have so done before them. The question then, is, can that gratification be found in supporting and maintaining an edifice that has been erected by others? Most certainly it cannot. (1.113–114)

The way to resist such men, and thereby secure the foundation of free government, is in one sense "simple"—a matter of swearing "by the blood of the Revolution, never to violate in the least particular, the laws of the country; and never to tolerate their violation by others" (1.112). But the deeper motions of Lincoln's argument work from the conviction that dutiful words and resolute action are not enough. The danger seems too great, too likely to reveal itself before it is detected, too difficult to appreciate in its full power, unless a new level of vigilance and duty—of wakeful submission to the unique task given to the postrevolutionary generation—is attained. What is needed, Lincoln argues, is an embrace of "political religion." The new devotion to the law and the institutions of self-government requires citizens "to be united with each other, attached to the government and the laws, and generally intelligent" (1.114).

Jackson had positioned his Farewell to resist disruption of the administration's muscular enforcement of the status quo. Van Buren had crafted his Inaugural to hold his narrow Democratic margin of victory by means of a call for unity. Lincoln attempted to mobilize the political imagination of a broad constituency for the defense of something that would die, he said, without a new reverence for the laws and a new and vigorous resistance to tyranny. As a youthful exaggeration, the idea seems insubstantial—but Lincoln is more serious than we might assume. In order to succeed, it seems, this new and militant devotion must be quasi-religious; ordinary caution, courage, and moderation are not enough. Citizens will not rise to the occasion unless they have a vivid sense of the tremulous state of their hold on freedom.

In the way Lincoln presents it, there is something almost demonic about this danger that makes it akin to the working power of the "towering genius" who would lure a free republic into taking its own life. The tyrant's attractive offer of nihilistic rebirth through destruction—his preference for defiant annihilation over subordination—is more in keeping with Milton's Satan or Shakespeare's Richard III or (the favorite of Lincoln's maturity) Macbeth than with the historical figures Lincoln cites directly in 1838:

> Many great and good men sufficiently qualified for any task they should undertake, may ever be found, whose ambition would aspire to nothing beyond a seat in Congress, a gubernatorial or a presidential chair; *but such belong not to the family of the lion, or the tribe of the eagle,* [.] What! think you these places would satisfy an Alexander, a Caesar, or a Napoleon. Never! Towering genius disdains a beaten path. It seeks regions hitherto unexplored. . . . It *scorns* to tread in the footsteps of *any* predecessor, however illustrious. It thirsts and burns for distinction; and, if possible, it will have it, whether at the expense of emancipating slaves, or enslaving freemen. (1.114)

Here Lincoln challenges Van Buren's quiescent view almost sarcastically: "What! Think you these places would satisfy . . .?" The perverse depth of the tyrant's shocking psychology (as though to say "Evil, be thou my good" along with Milton's Satan) gives the hyperbolic argument a strange gravity: what would such a man not do—and what must those who resist him summon up in themselves—to achieve or frustrate such designs? Ordinary vows, reverence, and reason do not seem to be enough.

Jefferson had suggestively (and more soberly) profiled the same three historical tyrants in his autobiography published in 1829. There he linked each tyrant to one of the "three epochs in history signalized by the total extinction of national morality." He exempted Caesar from the most serious charge, but he made clear that each era exhibited the world's most destructive displays of political and moral violence as a result of the infectious power of one man's will over the counsel of reason: "The first [epoch of disaster and extinction] was of the successors of Alexander, not omitting himself. The next the successors of the first Caesar, the third our own age . . . [leading up to] the enormities of Bonaparte partitioning the earth at his will, and devastating it with fire and sword."[18] Like Jefferson, Lincoln saw the danger in terms of unlimited ambition. But he includes Caesar (not his "successors") because he is interested in tyrannies more subtle and destructive to American freedom than fiery conquest. Jefferson's list does not anticipate the sinister genius or the strange method of fighting him that preoccupies Lincoln.

We need to recall that for Lincoln the subtle power of tyranny is evident in some seemingly ordinary citizens: those "lawless of spirit" who are capable of imitating the great vices of the greatly ambitious man. They are the ones who swell the influence of mobs by seeking the destruction of all government, both as an institution and as the internal operation of their rational faculties: "Used to no restraint" and "[h]aving ever regarded Government as their deadliest bane, they make a jubilee of the suspension of its operations; and pray for nothing so much as its total annihilation" (1.111). The malignant rioter's ambition creates its own apocalyptic nihilism, which so distorts other citizens' purposes that it awakens their "deep rooted principles of *hate*, and the powerful motives of *revenge*," which were fortunately channeled toward the external enemies of self-government during the Revolution (1.114).

If ordinary citizens can become nihilistic tyrants, those who resemble lions and eagles, according to Lincoln's analysis, are all the more sinister. They come to resemble Shakespearean tyrants, particularly Macbeth. When Lincoln refers to them as lions and eagles, he is echoing lines from Shakespeare's play, in its introductory description of Macbeth and Banquo as all-conquering heroes. (The 1838 speech might also be drawing from biblical sources—perhaps Jeremiah's likening of Nebuchadrezzar to a lion and his armies to eagles, or David's lament for Saul and Jonathan as swifter than eagles and stronger than lions.)[19] It is *Macbeth*, the play Lincoln later called his favorite Shakespearean drama, that provides the most powerful setting for the idea Lincoln is trying to project.

In *Macbeth* we have the one place in all the plays where Shakespeare's language includes the two kingly beasts in close proximity, in a context that is paradigmatic of tyranny's power to overthrow everything in its path. Macbeth and Banquo are likened to the lion and the eagle because their power to destroy Duncan's enemies seems to know no bounds: "Dismay'd not this [fresh assault] / Our captains, Macbeth and Banquo? / Yes, / As sparrows eagles; or the hare the lion."[20] Macbeth at first directs that power toward fighting the enemies of his king. But almost immediately we see him tempted to loose it upon Duncan and sweep away all competitors. It soon dwarfs the desire to rule as king. Indeed, Macbeth envisions the parricidal crime the moment he hears the prophecy of his triumph. The voices of the witches release an ambition in him that seeks to obliterate all opposition, including all those who might remind him of his crimes, even his own conscience. He is soon appalled at his own thoughts and actions, and his conscientious "human kindness," joined with his ruthlessness, makes him a far greater tyrant than he would have been had he not known the value of what he was destroying. The almost unnerving boundlessness of his ambition is an evil perversely benefiting from his sensitivity to virtue.

Shakespeare's play reveals the difficulty of resisting such a force when its evil begins to penetrate the imaginations of more ordinary men. It threatens to set good men against one another. Macduff and Malcolm, the eventual slayers of the tyrant, must overcome (and show that they can overcome) the specter of a profound distrust among disheartened men and the threat of self-doubt. They must meet the growing suspicion that all men are infected, as Macbeth is, with impulses so tyrannical there is no hope that the evil of willful defiance of the law can be resisted. Thus Shakespeare shows how Malcolm, the man who would be the next king, must test Macduff with purported tales of Malcolm's own perversity and of his unfitness to govern. It is not until he mines his own capacity to envision incipient evil in himself as well as others, recalls the religious memory of the healing king Edward the Confessor, and vows to fight for Scotland that Macduff is reassured and both men can resist Macbeth's horrors by besieging Dunsinane.

The parallels between the dramaturgical precedent and Lincoln's argument are striking. Malcolm's demonstration of self-rule in the face of an extreme yet insidious threat—Macbeth's psychological, political, and spiritual tyranny—meets power with power by invoking his own authority as the rightful king, by remembering the precedent of a great and religious monarch, and by joining with Macduff and others to resist the menace. Similarly, in the Lyceum Address Lincoln portrays an incipient, penetrating evil in such a way that it can stir his audience to act as self-governing citizens, draw strength from political religion, and form political friendships. They can then revere the laws not as conformists but as fraternal imitators of a higher model of self-governing citizenship embodied in Washington's heroic, revolutionary conformity to the laws. By such means they can break the spell that threatens the American polity.

What then is reverence? "*Political religion,*" as Lincoln presents it, would effectively educate and express the people's attachment to the laws if it could generate vigilance, endurance, and solidarity. But an effective political religion would need to raise those qualities to a new level, beyond the normal expectations for human nature. When he introduces the topic, Lincoln treats the forms and practices of political religion as almost ordinary. A vow, he says, will do. But the oath needs to be made "by the blood of the Revolution," imitating and incorporating each Founder's arduous pledge of "his life, his property, and . . . sacred honor." Transgression of the pledge is supposedly a sacrilege violating a familial as well as a political trust: "[L]et every man remember that to violate the law, is to trample on the blood of his father, and to tear the character of his own, and his children's liberty." (The sanguinary Macbeth is again an apt paradigm for the neglect of political religion.) Reverence for the Founders' revolutionary sacrifice gives devotion to the law a sacramental character, which Lincoln not implausibly assumes will increase civil worshipers' capacity to make their own sacrifices: "[L]et the old and young, the rich and the poor, the grave and the gay, of all sexes and tongues, and colors and conditions, sacrifice unceasingly upon its [the law's] altars" (1.112).

This hyperbole, which rings false to many modern ears, contains and expresses a strategy for overcoming a hidden, lethal danger of extraordinary proportions. Now that the inartificial, material proofs of founding virtue have "crumbled away" along with the immediate influence of the Founders and those who acted with them, their successors must supply a new devotion to self-government at least as formidable as the destructive impulse that arises out of Napoleonic genius.[21]

How is this new devotion possible if passionate excess is such a dangerous stimulant to the mobocratic spirit? Lincoln has prepared for this question by stressing reverence rather than devotion to duty. Reverence is by definition a joint exercise of reason and the higher, upward-looking passion of admiration. When we look at how Lincoln says reason will be exercised to overcome the tyrant passions, we see this pattern of rational and passionate synthesis extended to those activities that will preserve the republic. The materials for improvement are to be furnished by reason, which he hopes will be "moulded into *general intelligence,* [*sound*] *morality* and, in particular, *a reverence for the constitution and laws*" (1.115).[22] Here reverence is the confluence of "unimpassioned reason" and passion in a well-directed fear of tyranny and admiration for the law and its greatest authors.

Observed from one perspective, Lincoln's address is a bundle of opposites. Political religion is everything, and yet Lincoln also says that reason— "cold, calculating, unimpassioned reason"—must prevail (1.115). If we look closely at his language, we see that reason and political religion are somehow to be understood in terms of one another. Civil religion is here a mixture of reverence, passion, and reason. When he seems to reject all passion for "cold, calculating" reason, his language likens the work of self-government to stonecutting, masonry, and sculpture—artful expressions of reason in quasi-religious service to "the temple of liberty." The postrevolutionary republic must stand upon the "rock" of reason, as though it were a lesser version of "the only greater institution," the Church of Saint Peter. It cannot be an ordinary edifice since, "as truly as has been said" of Saint Peter's church, it too must withstand the political equivalent of "*the gates of hell.*" Otherwise it would not be able to resist an evil that menaces (and grows from) the very success of American self-government.

We are now in a position to review the speech's conclusion in detail:

> [The Founders] *were* the pillars of the temple of liberty; and now, that they have crumbled away, that temple must fall, unless we, their descendants, supply their places with other pillars, hewn from the solid quarry of sober reason. Passion has helped us; but can do so no more. It will in future be our enemy. Reason, cold, calculating, unimpassioned reason, must furnish all the materials for our future support and defence. Let those [materials] be moulded into *general intelligence,* [*sound*] *morality* and, in particular, *a reverence for the constitution and laws.* (1.115)[23]

Reason does not simply dictate. It accommodates "general intelligence," which is closer to sensible, reflective learning than disembodied reason. "Sound morality," in the context of the next sentences, is the stuff of self-governing freedom rather than ascetic adherence to a rational rule. "Reverence," so developed by Lincoln's blend of hyperbole and frank analysis, is an intellectual passion rather than a conceptual slavery or an automatic assent. In the light of Washington's precedent and the revolutionary origin of the laws, reverence is a wakeful subordination to something greatly and rightly admired.

Lincoln uses parallel phrasing to elucidate this mixed nature in each virtue of the self-governing citizen:

> Let those materials [of "unimpassioned Reason"] be moulded into
>
> (1) *general intelligence,*
>
> (2) *sound morality* and, in particular,
>
> (3) *a reverence for the constitution and the laws;*
>
> > (1) and that we improved to the last;
> >
> > (2) that we remained free to the last;
> >
> > (3) that we revered his name to the last;
>
> that, during his long sleep, we permitted no hostile foot to pass over or dese-crate [his] resting place; shall be that which to lea[rn the last] trump shall awaken our WASH[INGTON]. (1.115)[24]

Here "cold, calculating, unimpassioned reason" in three ways reinvests passion in reason and directs its energies toward self-government. In paired phrases, Lincoln lines up "general intelligence" with the capacity to "improve . . . to the last"—to discover, invent, debate, and formulate such things as material innovations and legislation, all being activities that can be presumed to be powered by aspiration, inspiration, and a desire to improve. He aligns "sound morality" with "remain[ing] free to the last"—not for the sake of moral conformity alone but for living in such a way as to perpetuate self-government within oneself as well as in the polity. Finally, there is "reverence for the constitution and the laws," elaborated not as dedication to the laws but as an imitation of that great sublimator of revolutionary fervor, George Washington, who in yielding his sword to the new civil power became the republic's embodiment of the rule of reason and the judge, as an enduring exemplar, of the inheritors of the republic.

The rhetorical language with which Lincoln reaches this conclusion is more than the instrument of his ideas; it often embodies his argument for reverence in its synthesis of reason and passion. Hugh Blair, the influential eighteenth-century orator and philosopher of rhetoric, defined "high eloquence" as an activity of mind and passion capable of ennobling the mind of speaker and audience. In the best practical activity of such speaking, the mind is thought to appeal to the passions by becoming more itself. Instead of reducing the passions to instruments or depending on demagoguery, the eloquent orator's mind is in this sense moved by its own high object in a way that inspires passion in others. The virtue of the speaker, his subject, and his audience are assumed to be intertwined:

> [H]igh eloquence . . . is always the offspring of passion. By passion, I mean that state of the mind in which it is agitated, and fired, *by some object it has in view*. A man may convince, and even persuade others to act, by mere reason and argument. But that degree of eloquence which gains the admiration of mankind, and properly denominates one an orator, is never found without warmth or passion. Passion, when in such a degree as to rouse and kindle the mind, without throwing it out of the possession of itself, is universally found to exalt all the human powers.[25] (emphasis added)

* * *

In framing his ideas of political religion, Lincoln may have drawn from the *Federalist Papers* 49, where Madison worries about how to cultivate the "veneration" that is necessary for the perpetuation of republican government. Long before Lincoln made his speech, Madison anticipated the problem Lincoln would attempt to address. The revolutionary period, Madison argued, had "repressed the passions most unfriendly to order and concord," passions that would thereafter endanger the institutions of self-rule. The practical solution to the difficulty, Madison argued, was to ensure that the people were consistently brought into contact with "examples" both "*ancient*" and "*numerous*" that would win their "prejudices" to the side of "rational government." Reverence, in other words, would be instrumental in the success of the regime through its power to link prejudice and rationality.[26] If that connection were more than purely instrumental—more than merely a means to an end—it would draw passions and prejudices toward a rational end. It would serve reason not simply as a device but as a way of directing the desire to imitate the Founders and so sustain the institutions of American self-government.

In the absence of encouragement to revere high models, Madison continued, the people would be drawn into perennial controversies over the Constitution, which "would carry an implication of some defect in the government." Lacking reverence, their reasonable faculties would be drawn into bickering and thence into irreverence that would make the principles and methods of dissent the measures of the Constitution. Madison was not arguing that citizens should not join in political debate; he was concerned that the government's dependence on public opinion as well as the guidance offered by the Constitution would be thrown out of balance if no care were taken to sustain political reverence.

As we have seen, Lincoln analyzes this problem in detail. He observes that the revolutionary struggle, which redirected destructive energies, has run its course, and he suggests, with the help of strategic exaggeration, that the danger of disruption is greater than what Madison described. That danger requires, in other words, a reverence closer to religion than what Madison recommended.

Much more than Jackson or Van Buren, Lincoln invites his audience into a discussion of the principles, tendencies, and sustenance of self-government. He concentrates on its vulnerabilities and the burden they place upon self-governing citizens. He avoids the constitutional questions surrounding slavery so as to consider the deeper and more complex problem of defending a free polity against itself. Rather than efface the issue of slavery, he refocuses and represents it in relation to the origins and pathologies of self-government. And he returns to the need for reverence, not as an unexplained or merely patriotic imperative but as the result of an inquiry into the power of self-destructive tyranny among free men.

Reverence—as Lincoln invokes and enacts it—is a means of awakening, humbling, ennobling, and redirecting the passions of citizens who do not anticipate, or do not adequately anticipate, tyranny's lethal dangers or their own resources for combating them. It comes from fear as well as admiration and emulation. Lincoln's vision of the Napoleonic genius within and without awakens an activating fear—of tyranny that is strangely familiar in the excesses of the mob, yet so terrible in its secret development that ordinary citizens who felt that fear in time would be drawn together, and to higher models of resistance, to meet the threat. They would need to conceive of the danger of Americans becoming their own versions of Macbeth or of the disillusioned and subsequently murdered Banquo. In effect, Lincoln adapts Madison's idea of reverence to promote an antityrannical association—a kind of political party—so as to preserve the Founders' institutions in new

"Temple of Liberty" (1834), Jared Bell, in the Library of Congress collection of reproductions: PC/US—1834.B444, No. 1; reproduction # LC USZ62-89564. A woodcut, presumably for printing copies on banners or other surfaces.

This 1834 vision of Liberty shows an airy, Edenic vision of harmony in which the goddess presides over the exchange of goods (the trader's grain and the Native American's game), under the incongruously urgent slogan "The Union Must and Shall be Preserved." The delicate structure does not need to be strong or massive: it houses the flame of liberty, and Minerva and Justice protect the temple's flanks, presumably to ward off threats we do not see. The scene contrasts with Lincoln's abstract, rock-hewn, and besieged vision of the Temple of Liberty set out in his 1838 Lyceum Address: "[The Founders] were the pillars of the temple of liberty; and now, that they have crumbled away, that temple must fall, unless we, their descendants, supply their places with other pillars, hewn from the solid quarry of sober reason" (1.115). If a self-governing people can become the supports of the new structure, it will be its own means of protection. The self-governing, tyranny-resisting character of the preserved nation, not merely its freedom of trade and guardian powers, will make it so. Lincoln might have had in mind an ethical and political version of the just-completed U.S. Capitol, or the massive Greek Revival federal building (under construction since 1834 and completed in 1842), which was being built, as he spoke, on the site of the demolished federal building in lower Manhattan, the very place where George Washington had taken the first presidential oath.

and sustaining acts of resolve and innovation. To serve that end, he uses passion, as all orators do, as an instrument—but, most remarkably, by identifying and appealing to passions conducive to self-government.

The peculiarly complicated political and moral difficulties of self-government must have contributed to Lincoln's fascination with *Macbeth*. It was the one play he called "wonderful," as though it were the master of the rest (6.392). Just before his death, he is reported to have read Macbeth's words in the moments before Duncan is killed, choosing a passage that permitted him to read Macbeth's mind feelingly, and—because the lines do this too—in sympathy with Duncan's innocent vulnerability.[27] We do not need to psychologize about subconscious motivations or speculate about Lincoln's deepest purposes to notice that his reading of the speech entailed his taking on of both roles. In the Lyceum Address he delivered a quarter of a century before, he had already outlined Macbeth's prospective history in the American polity. An aging and virtuous Duncan might die at the tyrant's hand; but if the warnings were heeded, a chastened Macduff—in the company of distressed and resolute friends—could overcome the usurper and live free of inner tyranny, if he met the inner and outer challenge at once.

3

The Temperance Address

Moral Reform and Emancipation

And when the victory shall be complete—when there shall be neither a slave nor a drunkard on the earth—how proud the title of that *Land,* which may truly claim to be the birthplace and the cradle of both those revolutions, that shall have ended in that victory. (1.279)

On February 22, 1842, Lincoln addressed the Washington Temperance Society of Springfield with a speech that enlarged his discussion of reason and tyranny in the 1838 Lyceum Address. His presentation was again ostensibly apolitical, though resonant with political implications. Most notably, it added shadow and light to the portrait of human nature and the task of self-government that he had begun to produce four years before. The Lyceum Address had sketched the disturbing advances of lawless passions and the arduous means with which their tyranny could be resisted by discovering unused resources of strength within American democracy. The temperance issue presented the problem in one of its most common, dramatic, and destructive forms. Alcohol was, after all, the proverbial fuel of anger and licentiousness, a notorious destroyer of self-governing activity. Habitual drunkenness was therefore a form of slavery, perhaps one of its most damaging forms because it worked to destroy even the free man's power to love liberty. The temperance movement was, in Lincoln's view, an opportunity to resist the encroachment of this broader tyranny—if temperance could be pursued without the movement itself becoming a tyrannical force.

There is much in this 1842 address to suggest that it served several purposes. The antebellum champions of temperance had a strong philosophical affinity for the work of the antislavery cause. In the late 1830s and early '40s, both movements were centered in churches, from which they drew vehement supporters such as Edward Beecher. In Illinois, the Presbyterians had played a major role in both movements, and it was in a Presbyterian church in Springfield that Lincoln spoke. Temperance and abolition forces were often entwined up to the mid-1850s, when vote-seeking Republicans began to downplay antidrinking sentiments that had antagonized voters they hoped to recruit to their cause, especially Irish and German immigrants.[1] In the early 1840s, long before the emergence of the Republican Party, Lincoln's brand of Whig politics explicitly favored attempts to alleviate the drinker's plight and emphasized principles he would incorporate into the explicitly antislavery speeches he began to deliver in 1854. The Temperance Address gave Lincoln an opportunity to venture, in a displaced context, ideas about emancipation and the prospects for a gradual abolition of slavery.

Both subjects were full of implications for the general topic of self-government, just as the idea of self-government had a bearing upon them. The impulse to read back into Lincoln's early speeches the philosophy of his mature political career should be seriously questioned. But so must be the assumption that in the early stages of his public life Lincoln had no significant intimation that his political and philosophical thinking might take the direction he later made evident to the world. From the time he proposed his antislavery resolution in the late 1830s, delivered the Lyceum Address, and faced an audience of temperance supporters in that Springfield church, he was projecting his political career.

As we have seen, the Lyceum Address is an important introduction to Lincoln's implicit treatment of slavery within an argument about broader principles. Mob rule, he argued, created a vulnerability to Napoleonic tyranny. If mob rule continued to work its way into the bloodstream of political life, constitutional self-government would degenerate into bondage: a slavery for all, or a false freedom under a lawless tyrant. Reason would be subordinated to anger and furious ambition. In the Temperance Address Lincoln told his audience that intemperance was also a kind of "fury," a lawless submission to passion that took reason prisoner. And like the temptation toward mob rule, its power was such that reformers could not and should not assume they were immune to it. If temperance reformers wished to have a practical and just effect, they needed to recognize and act upon their own fallibility and the self-governing potential of those they found at fault.

Just as intemperance was a common condition—actual or in potential—

for all, so was slavery, though in Lincoln's careful terms the latter connection was made almost entirely by implication. Reform would have to consist of politic means to cure the entire organism, in a treatment that could not and should not be carried out, Lincoln contended, by means of shame, fear, or ill-considered draconian laws. Only if the drinker's powers of self-government were recognized and his capacity to resist the temptation of alcohol acknowledged by himself and his friends, would temperance and self-governed liberty prevail.

In the case of alcohol, Lincoln explained, the incipient danger had been almost universally detected. It was deemed worthy of "total and final banishment" by "three-fourths of mankind" if only the right means could be found (1.276–277). But enlightenment had come many generations after alcohol had become accepted as "*a very good thing*," as an enrichment of ordinary life. The moral and political zeal of the reformers ignored the magnitude of this reversal of attitudes, and hence the depth of the drinker's addiction and his capacity to reform. Their efforts had created, in Lincoln's view, a cruelly moralizing and ineffective tyranny. Meanwhile, a new set of reformers, the Washingtonians, had established an association of reformed drinkers for the purpose of encouraging the drinkers' unextinguished desire to choose a sober life. Their fraternity held promise for preserving and restoring the grounds of self-government.

Lincoln framed his attacks on the preachers' zeal through the perspective of the suffering drinker, who he said believed that the preachers' efforts served a self-interested fanaticism in favor of combining church and state. The preachers' allies, the lawyers who created legal sanctions against the distribution and drinking of alcohol, were similarly dismissed as ambitious for office. Lincoln seconded that view by calling them "impolitic" and "unjust." In their advocacy of prohibition tantamount to immediate abolition, the preachers and lawyers ignored the weaknesses and strengths of the drinker's human nature. The Washingtonians, on the other hand, knew the drinker's plight and potential because they were drinkers who had risen to sobriety. They honored the principles of law and self-government and were ready to help drinkers who sought to become nobler versions of themselves.

As though these distinctions between zealous reformers and Washingtonians were not inflammatory enough, Lincoln made a point of urging the zealous nondrinkers in his audience to join him in lending sympathy and support to those whom the Washingtonians were aiding. Lincoln's law partner, William Herndon, recalled in his biography of Lincoln that nondrinking listeners felt insulted. Lincoln's speech, he claimed, raised the ire of the churches and damaged his political prospects for years after:

> I was at the door of the church as the people passed out, and heard them discussing the speech. Many of them were open in the expression of their displeasure. "It's a shame," I heard one man say, "that he should be permitted to abuse us so in the house of the Lord." The truth was the society was composed mainly of the roughs and drunkards of the town, who had evinced a desire to reform. Many of them were too fresh from the gutter to be taken at once into the society of such people as worshipped at the church where the speech was delivered. . . . The whole thing, I repeat, was damaging to Lincoln, and gave rise to the opposition on the part of the churches which confronted him several years afterwards when he become a candidate against the noted Peter Cartwright [a preacher] for Congress.[2]

Herndon was certain Lincoln's effort was a costly failure; but his information suggests that Lincoln, whether he succeeded or not, intended to take a risky path. Appealing to a large group of citizens beyond the pale of elite reformers, he seems to have been trying to reach both audiences, to affirm solidarity with common citizens and to detach relatively genteel, churchgoing supporters of temperance from their zealous leaders. (The typical Washingtonian, Lincoln assumed aloud, was not a churchgoer [1.272].) Standing in a Presbyterian church, noting the mistaken righteousness of the preachers but favoring their general goal, praising the reformed drinkers as models, recognizing the plight of the inebriates and even the legal claims of the dram sellers, he was taking a calculated risk. The Temperance Address established a controversial view of human nature and regeneration that might temper and inspire an enlargement of self-government.

By arguing that the preachers and lawyers are *"impolitic and unjust,"* Lincoln not only means that they ignore the history of the laws and the nature of political life. They also misunderstand human nature, and hence the religious principles they claim to uphold:

> When the dram-seller and drinker, were incessantly told, not in the accents of entreaty and persuasion, diffidently addressed by erring man to an erring brother; but in the thundering tones of anathema and denunciation, with which the lordly Judge often groups together all the crimes of the felon's life,

and thrusts them in his face just ere he passes sentence of death upon him, that *they* were the authors of all the vice and misery and crime in the land; that *they* were the manufacturers and material of all the thieves and robbers and murderers that infested the earth; that *their persons* should be shunned by all the good and virtuous, as moral pestilences—I say, when they were told all this, and in this way, it is not wonderful that they were slow, *very slow,* to acknowledge the truth of such denunciations, and to join the ranks of their denouncers, in a hue and cry against themselves.

To have expected them to do otherwise than they did—to have expected them not to meet denunciation with denunciation, crimination with crimination, and anathema with anathema, was to expect a reversal of human nature, which is God's decree, and never can be reversed. (1.272–273)

In the Lyceum Address, Lincoln had argued that a "political religion" of reverence for the law, combined with the political friendship of self-governing citizens, was the only adequate defense against the insidious and powerful tyrannies of mob rule and Napoleonic dictatorship. The Temperance Address makes a complementary case for respecting the drinker's complex humanity in the light of his God-given nature—not only his weaknesses but also his higher capacities, which can somehow withstand his addiction when he resolves to rise, with the moral support of his friends, to his fuller stature.

The old reformers confront the greatest problems in ignorance of their true difficulty, and without the means to draw from their followers' natures and associations the strengths they need to reform. They expect too much, and think too little, of the drinker's character:

> Another error, as it seems to me, into which the old reformers fell, was, the position that all habitual drunkards were utterly incorrigible, and therefore, must be turned adrift, and damned without remedy, in order that the grace of temperance might abound to the temperate *then,* and to all mankind some hundred years thereafter. There is in this something so repugnant to humanity, so uncharitable, so cold-blooded and feelingless, that it never did, nor ever can enlist the enthusiasm of a popular cause. (1.275)

If so many sober citizens regularly resist fiery threats of eternal damnation, how can anyone, especially those who are not sober, be urged to act for the sake of bringing temperance to the next generation? What good can come from strategies that ignore the natural tendency to resist looking ahead? Lincoln insists that effective reform depends upon fidelity to human nature, which requires the reformer to appeal to self-interest:

> Posterity has done nothing for us; and theorise on it as we may, practically we shall do very little for it, unless we are made to think, we are, at the same time, doing something for ourselves. What an ignorance of human nature does it exhibit, to ask or expect a whole community to rise up and labor for the *temporal* happiness of *others* after *themselves* shall be consigned to the dust, a majority of which community take no pains whatever to secure their own eternal welfare, at a no greater distant day? (1.275)

Here the censure of evangelical motives is, in its first impact, severe. Preachers who expect to convert their audiences to the cause of prohibition and universal temperance forget the limitations of their own preaching of redemption, which has little effect on most people even though it threatens them with horrible punishments. By Lincoln's estimate, the temperance preachers are doubly cruel: they abandon the sinner for the sake of securing grace for the nondrinker, and they offer the sinner no way to act upon his own redemption except to give himself up to the flames.

As a consequence, when they call upon their audiences to join the temperance movement, they do not concern themselves with the true plight of the drinker but rather fix their sights on the apocalyptic goal of complete prohibition, to be enjoyed by later generations. Callous toward the sinner and self-satisfied in identifying themselves with the already temperate, they see no reason to connect the work of the movement to the "interests" of those who labor in it. In order to avoid the appearance of validating the sinner's condition or lowering the status of the nondrinking party, the old reformers ignore the task of building support for a truly "popular cause."

The Washingtonians know, according to Lincoln, that each drinker needs "every moral support and influence, that can possibly be brought to his aid, and thrown around him" (1.277). They understand the converse: that he must first be convinced that the reformer is a "sincere friend." A "kind, unassuming persuasion" must be used—"ever adopted," as Lincoln says, as the guiding method of that association. Such persuasion must appeal to the heart, not as though it were a mechanism of passion but because it is "the great high road" to reason and assent. The true reformer needs to use "honey" rather than "gall" not for mere effect but in order to appeal to the drinker's needy vigilance. Despite his weaknesses, the inebriate's heart continues to serve and inform the reason, at least to the extent that it knows a hypocrite. Persuasion that is "kind," in the Shakespearean sense of the word that Lincoln would have known, would recognize the need for, and would embody, kindness: a confirmation of the mutuality of the reformer's and the drinker's condition. The genuine reformer would in this sense not only convey his deep identification with the drinker's need for assistance but also demonstrate his recognition that the drinker has a power to govern himself—to seek and choose sobriety—in his fallen state (1.273). This is what Lincoln means when he suggests that the Washingtonians have surpassed the preachers as examples of Christian forgiveness:

> *They* adopt a more enlarged philanthropy. They go for the present as well as future good. *They* labor for all *now* living, as well as all *hereafter* to live. *They* teach *hope* to all—*despair* to none. As applying to their cause, they deny the doctrine of unpardonable sin. As in Christianity it is taught, so in this *they* teach, that
>
> "While the lamp holds out to burn,
> The vilest sinner may return."
>   (1.276)

In keeping with the sentiments of the hymnal, they expose the hypocrisy of those who hold to religion only to punish others at a distance.

According to Lincoln's formulation of the problem, the drinker is likely to have a capacity for "genius and generosity":

> There seems ever to have been a proneness in the brilliant, and the warm-blooded, to fall into this vice. The demon of intemperance ever seems to have delighted in sucking the blood of genius and of generosity. What one of us but can call to mind some dear relative, more promising in youth than all his fellows, who has fallen a sacrifice to his rapacity? He ever seems to have gone forth, like the Egyptian angel of death, commissioned to slay if not the first, the fairest born of every family. (1.278)

The hyperbolic simile conflates the demon of alcohol with the "angel of death" as well as the story of the Hebrews' escape from their Egyptian slavery after the deaths of the Egyptians' firstborn sons. Lincoln's compact allusion makes alcoholic slavery afflict the firstborn sons in a manner that joins the enslaved chosen people and the firstborn slave master: both embody the curse of slavery and the prospect of redemption. In this combination of roles the genius drinker is a Washingtonian paradigm of the self-governing, self-enslaving sufferer who in his fallen condition retains the power to reform himself. And he is suggestively analogous to the master of real slaves, whose genius enslaves him to the passion to tyrannize while offering moral redemption if he would turn that genius toward emancipation.

Deftly analogizing the temperance campaign to gradual abolition, the speech makes another apposite point with regard to alcohol. A general recognition of the prevalence and acceptance of alcohol for many generations, Lincoln argues, ought to temper the reformers' zeal for laws that arbitrarily divide sober souls from drunken infidels and those who serve them liquor:

> I have said that denunciations against dram-sellers and dram-drinkers, are *unjust* as well as impolitic. Let us see.
>
> I have not enquired at what period of time the use of intoxicating drinks commenced; nor is it important to know. It is sufficient that to all of us who now inhabit the world, the practice of drinking them, is just as old as the world itself,—that is, we have seen the one, just as long as we have seen the other. When all such of us, as have now reached the years of maturity, first opened our eyes upon the stage of existence, we found intoxicating liquor, recognized by every body, used by every body, and repudiated by nobody. It commonly entered into the first draught of the infant, and the last draught of the dying man. From the sideboard of the parson, down to the ragged pocket of the houseless loafer, it was constantly found. Physicians prescribed it in this, that, and the other disease. Government provided it for its soldiers and sailors; and to have a rolling or raising, a husking or hoedown, any where without it, was *positively insufferable.* (1.274)

In America the idea of abolition or even the notion of limiting the range of slavery by law was also a remarkably late development, wrongly taken for granted as the norm when slavery had long been assumed to be "as old as the world itself."

One can see from these currents that Lincoln is adjusting the roles of religion and law so that they serve an association of temperance seekers who are aware of their imperfections and yet know and seek self-respect. He does not use antipreacher terminology simply to win over unchurched or disillusioned citizens, nor does he dilute the importance of law simply because he disagrees with coercive prohibition. By his own lights, Lincoln takes religion seriously because the Washingtonians do, and he honors the law as the work of custom and self-government with all their flaws and strengths. Rather than rely on the brimstone and draconian laws that in the hands of the old reformers denied drinkers their self-respect, he cultivates self-respect for the sake of political friendship. Among citizens who see themselves and each other as fellow human beings and citizens, a self-respecting association arises out of their mutual recognition of their strengths with their weaknesses. It seems reasonable to assume that reformed and struggling drinkers and their non-drinking friends would be more devoted to reform and the rule of law than those who submitted to the preachers' curses or the lawyers' arbitrary prohibitions.

According to Lincoln's description, the success of the Washingtonians is based on a renewed version of Christianity. They manage an earthly salvation that combines religious experience with scientific and political enlightenment:

> [T]hey, by experiment upon experiment, and example upon example, prove the maxim to be no less true in the one case than in the other. On every hand we behold those, who but yesterday were the chief of sinners, now the chief apostles of the cause. Drunken devils are cast out by ones, by sevens, and by legions; and their unfortunate victims, like the poor possessed, who was redeemed from his long and lonely wanderings in the tombs, are publishing to the ends of the earth, how great things have been done for them. (1.276)

The Washingtonians help bring about that redemption in imitation of the gospels' account of Jesus' ministering to a man "out of the tombs" who, possessed of an "unclean spirit," wanders alone, unsubdued by anyone but Jesus. Washingtonians greet him by calming his fears of retribution and calling out to his rejected spirit. The biblical parallel would have resonated among Lincoln's audience:

> And when [Jesus] was come out of the ship, immediately there met him out of the tombs a man with an unclean spirit, Who had his dwelling, among the tombs; and no man could bind him, no, not with chains: Because that he had been often bound with fetters and chains, and the chains had been plucked asunder by him, and the fetters broken in pieces: neither could any man tame

him. And always, night and day, he was in the mountains, and in the tombs, crying and cutting himself with stones. But when he saw Jesus afar off, he ran and worshipped him, And cried with a loud voice, and said, What have I to do with thee, Jesus, thou Son of the most high God? I adjure thee by God, that thou torment me not. For he said unto him, Come out of the man, thou unclean spirit. And he asked him, What is thy name? And he answered, saying, My name is Legion: for we are many. And he besought him much that he would not send them away out of the country.[3]

By displacing and redirecting biblical references to judgment (the Angel of Death, the Last Judgment) and allying his argument with scenes of New Testament healing, Lincoln once again throws down the gauntlet before preachers who would rather abandon the drinker to perdition than lower themselves to the exigencies of a politico-religious association that tries to bring about temperance step by step. Herndon's criticism of Lincoln may be pointing to a rankling passage on this subject in which Lincoln calls upon the nondrinking elite in his audience to imitate divine condescension, to join the unwashed, tainted society of the Washingtonians for the good of the temperance cause:

"But," say some," we are no drunkards; and we shall not acknowledge ourselves such by joining a reformed drunkard's society, whatever our influence might be." Surely no Christian will adhere to this objection. If they believe, as they profess, that Omnipotence condescended to take on himself the form of sinful man, and, as such, to die an ignominious death for their sakes, surely they will not refuse submission to the infinitely lesser condescension, for the temporal, and perhaps eternal salvation, of a large, erring, and unfortunate class of their own fellow creatures. Nor is the condescension very great. (1.277–278)

Lincoln's words test the border between persuasion and sarcasm. Joining the society of reformed drinkers as a supporter of the struggling drinker might seem a modest test of the churchgoers' faith; but the reversal of roles Lincoln advocates as though it were a little thing must have strained what remained of his influence with conventional leaders in the temperance cause.

There were differences among the Washingtonians, particularly over whether friendly persuasion was enough.[4] Lincoln chose to delineate the breach between the old and the new reformers in stark terms. To appreciate

Lincoln's choice and the relative delicacy of his maneuvering between sua-
sion and sarcasm, we can compare the Temperance Address to a Washingtonian tract that was published the year before by Jesse W. Goodrich.
Goodrich, seeking to establish a single credo for the Washingtonians based
on the Declaration of Independence, embedded his ambition in his sweeping title, *A Second Declaration of Independence; or, The Manifesto of All the
Washington Total Abstinence Societies of the United States of America.* He declared that he designed his pamphlet as part of his attempt to make the
Washingtonian creed the foundation of the republic, "to render [the original
Declaration] subservient" to "the cause of Temperance," the true "cause of
Patriotism."[5]

Goodrich's strange effort to supplant the Declaration shows us how
volatile and protean the temperance cause could be. Its champions could
fuse various political and moral arguments about the nature and destiny of
the republic. Goodrich goes so far as to justify the Washingtonians' project as
though it were the true Jeffersonian revolution, this time pulling down the
tyrant alcohol. Lincoln uses metaphors of tyranny and conquest to characterize temperance's enemy and goal, but his analogies are ostensibly apolitical: he draws them from the Bible. Goodrich is intent upon aggressive political action: the Washingtonians must attack those economic and political
forces that keep them down. He hurls abuse at the "Reign of Alcohol" and its
train of abuses, contending that legislators and retailers who have refused to
prohibit the liquor trade have created them. An evil combination "has en-
deavored to prevent the reformation of the 'inebriates' of these States; for
that purpose violating the laws for the regulation of his *Liquid Fires*—refusing to pass others to encourage their banishment hence,—rearing new
'Signs'—and spreading new temptations throughout the land."[6]

Lincoln draws attention to the greater incidence of drunkenness among
those who are unusually generous and brilliant; Goodrich zealously divides
the world into those who maintain or recover their native moderation, and
those who have lost it and refuse to reform. Inspired by the revolutionary
spirit of the Declaration, he prepares for a revolutionary judgment day. Paro-
dying Jefferson's phrases, he replaces Locke with Rousseau: "[A]ll men are
made *temperate,*" he says. They are "endowed by their Creator with certain
natural and innocent desires." In place of life, liberty, and the pursuit of
happiness, he inserts the kind of innocence that is exhibited in man's love

of pristine "cold water"—that "crystal element" from "Eden" which is now threatened by sinister powers within the republic. Like a tyrant king quartering troops in the colonies, alcohol must be condemned for "quartering in our Alms-houses and Penitentiaries large and expensive bodies of *rum-ruined* paupers and criminals among us."[7] The persons Lincoln never stigmatized, whom he criticized the preachers for abandoning, become in Goodrich's conception the troops of an alien power.

As a Washingtonian, Goodrich upholds the same organizational doctrine Lincoln praises: reformed drinkers have a special authority in the effort to convert others to the cause. But the pamphleteer turns that mission toward distinguishing between the sheep and the goats. The reformed drinker is the revolutionary patriot while the unregenerate man is a self-oppressed representative of the Old World: "[W]e have reminded [moderate drinkers] of the circumstances of the voyage of *our emigration*," he says; yet "[t]hey too, in vast numbers, are still deaf to the voice of reason and expostulation. We must, therefore, acquiesce in the necessity which announces our separation, and hold *them*, as we hold the *rest* of *inebriates*,—to themselves their own worst *enemies* in drinking,—in abstinence, their own best *friends*."[8] The drinker's task is his alone, while the association's priority is to smash the structures of oppression before it is too late. There must be a quick capture of the "Monster Demon." Alcohol must not be allowed "even a *foot-hold* or a single *throat-hold* among a free and sober people." Washingtonians must imitate the old colonists and "totally dissolve" their connections with "all the numerous branches of the *alcoholic Family*,"[9] by implication doing away with mercantile and political interests that support the alcohol trade.

We have seen that Lincoln's approach was far different. He opposed draconian legislation and the zealous coercion it would justify. Like Goodrich, he was not averse to using hyperbole to highlight and project the urgency of his case; but when he likened the temperance cause to war against a "demon," he looked to the inner strengths and limitations of the drinkers and their fraternal associations. These differences do not mean that he did not make use of religion. Steering away from Goodrich's strident political apocalypticism, he invoked the political religion of reverence for the Washingtonians' ideal: that exemplar of sobriety and self-government, George Washington. Because the foe of the drinker aspiring to sobriety is more powerful than a thing of human, political, or natural manufacture, the drinker needs something more than human power to fight it. The inspiring instance of that power, as in the Lyceum Address, is the man who was "*long since* the mightiest cause of civil liberty," and who is "*still* mightiest in moral reformation." The astral political exemplum of self-government in the republic's imagination, he is Lincoln's (and the Washingtonians') measure of the movement's success (2.279).

We can better understand Lincoln's entire argument by looking more closely at Washington's reputation, in which temperance was incorporated into the idea and practice of self-government. In Parson Weems's popular biography, Washington is heroically temperate but not a teetotaler.[10] His moral reformation is a self-conquest that exhibits and serves the cause of self- government. In governing himself, he turns outward to harden and temper the revolutionary ambitions of others. His triumph is first "over *himself,* then over the *British,* and uniformly to set . . . bright examples of *human perfectibility* and *true greatness.*" In early nineteenth-century America, Lincoln could evoke these proverbial ideas about Washington's qualities merely by speaking his name "in its naked deathless splendor."

For Weems the most famous instances of Washington's greatness were his victories over external tyranny *and* the temptation to become a tyrant. He "obtained for his countrymen the completest victory, and for himself the most unbounded power; and then . . . returned that power, accompanied with the weight of his own great character and advice to establish a government that should immortalize the blessings of liberty."[11] The temperance movement that emerged a generation after his death adopted his name and revolutionary legacy as the vanquisher of tyranny within as well as without. Another reformer in that movement put the argument succinctly: "We labor in the cause of freedom, from a greater tyrant than British taxation—a slavery that binds both body and mind—and could Washington speak to us from his starry home, he would bid us go on, as worthy sons and noble sires."[12]

Weems offers a surprisingly complex illustration of Washington's revolutionary self-control when he discusses his "benevolence," which the biographer associates with his hero's ability to take command over his anger and turn his feelings toward friendship. Temperance is not in this case mere abstention. It is the work of reason as it calms angry men and opens their hearts to admirable affection. Weems makes a point of showing how Washington, after being insulted by the speech and actions of an acquaintance, becomes friends with the man with whom he could easily have come to blows:

Reason whispered the folly of harbouring black passions in his soul, poisoning his peace; he instantly banished them, and went to a ball, to drink sweet streams of friendship from the eyes of happy friends. . . . In what history, ancient or modern, sacred or profane, can you find, in so young a man, only 22, such an instance of that true heroic valour which combats malignant passions—conquers unreasonable *self*—rejects the hell of *hatred,* and invites the heaven of *love* into our own bosoms, and into those of our brethren with whom we may have had a falling out?[13]

As the exemplar of reasoned resolve, Washington puts down his fury by listening to reason and then swiftly banishing the "black passions of his soul." Fighting against seemingly insuperable odds and his own will to power, he somehow calms himself and his followers, and then secures the peace with an even greater showing of restraint.

Of course, in Weems's time Washington was famous for having promoted humility as the watchword for the victorious revolutionaries. Weems is now notorious for writing an exaggerated, highly selective version of Washington's life. In Lincoln's time, by his own account, the influence of Weems's book had begun to fade among the young. But the resonance of Weems's sentiments in Lincoln's imagination cannot be so easily dismissed. Speaking before the New Jersey legislature on his way to his inauguration, Lincoln famously identified Weems's biography of Washington as one of the inspirations of his political career and his idea of the union:

May I be pardoned if, upon this occasion, I mentioned that away back in my childhood, the earliest days of my being able to read, I got hold of a small book, such a one as few of the younger members have ever seen, "Weems's Life of Washington." I remember all the accounts there given of the battlefields and struggles for the liberties of the country, and none fixed themselves upon my imagination so deeply as the struggle here at Trenton, New Jersey. The crossing of the river; the contest with the Hessians; the great hardships endured at that time, all fixed themselves on my memory more than any single revolutionary event; and you all know, for you have all been boys, how these early impressions last longer than any others. I recollect thinking then, boy even though I was, that there must have been something more than common that those men struggled for. I am exceedingly anxious that that thing which they struggled for; that something even more than National Independence; that something that held out a great promise to all the people of the world to all time to come; I am exceedingly anxious that this Union, the Constitution, and the liberties of the people shall be perpetuated in accordance with the original idea for which that struggle was made. (4.235–236)

Speaking the next day in Independence Hall, Lincoln defined that "something" as "liberty" and the "hope" of liberty that Washington's revolutionary struggle gave "to the world for all future time" (4. 240). Here, as we have seen in the early speeches, the securing of that liberty depends upon temperance in the face of provocation, at least as much as heroism in battle. Moving to the balcony to deliver yet another brief speech, Lincoln defined the "spirit that animated our fathers" in Weems-like terms, as a "fraternal feeling" that resists "passion, ill-temper, and precipitate action on all occasions" (4.241).

Lincoln draws from a similar stream of associations in 1842 when he describes the plight and heroic potential of the common drinker, whose liberty, like the liberty of the republic, derives from self-overcoming acts. In the Lyceum Address, Lincoln had treated the will to power as a phenomenon evident in rare individuals. In the Temperance Address, it is a potentiality within every drinker, whose appetite grows, Lincoln says, "a hundred fold stronger . . . than any natural appetite can be" as he tries to become sober. Success "requires a most powerful moral effort" because the appetite seems to exceed human proportions, as though it were a vampire-like "demon of intemperance," something clearly beyond human control (1.277–278). In their struggle for sobriety, drinkers are paradigms in this sense for nondrinkers; both must overcome an external tyranny—and resist a great tyranny within themselves—in order to secure their liberty.

* * *

Lincoln keeps the extraordinary danger of that tyranny before his audience by repeatedly referring to the demon of drink and by making a hyperbolic yet suggestive reference to the "fury" that reason must overcome if the drinker is to become sober. In a concluding allusion to *Macbeth,* he links demonic power and fury to moral and political tyranny. In the peroration to the address, he looks forward to the victory of Washingtonians as though it could reverse Shakespeare's paradigmatic history of intemperance: "Hail fall of Fury! Reign of Reason, all hail!" (1.279). The line repeats and reverses the meaning of the witches' greeting to Macbeth in the first act of the play, in which Shakespeare shows us the temptation that will ruin his dark hero:

3. Witch	Hail!
1. Witch	Lesser than Macbeth, and greater.
2. Witch	Not so happy, yet much happier.
3. Witch	Thou shalt get kings, though thou be none.
	So all hail, Macbeth and Banquo!
1. Witch	Banquo and Macbeth, all hail![14]

The alternation of "hail" and "all hail," found nowhere else in Shakespeare, is a signature of this famous scene.[15] Lincoln uses "all hail" to parody and redirect the demonic prophecy that Macbeth and Banquo will obtain kingly power.

Lincoln's attachment to *Macbeth* is well known. During the Civil War he told a White House visitor that it was his favorite Shakespearean play. He seems to have considered it Shakespeare's most comprehensive statement on the human condition. He had been reading it over for years. In 1842 it suggested an apt correspondence: the murderous Macbeth, intoxicated with and tormented by the assurance of his destiny as well as the liquor he shares with Lady Macbeth, is a spectacular negative instance of Washingtonian resolve and sobriety. Macbeth's complex and compelling tragedy is a powerful resource for Lincoln's effort to crystallize his thinking about the temptations of drink, the power of ambitious fury, and the resolve to turn back the tyrannical will. Shakespeare's hero is a boiling caldron of conflicting impulses—a fit point of reference for a speech about the demon of intemperance and the collective resolve that is needed to subdue him.

In the words of Shakespeare's Macduff, the man who will finally slay Macbeth, "[b]oundless intemperance / In nature is tyranny."[16] Macbeth is called tyrant twice as many times as any other figure in the plays. The crime he commits that turns the kingdom upside down—his murder of the head and ruler of the realm—is notoriously aided by drink. Macbeth's ambivalent nature, which his wife thinks is "too full o' th' milk of human kindness," tips toward murder when she displaces the milk with alcohol, and by "pour[ing]" her "spirits" (her intoxicating words) in his ear.[17] The metaphor becomes fact when she rings the bell that tells Macbeth his "drink" is ready, thus signaling him to kill the sleeping Duncan.[18] She drugs the drinks that put the king's guardians to sleep and uses the drink herself for the opposite effect: after imbibing, she and her husband become "bold" in their ambition to destroy all opposition.[19] In *Macbeth* drink is a dramatic agent of false, irrational resolve and a catalyst of the will to power.

Once the head of the kingdom is dead, Macbeth's rule is called a "distempered cause," having lost its subservience to measure and reason.[20] His actions arise from "fury," and his life becomes meaningless—"full of sound and fury"—as he succumbs to his intoxication.[21] He seeks to end all resistance to his will by suicidally combating the last proddings of his reason and conscience. Lincoln's double apostrophe, "Hail fall of Fury! Reign of Reason, all hail!" fittingly greets the demise of a Macbeth-like tyrant within the drinker. He is to be replaced by the rule of Reason—the governor of the reformed drinker's self-government.

* * *

The problem of intemperance, as Lincoln develops it in these various ways, is a version of the problem posed by the presence of slavery in the American republic. Its history offers a suggestive, displaced paradigm for the history of slavery agitation. As we have seen, Lincoln observes how a long period of toleration and indifference, even moral endorsement, was followed by repudiation—a fundamental but uneven shift in attitudes that amplified and aggravated old sectional differences and endangered, in various ways, the underpinnings of the laws and constitutional government itself. Lincoln observes that intemperance was long thought to resemble a "hereditary disease," to be treated as "a *misfortune,* and not as a *crime,* or even as a *disgrace*" (1.274–275).

> The universal sense of mankind, on any subject, is an argument, or at least an *influence* not easily overcome. The success of the argument in favor of the existence of an over-ruling Providence, mainly depends upon that sense; and men ought not, in justice, to be denounced for yielding to it, in any case, or for giving it up slowly, *especially,* where they are backed by interest, fixed habits, or burning appetites. (1.275)

Lincoln looks forward to a time when "[e]ven the dram-maker, and dram-seller, will have glided into other occupations *so* gradually, as never to have felt the shock of change" (1.279). But the belatedness of the northern reforms, a postrevolutionary phenomenon deeply influenced by the philosophy and experience of the revolution, meant that heedless reform that defied history and human nature could endanger the republic of laws within which the earlier reforms were possible. If the zealous reformer condemned intemperance in such a way that the drink-ridden citizen (and, by analogy, slave-owning citizens and tolerating states) would be set "adrift, and damned without remedy, in order that the grace of temperance might abound to the temperate" (1.275), the drinker and slave owner would be tempted all the more to embrace and defend the practices that their foes (and perhaps they themselves) found so repellant.

In the Temperance Address, Lincoln does not equate historical attitudes toward slavery and intemperance. But such a comparison hovers over his argument because his remarks on traditional views of alcohol so readily convert into an implicit reference to slavery's three-hundred-year history in the New World giving way within two generations, between the Declaration of Independence and the time of Lincoln's speech, to the expulsion of slavery from the northern states and growing resistance to change, under increasingly vehement denunciation, in the South. The confluence of the histories of alcohol and slavery, as well as their distinct differences, would have created stresses—and controversial opportunities for drawing analogies—that speakers on either subject would have found difficult to ignore. The very attempt to avoid such allusions across these divides would have forced an orator to cope with audiences' sensitivities to apparent analogies between proximate subject matters.

Speaking in Britain in 1846, Frederick Douglass framed the issue of slavery in terms that acknowledged the common opinion that there were important similarities between intemperance and slavery, while asserting his objection to the idea that they were the same: "It is common in this country to distinguish every bad thing by the name of slavery. Intemperance is slavery; to be deprived of the right to vote, says one, is slavery; to have to work hard is slavery, says another. . . . I do not wish for a moment to detract from the horror with which the evil of intemperance is contemplated. . . . But I am here to say that I think the term slavery is sometimes abused by identifying it with that which it is not."[22] In Lincoln's hands, the analogy was suggestive but not automatic. It drew out the tyrannical nature of each scourge without necessarily giving them the same moral weight. At the same time, it highlighted the peculiarly destructive power of each. Intemperance, as he presented it, revealed itself more fully to an audience that came to see its deeper resemblances to slavery. Conversely, the characteristic evil of slavery, as he implicitly treated it, was more apparent in the light of alcohol's demonic tyranny over the drinker, who embodies both the slave and the master in the way he becomes bound to his own tyrannical fury.

Lincoln is against promotion of the manufacture and consumption of intoxicating beverages, much as he is against—from an early stage in his career—the moral justification of slavery. Yet he appeals to a capacity to appreciate the deeply influential power of long-held common sentiments, even though they might in his time be considered by a majority to favor repellant practices. The ability to see the damage of intemperance or slavery, he implies, is not the same as a moral authority to condemn the drinker, the slave owner, or all laws protecting the peculiar institution. From many angles, Lincoln pushes his case that the newly won recognition of these twin evils does not confer a profound moral superiority on one potentially tyrannical human being over another. It reveals his listeners' kinship in their vulnerability to the depredations of drunken fury, just as it draws them together as champions of moral reform. If they do *not* see any significant analogies between intemperance and slavery, they are resisting Lincoln's characteristic invitation to consider the nature of self-government.

> When the victory shall be complete—when there shall be neither a slave nor a drunkard on the earth—how proud the title of that *Land*, which may truly claim to be the birth-place and the cradle of both those revolutions, that shall have ended in that victory. (1.279)

* * *

That victory, Lincoln warns his audience, will not come quickly. Isolated drinkers can do little by themselves to reform; the Washingtonians must become increasingly influential. The Lyceum Address had sought to combine "cold, calculating, unimpassioned reason " with political friendship in order to instruct and encourage sober citizens to array themselves against the tyranny of the mob and the singularly ambitious destroyer of the Founders' institutions (1.115). The Temperance Address supplies the missing steps to a more explicitly synthetic argument about the political and moral indispensability of developing strong sympathies and friendships in the pursuit of these ends. Not all passions are enemies. Sympathy and friendship are good passions informed by reason, and they support reason in turn to help the drinker return to sobriety.

This explanation is incomplete, however, without an account of the relation between friendship and the individual will. As we read the speech, we need to look for more evidence of Lincoln's understanding of the will in the self-governed life. For it is not clear how or when the drunkard chooses to become sober, and his reformation is neither instantaneous nor inevitable. The role of friendship in this transformation is not obvious. In a crucial passage, Lincoln adumbrates the function of the will at the moment the intemperate man resolves to become sober:

> [W]hen one, who has long been known as a victim of intemperance, bursts the fetters that have bound him, and appears before his neighbors "clothed, and in his right mind," a redeemed specimen of long lost humanity, and stands up with tears of joy trembling in eyes, to tell of the miseries *once* endured, *now* to be endured no more forever; of his once naked and starving children, now clad and fed comfortably; of a wife long weighed down with woe, weeping, and a broken heart, now restored to health, happiness, and renewed affection; and how easily it all is done, once it is resolved to be done; however simple his language, there is a logic, and an eloquence in it, that few, with human feelings, can resist. (1.272)

Our judgment of the meaning of this passage, in the context of the entire speech, will have an important bearing on our interpretation of the Temperance Address as a whole. If it is true that Lincoln is analogically addressing the issue of slavery, is he saying that reform will be spontaneous? The moment of the decision for temperance is freighted with implications for Lincoln's understanding of the prospects for a regeneration of slaveholders' attitudes and for a broadening of reformers' understanding of how tyranny is to be truly overcome. What role, if any, can political friendship and sympathy play in this revolution?

The decision to give up alcohol, Lincoln says, is in one sense easy—if the drinker's resolve is strong: "[H]ow easily it all is done, once it is resolved to be done" (1.272). But it is not at all clear how the drinker makes his resolution in the first place. When we demand to know Lincoln's understanding of the drinker's mind at this moment of truth, the way seems closed. The origin of the drinker's resolution resides somewhere in the disjunction between the long history of unhappiness that preceded the change and the evidence of his family's happiness after it. Why did he show his resolve when he did?

What exactly did he resolve to do? Lincoln says there are answers to these questions in what the reformed drinker says so convincingly with his simple "logic" and "eloquence."

We already know that as a Washingtonian the former drinker benefited from the supportive company of reformed drinkers. In Lincoln's hyperbolic sentence, there is another part of the answer: the reformed drinker seems to have known something about the suffering he was causing ("of a wife long weighed down with woe") before the change. But the grounds for the change are not clear: it is the ease of the transformation that the one-time drunkard finds worth communicating, not the reasoning behind the choice. He seems to have had a sense of what the change would be once he resolved to bring it about; the idea of his new life persisted in his nearly subhuman existence. But it is not obvious how that sense might have molded his resolve to become sober. Although Lincoln's brief and simple explanation imitates the reformed drinker's simple eloquence, he does not attempt to give his audience a reformed drinker's actual words. We get the impression that the intemperate man knew something about himself he could not fully articulate and then was able to make a choice. In what way that choice was informed by his reason and imagination, we do not know.

A review of Lincoln's correspondence with his friend Joshua Speed during the months before and after he delivered the Temperance Address tells us something about the method and meaning of the drinker's resolution to live in sobriety. Developing the power to make and keep resolutions was a problematic preoccupation of Lincoln's into his thirties. *Honor's Voice,* Douglas L. Wilson's detailed examination of the biographical evidence of this period, reveals the complexity of Lincoln's struggle to regain confidence in his power of resolve, especially in affairs of the heart leading up to his final decision to marry Mary Todd.[23] Here it is worth focusing on a few discursive clues about the meaning Lincoln attached to the act of resolution in his own affairs of the heart, and then seeing whether they help us understand his thinking about temperance and slavery.

January 1841 marked the beginning of Lincoln's strange descent into a melancholia that alarmed his friends. If we consult his own account of his condition during that time, we see him attributing his melancholy to his profound disappointment in his lack of resolve. The good guess of biographers is that Lincoln was paradoxically obsessed with his inability to persist in his courtship of Mary Todd. In a letter to his friend Joshua Speed a year after the engagement had been broken off, he set out his dilemma as one caught between his desire to be faithful to his purposes and his painful awareness that he was failing in that resolve:

> I must regain my confidence in my own ability to keep my resolves when they are made. In that ability, you know, I once prided myself as the only, or at least the chief, gem of my character; that gem I lost—how, and when, you too well know. I have not yet regained it; and until I do, I can not trust myself in any matter of much importance. (1.289)

Toward the end of 1841 and in the months after delivering the Temperance Address, Lincoln recovered enough to offer his friend some remarkable advice in response to Speed's similar hesitations regarding his engagement and marriage to Fanny Henning. It would seem to be overreaching to link such sentiments with Lincoln's formal address to the Washingtonians were it not for Lincoln's efforts to signal such a connection. In his letters of advice he refers to the address several times, requesting that Speed and his wife read it aloud "as an act of charity to me" (1.283), and then explaining that he is sending them a copy of the speech (1.290).

It is likely that Lincoln's letters to Speed drew from what he had learned about his own difficulties, and from his hope that a happier outcome was possible:

> Again, you say you much fear that that Elysium of which you have dreamed so much, is never to be realized. Well, if it shall not, I dare swear, it will not be the fault of her who is now your wife. I now have no doubt that it is the peculiar misfortune of both you and me, to dream dreams of Elysium far exceeding all that any thing earthly can realize. (1.280)

Speed's problem, Lincoln argues, was to distinguish between two passions, one that was tyrannizing over his capacity for earthly love, the other that he was experiencing in the sight of his beloved's "heavenly *black eyes*" (1.266). Tempting him with the prospect of a happiness without limit, the first passion consisted of dreams of perfection that were acting upon him like a supremely intoxicating liquor or a furious ambition. The intensity and boundlessness of his imagined happiness, Lincoln told him, had made earthly happiness seem unattainable.

Speed had therefore convinced himself, Lincoln writes, that he had "*reasoned*" himself into the marriage rather than acting upon love. He had suffered from "an apprehension," before the wedding and apparently for a brief time after, that he did not love his beloved "as [he] should" (1.266). His resolve was in danger of failing, Lincoln argues, because it did not rely upon his real love, the heartfelt aspiration that drew him to his beloved's beauty. To make the distinction between the two passions, Speed would need the power to remember, discern, and enjoy the combination of heaven and earth in his beloved's eyes, those proverbial windows on the soul that are the physical attributes of the beloved's inspiring yet earthly beauty. "Say candidly, were not those heavenly *black eyes*, the whole basis of all your early *reasoning* on the subject?" (1.266) In order to escape his conviction and dark foreboding that his mere reason had led him to love, Speed needed to reason more carefully and realize that his beloved's beauty had spurred his early, confident thoughts about courting and marriage. He could then see that his love, grounded in something terrestrial as well as transcendent, was real. It had begun in the heart, where he was afraid he did not love. And it had engaged his reasoning power thereafter because it was real. It had directed his thoughts in the sense that he became "unable to *reason* [himself] *out* of it." The point is humorous and apt. Speed did not rationalize after all. Lincoln was telling him that his reason, as it was led by his true apprehension of his beloved's eyes, could guide him back into love, out of his melancholy. Speed needed, in other words, a kind of reverence, a compound of reason and passion that would inspire and yet temper him as he entered into matrimony. Rather than being torn between dreams and reason, he needed reverence in order to make real his resolve to court and marry his beloved.

This private reverence, with the power to overcome the lover's melancholy slavery to a tyrannical passion, hearkens back to Lincoln's conception of the drinker's reverent turn, in his thoughts of his family and its lasting happiness, toward sobriety. It reminds us of Lincoln's emphasis on the goodness of the heart, "the great high road" to reason (1.273), and his treatment of public reverence in the Lyceum Address, which turned upon the idea that political religion—reverence compounded of humility and resolution—could encourage the right combination of moderation and desire to resist the tyranny within as well as without. All these kinds of reverence, as Lincoln presents them, are capable of freeing the vulnerable sufferer or imperfect citizen to live a self-governed, devoted life. His power to act well grows with his capacity to be thus inspired in a world he knows to be mortal yet in some sense beyond mortality, and in need of his resolve. Then he can throw off the tyranny of intemperance in love, in the consumption of alcohol, and in the mob's and the genius's attempts to make their furious passions the law for all.

These are, of course, patterns of inference rather than records of resolute deeds. We cannot conclude that Lincoln or Speed became more resolute because he thought or read such things. Douglas L. Wilson's account of Lincoln's courtship of Mary Todd shows how an intricate combination of events interacted with his hesitations and choices on the road to matrimony and resolution. But thinking—certainly the power of thought as Lincoln used it— is a kind of deed. Lincoln's life in politics, one could say, is a story of the power of "resolves" that largely derived from his ideas about human nature, love, friendship, self-government, and human beings' capacity to rise or descend according to how well those ideas were understood and defended.

The more closely we look at Lincoln's early speeches, the more difficult it is to dismiss their eccentricities as the immature or unguarded displays of an ambitious yet obscure Whig. In 1838 and 1842, Lincoln invoked and developed various ideas of reverence in his attempts to resolve crucial problems. He expressed himself in private and public environments in which the meaning of self-government and the problem of promoting self-government generated a high order of controversy. And he presented his ideas persuasively, trying to change, temper, and draw forth minds and dispositions, suggestively embodying what he was saying in the way he was saying it. Rather than giving us symptoms of his prepresidential insufficiency or a distant preview of his grand presidential persona, the Temperance Address is a window on Lincoln's understanding of issues and modes of eloquence that he was to develop with momentous consequences in later years.

The Speech on the War with Mexico
and the Eulogy for Zachary Taylor

Injustice and Heroic Virtue

Before [my letter] reaches you, you will have seen and read my pamphlet speech, and perhaps, [been] scared anew, by it. After you get over your scare, read it over again, sentence by sentence, and tell me honestly what you think of it. (1.448)

It has been the custom of historians to think Lincoln's 1848 congressional speech on the Mexican War was unwise, or at least impolitic. In Washington barely a month when he delivered the speech on January 12, the new congressman risked attacking President Polk's justification for a war that was popular in many parts of the country, and which had already led to victorious battles and the occupation of Mexico City by American troops. Although the Whigs of the northeast had opposed Polk's actions, many Whigs—including many in Illinois—had joined the ranks of volunteers. The Whig and sometime rival John J. Hardin, who held Lincoln's chair in Congress two years before, had been killed at the Battle of Buena Vista and was now among the honored dead.[1] Lincoln risked being condemned for betraying the memory of the war heroes of Illinois.

After reading the speech, Lincoln's law partner Herndon made Lincoln know that others who had been his supporters did not like it. But the general Whig reaction in Lincoln's district was not necessarily negative. Although we know that several prominent citizens joined Herndon in their criticism, the evidence is much more favorable to Lincoln's position than we might suppose. G. S. Borit has shown that Illinois Whig newspapers supported the general views Lincoln had espoused.[2] Those commentators who suggest that the speech contributed to Lincoln's failure to win renomination to the House must take into account other contrary evidence. It is true that although he had pledged himself not to seek a second term, he had not closed the door to running again. And we know that in a letter to Herndon written just before he delivered the Mexican War Speech, he had hinted strongly at the possibility of running if no other Whig candidate was brought forward. There was such a candidate, and under the Illinois Whigs' general rule of passing the baton among their leaders, the new man stood for the election. The replacement candidate's loss to the Democrats, an outcome some historians contend was influenced by public response to Lincoln's position on the war, was no clear rejection of Lincoln's views, as G. S. Borit has documented.[3]

We might frame the question somewhat differently: why did Lincoln risk giving a speech that many since have thought jeopardized or ended his congressional career? Was he so indifferent to the possibility of failure that he did not realize that his words could be used against him by Democrats, some of his friends, and the guardians of the historical record? In his recent, massive biography of Lincoln, David Donald concludes that Lincoln's motive was primarily tactical, partisan, and mistaken: "Now that the fighting was over and the peace treaty was expected in Washington momentarily, the only purpose that Lincoln and other Whigs had for assailing the President's course in beginning the war was political. Their object was to hurt the Democrats in the next presidential election."[4] The speech was unwise, Donald implies, because it was an ineffective tactic. Lincoln had not given much thought to the war until it became a useful lever for his party.[5] Worse, Lincoln's high hopes for the address, coupled with its failure to win emphatic support for his position in central Illinois, gave him the appearance of overreaching.[6] The Whigs, looking for a "pretext" to attack the president, used Polk's self-congratulatory message on the Mexican War as their wedge issue for the 1848 elections.[7] Lincoln's speech on the Whigs' behalf was therefore, Donald concludes, opportunistic as well as ineffectual, and his satisfaction with his effort was a symptom of political immaturity, if not vanity.

Speaking at an inopportune time on a murky subject, Lincoln—according to Donald—had "speculated with a freedom that he would never have permitted himself in a courtroom." He was "proud of his effort," which he "hoped would establish his place in the House of Representatives." Basking in supposed triumph, he had "regretted his pledge that he . . . would serve only one term," and thus found to his chagrin he did not have support for a second.[8] Lincoln's partisan spirit, expressed in his maneuvering to redefine Whig "ideology" in order to defeat Polk, "led him to advocate policies [such as the right of revolution for 'any people anywhere' (1.438)] that would later come back to haunt him."[9]

Having set up an essentially partisan context and motive for the address, Donald analyzes Lincoln's most important ideas as though they too were tactically misguided. The reason Lincoln is supposed to have insisted on Polk's proving that the war started on a "spot" that was American soil is that he wanted to embarrass the Democratic president, not so much because—as Lincoln himself argues—the outbreak of war could be justified only if the Mexicans' attack took place within American borders. Donald passes with one sentence over the territorial question that Lincoln makes the centerpiece of his case.[10] The attempt to ascertain in public debate whether the "spot" of the first battle was on American or Mexican soil is assumed to be questionable because it was unsuccessful. The fact that for years afterward, and as late as the 1858 Senate campaign against Douglas, Lincoln was subjected to the nickname "Spotty Lincoln" lends a measure of support to Donald's interpretation. The label implied that he had been tainted by an erratic, self-serving argument about an insignificant point.

For Donald, the speech shows Lincoln in an immature state. He is a reckless conformist, adhering to the national party line and then setting out risky, impertinent ideas about the right of revolution and the limits on presidential power—ideas whose consequences he would later regret. Thus we have Lincoln's apparent anger at Herndon's unenthusiastic response, which in Donald's estimation "reflected his discomfort" with his speech's claims.[11] Likewise, Lincoln's famous argument for a legitimate right of revolution is in Donald's estimate "a curious digression," unnecessary and risky because it is not sufficiently germane to Lincoln's partisan attack on Polk.[12] It is another overreaching "speculation," like Lincoln's assertion that Polk provoked the war because of his desire for "military glory."[13] Lincoln's Whiggish distrust of presidential initiative is indicative, in this view, of a disposition that prevented him from acting more decisively in the early stages of his presidency.[14]

The evidence for Donald's conclusion is interesting but insufficient if we give the speech a close reading. There is little question that Lincoln was a faithful Whig, that the party was preparing for the presidential contest later in the year, and that he would have been deeply involved in a plan to build a case against the Democrats based on the nature of Polk's decision to go to war. It is likely that a tactical failure on Lincoln's part would have had a negative effect on the next campaign. But we do not know that the speech was a failure, and we should not assume that Lincoln wrote with such partisan dutifulness that he articulated none of his own ideas, or that he made no significant contribution to the debate. There is another way to read the speech: "sentence by sentence," in the way Lincoln himself asked Herndon to read it in his letter of February 2, 1848, quoted in the epigraph to this chapter.

A knowledge of the context of Lincoln's oratorical effort is indispensable, for he joined a debate that had begun several years before. A sense of the conditions that brought the matter to a head in Lincoln's first months in the House is also important. So is our knowledge of Lincoln's fabled interest in newspapers and periodicals, which should caution us not to underestimate his comprehension of the wider scope and historical roots of the 1848 debate. But the explicit interpretive advice Lincoln gave to Herndon suggests that we should go back to the speech itself, to see whether there is something our historical contextualizations have missed. G. S. Borit's impressive 1974 study, which yields a mountain of evidence for Lincoln's careful framing of the speech in light of general Whig support for his views, ought to have encouraged modern readers to make a much broader reassessment of Lincoln's rhetorical and political purposes.[15]

On May 11, 1846, during the Congress's first discussion of going to war against Mexico, the Whig senator Crittenden posed the very question that Lincoln addressed in 1848: American blood had been shed, but had it been shed on American soil? That was the claim, but the Whigs wanted to know it was true. An inquiry was needed, the senator explained, because the border of Texas had not been clearly defined at the time of Texas's admission to the union: "[T]he resolution [for annexation] passed in this body was cautiously worded and framed in general terms, with the knowledge of every man then here, and the most of them now here; and this Government then hesitated to say what was then the boundary between Mexico and the province of Texas. And if I was not mistaken, there were few of those who are here now who then thought the boundary of Texas extended to the Rio Grande [on the banks of which the conflict had begun]."[16]

Crittenden's position differed considerably from the one that was delineated the next day by the Democratic senator Cass, the man who was to become his party's nominee for the presidency in 1848: "I have no doubt the boundary of Texas goes to the Rio del Norte [the Rio Grande]. But I do not place the justification of our Government upon any question of title. Granting that the Mexicans have a claim to that country, as well as we, still the nature of the aggression is not changed. We were in the possession of the country—a possession obtained without conflict. And we could not be divested of this possession but by our own consent, or by an act of war. The ultimate claim to the country was a question of diplomatic adjustment. Till that took place, the possessive right was in us."[17]

It is important to appreciate the articulate complexity of the Whig position, as well as the force of the Whigs' popular Democratic opposition, which was led by President Polk and (between 1845 and 1847, just before Lincoln's arrival) a Congress dominated by Democrats.[18] Many congressional Whigs questioned the president's actions on the grounds that the war had begun in territory of disputed ownership. Unlike Cass, the Whigs did not take American possession of the land for granted. The border between newly annexed Texas and the republic of Mexico was to be fixed by negotiation with Mexico, not by a war to restore possession. In fact, before hostilities had commenced, the new constitution of Texas had acknowledged the need for such an adjudication; it did not claim the Rio Grande as its border. Although the Democrats met the Whigs part way on the border question, they were quick to dispense with the idea of arbitration. Mexico (they alleged) had initiated the attack, and many thought Texas was entitled to the Rio Grande border it had proclaimed for itself in its days as an independent republic. Democratic support for annexation of the land extending to the river was strong, despite disagreement over its title.

Among the Whigs, positions on the border question were not entirely harmonious. Some Whig congressmen moved into Polk's camp. In a House speech delivered two days before Lincoln's, Reverdy Johnson, a lonely Whig defender of the president, declared that the border issue was secondary to the right of fighting one's enemies: "But it is said that the place of conflict was Mexican territory. If it was, the argument in our behalf would not be in the least enfeebled. [Mexico] was there intending to go further," presumably to reconquer Texas. "Whether this portion of the territory was or was not rightfully a part of Texas, was, at least, a matter of dispute." What mattered was that the United States had met the enemy and won the spoils. Other Whigs alleged that the war was provoked to extend the boundaries of slavery. (Lincoln perhaps indicates his agreement with this view in his allegation that Polk had "some strong motive" in provoking the war that he [Lincoln] "will not stop now to give my opinion concerning" [1.439].) In the Senate, John Hale from New Hampshire warned that the war risked wider conflict and even divine retribution; it had sowed "the seeds of war and slavery."[19]

The Democrats, for their part, were not unanimous. Most notable in dissent was Senator John C. Calhoun, who joined the more outspoken Whigs in questioning Polk's actions from their beginnings in 1846. One week before Lincoln's January 1848 speech in the House, the South Carolinian answered Polk's call for tens of thousands of new soldiers by arguing that the administration had carried out a war of conquest for the aggrandizement of federal power and patronage, not merely for the purpose of defending the Texas border or securing reparations from Mexico. Polk had risked, said Calhoun, the creation of an American empire that threatened American liberty, and he had unnecessarily stirred conflict over the status of slavery in the conquered territories. Calhoun feared that a forced incorporation of a numerous and ungovernable nation of nonwhites was becoming more likely. The total conquest of Mexico seemed to be, therefore, the only way to satisfy Polk's conditions for bringing the war to an end.[20] It was better to pull back to a defensive line near the original battle, and from there to commence territorial negotiations, than to become an army of occupation for an indefinite period throughout Mexico.

Calhoun's argument included ideas that Whigs, particularly Whigs in the North, would not have endorsed; but a leading northern magazine, the *American Review,* respectfully reviewed his speech two months later, citing him as an ally in the struggle against Polk's initiative to expand the occupying force.[21] For the northeastern Whig editors of the review, the war was a vain exercise of the right of conquest that would exacerbate disagreements over slavery. Would Americans be satisfied, they asked, "by being told that it is our 'destiny' that has led us into war with Mexico; that the superiority of our Anglo-Saxon blood impels us to overrun and thus refine and civilize the feebler and inferior race dwelling on our border; or, in fine, by the assurance that we have in the contest displayed such remarkable war-like propensities and capacities, that we shall thereby become a terror to all other nations?" The better course would be to show "the example as well as the principle of contented liberty, of prosperous industry, of overflowing happiness, and of equal justice within our borders."[22] In the *American Review* appearing in January 1848, the month Lincoln gave his speech, the editors specifically referred to Polk's "schemes of conquest" as harmful to the Constitution.[23]

The arrival of the Whig-laden Thirtieth Congress, combined with Polk's request in late 1847 for a new infusion of millions of dollars and thousands of troops for a more forceful occupation of Mexico, gave the congressional opposition renewed impetus. The war was ongoing, the date and mode of its ending unclear. The *Congressional Globe* indicates that at the end of 1847, contrary to Donald's account, congressional debate indicated there was no forceful consensus that the war was about to be terminated. The Mexican authorities would not accept American terms. Polk's negotiator, Nicholas P. Trist, had been sent orders to terminate his diplomatic efforts and return to the United States. Military action had resumed. Trist, who was staying on in Mexico against his instructions, managed to formulate a treaty anyway, but the Mexicans did not sign it until February 2, 1848, more than two weeks after Lincoln's speech. News of the agreement did not arrive for days, and the Senate did not receive it for consideration until February 23.

At the time Lincoln was preparing his speech, the question before the Congress was whether to send a large new force to win what the president considered to be satisfactory territorial concessions. The question was naturally charged with election-year maneuvering, with each party attempting to embarrass the other. The Democrats attempted to make the Whigs seem unpatriotic or merely pliant; the Whigs defended themselves by attempting to separate their support for troops and supplies from their repudiation of Polk's commencement of hostilities. The point of Lincoln's opening declaration is that the president had tried "to argue every silent vote given for supplies, into an endorsement of the justice and wisdom of his conduct." Lincoln wanted to resist Polk's pressure by basing his vote on the truth of the case (1.432).

Almost immediately after Lincoln's arrival in Washington, Congressman Richardson (a Democrat from Illinois) had introduced a resolution that the war was "just and necessary" and "prosecuted with the sole purpose of vindicating our national rights and honor."[24] The Whigs replied by passing their own resolution critical of Polk's role in the beginning of the conflict. A series of Whig resolutions came to the floor: "that the present war with Mexico should not be waged or prosecuted 'with a view to conquest'"; that the

House was against " 'right makes right' " and for " 'life, liberty, and the pursuit of happiness' " as "inalienable rights of man"; that no territory should be taken beyond the borders of Texas set at the annexation date; that the president should ask the people's consent for new taxes to pay for the war. Lincoln himself moved, acting as a Whig subcommittee chair, the adoption of a resolution calling on the president to answer a series of interrogatories about the legal status of the "spot" on which the fighting had begun.[25]

Lincoln's speech, delivered days after his submission of that resolution, addressed itself directly to the charge that the Whigs' maneuvering was mere politicking:

> I admit that such a vote should not be given, in mere party wantonness, and that the one given, is justly censurable, if it have no other, or better foundation. I am one of those who joined in that vote; and I did so under my best impression of the *truth* of the case. How I got this impression, and how it may possibly be removed, I will *now* try to show. (1.432)

Without presuming to claim that he has no partisan motives (he makes "allowance" even for Polk's partisan bias, which he implies is not in itself vicious [1.438]), Lincoln maintains that partisan votes are condemnable if they conceal or express serious misjudgments. To some degree, this was the traditional claim of Lincoln's fellow Whigs—arguably a partisan claim, but one that aspired to transcend partisanship. Since the days of John Quincy Adams, before they had begun to call themselves Whigs, the party had argued for principle over interest in their fight against the powerful party machinery of Jacksonian Democrats. What looked like principle to them, of course, was often what Jacksonian Democrats tended to think was genteel prejudice. But this does not mean that both parties did not think of themselves, perhaps rightly, as the keepers of at least some traditions and ideas that were above partisan affiliation. Paradoxically, a belief in principle was one of the convictions that had made the Whigs a party.

The notion that all political ideas are essentially prejudiced, that one must either do away with such things or choose which prejudice to support, has the effect of prejudicing our own reading of political speeches. We become oblivious to the possibility that they invoke and develop genuine ideas. Without resorting to high-toned Whiggery patented by Daniel Webster and Henry Clay, Lincoln here assumes the voice of a partisan who is yet willing to place himself at risk of defeat over a question of principle and the facts that support it. He approaches the debate as though it were a judicial contest in which opponents keen on finding contradictions and contrary facts might overturn specific points of evidence in an argument. Conceived of as a legislative court of justice, the House becomes a place where partisans clash in deliberate debate to establish the truth of what has happened—in the tradition of the American courtroom's combination of advocacy and judgment. Did Polk unjustly provoke the war, or didn't he? The president is his own lawyer, and both partisans are in the dock as well. To ascertain that truth, Lincoln implicitly argues, is to establish something central to all other deliberations about the war. Both men's standings are at risk on a point of truth and honor.

By framing the speech according to the "spot" question—the issue of who had jurisdiction over the land where the first battles were fought—Lincoln placed himself on dangerous ground. Contrary facts or inadequacies in logic might easily destroy his case. He had to be confident that the available evidence had revealed a pattern so telling it was unlikely to be overturned. At the same time, his judicial approach enabled him to avoid direct treatment of more problematic aspects of the controversy, especially the question of slavery and the problem of incorporating territories newly acquired by conquest.

> The President, in his first war message of May 1846, declares that the soil was *ours* on which hostilities were commenced by Mexico; and he repeats that declaration, almost in the same language, in each successive annual message, thus showing that he esteems that point, a highly essential one. In the importance of that point, I entirely agree with the President. To my judgment, it is the *very point*, upon which he should be justified, or condemned. . . . [I]t seems to have occurred to him, as is certainly true, that title—ownership—to soil, or any thing else, is not a simple fact; but is a conclusion following on one or more simple facts; and that it was incumbent upon him, to present the facts, from which he concluded, the soil was ours, on which the first blood of the war was shed. (1.433)

As we have seen, the border issue was not an original topic. Many of its intricacies had already been presented in pamphlet and speech, most prominently by Albert Gallatin and (much more briefly) by Henry Clay.[26] Speaking in November 1847, Clay had referred twice to the border question, but only in terms of its being the "immediate," not the "primary," cause of the war.[27] The fundamental cause, he said, was the annexation of Texas and the love of conquest, perhaps fueled (Clay does not exactly say) by a desire to expand slavery. The ensuing war with Mexico had at least opened the possibility of "propagating slavery" in the conquered lands, a purpose Clay says Americans must "positively and emphatically, disclaim and disavow."[28] His speech is full of foreboding over intractable subjects Lincoln would largely avoid in his own oratorical effort: "The day is dark and gloomy, unsettled and uncertain, like the condition of our country, in regard to the unnatural war with Mexico. The public mind is agitated and anxious, and is filled with serious apprehensions as to its indefinite continuance, and especially as to the consequences which its termination may bring forth, menacing the harmony, if not the existence, of our Union."[29]

Lincoln gave these Whig concerns a highly specific forensic focus conducive to the discovery and evaluation of facts. Again, though his speech was self-consciously political, it was designed to resist being dismissed as a merely partisan effort. Without bringing up many of the difficult circumstances of the war, he appealed to common sense and accessible notions about property law and honorable dealing, and he exercised his courtroom talents in a political debate he knew would be overheard by the voting public. The approach took him closer to Daniel Webster than to Clay, both in terms of style and his point of departure. On March 1, 1847, Webster had addressed the Senate on the war without mentioning the border question; but his introduction contained a tantalizing invitation to anyone interested in discovering what Polk's role was in the origin of the conflict: "The true origin of the war with Mexico, and the motives and purposes for which it was originally commenced, however ably discussed already, are subjects not yet exhausted. I have been particularly desirous of examining them. I am greatly deceived, Mr. President, if we shall not ere long see facts coming to light, and circumstances found coinciding and concurring, which will fix on the executive government a more definite and distinct purpose, intended to be effected by the cooperation of others, in bringing on hostilities with Mexico, than has as yet been clearly developed or fully understood."[30] Webster said he was too tired to follow the matter up.[31] To Lincoln, who had been elected to Congress in August 1846, and who, under the slow-moving transition that was customary in those days, was preparing to take up his duties in Washington at the end of 1847, Webster's speech would have been a tantalizing signal that the Whigs' political agenda in the next Congress would need an inquiry into the events leading up to the war's first battle. Delivered just weeks after his arrival in Washington, Lincoln's speech took up the task of testing Webster's hypothesis.

Although not the first Whig to focus on the border issue or the general cause outlined by Webster, Lincoln made use of the venerable Whig's hypothesis with a distinctively forensic energy. Almost immediately after the congressional terms began, he presented the Whig subcommittee's "spot" resolutions (1.420). He prepared himself to act as a deliberate prosecutor, framing the debate so that it would issue in a public determination of whether Polk was guilty or innocent of provoking an illegal war. The procedure was risky because there was no obvious *corpus delicti*. The border question was vexed. Lincoln's grand jury rhetoric ran the double risk of trivialization and overstatement, of seeming to reduce a political question to the terms of a civil court or blowing the proceeding out of proportion when American forces in Mexico were in need of material and moral support.

By promoting a contest of inquiries by both sides that would bring more such evidence before the House, Lincoln enlarged the field of deliberation to include matters that were more amenable to political debate than the tangled history of Texas. The forensic approach not only played to his strengths as a courtroom lawyer; its relatively narrow focus enabled him to make a unique contribution that the general public could follow while identifying with his efforts. He could leave the treatment of the full sweep of the Texan story to his more experienced colleague in the Whig caucus, Alexander Stephens, whose wide-ranging speech a few weeks later moved Lincoln to say it was "the very best . . . of an hour's length" he had "ever heard." "My old, withered, dry eyes," he wrote Herndon, "are full of tears yet" (1.448).[32] For himself, Lincoln had chosen the relatively narrow forensic path.

The resolutions from Lincoln's committee were questions for the president and were tantamount to detailed charges. In presenting them and delivering his speech on the issue a few weeks later, he ventured a frontal attack that sought victory and risked being proved wrong. Like other Whigs, he had been reticent about questioning Polk's motives and actions while the war was in progress: "When the war began, it was my opinion that all those who, because of knowing too *little*, or because of knowing too *much*, could not conscientiously approve the conduct of the president, in the beginning of it, should, nevertheless, as good citizens and patriots, remain silent on that point, at least till the war should be ended" (1.432). But now, he argued, vindication or correction was inevitable. The Democrats had come to insist that the Whigs vote their explicit approval of the war as "just and necessary . . ., prosecuted with the sole purpose of vindicating our national rights and honor, and of securing an honorable peace" (1.432). Framed on December 20, 1847, the latest such resolution had forced Lincoln to endorse Polk or pursue his political indictment. The "spot" resolutions and the speech three weeks later were the resolution of his dilemma (1.432).[33]

Was Lincoln's argument that he was compelled to act strong enough to meet the difficulty of speaking against Polk while the war continued? The speech he prepared was an attempt to blunt objections by concentrating on the specific evidence of Polk's published speeches, not the general doubts and speculations that Polk's opponents had used since 1846. He went further, saying he would accept "for true, all the President states as facts" so that he could scrutinize and judge the argument as much as possible on its own terms. And he would study Polk's words for reasons to believe the president (1.433). If Polk's position were found defective by its own standards of proof, the rival party would certainly have taken special pleasure in his self-contradiction. A fellow Whig, James Dixon, had already analyzed Polk's speeches and executive orders in that way: "[I]t happens, very frequently, that when the President in a message to Congress makes a statement unfounded in fact, he furnishes us the means of proving the statement untrue—in the documents, at the same time, laid before us."[34] Lincoln was attempting something more ambitious: a test of Polk's arguments on the basis of Polk's own respect for the truth. In the midst of the speech he would argue that the president "would have gone farther" to defend the justice of the war "if it had not been for the small matter, that the *truth* would not permit him." Lincoln was attempting to show that the jigsawed shape and substance of the president's speeches, informed by Polk's residual sense of shame and his resistance to falsehood, had created his own indictment (1.433).

Does Lincoln defeat Polk rhetorically on such terms, or does his partisanship reduce his deliberation to hackwork, as some historians have assumed? At first glance, the evidence seems entirely mixed. The speech is no schoolroom model of polite debate. It contains hardly concealed invective. Lincoln accuses Polk of dangerous deception, then murder (1.438, 439). Yet he takes extraordinary steps to weigh the truth of the words and documents Polk uses in justifying his actions, and he restricts his conclusions to what he admits is limited evidence that needs Polk's reply so that Lincoln's charges can be confirmed or denied. Sarcasm and prosecutorial logic force the issue, and yet they are regularly subordinated to the desire to enlarge the deliberative grounds of the debate.

To determine the outcome of these competing impulses, a closer reading of the speech is called for. We return to Lincoln's crucial paragraph:

> The President, in his first war message of May 1846, declares that the soil was *ours* on which hostilities were commenced by Mexico; and he repeats that declaration, almost in the same language, in each successive annual message, thus showing that he esteems that point, a highly essential one. In the importance of that point, I entirely agree with the President. To my judgment, it is the *very point*, upon which he should be justified, or condemned. (1.433)

Lincoln tries to establish common grounds upon which his disagreement with President Polk can be tested, not only with regard to his published words, but also according to what the president did not say. Polk knows, Lincoln argues, the importance and complexity of the boundary question. Here we should recall Lincoln's appeal to what he believes is the president's persistent though errant sense of truth:

> [I]t seems to have occurred to him, as is certainly true, that title—ownership—to soil, or any thing else, is not a simple fact; but is a conclusion following one or more simple facts; and that it was incumbent upon him to present the facts, from which he concluded, the soil was ours, on which the first blood of the war was shed. (1.433)

The test immediately follows. Polk's actual starting point and the evidence he gathers to prove it are "the sheerest deception," Lincoln says, because Polk fails to declare his true position or prove it with adequate evidence. Most importantly, the president avoids the evidence that would expose him. The geographical basis for the defense of American soil is strangely lacking: "[T]here is not one word in all the President has said, which would either admit or deny the declaration" that he commenced hostilities on Mexican, not American, territory (1.433–434). The beauty of Lincoln's carefully focused point of contention is that it could be confirmed by reviewing Polk's other widely circulated messages of 1846 and 1847.[35] In those texts, after describing the history of purchase, revolution, and treaty that determined the boundary of Texas (which Lincoln argues left the boundary question unresolved), Polk added arguments based on less decisive evidence, as though he too doubted the force of his best conclusions.

Only after this careful preparation does Lincoln venture to raise the vexed issue of borders. The crux of the issue was whether American territory extended beyond the Nueces River, all the way to the Rio Grande (their mouths being approximately 150 miles apart), or whether it ended somewhere in between, where the border was yet unmarked by a treaty both governments recognized.

> The issue, as he [Polk] presents it, is in these words "But there are those who, conceding all this to be true, assume the ground that the true western boundary of Texas is the Nueces, instead of the Rio Grande; and that, therefore, in marking our army to the east bank of the latter river, we passed the Texan line, and invaded the territory of Mexico." Now this issue, is made up of two affirmatives and no negative [no means of affirming *or denying* a proposition]. The main deception of it is, that it assumes as true, that *one* river or the *other* is necessarily the boundary; and cheats the superficial thinker entirely out of the idea, that *possibly* the boundary is somewhere *between* the two, and not actually at either. A further deception is, that it will let in *evidence,* which a true issue would exclude [evidence outside of the question whether the land was owned by one party or the other]. A true issue, made by the President, would be about as follows[:] "I say, the soil *was ours,* on which the first blood was shed; there are those who say it was not." (1.433)

Analyzing Polk's evidence for the location of the border at the Rio Grande, Lincoln first argues that the president has ignored the legal understanding of buying and selling territory:

> His [Polk's] first item is, that the Rio Grand was the Western boundary of Louisiana, as we purchased it of France in 1803; and seeming to expect this to be disputed, he argues over the amount of nearly a page, to prove it true; at the end of which he lets us know, that by the treaty of 1819, we sold to Spain the whole country from the Rio Grande eastward, to the Sabine. Now, admitting for the present, that the Rio Grande, was the boundary of Louisiana, what, under heaven, had that to do with the present boundary between us and Mexico? How, Mr. Chairman, the line, that once divided your land from mine, can still be the boundary between us, after I have sold my land to you, is, to me, beyond all comprehension. (1.434)

History, by way of the Mexican Revolution, had taken the land from Spain. But that event in itself did not reopen the border question. At this point Lincoln placed a complex but clarifying assertion in the *Congressional Globe:*

> The outrage upon common *right,* of seizing as our own what we have once sold, merely because it *was* ours *before* we sold it, is only equaled by the outrage on common *sense* of any attempt to justify it. (1.434)

For some reason, this clarification does not appear in the speech Lincoln circulated widely in pamphlet form. He may have had the pamphlet set in print from his original draft. (Another important added passage, to be discussed, met the same fate.) It is possible that he concluded that his phrasing, upon reflection, lent by analogy an unintended support to slavery advocates and their argument that *persons* "sold" by those who brought slaves to America could not be liberated, even for compensation, on the basis of an inalienable right that revoked the sale. Whatever the case, the gloss's eloquent expression of moral outrage fixes the double point: Polk's reasoning not only ignores the law; it is obtuse, an insult to the common intelligence.

Lincoln accuses Polk of employing similar reasoning regarding the history of the Texas Republic. The Texas constitution, which Polk refrained from mentioning, declared the state's western borders were still to be determined. Yet the president had tried to argue that the prior republic's assertion of control was authoritative, and that the document signed by Santa Anna years before, when he was a prisoner of war at the end of the battles for Texan independence, set the boundary at the Rio Grande. Lincoln points out that just because that document stipulated that the Mexican army should withdraw to that river's western banks, it did not establish a border, only a means of separating the two armies. It was not a treaty and was not labeled as such in the relatively obscure collection of state papers in which Polk had found it (1.436).

The next point of the president's evidence, that "Texas *before,* and *after,* annexation had *exercised* jurisdiction *beyond* the Nueces—*between* the two rivers," is close to the heart of the issue. At this point Lincoln assumes the voice of a country lawyer humbling an oversophisticated opponent's pretensions:

> This actual *exercise* of jurisdiction, is the very class or quality of evidence we want. It is excellent so far as it goes; but does it go far enough? He tells us it

went *beyond* the Nueces; but he does not tell us it went *to* the Rio Grande. He tells us, jurisdiction was exercised *between* the two rivers, but he does not tell us it was exercised over *all* the territory between them. Some simple minded people, think it is *possible,* to cross one river and go *beyond* it without going *all the way* to the next—that jurisdiction may be exercised *between* two rivers without covering *all* the country between them. I know a man, not very unlike myself, who exercises jurisdiction over a piece of land between the Wabash and the Mississippi; and yet so far is this from being *all* there is between those rivers, that it is just one hundred and fiftytwo feet long by fifty wide, and no part of it much within a hundred miles of either. He has a neighbour between him and the Mississippi,—that is, just across the street, in that direction—whom, I am sure, he could neither *persuade* nor *force* to give up his habitation; but which nevertheless, he could certainly annex, if it were to be done, by merely standing on his own side of the street and *claiming* it, or even, sitting down, and writing a *deed* for it. (1.437)

Likewise, the terms of the admission of Texas to the Union, by leaving adjudication of the border to "future adjustment," fail to support Polk's attempt to ignore or deflect attention from the lands between the two rivers.

Lincoln's reading of the presidential messages regarding the war draws attention to a real vagueness in Polk's description of the crucial period leading up to the beginning of hostilities. The presidential language claims that troops were sent to protect the border at the Rio Grande and avoids considering the possibility that the American army had been ordered into territory that had always been foreign to effective American jurisdiction: "[O]ur squadron had been ordered . . . to take a 'position between the Nueces and the Del Norte' or Rio Grande and to 'repel any invasion of the Texas territory which might be attempted by the Mexican forces.' "[36] Then "it was deemed proper to order the Army under the command of General Taylor to advance to the western frontier of Texas and occupy a position on or near the Rio Grande," which Polk then calls "our own soil."[37] Because the Mexican troops crossed the river and attacked Taylor's forces, the enemy is said to have "commenced aggressive war" (1.487).[38] A similar account of events was the basis for Polk's claim in his 1846 speech that "Mexico has passed the boundary of the United States, has invaded our territory and shed American blood upon the American soil."[39]

The crucial information Lincoln says is missing has to do with the village

Taylor occupied, which Lincoln says had never before been subjected to American jurisdiction:

> [I]t is a singular fact, that if any one should declare the President sent the army into the midst of a settlement of Mexican people, who had never submitted, by consent or by force, to the authority of Texas or of the United States, and that *there,* and *thereby,* the first blood of the war was shed, there is not one word in all the President has said, which would either admit or deny the declaration. In this strange omission chiefly consists the deception of the President's evidence—an omission which, it does seem to me, could scarcely have occurred but by design. (1.437–438)

The charge is that Texan officials and the Polk administration had *wished* for the border to be on the Rio Grande but had not established that fact except by the military means they had employed to confirm it. If they had not established that fact, then the law of conquest, not a previously won right of jurisdiction, was what supposedly made the land theirs.

In following this argument through its next stages, Lincoln brings to light, in the center of his speech, a deeper issue that puts his own argument into question: are all conquests, even when they are won by revolutionary governments, illegitimate? Both Mexico and the United States could claim to be such governments. What, if any, was their right to claim control and to expand their region of control, even over areas that did not directly participate in their revolutions? What, in other words, were the respective rights of the competing Mexican and Texan/American claims over the land between the Nueces and the Rio Grande?

Lincoln says that jurisdiction is exercised by the government that has *effective* civil control over a specific locale—as though the legitimacy of that government's claim could indeed derive from power as well as principle. Given that such effectiveness secures the consent or at least the submission of the people of the area, Lincoln argues, jurisdiction over the area west of the Nueces before the beginning of hostilities depends upon the respective territorial reaches of the revolutionary Mexican and Texan governments. Polk acknowledges the importance of this idea by mentioning the existence of American roads and administrative functions such as revenue collections west of the river (just how far west he does not say).[40]

Lincoln is much more particular than Polk. He claims that possession is not the same as jurisdiction. Claims of possession can be empty. Jurisdiction is a proven power to govern. Boundaries changed when Mexico "revolutionized" against Spain, and when, in the 1830s, Texas "revolutionized" against the government of Mexico before it gained statehood in the United States. The new governments had claimed various boundaries, some overlapping. The true line of separation between Mexico and Texas, whether it was the Nueces, the Sabine, the Rio Grande, or some point between, was vague, and so had to be determined by each government's effective reach. That influence depended, in other words, upon force as well as principle, and so was related to the kind of revolution that brought it about. What mattered, in other words, was the meaning of "revolution." Lincoln's definition is a mixture of *Realpolitik* and principle: "[J]ust so far as [Texas] carried her revolution, by obtaining the *actual,* willing or unwilling, submission of the people, *so far,* the country was hers, and no farther" (1.439).

Is Lincoln therefore sanctioning a right of conquest like the one the Whigs condemned Polk for exercising? His answer is again a form of realism blurring into qualification. He is ostensibly unyielding: revolutionary force would seem to be the principle of rule, and the people's endorsement of revolution would not have to be decisive. A small group ("any portion") could exercise its "sacred right" to rise up against an existing government, imposing its will on others. But this almost nihilistic hardness in Lincoln's position mixes with deeper considerations. His definition of revolution intersects with his understanding of self-government, and his preoccupation with the securing of self-government through the American Revolution and its imitators. The right of conquest, more fully understood, has to do with a prerevolutionary "sacred" right to create self-determining government:

> The extent of our territory in that region depended, not on any fixed *treaty-fixed* boundary (for no treaty had attempted it) but on revolution. Any people anywhere, being inclined and having the power, have the *right* to rise up, and shake off the existing government, and form a new one that suits them better. This is a most valuable,—a most sacred right—a right, which we hope and believe, is to liberate the world. Nor is this right confined to cases in which the whole people of an existing government, may choose to exercise it. Any portion of such people that *can, may* revolutionize, and make their *own,* of so much of the territory as they inhabit. More than this, a *majority* of any portion of such people may revolutionize, putting down a *minority,* intermingled with, or near about them, who may oppose their movement. Such minority,

was precisely the case, of the tories of our own revolution. It is the quality of revolutions not to go by *old* lines, or *old* laws, but to break up both, and make new ones. (1.438–439)

Force is a fact but not, as a rule, the determining fact. Deeper revolutionary motions are at work. Revolutionary jurisdiction arises from the revolutionaries' subsequent control over the territory they inhabit *and govern.* To govern it, they must "make" it their own, not merely declare it is theirs: "Any portion of such people that *can, may* revolutionize, and make their *own,* of so much of the territory as they inhabit" (1.438). The right of revolution, when not exercised, can in some circumstances legitimize the government that maintains itself among those who might easily revolutionize but do not.

Revolution does not create a right of conquest over territories beyond the revolutionaries' self-ruled settlements. What counts is that the people in that region have "submitted themselves" to the revolutionary government. Whether it is by compulsion or choice, the *act* of submission is in principle pivotal, even though it is not always controlling. Because effective control manifests itself in the effective functioning of "civil authority" within the subordinate or consenting people's territory (1.439), it at least *tends* to have something to do with self-determination. Thus it is not surprising that, in the transcript of his remarks on the House floor, Lincoln is reported to have asserted the importance of the converse act of resistance—the act of remaining as one is—as something also "in conformity with natural right." If the reporter for the *Congressional Globe* recorded the words correctly, Lincoln elaborated upon his prepared remarks by saying that if there were Mexican settlements between the Nueces and the Rio Grande that managed to remain beyond the effective reach of Texan authority until the arrival of the American army, they were not part of Texas:

> [I]f there were an isolated portion of people who took no part in the movement, over whom the revolutionary party, by force or otherwise, had never been able to extend their power, then that people and the country they occupied were not included within the boundaries of the territory revolutionized. No rule could be more just, more republican, more in conformity with natural right. Why, under the rule that one portion of the people have the right to rise and shake off their government, another portion have precisely the same right to remain as they were. . . . But if there were on the Rio Grande, a por-

tion of people who had never been disturbed by them [the revolutionary Texans]—at least successfully—who had never consented to go, it seemed to him [Lincoln] a violation of common sense to claim that the people who chose to remain there, and who did remain there notwithstanding all the force that could be brought to bear upon them, belonged to the [Texan] revolutionary government.[41]

We do not know if the transcript is perfectly reliable. The recorder occasionally notes during various debates that he misses a comment. The obvious disparities between the transcripts of congressional speeches and their formal appearance in the *Congressional Globe Appendix* is a likely indication of inaccuracy. The *Globe*'s transcripts are, according to the collection's title page, "Sketches of the Debates and Proceedings," while the appendix preserves "Speeches and Important Papers." Still, the transcriber's record consists of the tracings of a living witness who would be uniquely situated to pick up and flesh out extemporaneous and clarifying remarks that might not find their way into the edited version published in the appendix. If Lincoln indeed made this interlinear comment, he was confirming his own edited argument—about revolution and consent—that surrounds it.

If Lincoln is here anticipating, as others did during the Mexican War debate, the possibility of sectional revolt and civil war within the United States, his doctrine of the right to revolution does not appear to be an inadvertent justification for what would become the Confederate cause, as Gore Vidal and others have long contended. It is not at all clear that Lincoln goes this far. Although he defends the right of revolution even for minority causes, he distinguishes—as we have seen—between legitimate and illegitimate revolutionary claims to territory.[42] To the degree that an internal rebellion claimed to have jurisdiction only over a section of the old Union, the revolutionizing states would have to overcome not only local opponents but also the claims of the Union—another revolutionary government—by ending that government's resistance, and the resistance of its people, to having the Constitution and its jurisdiction overturned. Much like the Texas revolution's claim to have civil influence over territory beyond its power to rule, the southern rebellion, when it finally came, would claim a constitutional ground the North would not relinquish. For Lincoln, the notion that "might makes right," when wrongly understood, is a corrupt axiom of government. Rightly apprehended, it can be a principle for establishing, preserving, and moderating self-government. Rather than a flaw in Lincoln's prepresidential think-ing, these passages in the Mexican War Speech contribute to our under-standing of Lincoln's emerging conception of constitutional government in a self-governing polity that honors the right of revolution.

In the speech on Mexico, the rhetorical effect of Lincoln's argument about revolution and jurisdiction is to transfer the burden of proof to Polk. If Polk chooses to respond, he must supply evidence that the charge of unlaw-ful conquest is *in*correct.

> Let him answer, fully, fairly, and candidly. Let him answer with *facts,* and not with arguments. Let him remember he sits where Washington sat, and so re-membering, let him answer, as Washington would answer. As a nation *should* not, and the Almighty *will* not, be evaded, so let him attempt no evasion—no equivocation. (1.439)

Lincoln is on trial too. Because the facts might have a meaning other than what he has given them, or because new evidence could be brought forward to make Polk's case, Lincoln's argument might fail. If the connection be-tween Texas's revolution and its jurisdiction beyond the Nueces is the foun-dation for determining the justice of the war, then Lincoln places himself in a position to gain, or lose, his party's case on the basis of interpretable facts.

* * *

It is important to understand the political parameters of Lincoln's rhetorical gestures. Lincoln made a forceful and ingenious case, and Polk never gave an answer. We have no evidence that he noticed the challenge from the fresh-man representative from Illinois. Lincoln's forensic persuasiveness and openness to refutation, when we view it in this light, is likely to have been di-rected far more to Whigs and Whig sympathizers than to Polk and his Dem-ocratic supporters. Polk and his party interpreted the facts differently and did not rise to the bait of Lincoln's demands for information. The "spot" res-olutions had posed eight queries that were carefully framed rhetorical ques-tions—interrogatories that in the absence of reply were incisive accusations to encourage Whig stalwarts, if no one else, to press the attack on the Demo-crats. (The president was asked to reveal, among other things, self-indicting information about "Whether that spot ['on which the blood of our *citizens* was shed'] is, or is not, within a settlement of people, which settlement had existed ever since long before the Texas revolution, until it's inhabitants fled from the approach of the U.S. Army" [1.421]). But this did not mean that Lincoln did not care about persuading others to take up the Whig cause. The Democrats had resisted answering such questions since 1846; but the general public might be ready to pursue Lincoln's questioning now that the war had come to a dangerous turning point that threatened to commit the country's armed forces to a lengthy occupation of Mexico.

G. S. Borit has discovered that Lincoln spent more on printing and circulating his speeches than almost any other congressman of that session. He devoted roughly half of his budget to publishing thousands of copies of the Mexican War Speech,[43] which, as he intimated to Herndon the month before, was his first major effort "to distinguish" himself in the Congress (1.420). The speech he sent to constituents was not just a contribution to the House debate; it was, as we have seen, a dramatization of a forensic inquiry into the president's actions, before a kind of jury, along the familiar and intriguing lines of a criminal trial. Readers could observe Lincoln confronting the suspect, offering him a chance to exonerate himself, then closing the trap as exculpatory evidence seemed less and less likely to be found. Polk's silence could win Lincoln electoral support as long as the spell of his indictment maintained creditable force:

> My way of living leads me to be about the courts of justice, and there, I have sometimes seen a good lawyer, struggling for his client's neck, in a desparate case, employing every artifice to work round, befog, and cover up, with many words, some point arising in the case, which he *dared* not admit, and yet *could* not deny. . . . [J]ust such, and from just such necessity, is the President's struggle in this case. (1.438)

Was Lincoln discrediting his search for truth by dramatizing his claims for public consumption? The answer depends in part on our assessment of the heuristic power of his apparent exaggerations. Rhetorical drama can be misused. On the other hand, it has a capacity to draw out from a case what otherwise might have been missed. A closer reading is necessary to clarify and judge Lincoln's uses of rhetorical appeals.

Some of the most questionable and gallery-reaching dimensions of Lincoln's approach are his embellishments of the theme that Polk is a Shakespearean tyrant. The president is the leading suspect in the fratricidal murder of an innocent Abel (1.439). Lincoln makes Polk akin to Shakespeare's Claudius, who—in one of Lincoln's favorite speeches—prays for forgiveness while holding on to the fruits of his crime. In his attempt to suppress evidence, he is said to betray a guilty conscience, which in the fashion of Macbeth's conscience forces him to pursue greater crimes. Lincoln gives Polk other qualities of Macbeth:

> He is a bewildered, confounded, and miserably perplexed man. God grant he may be able to show, there is not something about his conscience, more painful than all his mental perplexity! (1.442)

Like the Thane of Cawdor, the president is the prisoner of his own equivocation (the theme of the Porter's ironic parody of Macbeth's torment). His bewilderment reflects the confusion of his evidence for going to war (1.439). In his overreaching fury, the Polk of Lincoln's imagination imitates Macbeth's vain, sleepless attempt to lash out in order to confirm the bewitching predictions of triumph:

> [F]ixing the public gaze upon the exceeding brightness of military glory—that attractive rainbow, that rises in showers of blood—that serpent's eye, that charms to destroy—he plunged into it [the war], and has swept, *on* and *on,* till, disappointed in his calculation of the ease with which Mexico might be subdued, he now finds himself, he knows not where. How like the half insane mumbling of a fever-dream, is the whole war part of his late message! (1.439–440)

What Polk says on the subject, in other words, is sound and fury. In Macbeth's famous estimate of his own fever dream, which Lincoln could assume was familiar to many in his audience, the mad compulsion to continue fighting signifies nothing.

Lincoln's colleague Alexander Stephens was moved to affiliate Polk with Macbeth a few days later when he invoked the famous line "Out, damned spot," to suggest that the president was having difficulty keeping down a guilty conscience despite his power to suppress crucial evidence. Guilt is upon Polk's brow, Stephens argued, "as indelibly as that stamped upon the brow of Cain by the finger of God. He and his friends may say, 'out, foul spot,' but it will not 'out.'"[44] A similar analogy might have stimulated Lincoln to use the word *spot* four times in his December 1847 presentation of the interrogatories that came to be known, notoriously, as the "Spot Resolutions." The spot is the imaginative and physical space where the crime and the tainted land combine.

For modern readers, these rhetorical maneuverings are likely to put a strain on Lincoln's reputation. But we should be willing to consider the possibility that Lincoln is building up Polk to Shakespearean dimensions so as to puncture his pretensions. The purple passages are devices, the sort of partisan ridicule that Lincoln used most freely in the first parts of his political career. But the station and character of the man he attacks, as well as the charged circumstances of the occasion and the absorbing disclosures of the documents under Lincoln's examination, permit the allusions to capture much of the shape and substance of Polk's two speeches in defense of the Mexican War. For all its excesses, Lincoln's hyperbole is dramatic shorthand for what he shows to be suspicious lacunae in the president's case. In the context of his far more sober investigation of the issue in the speech as a whole, these passages are half-satirical pauses in the main argument. In another sense, they are exaggerations that serve the roughhewn deliberative purpose of identifying Polk's deeper political weaknesses, exposing an incoherence that might betray a bad conscience's inability to supply exculpating information.

* * *

There are two parts to the story of the Mexican War Speech, the second being Lincoln's eulogy for Zachary Taylor two years later. Not to be surpassed by the Democrats once peace was declared, the Whigs had sought to defuse the opposition's attacks on their patriotism by nominating Polk's first general in the conflict, Zachary Taylor, for the presidency. Victor of the war's first battles, he was the man who had followed orders to fight on the spot Lincoln had said was outside American jurisdiction. But he was not a defender of Polk's administration. Writing in June 1848 to Herndon, Lincoln celebrated the shrewdness of his party's turnabout tactic: "Taylor's nomination takes the locos on the blind side. It turns the war thunder against them. The war is now to them, the gallows of Haman, which they built for us, and on which they are doomed to be hanged themselves" (1.477). The gamble worked to win the Whigs the presidential chair when Taylor won the election. Issues of principle were involved as well. Hardly a Whig partisan, Taylor shared a distrust of territorial ambitions that might enflame the issue of slavery in the territories. As president, he went so far as to threaten sending federal troops to fight Texans if they attempted to extend the new slave state's territory into New Mexico. His spirited yet restrained character embodied attributes Lincoln had long admired as exemplary virtues for the self-governing citizen.

Soon thereafter, of course, in the midst of the constitutional crisis of 1850 in which the slavery debate was inflamed by disagreement over the status of slavery in the territories acquired from Mexico, President Taylor died. The eulogy Lincoln delivered on short notice in Chicago in July 1850 drew from the substratum of the Mexican War Speech; but it did much more to describe the dead president as Polk's antitype—as a victorious yet stoic and moderate hero who resisted the temptations of conquest throughout his life. How was it possible to make such a case? Lincoln rises to the occasion by expanding upon themes he introduced in the Lyceum and Temperance speeches. Speaking in the form of the eulogy, he is able to step beyond the satirical polemics of his congressional address in order to give his attention to the war's military and political hero.

Taylor possessed, Lincoln argues, a "sober and steady judgment" as his "rarest military trait": "a combination of negatives—absence of *excitement* and absence of *fear*." The heroic general "could not be *flurried,* and he could not be *scared*" (2.87). Unlike many military men, he did not duel and was not quick to quarrel. He "pursued no man with *revenge*" (2.87). He shunned applause and public display. His devotion to duty was "unostentatious, self-sacrificing, long enduring" (2.89). In consideration of his sympathetic relations with his fellow soldiers, "none can be found to declare, that he was ever a tyrant anywhere, in anything" (2.88). He was capable of ambition, even of rising to the presidency, but only after "repeated, and steady manifestations in his favor" gave him the nomination and "[did] beget in his mind a laudable ambition to reach the high distinction of the Presidential chair" (2.88). His patience and self-overcoming, in Lincoln's emphasis, were as important as what he won. If we remember Lincoln's earlier speeches, it is difficult to ignore the resemblance of Taylor's virtue to Lincoln's method of self-presentation. Taylor seemed to be a sum of negatives, an immovability that derived from "a dogged incapacity to understand that defeat was possible." He entered each battle at a significant disadvantage and triumphed by *holding to* something rather than seizing it:

> It did not happen to Gen. Taylor once in his life, to fight a battle on equal terms, or on terms advantageous to himself—and yet he was never beaten, and never retreated. In *all,* the odds was greatly against him; in each, defeat

seemed inevitable; and yet in *all,* he triumphed. Wherever he has led, while the battle still raged, the issue was painfully doubtful; yet in *each* and *all,* when the din had ceased, and the smoke had blown away, our country's flag was still seen, fluttering in the breeze. (2.87)

The triumph is indisputable yet almost passive, and the hero is like the flag he saves. Both declare themselves from their fixed place, through the smoke.

Two years before the eulogy was written, and a week before Lincoln had delivered his 1848 Mexican War Speech, Senator Cass, the Democrat who was to run against Taylor for the presidency, described Scott's and Taylor's campaigns in conventional hyperbolic terms that do not capture Lincoln's insight: "[T]he movement of our army . . . [was] one of the most romantic and remarkable events which ever occurred in the military annals of our country. [Outnumbered and cut off from communication] a veil concealed them from our view. They were lost to us for fifty days. . . . The shroud which enveloped them gave way, and we discovered our glorious flag, waving in the breezes of the [Mexican] capital, and the city itself invested by our army. And similar circumstances marked the very commencement of the war, when the Mexicans first surrounded our [Taylor's] troops."[45] Lincoln appears to have appropriated Cass's description for his deeper purposes. The eulogy portrays Taylor's military heroism as a virtue that emphatically resists the Macbeth-like excesses of Polk and his most vehement supporters. Both Lincoln and Cass rely on "The Star-Spangled Banner" effect: the flag emerges in triumph from the smoke of battle, after a period of distressing uncertainty. But Cass merely reveals an American flag planted on foreign soil—as American forces had indeed placed it—as the mark of conquest. Lincoln refrains from saying exactly *where* Taylor's flag waves, except that it marks the location of the American troops. The flag is not used to settle the territorial question. Taylor's victory is a self-overcoming triumph, not a conquest. Taylor's virtuous and victorious persistence under adversity is Lincoln's theme.

This effect is developed further in Lincoln's description of Taylor's battle of Palo Alto. In a few sentences, the eulogy sets out the way Taylor fought to *rescue* one part of his army with the other—not so much to conquer a foreign foe as to redeem his fellow soldiers, through military victory, from death. Each part of the divided American force holds out for the other, and the victory at the end is one of reunion rather than domination of territory.

One American force had been stationed, under Polk's orders, in an earthwork fort in disputed territory; the other, under Taylor, had gone back for supplies. Taylor had fought his way back to the stronghold, engaging in two battles with Mexican forces that attempted to block his advance. Quickly handling these details, Lincoln concentrates on the experience of the final stage of the battle in the imaginations of each group of Americans—those inside and those outside the fort, at a considerable but closing distance from each other. Rather than dwell upon military strategy and the cause and effect of the conflict, he focuses on the hour of fighting before Taylor's victory:

> A brief hour before, whether all *within* the fort had perished, *all* without *feared, but none could tell*—while the incessant roar of artillery, wrought those *within* to the highest pitch of apprehension, that their brethren *without* were being massacred to the last man. And now the din of battle nears the fort and sweeps obliquely by; a gleam of hope flies through the half imprisoned few; they fly to the wall; every eye is strained—it is—the stars and stripes are still aloft! Anon the anxious brethren meet; and while hand strikes hand, the heavens are rent with a loud, long, glorious, gushing cry of victory! victory!! victory!!! (2.85)

There is method in this excess. Lincoln himself "sweeps obliquely" by the conventional details of the battle, featuring instead the anxiety and relief that accompany the American rescue of Americans. The battle is a fog of noise passing beyond the fort. We do not see the fleeing Mexicans. They are simply "routed" (2.85). American heroics are embodied in the flag "still aloft" rather than specific deeds of battle. The cry of triumph, "victory!" becomes the shout of triumphant Americans from the fort and the scouting force rejoining them, each group seeing the other free from harm. This rendering of the last moments of the battle is quite possibly a careful reinterpretation of the account given by T. B. Thorpe in his book *Our Army on the Rio Grande,* published in 1846, which concentrates not on the mechanics of victory but on the echoing effect of cheers from each group of American soldiers.[46] Elsewhere in the speech, Lincoln tempers his description of Taylor's victories by citing the names of prominent men killed in the battles. Here, in his most extensive description of Taylor's military operations, he mutes the fact of conquest with an affirmation of faithful friendship between "half-imprisoned" and happily spared men. The facts of liberation and brotherhood amid suffering and death muzzle the impulse to glorify territorial acquisition.

Some of the lines of the passage achieve a rhythmical form that helps Lincoln shift attention away from territorial gains and toward the elation of the liberated Americans:

> And now the din of battle nears the fort
> and sweeps obliquely by;
> a gleam of hope flies through
> the half-imprisoned few . . .

The concluding lines can be broken into blank verse: a pair of eight syllable lines that link the flag with the reunion of brothers in arms, and then three pentameters about the sounds of celebration for a victory of reunion more than conquest.

> the stars and stripes are still aloft!
> Anon the anxious brethren meet;
> and while hand strikes hand, the heavens are rent
> with a loud, long glorious, gushing cry
> of victory! victory! victory!!

What then can be learned from the life and death of a man with such a "great, and well known name" if, as Lincoln argues, it tells us far more than what we learn from "*many* undistinguished" lives and the accomplishments of aggressive heroes? Pondering Taylor's mortality prepares us for "contemplation of our own mortal natures," not simply that we are finite creatures but that we might learn about our mortal natures from an admirable model whose greatness was a heroic acknowledgment of mortality. It is not enough to conclude that his death like anyone else's is useful to reflect upon, or that it is beyond anyone's comprehension. Taylor's heroism does something more

> in reminding us that *we*, too, must die. Death, abstractly considered, is the same with the high as with the low; but practically, we are not so much aroused to the contemplation of our own mortal natures, by the fall of *many* undistinguished, as that of *one* great, and well known, name. (2.90)

Taylor is not simply great; his stature and mortality embody a deeper truth about wise patriotism.

Building upon his argument in the Temperance Address that men are generally indifferent to the prospect of death, Lincoln crafts a quotation from one of his favorite poems to support his idea that Taylor's heroic legacy, rightly considered, can help to remove the complacency that denies the urgency of mortal life. He selects lines from William Knox's "Oh, Why Should the Spirit of Mortal Be Proud," which a few years before he had called "so fine a piece" that he would have given "all I am worth" to have written it (1.378).[47] David Donald reports that Lincoln memorized the poem in its entirety.[48] For the purposes of the eulogy Lincoln uses only the second half of the poem, placing it at the end of the speech to fortify his contention that by identifying with Taylor as "a great, and well known, name" we who are not such heroes can come to know our mortality with a new conviction:

> So the multitude goes, like the flower or the weed,
> That withers away to let others succeed;
> So the multitude comes, even those we behold,
> To repeat every tale that has often been told.
>
> For we are the same, our fathers have been;
> We see the same sights our fathers have seen;
> We drink the same streams, and view the same sun,
> And run the same course our fathers have run.
>
> *They* lived; but the story *we* cannot unfold;
> They scorned, but the heart of the haughty is cold;
> They grieved, but no wail from their slumbers will come,
> They joyed, but the tongue of their gladness is dumb.
>   (2.90)

The gap between humble folk and great figures like Taylor is erased in death and yet reaffirmed in a manner that stimulates emulation of virtues that can be ours ("we are the same, our fathers have been") while we recognize that we cannot know and so cannot duplicate the story of precisely how the hero acquired those virtues. We must find them ourselves, inspired by men like Taylor. After three more verses, the poem closes with the line it was known by: "Oh, why should the spirit of mortal be proud!"—the paradoxical point being, if we follow Lincoln's preface, that precisely because Taylor was a particular sort of great man, and because his legacy should be recognized, his death bestirs in us a sense of our own mortality—amid our admiration and emulation of virtue—far more than our contemplation of ordinary men's deaths.

In making this point, Lincoln shifts Knox's meaning so that he does not reduce Taylor to an Everyman. The first half of the original poem, which Lincoln leaves out of the elegy, consists of markedly unheroic comparisons:

> The thoughts we are thinking our fathers could think;
> From the death we are shrinking our fathers would shrink;
> To the life we are clinging they also would cling;
> But it speeds for us all, like a bird on the wing.[49]

The effect of Knox's original opening is to level completely the difference between the living and the dead: all share the same thoughts and fears. Lincoln, in contrast, selects lines from the elegy that stress sameness and distance: each generation follows the same path, but we *cannot* know the previous generations' full story. Our imitation of previous generations is an apprehension of what they endured; but it is discovered in our own experience, *as we endure it wisely*. Our capacity to endure seems to depend, as the speech teaches, upon an emulation of virtue aware of its own mortality. In the principled action and restraint of Taylor's life we are invited to see that wise encounter with mortality.

Taylor's achievements win praise because they are said to have proceeded and ended with heroic self-overcoming. "The conqueror at last is conquered. The fruits of his labor, his name, his memory and example, are all that is left us—his example, verifying the great truth, that 'he that humbleth himself, shall be exalted,' teaching, that to serve one's country with a singleness of purpose, gives assurance of that country's gratitude." His quasi-Christian yet heroic ambition is a model for the ways the country must steel and humble itself for the tests to come. Like Washington, Taylor is an exemplar of "sterling, but unobtrusive qualities." He is "a sleepless sentinel," a man "always at his post," whose "unostentatious, self-sacrificing, long enduring devotion to his *duty*" rebukes tyrannical desires and wins the field by outlasting danger, conquering foes with a generally undemonstrative yet eagle-like vigilance (2.89–90).

As the conqueror who overcomes and governs himself, Taylor embodies Lincoln's attempt to forge in himself and in the public an unwavering devotion to "*wisdom* and *patriotism.*" That combination of restraint and passion is what is needed to face "the one great question of the day," which Lincoln does not need to name—the determination of the status of slavery in the territories. Under Taylor, Lincoln says, there was a greater likelihood that the emerging settlement now called the Great Compromise of 1850 would have been "partially acquiesced in by the different sections of the union." That is, there was hope that Taylor would somehow preside over a principled concession—an act of strong-minded magnanimity—that would have enforced a political settlement consistent with Taylor's character (2.89–90). Now that he is gone, the situation is more dangerous. But Taylor remains a model of granitic humility and patient, unwavering resolution, an exemplar whom Lincoln, speaking in 1850, desires his country, and himself, to imitate. In the following years, after the Whig Party itself died and Lincoln helped form the Republican movement, the general pattern of Taylor's precedent—as Lincoln molded it in this eulogy—informed the substance and shape of his later oratory.

5

The Eulogy for Henry Clay

Persuasion and/or Principle

Mr. Clay's predominant sentiment, from first to last, was a deep devotion to the cause of human liberty—a strong sympathy with the oppressed every where, and an ardent wish for their elevation. With him, this was a primary and all controlling passion. Subsidiary to this was the conduct of his whole life. He loved his country partly because it was his own country, but mostly because it was a free country; and he burned with a zeal for its advancement, prosperity and glory, because he saw in such, the advancement, prosperity and glory, of human liberty, human right and human nature. He desired the prosperity of his countrymen partly because they were his countrymen, but chiefly to show to the world that freemen could be prosperous. (2.126)

Henry Clay, the great orator and politician who died in 1852, was Lincoln's "beau ideal of a statesman" (3.29). On July 6, 1852, a week after the Great Pacificator's death, Lincoln presented an unusually pointed commemoration of Clay's life to a statehouse audience of various political persuasions. The text comes down to us from the *Illinois Weekly Journal,* which printed it under Lincoln's supervision. At first glance, its words seem to have little to do with the mature political philosophy that emerged in the later years of Lincoln's competition with Stephen Douglas. In 1852 Lincoln was speaking during a period of relative quiescence, two years after the Great Compromise of 1850 and two years before Lincoln's forceful return to the political arena in opposition to Douglas's Kansas-Nebraska Act. In fact, the eulogy to Clay is agonistic, an intellectual engagement with those who contend over the mantle of his legacy. It is a remarkable fount of ideas about political leadership and the nature of political eloquence that distinguishes Lincoln from those—especially Stephen Douglas and his Democratic supporters—who would appropriate the Great Compromiser's precedent as an excuse for accommodating slavery. It provides a preview, in method and substance, of lines of reasoning that emerge a few years later in Lincoln's more explicit antislavery oratory.

It is worth remembering that Henry Clay was widely considered to be a very great speaker, Edward Everett's judgment notwithstanding. Everett had found fault in Clay's being so "negligent of fame" he had not carefully edited and printed all his speeches. Although Clay was "second to none in the originality, power, and versatility of his intellect," he had neglected "literary execution and rhetorical finish." His printed speeches were, in Everett's estimate, more like unrevised "reports" than speeches, and so were "not to be considered as models."[1] But Clay's reputation as an eminent statesman remained strong all his life. To take up the task of speaking appropriately in his memory was to invite comparison with one's own oratorical efforts, particularly when the audience knew the eulogist was a man with his own political ambitions. Adding to that challenge was Lincoln's awareness of Clay's reluctance to make commemorative speeches. Daniel Webster had thrived on such occasions. Clay, as Lincoln notes, "never delivered a Fourth of July Oration, or an eulogy on an occasion like this." Clay did not speak "merely to be heard," but sincerely, "for practical effect, . . . for the good of the whole country" (2.126). How then was Lincoln to speak in the high oratory demanded of the situation when the man he was eulogizing was disposed against such displays? Could he imitate his model and speak with "practical effect" on such an occasion, even though oratory that was manifestly political would be inappropriate? Lincoln responded to this challenge by arguing that Clay's achievement and his love for his country were animated by a sympathy and moral fervor for "human liberty, human right and human nature." He did not indulge in superficial patriotism: Clay "loved his country partly because it was his own country, but mostly because it was a free country" (2.126). A eulogy to the Great Compromiser might secure its legitimacy by joining in that sentiment, in this case converting the ceremonial occasion into one that served what Lincoln alleged to be Clay's highest purposes. Lincoln does this by trying to show that Clay's antislavery credentials were not only laudable but fundamental to his political legacy. A eulogy that made such an argument could claim to affirm Clay's legacy and extend it into a new generation of political leadership.

To proceed without recognizing the formal gravity of the occasion would have violated the just expectations of a bipartisan gathering in a time of grief. Yet the occasion of national bereavement, over the loss of the man who many believed had saved the nation from civil war, might easily have stirred in Lincoln's Springfield audience a keen interest in the eulogist's performance. There was the political question of whether Lincoln's Whigs could prevail over resurgent Democratic fortunes, which had benefited from the leading Democrat Stephen Douglas's skillful molding of Clay's proposals into the final language of the Great Compromise of 1850. It would have been hard to ignore the larger challenge Clay's death posed to the Whig Party as well as to the country. Would his legacy continue? Which party—the Democrats or the Whigs—would be better suited to extend or use Clay's work? Had Clay completed the arduous political task of reconciling the slave and free states within the union, or would his death mark the end of an era of compromise, to be followed by greater conflicts that would call for even greater leaders? If Clay's achievement was unsurpassable, how would that need be fulfilled?

According to available records, the dozens of eulogies that were delivered elsewhere in the country avoided or only vaguely hinted at such concerns. Almost none of them mentioned slavery, despite its role in the conflicts that Clay tried to resolve.[2] Lincoln's response was, in form and substance, a daring innovation. Although he was extremely deferential to Clay's public contributions as a maker of compromise, he attempted to show that Clay's opposition to slavery was long-standing, principled, and at the heart of his legacy. More than an engineer of compromise, Clay was to be understood as a defender of the union who loved his country as the best hope for securing human liberty for all everywhere.

Lincoln's bold design becomes evident slowly, but it suggests itself in every part of the speech. Without naming or praising any of Clay's particular virtues, it focuses on the proximity of his birth date and America's—with Lincoln forcibly assuming that the nation emerged in 1776 with the Declaration and its propositions about liberty and equality:

> On the fourth day of July, 1776, the people of a few feeble and oppressed colonies of Great Britain, inhabiting a portion of the Atlantic coast of North

America, publicly declared their national independence, and made their appeal to the justice of their cause, and to the God of battles, for the maintainance of that declaration. (2.121)

Clay's humble origin "of undistinguished parents, and in an obscure district of one of those colonies," identifies him with "[t]he infant nation" and its rise from oppression to free and independent citizenship in the company of other nations (2.121-122). His education, though "comparatively limited," demonstrates how those born in obscurity and of low birth can rise in such a nation to respectability—to the sort of independence that wins the esteem of independent peers: "Mr. Clay's lack of a more perfect early education, however, regretted generally, teaches at least one profitable lesson; it teaches that in this country, one can scarcely be so poor, but that, if he *will*, he *can* acquire sufficient education to get through the world respectably" (2.124). Now the nation with its original aspirations survives the man, and so by implication needs a new set of champions: "In all that has concerned the nation the man ever sympathized; and now the nation mourns for the man" (2.122). What Lincoln finds most remarkable is not so much Clay's history—that he saved or healed the country's torn political fabric—but that he sympathized with "all that concerned" the nation, and should concern his successors, especially the freedom that advances "liberty, human right and human nature" (2.126).

Instead of pursuing all of these ideas in the first part of his speech, Lincoln reads from a lengthy eulogy for Clay printed in a rival party's newspaper. He begins with commonplaces supplied by his political opponents, in a characteristic attempt to find common ground while seeking advantage for his case. This gesture enables him to begin speaking in the usual eulogistic mode without thoroughly adopting it as his own. Praising the substance and expression of this inserted text (calling it a "pathetic and beautiful . . . high and exclusive" praise of Clay), he proceeds without apparent equivocation to devote two pages—a fifth of his speech—to a rival's words: "I could not, in any language of my own, so well express my thoughts." Full of hyperbole, the newspaper's version praises Clay as the indispensable leader whose "power to move the heart of man" through his eloquence was "without equal":

[H]e has quelled our civil commotions, by a power and influence, which belonged to no other statesman of his age and times. And in our last internal discord, when this Union trembled to its center—in old age, he left the shades of private life and gave the death blow to fraternal strife, with the vigor of his earlier years in a series of Senatorial efforts, which in themselves would bring immortality, by challenging comparison with the efforts of any statesman in any age. He exorcised the demon which possessed the body politic, and gave peace to a distracted land. Alas! The achievement cost him his life! He sank day by day to the tomb—his pale, but noble brow, bound with a triple wreath, put there by a grateful country. (2.123)

The newspaper's hyperbole moves in a direction that Lincoln will eventually resist. But Lincoln's extensive use of his opponents' tribute to Clay is a generous compliment to the sensibilities of the Democrats. In this sense, his praise for the article is not disingenuous, and his praise for its sentiments is sincere. As he acknowledges, the circumstances militate against any effort he might make as one of Clay's Whig friends to praise the departed leader with such language, even when exalted rhetoric is appropriate: a "high and exclusive eulogy, originating with a political friend, might offend good taste" (2.122). His performative reading of the Democratic eulogy helps him discharge his preliminary responsibilities without himself indulging in the kind of ceremonial eulogy he says Clay never deigned to give.

But the more Lincoln speaks for himself after reading the article aloud, the more he implicitly distinguishes his own method and subject from the Democratic newspaper's "pathetic and beautiful language," which he soon contrasts with Clay's plainness. The Democratic eulogy is not, we begin to see, the speech that Clay's aversion to eulogy demands. Lincoln's long quotation sets the scene for him to try out his own plain effort to eulogize Clay's virtues more accurately.

Clay's preservation of the Union, according to the Democratic eulogist, seems to be a miraculous achievement of nonpartisanship. It appears to be utterly beyond politics, and so his work might be taken up by a rising Democrat like Stephen Douglas who has a similarly nonpartisan aura. When Lincoln assesses Clay's legacy, the "miracle" he sees in Clay's life is more personal and political, a result of his character and persuasive power: "[T]he long enduring spell—with which the souls of men were bound to him, is a miracle" (2.125). Clay's enlightened partisanship began in these long-lasting attachments, and reached beyond itself to enlarge his circle of influence. He was a Whig who found additional allies beyond his party. The Democrat waiting in the wings (the newspaper eulogist did not use a name but most likely had Douglas in mind) would be—if he followed the newspaper eulogist's gist—a very different kind of politician: one who could win allies by seeming not to be a Democrat. Here is that insinuation in the article Lincoln quotes and later gradually undermines:

> Perchance, in the whole circle of the great and gifted of our land, there remains but one on whose shoulders the mighty mantle of the departed statesman may fall—one, while we now write, [who] is doubtless pouring his tears over the bier of his brother and his friend—brother, friend ever, yet in political sentiment, as far apart as party could make them. Ah, it is at times like these, that the petty distinctions of mere party disappear. (2.122)

Void of particularities, the newspaper eulogy amplifies Clay's powers to such a degree that they seem inimitable, hence obsolete, unless another miraculously nonpartisan politician should appear. Of course it is appropriate, as Lincoln later notes, to abstain from particular political details concerning matters of relatively minor importance in a time of grief. But the newspaper eulogy indirectly expresses opposition to Clay's accomplishments as a Whig leader and statesman by discouraging the idea that Clay was in any important sense a politician:

> Henry Clay belonged to his country—to the world, mere party cannot claim men like him. His career has been national—his fame has filled the earth—his memory will endure to "the last syllable of recorded time." (2.122)

Lincoln soon dissipates the odor of Democratic enthusiasm by noting that, yes, the ability to rise above partisanship is to be highly praised, but that to understand Clay's true virtue one must begin with his partisanship, and then see his greatest achievements as rising from and beyond party by winning support for causes of grave national importance:

> A free people, in times of peace and quiet—when pressed by no common danger—naturally divide into parties. At such times, the man who is of neither party, is not—cannot be, of any consequence. Mr. Clay, therefore, was of a party. Taking a prominent part, as he did, in all the great political questions of his country for the last half century, the wisdom of his course on many, is doubted and denied by a large portion of his countrymen; and of such it is not now proper to speak particularly. But there are many others, about his

course upon which, there is little or no disagreement amongst intelligent and patriotic Americans. (2.126–127)

When he declares that Clay's hold over his followers was "a miracle," Lincoln means to analyze it—with deference toward Clay's achievements but also with a resolve to perpetuate and expand them on the basis of an analysis of Clay's expansive partisanship regarding the Declaration's fundamental propositions (2.125). Juxtaposition rather than rigorously logical demonstration serves this purpose in emphasizing Clay's most important political virtue: his "predominant sentiment" was, "first to last, . . . a deep devotion to the cause of human liberty—a strong sympathy with the oppressed every where, and an ardent wish for their elevation" (2.126).

Lincoln's spirited pursuit of this goal is evident in the manner in which he lists Clay's great accomplishments. He says nothing of Clay's lifelong interest in public works, for decades a staple of Whig political platforms. The Democrats' eulogy had listed three landmarks: the Missouri Compromise, the resolution of the nullification crisis, and the Great Compromise of 1850. Lincoln almost archly inserts a fourth—the decision to fight Britain in the War of 1812, which shows the Pacificator in a decidedly militant light, taking a controversial position and persuading others to adopt it:

In 1812 Mr. Clay, though not unknown, was still a young man. Whether we should to go war with Great Britain, being the question of the day, a minority opposed the declaration of war by Congress, while the majority, though apparently inclining to war, had, for years, wavered, and hesitated to act decisively. . . . By Mr. Clay, more than any other man, the struggle was brought to a decision in Congress. . . . [H]e aroused, and nerved, and inspired his friends, and confounded and bore-down all opposition. (2.127)

The virtue of Clay's accomplishment emerges *out of* partisanship, not in the abandonment of political friendship. Against the view of Edward Everett, who had contended that Clay's contribution was not widely approved, and that the war's unpopularity in New England had contributed to the demise of the Federalist Party, Lincoln insists that Clay was heroic: he enlivened a supine majority to act upon its convictions and do what almost all "intelligent and patriotic Americans" later believed was wise (2.127).

Whereas the Democratic eulogy had said nothing about Clay's role in the war, Lincoln's account takes up almost a tenth of his text—far more than his discussion of Clay's role in the nullification controversy and the Compromise of 1850. The historical distance of the 1812 decision, as well as its remoteness from the debate over slavery, gives him the opportunity to pull out a few oratorical stops when he describes the lost oration with which Clay won the day:

> The precise language of this speech we shall never know; but we do know—we cannot help knowing, that, with deep pathos, it pleaded the cause of the injured sailor—that it invoked the genius of the revolution—that it apostrophized the names of Otis, of Henry and of Washington—that it scorned, and scouted, and withered the temerity of domestic foes—that it bearded and defied the British Lion—and rising, swelling, and maddening in its course, it sounded the onset, till the charge, the shock, the steady struggle, and the glorious victory, all passed in vivid review before the entranced hearers. (2.127)

Lincoln's inhibitions about making a partisan eulogy momentarily evaporate as he recreates himself in honor of the assertive, principled, partisan performance of his Whig ideal. Clay, it seems, was himself a partisan capable of mustering a martial spirit: he achieved, in this case, a consensus for war based on decisive principles. We are briefly caught up in the celebratory, carefully limited martial language Lincoln used in his 1850 eulogy for Zachary Taylor, that speech being an antidote to the Democrats' charge that Clay's party, made up of recent opponents of the Mexican War, housed the wrong kind of pacificators.[3] Lincoln here makes Clay a more principled compromiser and a more insistent warrior than the Democratic eulogist had imagined.

A biographer of Lincoln who writes appreciatively of his eloquence in other speeches has found the eulogy to Clay to be a perplexing disappointment. In Lord Charnwood's view, it is a disturbing departure from the oratorical methods and philosophical principles of his other speeches: "[T]he occasion and the subject are used with rather disagreeable subtlety to insinuate opposition to slavery into the minds of a cautious audience. The speaker himself seems satisfied with the mood of mere compromise, which had governed Clay in this matter, or rather perhaps he is twisting Clay's attitude into one of more consistent opposition to slavery than he really showed."[4] Charnwood identifies the problem of coordinating the two lines of argument that Lincoln pursues: a highly deferential view of Clay's abilities as the Great Pacificator (which required him to place compromise over confrontation regarding slavery), and a seemingly contradictory attempt to push Clay toward an antislavery position that to Charnwood seems beyond the facts. The biographer registers discomfort at Lincoln's ingenuity, his mode of presentation, which seems to rely uncharacteristically on a form of indirection—insinuation—to make these points, and which this sympathetic historian finds inappropriate and unsettling.

Does the eulogy show Lincoln distorting Clay's legacy to complement his own? Charnwood's suspicions, reluctantly expressed in the context of his high expectations for Lincoln's antebellum rhetoric, deserve serious consideration. Does the eulogy go too far in making the Great Pacificator a champion of emancipation? To judge the issue, we need to examine Henry Clay's complicated position on the slavery question, and Lincoln's particular use of Clay's words. A good place to begin is the speech from which Lincoln draws his most important, climactic quotation from Clay's oratory: the 1827 address on the subject of emancipation and the colonization of Africa.

In that speech Clay explains that he is seeking a solution to the problem of slavery that avoids "the two extremes of public sentiment"—the view of the abolitionist who demands immediate and unconditional emancipation at the price of jeopardizing the Constitution and the Union, and the position of the diehard slave owner who, he says, "trembles with aspen sensibility at the appearance of the most distant and ideal danger to the tenure by which that description of property is held."[5] This is the view Lincoln emphatically endorses and elaborates in the 1852 eulogy:

> Cast into life where slavery was already widely spread and deeply seated, he did not perceive, as I think no wise man has perceived, how it could be at *once* eradicated, without producing a greater evil, even to the cause of human liberty itself. His feeling and his judgment, therefore, ever led him to oppose both extremes of opinion on the subject. Those who would shiver into fragments the Union of these States; tear to tatters its now venerated constitution; and even burn the last copy of the Bible, rather than slavery should continue a single hour, together with all their more halting sympathizers, have received, and are receiving their just execration and the name, and opinions, and influence of Mr. Clay, are fully, and as I trust effectually and enduringly, arrayed against them. But I would also, if I could, array his name, opinions, and influence against the opposite extreme—against a few, but an increasing number of men, who, for the sake of perpetuating slavery, are beginning to as-

sail and to ridicule the white-man's charter of freedom—the declaration that "all men are created free and equal." (2.130)

In defining a middle path between extremes, Clay, like Lincoln, does not deny himself the expression of outrage over slavery. In his colonization speech he calls slavery a "curse" by means of which "the unhappy portion of our race is doomed to bondage." It is the "deepest stain upon the character of our country."[6] When Lincoln responds in the eulogy to the emergent view that the Declaration is a false authority on these issues, he harmonizes with Clay's willingness to insist on the moral sense of the case: "This [rejection of the Declaration] sounds strangely in republican America. The like was not heard in the fresher days of the Republic" (2.131).

The strength of Clay's legacy, as Lincoln saw it, was its identification of contemporary hopes for liberty with the moral substance of the American founding. The Union, as Clay set it forth in 1827 in a moment of uncharacteristically unguarded enthusiasm, was informed by the principle of liberty, which the American experiment in self-government offered to the entire human race. Lincoln quoted the passage in the 1852 eulogy and used it in speeches later in the decade:

> If they would repress all tendencies towards liberty, and ultimate emancipation, they must do more than put down the benevolent efforts of this society. They must go back to the era of our liberty and independence, and muzzle the cannon which thunders its annual joyous return. . . . They must blow out the moral lights around us, and extinguish that greatest torch of all which America presents to a benighted world—pointing the way to their rights, their liberties, and their happiness. And when they have achieved all those purposes their work will be yet incomplete. They must penetrate the human soul, and eradicate the light of reason, and the love of liberty. Then, and not till then, when universal darkness and despair prevail, can you perpetuate slavery, and repress all sympathy, and all humane, and benevolent efforts among free men, in behalf of the unhappy portion of our race doomed to bondage. (2.131)[7]

Clay clearly has the Declaration of Independence in mind. The cannon's blast marks the day of "liberty and independence." The torch of "rights, their liberty, and their happiness" draws its meaning from the language of Jefferson's opening sentences. Like Jefferson, Clay does not conceive of the revolution of liberty and rights as a purely local development. The American torch has ignited a "moral revolution" across the world and in the souls of humankind. Those who remain slaves are, like free men, "a portion of our race." They can expect to benefit from those "tendencies" toward "ultimate emancipation." Emancipation is the legitimate expectation of American slaves because the idea of liberty entails an idea of equality—of each person's right to liberty and potential for self-government. Slavery therefore cannot be a natural sinew of the American polity despite its protections under American law.

These ideas buttressed the work of Clay's colonization society. To reject the society's goals, he said, was to put down "all tendencies toward liberty and ultimate emancipation." The work of the colonization society was the least offensive and most practical emancipatory effort one could reasonably imagine. To reproach it for endangering the institution of slavery was to deny the very spirit of liberty and the moral meaning of the American founding. If no such effort to lessen the curse of slavery were permissible (Calhoun, for example, was opposed to the society's activities, as were radical abolitionists), there could be no moral principle directing America's revolution.

Could Clay have been serious about colonization, and Lincoln serious in his support of Clay's efforts, given the unlikelihood of success? Colonization was the means, Clay argued, for the disgrace of enslavement to end. He thought it offered a way of ending slavery slowly, without disregarding the slaveholder's fears, the bonds of Union, or the volition of freed blacks. The repatriation of hundreds of thousands of freedmen to Liberia would show the South that there existed a safe means of freeing surplus slaves, thus keeping them apart from persons remaining in bondage and far from the owners who held them there. He assumed that voluntary colonization would encourage slave owners to emancipate more of their slaves as the virtues of free labor, replacing slavery, became clear. The fulfillment of the society's plans would be "instrumental in eradicating this deepest stain upon the character of our country, and removing all cause of reproach on account of it, by foreign nations."[8]

Speaking in 1852, Lincoln calls the colonization society's aspirations laudable and practicable. But he does not share Clay's industrious enthusiasm for working out the details of colonization project. The great Whig statesman had shown his seriousness by laboriously calculating the rate of colonization that would be required and the capacity of available ships to carry freedmen back to Africa. In his 1827 speech he had hopefully predicted that repatriation of 52,000 persons a year would end the growth of the entire black population, slave and free. But by 1850, only a few thousand had made the journey to Liberia, and in America planters were using an increasing slave population to expand their territory and feed their gins. In the time between Clay's speech and Lincoln's eulogy, the slave population had increased by half.

Lincoln risks asserting that "[e]very succeeding year has added strength to the hope" that the "redemption of the African race and African continent" will be realized (2.132).[9] But his eulogy replaces Clay's confident predictions with a hypothetical generality. He expresses his hope with an elaborately conditional syntax that focuses on the power of goodwill, the desirability of ending slavery (not of emancipation per se), and the principle of gradualism more than the importance of colonization itself:

> If as the friends of colonization hope, the present and coming generations of our countrymen shall by any means succeed in freeing our land from the dangerous presence of slavery; and, at the same time, in restoring a captive people to their long-lost father-land, with bright prospects for the future; and this too, so gradually, that neither races nor individuals shall have suffered by the change, it will indeed be a glorious consummation. (2.132)

Lincoln's caution had a precedent in Clay's own oratorical record. Speaking in 1839, a little more than a decade after the experiment in colonization had commenced, Clay had said that there might not be an "entirely practicable" means effecting emancipation: "[N]o practical scheme for [the slaves'] removal or separation from us has been yet devised or proposed." The advantage of the colonization scheme, which began with blacks already free and willing to go, was not so much its proven practicality as its "unmixed humanity and benevolence" when compared with other plans.[10]

Clay's deference to all sides had given his colonization society an opportunity to invoke the Declaration without seeming allied to the abolitionists. But it had also been a symptom of Clay's reluctance to make emancipation a decisive political issue. The meaning of the Declaration's authority could become clouded when he embedded it in his efforts to reach compromise. His ability to structure consensus among divergent parties and sections had much to do with his cultivation of moral *ambiguity*, as a recent interpreter of the 1850 negotiations has noted: "[T]he best strategy for saving the Union seemed to him to be getting men to agree to an ambiguous proposition for nonintervention in the territories, even knowing full well that many agreed to it in the belief—directly counter to his own—that this sanctioned the spread of slavery into the territories. Clay preferred to accentuate the ambiguity to secure agreement."[11] Lincoln, we know, would soon become more insistent than Clay on such matters. In 1852 his eulogy shows him less strident than he is in 1854. Nevertheless, his interest in protecting Clay's antislavery credentials from the charge of moral ambiguity is urgent in 1852. By various ingenious means he gradually uncovers Clay's moral position within his political devices.

The gist of this approach is evident in Lincoln's comparison of the Great Pacificator with other American leaders he surpassed in the length of time he held sway over national affairs. Clay's superior achievement, Lincoln argues, had to do with his power to combine eloquent speech, good judgment, and a strong will. His political compromises were in themselves not as important as his principles and his approach. Indeed they were forms of political technology, or "mode[s] of adjustment" (2.129) that therefore did not contradict or cancel Clay's moral ideas. His success stemmed from the predominance in his oratory of his conviction that his cause was just. It neglected the "types and figures" of rhetoric because it sought to express instead his "deeply earnest and impassioned tone, and manner, which can proceed only from great sincerity and a thorough conviction, in the speaker of the justice and importance of his cause." Clay's judgment therefore led him not only to "avoid all sectional ground"; it allowed him to "weigh every conflicting interest" in order to preserve the Union on terms that would keep it worth the saving (2.126).

Lincoln maintains this precedence of ideas over the political technology in Clay's achievements by mentioning almost no details about the complex arrangements he helped bring about in his compromise legislation. The morally ambiguous and ingenious provisions of the Missouri Compromise of 1820, which admitted Missouri as a slave state above the new Mason-Dixon line but prohibited slavery elsewhere in that northern region, are absent from the speech. Lincoln stresses Clay's "inventive genius, and his devotion to his country in the day of her extreme peril," not the arrangement itself (2.129). He has nothing to say about the nullification crisis, or the Compromise of 1850, the latter (with its multiple provisions and ambiguities about the basis on which new states could enter the Union as slave or free) being difficult to secure in one's judgment according to moral principle—as the Kansas-Nebraska crisis proved in 1854.

Clay had contributed to the Great Compromise's inclusion of some congressional prohibitions on slavery in the territories; but Lincoln's eulogy does not attempt to winnow that accomplishment from the complications of the multiauthored settlement of 1850. In his effort to build his case for Clay's heroic leadership in the light of his crucial *ideas,* Lincoln quotes from Jefferson's April 22, 1820, letter to John Holmes, in which the author of the Declaration expresses his horror at the prospect of a dispute over slavery that would divide the country with a line on the map. The eulogy uses Jefferson's words to trump consideration of the details of the 1820 and 1850 agreements so that Clay's larger effort can be seen to uphold antislavery ideas— ideas that Lincoln in later speeches would explicitly connect to the Founder's support of slavery prohibitions in the Northwest Ordinance (2.127– 128). Jefferson's letter famously invokes antislavery sentiments in the complicating context of his analogy about holding a wolf by the ears:

> [T]his momentous question, like a fire bell in the night, awakened, and filled me with terror. I considered it at once as the knell of the union. . . . A geographical line, co-inciding with a marked principle, moral and political, once conceived, and held up to the angry passions of men, will never be obliterated; and every irritation will mark it deeper and deeper. I can say, with conscious truth, that there is not a man on earth who would sacrifice more than I would to relieve us from this heavy reproach, in any *practicable* way. The cession of that kind of property, for so it is misnamed, is a bagatelle which would not cost me a second thought, if in that way, a general emancipation, and *expatriation* could be effected; and, gradually, and with due sacrifices I think it might be. But as it is, we have the wolf by the ears and we can neither hold him, nor safely let him go. Justice is in one scale, and self-preservation in the other. (2.128–129)

Jefferson's scruples, embodied in the quotation that Lincoln places within his account of Clay's actions, harmonize with Clay's. And Clay's solution to the Missouri question, whereby he resisted a strictly sectional division, addresses Jefferson's anxieties about a provocative, permanent line. One state north of the line would enter the union allowing slavery, in exchange for keeping slavery out of the rest of the northern region under discussion. Lincoln maintains the importance of Clay's moral stance by calling the 1820 settlement a resolution of the "Missouri question," not the Missouri Compromise. Throughout his speech, he denies the word *compromise* the status of a noun. The point is that Clay's principles prevailed. It is probably for this reason that Lincoln gives much more attention to Clay's advocacy of Greek and South American liberty than he does to the details of Clay's role in the later, messier Great Compromise of 1850. (When we look closely, we see that Lincoln dispatches the topic in a single sentence.) To go into detail would have clouded Lincoln's defense of Clay's principles, for it would raise constitutional and practical issues about the relation between the states, territories, and the federal government in the famous trade-offs of 1850, the meaning of which would have to be sorted out by Lincoln and his contemporaries.

The thesis Lincoln sets out to prove is as clear as it is problematic: Clay "ever was, in principle and in feeling, opposed to slavery" (2.130). Phrased as a simple declaration, the proposition entails three separate claims about Clay's philosophical position: its longevity, its basis in good judgment, and its origin in powerful conviction. And yet Clay had been reluctant throughout his career to delineate and specifically address slavery with a legislative agenda. Lincoln prods Clay's views into confrontation with proslavery views without claiming that Clay clearly attempted to *legislate* that principle and feeling, directly or indirectly, into the compromises he helped to construct. In the most notably recent instance—the debate over the compromise measures of 1850—Clay had made his dislike of slavery clear, but without immediate political consequence in the language of the final bill.[12]

Lincoln notes that Clay had set forward, at the beginning and end of his career, legislation for gradual emancipation in Kentucky (2.130). For Clay, however, the rights of the states and the jurisdiction of the federal government under the Constitution were almost hermetically sealed from one another. The legacy of the Declaration informed the moral consciousness of its inheritors, but it could have no decisive purchase in federal law under the sway of a neutral Constitution. This gap in legislation and conception at the federal level was the loophole through which Stephen Douglas would pilot the Kansas-Nebraska Act of 1854—a gap Lincoln would rise to fill, in opposition to what he considered Douglas's adventurism.

As an owner of slaves, Lincoln notes, Clay submitted to a regrettable necessity, much as the Founders did. He refrained from making the matter worse, despite his aversion to the institution, by indulging in precipitous action: "[H]e did not perceive, as I think no wise man has perceived, how it [slavery] could be at *once* eradicated, without producing a greater evil, even to the cause of human liberty itself" (2.130). ("The slaves are here," Clay had said. "[N]o practical scheme for their removal or separation from us has been yet devised or proposed; and the true inquiry is, what is best to be done with them.)[13] Hence the importance of colonization schemes, which were falling so far short of their goals that it was difficult to see how they could determine the question.

One does not have to read far in Clay's writings to see melancholy speculations about what could go wrong if no more effective solution could be found: "[B]eneath the ruins of the Union would be buried, sooner or later, the liberty of both races."[14] He blames abolitionists as well as uncompromising slaveholders for increasing the chances of civil war: "Abolitionists themselves would shrink back in dismay and horror at the contemplation of desolated fields, conflagrated cities, murdered inhabitants, and the overthrow of the fairest fabric of human government that ever rose to animate the hopes of civilized man."[15] But Lincoln does not quote from such texts in his optimistic eulogy. He lets Jefferson, not Clay, paint the prophecy of war, and he expresses an aversion to radical abolitionism in a carefully targeted condemnation of their disrespect of the Constitution and the Bible: they endanger "the cause of human liberty itself" by showing contempt for its foundational texts (2.130).

As we look more closely at the eulogy, we begin to see a profound difference in the strategy of the two men. Lincoln ostensibly agrees with Clay's reluctance to think in federal, antislavery terms. He characterizes outspoken criticism of the Declaration as a new thing, not an embedded regional prejudice (2.130). He goes so far as to characterize the Declaration as "the white man's charter of freedom" (2.130). And he uses the less inflammatory, vernacular version of Jefferson's phrasing when he states that "all men are created free and equal," thus joining equality with the complementary principle of liberty most cited by opponents of equality. In the quoted passages from Clay there is no invocation of the words *equal* or *equality*. Clay is intent upon "freedom," "rights," "liberties," and "happiness." Throughout the speech Lincoln never repeats the Declaration's sentence about equality, although he carefully misquotes it when he reads the proslavery words of a southern clergyman. His closest attempt to show that Clay directly endorsed the Declaration's principle of equality is a complex double negative with moral force but without direct reference to equality: "[Clay] did not perceive, that on a question of human right, the negroes were to be excepted from the human race" (2.130). In the second half of the eulogy, however, Lincoln supplies a more daring argument: an implicit defense and adaptation not only of Clay's principles but also of his *strategies of compromise* as instruments available for more assertive purposes. Lincoln suggests that the powers—the instrumentalities—that Clay used to effect the compromises might be used, when rightly understood and applied, to even greater effect for the sake of those sympathies.

As we have seen, Lincoln thought those means were more than rhetorical. They were not confined to the skills of eloquence. *Genius and its instruments,* along with devotion to the Union, comprised a vaster subject than rhetoric. Unlike Lincoln, the Democratic eulogist had missed this point by consistently staking Clay's reputation only on his eloquence:

> His eloquence has not been surpassed. In the effective power to move the heart of man, Clay was without an equal, and the heaven born endowment, in the spirit of its origin, has been most conspicuously exhibited against intestine feud. . . . [H]e has quelled our civil commotions, by a power and influence, which belonged to no other statesman of his age and times. (2.123)

The Democrats' favored successor, Douglas, was supposed to follow in Clay's footsteps because he was another great speaker whose powers of eloquence would overcome all political differences. Even though the two men were, "in political sentiment, as far apart as party could make them," their mutual power over words made them brothers and spread brotherhood across the nation (2.122). But Lincoln's analysis leads to a different conclusion. It was Clay's "inventive genius" of adjustment, along with "his devotion to his country in the day of her extreme peril," that tantalizingly defined his greatest achievements (2.129). His genius was far more significant than his eloquence, which for all its usefulness was a means, not an end: "[I]t was now perceived that his great eloquence, was a mere embellishment, or at most, but a helping hand" to genius and patriotism (2.129).

> He was surpassingly eloquent; but many eloquent men fail utterly; and they are not, as a class, generally successful. His judgment was excellent; but many men of good judgment, live and die unnoticed. His will was indomitable; but this quality often secures to its owner nothing better than a character for useless obstinacy. These then were Mr. Clay's leading qualities. No one of them is very uncommon; but all taken together are rarely combined in a single indi-

vidual; and this is probably the reason why such men as Henry Clay are so rare in the world. (2.125–126)

These ingeniously combined *multiple means* of activating political majorities and passing such measures, when understood in the light of Clay's power to wield them and their potential for carrying certain principles into practice, point the way for a successor to surpass Clay.

Thus we come to understand Lincoln's praise of Clay's skill, while effacing the political details of Clay's interventions, as an affirmation of the flexibility and power available to political genius. Informed by Clay's moral principles, that skill could direct those resources more effectively than Clay did if one could understand political genius more thoroughly. Antislavery principles might not have informed Clay's actions in any particularly identifiable way, as Lincoln's silence on the subject seems to concede; but the successor who understands Clay's genius and instrumentalities might thereby secure gradual emancipation by marshaling majorities that perhaps already desire such a thing. As in the case of Congress at the beginning of the War of 1812 or during the Missouri crisis, such majorities are to be found by a leader who knows how to help them coalesce and act (2.127, 129)—thus the need for a heroic leader whose genius serves his devotion to freedom and emancipation. The prosperity of the Union would then "show the world," as Clay wanted it to do, "that freemen could be prosperous" (2.126). In particular, the possibility of federal territorial legislation prohibiting the spread of slavery—whether Clay wanted it or not—might be made to seem more plausible and just.

It is right to feel, with Charnwood, that Lincoln presses these issues with unsettling subtlety. His appropriation of Clay pushes both men beyond their normal rhetorical limits. In his penultimate paragraph, Lincoln allows himself to imitate his favorite passages from Clay in a manner that refers to and exercises some of the "means" that he himself might discover in order to effect Clay's vague desire for universal emancipation:

> Pharaoh's country was cursed with plagues, and his hosts were drowned in the Red Sea for striving to retain a captive people who had already served them more than four hundred years. May like disasters never befall us! If as the friends of colonization hope, the present and coming generations of our countrymen shall *by any means,* succeed in freeing our land from the dangerous presence of slavery; and, at the same time, in restoring a captive people to their long-lost father-land, with bright prospects for the future; and this too,

so gradually, that neither races nor individuals shall have suffered by the change, it will indeed be a glorious consummation. And if, to such a consummation, the efforts of Mr. Clay shall have contributed, it will be what he most ardently wished, and none of his labors will have been more valuable to his country and his kind. (2.132; emphasis added)

Full of twists and provisos, these lines shift attention away from Clay's plans for colonization, elevate his antislavery sympathies, and subtly recognize the possibility of finding ways of implementing the gradual emancipation of American slaves—not simply as a first step to colonization but as an emancipatory action in its own right.

The final words of Lincoln's hyperbole echo lines from *Hamlet,* which he turns from despair toward hope. His elevated syntax and vocabulary overlap with Hamlet's famous contemplation of suicide, his wish for death and sleep that he describes as a "consummation / Devoutly to be wished." Hamlet thinks of escaping "the heartache, and the thousand natural shocks / That flesh is heir to" as he mourns the loss of his father.[16] But then he concludes that he cannot escape. "'Tis a consummation / Devoutly to be wished" that Hamlet concludes is unavailable to suicides or even to sleepers. Their fearful dreams of death might be true. In Shakespeare's play the hoped-for consummation is famously beyond Hamlet's ability to act. Lincoln's hope is different, running contrary to Hamlet's sentiment, Clay's bouts of melancholy speculation, and the nightmare vision of Jefferson's letter. He seeks "a glorious consummation" of "what [Clay] most ardently wished." Clay's ideas of human freedom remain within reach. They live in the Declaration and can be acted upon by new generations, perhaps "in future national emergencies" (2.132).

In his conclusion, Lincoln directs attention to the change in circumstances that accompanies Clay's death. New "instruments" (human and otherwise) will be needed to carry on:

But Henry Clay is dead. His long and eventful life is closed. Our country is prosperous and powerful; but could it have been quite all it has been, and is, and is to be, without Henry Clay? Such a man the times have demanded, and such, in the providence of God was given us. But he is gone. Let us strive to deserve, as far as mortals may, the continued care of Divine Providence, trusting that, in future national emergencies, He will not fail to provide us the instruments of safety and security. (2.132)

New trials will come, and Clay's principles, insofar as they were embodied in the legislative machinery he fashioned with them, will not be enough to resist them. New "instruments of safety and security"—leaders and legislation— will be needed. The gushing Democratic obituary in the newspaper addressed this problem with hyperbole and the claim that Clay had "exorcised the demon which possessed the body politic." Lincoln implicitly scorns this newspaper sentiment by forcefully assuming that no one, by himself, can presume to succeed Clay, that when the strife and the demon of disunity rise again, human effort itself will not be enough. The successor will be determined by "the providence of God," which will provide the human and legislative "instruments." Mortals can seek that favor, but only in the self-effacing belief that "He will not fail to provide us" such things.

In the months and years following Clay's death, Lincoln's prediction would in a sense be realized. Clay's compromises would demonstrate their vulnerabilities. The Great Compromise of 1850, which was negotiated through Congress by Stephen Douglas, would discandy, revealing deepening sectional divisions over slavery that were splitting the Whigs and threatening to break up the Democrats.[17] Clay's Whigs would disintegrate as a united force in a few years and would fail to nominate a candidate for the presidency in the next election. In the 1852 elections, Douglas's Democrats would win overwhelmingly, taking the presidency away from Lincoln's party, along with many congressional seats. In the attempt to resolve the status of slavery in the territories without taking up the question of slavery, the Douglas-sponsored Kansas-Nebraska Act of 1854 would pass at the cost of repealing Clay's Missouri Compromise, which Douglas had defended in 1849 as a sacred principle "canonized in the hearts of the American people as a sacred thing which no ruthless hand would ever be reckless enough to disturb."[18] By 1860 the old Democratic Party would itself disintegrate, unable to avoid the issue that had split it along sectional lines.

Eulogizing Clay on a Springfield platform in July 1852, Lincoln was preparing himself, his fellow Whigs, and his general audience for a new political alignment. We do not know precisely what he had in mind as he looked ahead. But we do know that in that speech he was beginning to make antislavery sentiments like Clay's politically consequential on a national level. Joined with the old Whig defense of the Union as the greatest hope for self-government, the two positions were to be adjusted to make room for a politics of principled compromise. Many Americans would not agree with the principles or the synthesis; but with further adjustments, Lincoln's position would contribute to a new political philosophy that appealed to the increasing numbers of antislavery Whigs, Free-Soilers, and unionist Democrats, without advocating forced emancipation or acceding to the perpetuation of slavery. In form and substance, the eulogy for Clay intimated Lincoln's own prescient ambition to serve, if called upon, as an instrument of that political transformation. We might now say that it was indeed Lincoln, not Douglas, who, as the Democratic eulogist said, was mourning for Clay and carefully anticipating the succession. Despite itself, the newspaper has the last word:

> Perchance, in the whole circle of the great and gifted of our land, there remains but one on whose shoulders the mighty mantle of the departed statesman may fall—one, while we now write, [who] is doubtless pouring his tears over the bier of his brother and his friend—brother, friend, ever, yet in political sentiment, as far apart as party could make them. Ah, it is at times like these, that the petty distinctions of mere party disappear. (2.122)

6

The Kansas-Nebraska Speech

Popular Sovereignty and Self-Government

If you hear me at all, I wish you to hear me through. (2.247)

According to a letter Lincoln wrote to a political friend, it was not until late summer of 1854 that he delivered a speech dedicated to the issue of slavery and prepared with publication in mind.[1] The relative clarity of this information entails a complex and characteristic qualification: Lincoln is implying that his antislavery career did not necessarily begin as late as 1854. When he wrote in 1860 to James Putnam that the Kansas-Nebraska Speech, delivered on October 16, 1854, was the "first printed speech of mine, on the Slavery question," he did not say that he had taken no previous position, or that there were no other speeches or documents that had at least an indirect bearing on the question. We know that Lincoln risked controversy in 1852 when he praised Henry Clay's antislavery feelings, and so distinguished himself from scores of eulogists who said nothing about slavery. Several years before, he had expressed antislavery sentiments in a public document: his 1849 proposal, in the U.S. House of Representatives, to abolish slavery in the District of Columbia. Although there is no recorded speech by him in support of that measure, we know that during Lincoln's brief career in the House he voted numerous times for the Wilmot Proviso, an amendment to prohibit slavery in the newly acquired territories.

What is important to notice is that, although these and other documents give us evidence that Lincoln's antislavery sentiments existed long before 1854, his letter to Putnam is carefully correct in its contention that no "printed speech ... on the Slavery question" existed prior to 1854. When he did finally speak in the summer and fall of that year, the result was a powerful performance. His lengthy, calculated, sometimes passionate arguments brought years of thought to fruition in a public forum. What to Herndon seemed a sudden transformation in the face of crisis was a galvanizing moment, a manifestation of the secret processes Herndon had always thought were at work within his partner's silences.[2]

The passage of the Kansas-Nebraska Act was the turning point. Here is how Lincoln characterized it as a sinister innovation when he spoke at Peoria:

> A controversy had arisen between the advocates and opponents of slavery, in relation to its establishment within the country we had purchased of France. The southern, and then best part of the purchase, was already in as a slave State. The controversy was settled by also letting Missouri in as a slave State; but with the agreement that within all the remaining part of the purchase, North of a certain line, there should never be slavery. As to what was to be done with the remaining part south of the line, nothing was said; but perhaps the fair implication was, that it should come in with slavery if it should so choose. The southern part, except a portion heretofore mentioned, afterwards did come in with slavery, as the State of Arkansas. All these many years since 1820, the Northern part had remained a wilderness. At length settlements began in it also. In due course, Iowa, came in as a free State, and Minnesota was given a territorial government, without removing the slavery restriction. Finally the sole remaining part, North of the line, Kansas and Nebraska, was to be organized; and it is proposed, and carried, to blot out the old dividing line of thirty-four years standing, and to open the whole of that country to the introduction of slavery. Now, this, to my mind, is manifestly unjust. After an angry and dangerous controversy, the parties made friends by dividing the bone of contention. The one party first appropriates her own share, beyond all power to be disturbed in the possession of it; and then seizes the share of the other party. It is as if two starving men had divided their only loaf; the one had hastily swallowed his half, and then grabbed the other half just as he was putting it to his mouth! (2.261–262)

Lincoln's great rival Stephen Douglas had engineered legislation for the remaining Louisiana Purchase territories by replacing the Missouri Compromise with the principle of popular sovereignty. The people of the territories, not Congress or previous legislation, would decide whether the new lands were to be slave or free. In response, Lincoln wagered his political fortunes on his ability to defend a carefully crafted antislavery argument. Was he acting prematurely? Too late? Should he have spoken at all? His speech would have to justify the timing of his argument as well as its substance.

Up to the time he left political office in 1849, Lincoln's affiliation with the Whig Party, which drew supporters from all sections of the country, was no obvious guide to his position regarding slavery. As we have seen, Clay and Webster, Lincoln's greatest Whig heroes, had attempted to maintain antislavery positions that did not alienate a broad range of Whig supporters in the South. In Congress, Lincoln had voted against extending slavery into the territories, but he had not participated in the public debate on the issue. Before 1850 the Whigs would probably not have survived as a formidable alternative to the Democrats if they had adopted an antislavery platform. It is true that in the aftermath of the Mexican War, President Taylor—a hero of that war, a Whig, and a slave owner—had confronted southern interests over the status of slavery in the American lands bordering Texas. But his death in 1850, in the midst of that controversy, had temporarily allayed the crisis. In the next few months, under the more accommodating administration of his successor, President Fillmore, it was the old Whig champion Henry Clay, with the tactical assistance of the Democrat Stephen Douglas, who managed to legislate a series of ameliorative agreements that dropped the Wilmot Proviso and obscured the realignment of national politics that the Mexican War and its aftermath had begun to bring about.

The result of that work—the agreements of 1850—rejected the Wilmot Proviso and traded preferences between northern and southern interests. They did not disturb the Missouri Compromise. Stephen Douglas had himself praised both compromises of 1850 and 1820 as bulwarks of a strengthened union. The old party arrangements, even though they were weakened by the increasingly sectional nature of national politics, remained at least superficially intact. Both measures offered the North and the South grounds for hoping that the slavery controversy would subside. After 1850 the doctrine of abolitionism—though it was influential among northeastern Whigs—still had no substantial position among Whigs in the South and was not a decisive concern in the old Northwest. It is true that antislavery sentiment was growing in the relatively broad-based Free-Soil Party, which had run the Whigs' old enemy Martin Van Buren for president in 1848. But the Free-Soilers lacked the coherence they needed to become a sustained political movement. "Barn-burning" defectors from the Democrats, joining with some abolitionist Whigs as well as rebels from both parties in the West, had fought for the goal of keeping the territories free from slavery and, in fact, had drawn many votes away from the two major parties. But their coalition could not attract and hold enough supporters from the traditional parties to re-shape the political map. By 1854 the Free-Soilers' influence had begun to dissipate.

The controversy over Douglas's legislation had, of course, put a severe strain on the Whig Party, which depended for its influence on the joint action of southern as well as northern supporters. What some northern Whigs saw as a breach in the Missouri line that threatened their free soil did not severely agitate their southern brethren. Conversely, as slavery moved toward the center of debate, southern Whigs found they had less to hold in common with their northern friends. Sectional divisions had begun to tear at the Democrats too, as could be seen in the eagerness with which many of them joined the loose coalition of Free-Soilers. Lincoln's speech took advantage of this volatility while attempting to hold as much Whig support, and southern Democratic respect, as possible.

It is reasonable to assume that Douglas had not intended to stimulate such a formidable opposition, and that he wished to open the remaining Louisiana territories as quickly as possible for settlement and the construction of railroads, in a manner that would defuse the slavery question as settlers moved west. Not incidentally, the success of the measure would have strengthened his national appeal in the upcoming presidential election. In its specific provisions, the new law redefined the status of the lands in the Louisiana Purchase that had not yet become states. It stipulated that the Missouri Compromise was no longer operative and entrusted the authority for determining the status of slavery to expressions of popular will, without clarifying what role the territorial legislatures or specific electoral procedures would play. The author of the Kansas-Nebraska Act had managed to convince a majority in Congress that "popular sovereignty" would decide whether the new territories would be "slave" or "free." Popular sovereignty was for him "that great principle of self-government" that "teaches every people to do that which the interests of themselves and their posterity morally and peculiarly may require"—to exercise a right "to establish and abolish such institutions as they thought their own good required."[3] The Compromise of 1850 had recognized rights of self-determination in several of the territories that were wrested from Mexico, had it not? What greater principle could there be for resolving the slavery question than the rights of free men to determine their own destinies? But the reaction to the new law in the country at large, as well as among those who resisted it in Congress, revealed different understandings of what "their own good required," and disagreement over the legislation that would best secure that good. Lincoln, joining others, called the 1854 law an act of personal ambition. In the name of self-determination, he argued, Douglas had created an engine that was heedless of the Founders' intentions and the hallowed history of compromise. In the words of Thomas Hart Benton, a breakaway Democrat from Missouri, it was "a monstrosity, born of timidity and ambition, hatched into existence in the hot incubation of a presidential canvas, and revolting to the beholders when first presented."[4]

President Pierce signed the bill on May 30, 1854. By August, Lincoln was engaged in an intense public campaign to repeal it. Toward the end of that month he delivered an elaborate speech on the question in Winchester, and several days later spoke for two hours in Carrollton (2.226–227). On September 7 he wrote to John Palmer, a disillusioned Democratic leader, offering him sympathy and support for his rejection of Douglas's maneuver (2.228–229). He was the likely author of a homespun, biting parable in an unsigned editorial that appeared in the *Illinois Journal* on September 9. The language of that witty argument tells us a great deal about the direction Lincoln would take on the speaker's platform. Exhibiting his characteristic powers of satire and storytelling, the editorial mocked the language of the Kansas-Nebraska Act in its tale of a dispute between an obtusely disrespectful cattle farmer named John Calhoun and his incredulous neighbor, one Abraham Lincoln.[5]

> The state of the case in a few words, is this: The Missouri Compromise excluded slavery from the Kansas-Nebraska territory. The repeal [brought about by the Kansas-Nebraska Act] opened the territories to slavery.... The Kansas and Nebraska territories are now as open to slavery as Mississippi or Arkansas were when they were territories.
>
> To illustrate the case—Abraham Lincoln has a fine meadow, containing beautiful springs of water, and well fenced, which John Calhoun had agreed with Abraham (originally owning the land in common) should be his, and the agreement had been consummated in the most solemn manner, regarded by both as sacred. John Calhoun, however, in the course of time, had become owner of an extensive herd of cattle—the prairie grass has become dried up

and there was no convenient water to be had. John Calhoun then looks with a longing eye on Lincoln's meadow, and goes to it and throws down the fences, and exposes it to the ravages of his starving and famishing cattle. "You rascal," says Lincoln, "what have you done? what do you do this for?" "Oh," replies Calhoun, "everything is right. I have taken down your fence; but nothing more. It is my true intent and meaning not to drive my cattle into your meadow, nor to exclude them therefrom, but to leave them perfectly free to form their own notions of the feed, and to direct their movements in their own way!"

Now would not the man who committed this outrage be deemed both a knave and a fool,—a knave in removing the restrictive fence, which he had solemnly pledged himself to sustain;—and a fool in supposing that there could be one man found in the country to believe that he had not pulled down the fence for the purpose of opening the meadow for his cattle? (2.229–230)

In the character of Calhoun, the story blends the hypocritical slaveholder with the high-minded champion of popular sovereignty, exposing his rapacious behavior. Thus Lincoln tars Douglas as a man who, like Calhoun in the story, excuses that behavior by arguing from principle: the cattle, not the man who throws down the fence, should be allowed to decide who will eat Lincoln's grass. Thus the cattle are several things at once: (1) the appetite of the slave system, which competes with free farmers for land as it exhausts its own resources and "breeds" more slaves, and (2) those territorial voters (some to be herded there to vote for slavery) to whom is entrusted their neighbors' well-being, without regard for legal precedent and without a principle to guide their appetites ("their own notions of the feed").

It is difficult to ignore the feeling that Lincoln is trading on an impression or prejudice in his audience that men who are enslaved under Calhoun behave like cattle, moving over the land like voracious herds. Negrophobia had deep roots in the North, and here it is not meticulously ignored. But by taking the more dangerous route of likening the animals not just to slaves but to free voters who trample their neighbors' rights after Calhoun destroys the fence, Lincoln's story suggests that popular sovereignty, uninformed by any idea but narrow self-interest, becomes a cattle-minded expropriation of others' rights to their land, perhaps even of their own rights to themselves. The editorial thus forecasts the arguments Lincoln would soon make in his own name: just as the enslaved man is treated as a grazing animal by his master, the free voter—whose liberty is curtailed by the repeal of the Missouri Compromise and the abandonment of traditional resistance to the perpetuation of slavery—becomes a kind of slave, either a man whose land is taken away from him or a kind of beast who roams westward without care for the damage he does to the rights of others.

Characteristically, Lincoln tells the humorous fable at his own expense. He identifies with his audience as a person caught unawares, dumbfounded by the shameless rapidity of his acquaintance's actions. He constructs the story so that the patently false explanation offered by the encroaching cattle herder is a triumph of hucksterism over Lincoln's belated powers of indignation. But instead of reducing the offended farmer to a buffoon, or interpreting Calhoun's action as a profound moral offense against the principles of freedom and equality, the story ridicules the cattle herder by focusing on his humorously lame excuse. Calhoun's reason is made to seem transparent to everyone. Farmer Lincoln's rejoinder—"You rascal"—is in this sense a folksy reprimand directed toward a mere conman. He appeals to free farmers' capacities to see the joke, to identify with his desire to protect what he owns, and to see their own vulnerability in the face of the legislation and animal hunger that have annulled the Missouri Compromise.

In Bloomington on September 12 and again on September 26, Lincoln gave the oratorical version of his parable in lengthy speeches. Springfield heard him on October 4, and Peoria on October 16. Newspapers printed his words (in truncated form) in transcribed or transliterated accounts he may have supervised. (See 2.230–233, 234–240, 240–247.) This process culminated in the lengthy, carefully printed Peoria speech, which now makes up one of the lengthiest oratorical performances in the *Collected Works*. It ran in installments for eight days in the *Illinois Journal.*

In the Peoria speech Lincoln tried to defuse Douglas's arguments without fundamentally questioning the principle of self-government or assuming the role of an abolitionist. He addressed his audience as independent voters, and he invoked the Declaration of Independence, the Northwest Ordinance, and the tradition of legislated compromise in order to question Douglas's faith in the uninhibited expression of self-interest and private judgment. Although he clearly adopted a number of abolitionist tenets, Lincoln did not take up the tone and substance of radical abolitionism. The indignant triumphalism of the abolitionist Theodore Parker's widely circulated oration, "The Nebraska Question" (February 12, 1854), offers a remarkable example of what Lincoln did *not* do in his Kansas-Nebraska speech, even though Parker coins a phrase about government by the people that will echo in the Gettysburg Address. One sentence will serve for comparison: "One day the North will rise in her majesty, and put Slavery under our feet, and then we shall extend the area of freedom. The blessing of Almighty God will come down upon the noblest people the world ever saw—who have triumphed over Theocracy, Monarchy, Aristocracy, Despotocracy, and have got a Democracy—a government of all, for all, and by all—a Church without a Bishop, a State without a King, a Community without a Lord, and a Family without a Slave."[6] Although Herndon made a habit of supplying his partner Lincoln with abolitionist publications, Parker's conception of the issue, his audience, and the prospects for a quick resolution of the slavery question are fundamentally at odds with the tone and substance of Lincoln's words.[7] The abolitionist not only calls for a conquest of the South, and the crushing of the Slave Power that would gain its justification from theological and political imperatives. He also conflates the hope of conquest with territorial expansion, and joins both these ideas under the aegis of an unstoppable religious crusade.

Charles Sumner's senatorial restraint did not conceal a similarly militant conviction that the Slave Power threatened the security and well-being of the North, as though the Kansas-Nebraska contest were between alien powers engaged in armed conflict. He saw its repeal of the Missouri Compromise as a destruction of the prospect of compromise in any form:

> Freedom is suddenly summoned to surrender even her hard-won moiety. Here are the three stages: at the first, all consecrated to Freedom; at the second, only half; at the third, all grasped by Slavery. The original policy of the government is absolutely reversed.[8]

> [The Kansas-Nebraska bill] annuls all past compromises with Slavery and makes any future compromises impossible. . . . [Yet] Freedom will be established by Congress everywhere, at least beyond the local limits of the States.[9]

Although he differed from Parker in accepting the limitations on Congress's power to abolish slavery where it existed, Sumner belligerently predicted that the rising conflict would "break" the Slave Power.[10]

Compared with Parker's and Sumner's abolitionist attacks on the bill, the abolition-leaning William Seward's senatorial speeches were relatively moderate. He defended the "dignity" of the tradition of compromise, which the Kansas-Nebraska bill had presumed to repeal with mere legislation. Recalling the words of Daniel Webster, he claimed that the Missouri Compromise was "irrepealable." Injured though it might be, the cause of compromise was not dead. But Seward, like Parker and Sumner, did not resist the temptation to threaten the defenders of slavery. Although he did not make his famous speech about an "irrepressible conflict" until 1858, in 1854 he was ready to remind the rival section that waves of immigrants—twelve thousand in a single day, according to his personal observation—were arriving in New York harbor, many on their way to the western lands.[11] By setting the raw number of northern immigrants against the slower increase in southern slaves, he arrayed the power of northern demographics against the frustrating record of sectional animosity and national legislation. He argued as though the force of numbers would sooner or later cancel the need to deliberate differences over the status of slavery in the territories or anywhere else.

To the extent that the abolitionists resorted to appeals to force over deliberation, they shared with Douglas a distaste for the prolongation of debates that they thought were threatening the principles of democratic government. Whether they relied on the arithmetic of demography or territorial plebiscites, both sides were proposing solutions that would replace deliberation and persuasion with a mechanism—a war of liberation or a territorial ballot. (Within two years, Kansas would see both mechanisms in deadly combination.) Lincoln takes a different tack. He does not avoid controversial statements; in fact his speech incorporates aspects of abolitionist philosophy, and it includes some of the vehement spirit of abolitionist assertions. But rather than ignore or berate the South, he alludes to the universal moral discomfort that accompanies the slave dealer. He takes this to mean that most Americans North and South apparently believe that slaves are human beings. In a similar spirit he reopens deliberation by appealing to moderate Whigs and Democrats who identify with free institutions and the American tradition of territorial law.

To appreciate the distinctive tenor and weight of Lincoln's argument, it is necessary to read it as a revision of Clay and Webster, and then to notice the ways in which Lincoln wrestles the issue from Douglas's control. There are of course affinities between Lincoln's Kansas-Nebraska Speech and the great speeches that Henry Clay and Daniel Webster devoted to the Compromise of 1850. But by 1854 the old Whigs' speeches were philosophically and rhetorically obsolete. The most effective legislative advocate of the 1850 law was now the author of the disastrous 1854 innovation. Lincoln had to do more than Clay and Webster had done, not only to protect the tradition of compromise from radical reinterpretation, but to ensure that further compromises over slavery did not have the effect of neutralizing the very idea that slavery was immoral, that it damaged the self-governing character of the republic.

In order to secure the 1850 agreement, Clay had regretfully but characteristically temporized, despite his dislike for slavery, over the principle of congressional prerogative in the territories. He had to rely on Douglas's energy to get the complex legislation passed in pieces, in a form that did not feature a set of guiding principles.[12] Webster had run into a different difficulty. In his famous speech of March 7, 1850, he had tried to adopt an inclusive position but had lost many of his old northeastern friends. By energetically endorsing the Fugitive Slave Law and condemning abolitionists, he seemed, in the eyes of many of his antislavery constituents, to be trafficking with the devil.

Webster's speech had condemned slavery as a "moral, social, and political evil." But he had explained that it was better understood in terms of the political and social arrangements that he said were at the foundation of the original consensus that joined North and South in the early days of the republic.[13] To many of his friends, this line of reasoning seemed to sacrifice the moral question. In his Clay-like faith that free labor would inevitably demonstrate to everyone its superiority to slave labor, Webster tried to stand above the fray. He took the un-Clay-like step of entirely avoiding the question of slavery in the territories, and he expressed his distaste for further territorial acquisition even though new lands were likely to be added to the American frontier.[14] Like Clay, he provided his political heirs with a formidable model of antislavery and unionist rhetoric. But his words failed to address Douglas's challenge.

Douglas's innovation was not merely a tactical maneuver, a way of gaining advantage on the national stage after the sequent deaths of Taylor, Clay, Webster, and Calhoun. The Kansas-Nebraska Act was a means for him to put on the mantle of Clay and Webster. The speeches Douglas delivered in favor of the 1854 legislation depended on arguments from principle that he said were derived from the 1850 compromise itself. The Kansas-Nebraska Act was, he argued, an extension and perfection of the 1850 law, an incorporation of the old Whig legacy within a Democratic superstructure. Lincoln characteristically chose to meet Douglas on this ground. Which man of principle could claim to inherit and extend the legacy of Clay, Webster, and the Founders themselves?

* * *

In his speeches and writings defending the 1854 legislation, Douglas had arrayed his argument with powerful assumptions that operated like rhetorical tropes. Each challenged his opponents' abilities to engage his remarks without losing their own concentration on the issue at hand:

Trope 1

Assumption: *Certain laws are designed to settle issues once and for all.* The Compromise of 1850 is one such law, for "We all know that the object of the compromise measures of 1850 was to establish certain principles which would avoid the slavery agitation in all time to come."[15]

Trope 2

Assumption A: *New legislation that limits the reach of a previous law repeals it.* This is the converse of Trope 1. Certain laws must be comprehensive. If they are not, they are invalid. Thus a new law can nullify an old one simply by denying that the old one applies to new lands beyond its original jurisdiction. Douglas's leading example is the 1848 congressional vote *not* to extend the Missouri Compromise's Mason-Dixon line beyond the Louisiana Territory. For Douglas, that vote was tantamount to a repeal of the Missouri Compromise.[16] One comprehensive law left no room for another.

Assumption B: *New legislation can repeal old law if it introduces, even parenthetically, a new way of deciding such questions.* Thus Douglas argues that the Great Compromise of 1850, in allowing some territories to become states, which then determine the status of slavery according to their local preferences, replaced the Missouri Compromise and opened the path for the 1854 law that enshrines popular sovereignty.[17]

Trope 3

Assumption: *Popular sovereignty, the voice of the people, is the maker of law.* Therefore the people of the territories ought to be allowed to resolve the question of slavery by acting as sovereign without regard for any competing principle or law but the Constitution, which itself enshrines the principle of popular sovereignty.[18]

Trope 4 (a corollary, matching trope 1)

Assumption: *The judgments of popular sovereignty are self-sufficient and final.* The people's law, the fruit of popular sovereignty, is all, and is to be understood according to tropes 1–3. "The real gist of the matter is this: Does it require any higher degree of civilization, and intelligence, and learning, and sagacity, to legislate for negroes than for white men? If it does, we ought to adopt the abolition doctrine. . . . If it does not—if we are willing to trust the people with the great, sacred, fundamental right of prescribing their own institutions, consistent with the Constitution of the country—we must vote for this bill."[19]

The rhetorical and political force of these assumptions has the effect of equating the settlers' will, and the will of any designated majority, with that of the American democracy, without regard for legislated precedent or point of reference outside of the procedures of the Constitution. A change in that popular will, preferred only on the basis of its newness, therefore makes changes in the law routinely capable of erasing past agreements and determining what new ones are acceptable. Concerning such issues, the popular will is all one thing, or the opposite. Mixed positions are logically impossible. New laws necessarily obliterate the old yet are highly susceptible, under the power of Douglas's tropes, to being erased in turn. The democratic sovereign's lawmaking power, as Douglas conceives of it, is therefore fundamentally indifferent to what that power does as long as it is free to swing between opposite poles and does not violate constitutional provisions.

In his Peoria speech, Lincoln ventures into the argument with the aid of matching tropes of his own:

Trope 1: Agreeing with Douglas, he believes that some forms of legislation regarding slavery are attempts to resolve, not temporize over, crucial issues. But whereas Douglas argues that a new law can—and should—establish principles that will bring the controversy to an end, Lincoln looks back to a history of compromise that has already required mutual forbearance, in the light of hallowed principles of the Revolution found in the Declaration of Independence, not just popular sovereignty's declaration of independence or the Constitution.

Trope 2: For Lincoln, therefore, the power of legislation is both more limited and more fundamental than it is for Douglas. He understands the new laws as extensions or abrogations of precedents, some more fundamental than others. Even the Constitution is illuminated and conceptually conditioned by the Declaration of Independence and the Northwest Ordinance. Some precedents are so important that they inform and judge succeeding legislation on the basis of something more than technical jurisprudence or the expression of the popular will. New laws that introduce exceptions to those precedents therefore need arguments to justify them, and they ought to be reversed by corrective legislation if they are in error. The old laws, at least the ones based on more fundamental principles, have an existence in several dimensions and can outlive aberrant legislation, if only by stirring legislators to repeal their mistakes. Contrary to Douglas's assumptions, they are neither irreducible substances nor soulless bodies mortified by a single shot. The Missouri Compromise lives on to animate opposition to Douglas's appeal. The Kansas-Nebraska Act's cancellation of the Missouri Compromise should itself be repealed.

Trope 3: In this sense, the law is greater than the lawmaker, and the people are subordinate to what they and their predecessors have legislated. More than a practical deference to what is on the books, this subordination is or ought to be a recognition of the existence of claims on human action that derive from sources beyond the reach of the popular will. The law, as we heard in the Lyceum Address, is itself a claim upon the will even when there is a conviction that the law is wrong. The Missouri Compromise of 1820, despite its lack of a clear antislavery principle, is not to be lightly abandoned. Analogously, there is legislation that in a sense takes precedence over other laws because of its political and philosophical sweep, and its venerable origin—for example, the Northwest Ordinance of 1787, which prohibited slavery in the old Northwest Territories and manifested, in Lincoln's view, the Founders' intention to limit the expansion of slavery in all territories. That

Well, I too, go for saving the Union. Much as I hate slavery, I would consent to the extension of it rather than see the Union dissolved, just as I would consent to any great evil, to avoid a greater one. But when I go to Union saving, I must believe, at least, that the means I employ has some adaptation to the end. To my mind, Nebraska [the Nebraska Bill] has no such adaptation. (2.270)

As we have seen, the chief purpose of Lincoln's Kansas-Nebraska Speech seems to be to prove that Douglas's measure is wrong because it jeopardizes the political *and* philosophical bases of union (2.254). By permitting the wholesale expansion of what Lincoln argues is an intractably self-interested ownership of men, the Nebraska bill seems to preserve the Union by sacrificing its reason for being, which for Lincoln is something more than the perpetuation of a compact of self-interested citizens and something greater than a confederacy of self-interested states. It would be wrong, however, to assume that Lincoln here wars against self-interest, which he insists is part of human nature. What is needed is moral principle that is *not confined* by self-interest. Self-interested devotion to the Union is a good thing, for instance, even if it accepts the idea of allowing the extension of slavery in some portion of some territories (as was the case in the 1850 compromise)—as long as the principle of restriction can still be effectively enforced in the territories overall.

This connection between self-interest and principle receives elaboration in each phase of Lincoln's argument. He pushes it into view whenever he can, sometimes begrudging its importance. It influences his toleration of slavery where the institution exists. The very ubiquity of self-interest and the tendency to exercise it unjustly where slavery has already been introduced are for Lincoln telling arguments against allowing slavery into the territories. Rather than condemning southerners who exercise what amounts to a tyrannical self-interest in their possession of property in slaves, Lincoln suggests that self-interest can corrupt even well-meaning citizens. One cannot merely abolish slavery, for one cannot do away with self-interest: "They [the southern slave owners and defenders of chattel slavery] are just as we would be in their situation" (2.255). On the other hand, the very intractability of self-interest could work to end slavery. The supporters of the Wilmot Proviso prohibiting slavery in the old Mexican territories were not hypocritical, as Douglas insists, simply because they were willing to allow slavery south of the Mason-Dixon line in the Louisiana territory. They maintained their fealty to the Missouri Compromise, Lincoln says, out of principled self-interest. They desired to hold what was won for freedom there—if only north of the lower Missouri line and without Missouri—while fighting to secure greater freedom elsewhere.

Lincoln resists Douglas's accusation of hypocrisy by using a destabilizing illustration. He likens Wilmot supporters and opponents of the Nebraska bill to the owner of a house, who by definition is keenly interested in holding title to his possession against those who might take it away simply because he does not wish to add a room:

> When we voted against extending the Missouri line [by insisting upon Wilmot's principle that all the Mexican lands taken in the war should be free] little did we think we were voting to destroy the old line, then of thirty years standing. To argue that we thus repudiated the Missouri Compromise is no less absurd than it would be to argue . . . that because I may have refused to build an addition to my house, I thereby have decided to destroy the existing house! And if I catch you setting fire to my house, you will turn upon me and say I INSTRUCTED you to do it! (2.258)

For Lincoln, the matter is one of logic and common sense, as well as self-interest. In the metaphor of property we have the nexus of what Tocqueville referred to as "self-interest properly understood," only here Lincoln is giving that principle the sort of shrewd application that Tocqueville said Americans did not adequately consider. The folksy story is designed to provoke his audience's jealous desire to defend its property rights, and the self-determination that protects them. The story also ingeniously stigmatizes Douglas's view as a bullying sharper's attempt to expropriate property in the name of the popular will.

Lincoln extends his revision of Douglas's view of popular sovereignty by showing the insufficiency of property rights when they are understood merely as one man's possession. If the right of possession applies, as he argues, not only to the individual citizen but to the Union's self-interested relation to the territories, it has to do with a larger, national sovereignty that transcends territorial citizens' right to determine whether a territory will be slave or free: "[I]f we surrender the control of it [the Nebraska Territory], do we not surrender the right of self-government?" (2.267). Insofar as self-interest is the principle of free citizens' actions, the Union's self-interest trumps the individual's when the issue is territorial government. The call for collective responsibility still depends on an understanding of each person's right of (and capacity for) self-government, but in the national frame regarding this question—not the frame of the isolated territorial voter. The alternative is a reductio ad absurdum:

> But you say this question should be left to the people of Nebraska, because they are more particularly interested. If this be the rule, you must leave it to each individual to say for himself whether he will have slaves. What better moral right have thirty-one citizens of Nebraska to say, that the thirty-second shall not hold slaves, than the people of the thirty-one States have to say that slavery shall not go into the thirty-second State at all? (2.267)

A moral tyranny of the few over the many would entail constitutionally protected voting rights that would give the citizens of a new slave state an additional advantage, reducing the self-interested, self-governing citizens in the free states to a slavish fraction of themselves—much as slaves are reduced to three-fifths of a person according to the representational rules of the Constitution (2.269).

The "moral rights" of the states in the Nebraska issue are superior to the Douglas-designated "sacred right" of the individual settler when a situation arises in which the champions of the settler's sovereignty would degrade other men, either by owning slaves or repealing the protective national compromises that have helped free citizens resist the extension of slavery and the dilution of their votes. Self-government is not possible for a slave or a free citizen so limited in his exercise of his self-interest that he must accept the expropriation of his union home. Likewise, the Nebraska settler's unfettered freedom to own slaves, beyond any clear power of the territorial legislature to prohibit the importation of slaves during the formative phase of that territory's rise to statehood, is an expropriation of other citizens' liberties. By creating an almost irresistible pressure among law-abiding citizens to pass and enforce laws protecting property in slaves, that freedom expropriates the homes of northern citizens as well as the free residents of the territory.

Of course, none of this argumentation makes sense in the American polity unless, as Lincoln points out, it is granted that the man held in bondage is a man, not chattel. Otherwise, the analogy between slave-owning and expropriating northern interests is eclipsed by property laws. If slaves are essentially property and Americans can move their property anywhere in the Union (as had been recently stipulated by the Dred Scott Decision) the grounds for resisting the extension of slavery through national, and perhaps even local, legislation would remove the grounds for Lincoln's case. Once it is granted that the bondman is a man, Lincoln argues, the Declaration enjoins Americans to recognize the precedence of certain rights in his possession. Douglas misinterprets Genesis when he says that

> the Nebraska bill was very old, that it originated when God made man and placed good and evil before him, allowing him to choose for himself, being responsible for the choice he should make. At the time I thought this was merely playful; and I answered it accordingly. But in his reply to me he renewed it, as a serious argument. In seriousness then, the facts of this proposition are not true as stated. God did not place good and evil before man, telling him to make his choice. On the contrary, he did tell him there was one tree, of the fruit of which, he should not eat, upon pain of certain death. I should scarcely wish so strong a prohibition against slavery in Nebraska. (2.278)

* * *

It is clear early in the speech that Lincoln is not arguing for the abolition of slavery. As with opening up the territories to armed agents for both sides of the controversy, abolition would set one part of nature (and one region) against the other. The defender of one principle of human nature would confront defenders of the other. Once again we see Lincoln's unwavering gradualism, which is really a habit of concession punctuated by disclosures of nonnegotiable principle. We catch something of the deeper form of his alternative position in the way he limits his call for equal rights without extinguishing hope for emancipation:

> Let it not be said I am contending for the establishment of political and social equality between the whites and blacks. I have already said the contrary. I am not now combating the argument of necessity, arising from the fact that the blacks are already amongst us; but I am combating what is set up as moral argument for allowing them to be taken where they have never yet been—arguing against the extension of a bad thing, which where it already exists, we must of necessity, manage as best we can. (2.266)

In the 1858 debates with Douglas, Lincoln will make an extended argument in favor of enslaved blacks' economic rights to possess the fruit of their labors. In 1854 he does so by implication, leaving out the word *economic* in

his statement of what he is *not* doing. (The trio of adjectives, "political, social, and economic," was the formula he would use several times in 1858.)
Here he bows to what he calls a "universal feeling" among whites that resists
the granting of political and social equality to blacks. But in the sentence in
which he agrees with that sentiment, saying "my own feelings will not admit
of this," he considers the possibility that his feelings *would* admit of it: "[I]f
mine would, we well know that those of the great mass of white people will
not" (2.256). In concluding that the universal feeling against emancipation
"can not be safely disregarded" even if it is a feeling separate from a sense of
justice and sound judgment, he backhandedly shifts the question from a
moral to a practical basis, depriving that feeling of a claim to justice.
"Whether this feeling accords with justice and sound judgment, is not the
sole question, if indeed, it is any part of it" (2.256). He raises the possibility
that if safety could be assured (for example, by means of the gradual emancipation he briefly advocates in a following paragraph), the prejudice against
emancipation might itself be affected (2.255). The possibility that freedmen
could be transported to Liberia is only momentarily considered, then rejected out of concern for their survival and the shortage of resources for un-
dertaking such a task. This temporizing saves the possibility of freedom for
all, as does Lincoln's refusal to retreat from the seemingly accidental territorial question, which is, arguably, the key to arresting the spread—and hence
the perpetuation—of slavery.

At the center of the Kansas-Nebraska Speech, these various lines of argument are joined in a hyperbolic yet carefully focused passage that enlarges
and hones their significance. Standing with one foot outside of the debate on
the immediate question, Lincoln focuses the controversy upon "human nature," which he says will always be made up of two antagonistic forces: self-
interest and a love of justice. The calculated outburst is of a type we know
Lincoln carefully rations, not only because he is suspicious of hyperbolic
rhetoric but because he can use it in small and powerful doses to expand and
deepen his rational argument:

> Slavery is founded in the selfishness of man's nature—opposition to it, is
> [in?] his love of justice. These principles are in eternal antagonism; and when
> brought into a collision so fiercely, as slavery extension brings them, shocks,
> and throes, and convulsions must ceaselessly follow. Repeal the Missouri
> compromise—repeal all compromises—repeal the declaration of independ-

ence—repeal all past history, you still can not repeal human nature. It still will be the abundance of man's heart, that slavery extension is wrong; and out of the abundance of this heart, his mouth will continue to speak. (2.271)

The logic of the hyperbole follows the pattern of Lincoln's important speeches. It concedes most of Douglas's points, adding to the list, for good measure, the hyperbolic repeal of history itself if Douglas so wills it. Then it rests its case on an apparently irreducible axiom: the unchangeableness of human nature. But the rhythm, substance, and context of these lines enlarge the argument allusively, with embedded references to Shakespeare and the Bible.

Whether or not many members of Lincoln's audience detected the specific allusions (the sources of which the speaker characteristically omits), their presence here evokes famous lines from *Henry IV*, Part 1, on the conflict between principle and appetite, and from the Gospel of Matthew on the source of faith in the highest of principles. We are led to the first of these associations by the cadences of Lincoln's four uses of "repeal," followed by the idea that human nature's love of justice is impossible to banish. The pattern of the repetition, when it joins with the substance and context of Lincoln's argument, calls up the famous speech in which Falstaff uses "banish" five times in his argument that to exile him from Prince Hal's company would be to banish the world itself: "If sack and sugar be a fault, God help the wicked! If to be old and merry be a sin, then many an old host that I know is damned. If to be fat be to be hated, then Pharaoh's lean kine are to be loved. No, my good lord: banish Peto, banish Bardolph, banish Poins; but for sweet Jack Falstaff, kind Jack Falstaff, true Jack Falstaff, valiant Jack Falstaff, and therefore more valiant being, as he is, old Jack Falstaff, banish not him thy Harry's company, banish not him thy Harry's company. Banish plump Jack, and banish all the world!"[22]

Whether or not it was detectable to many of those who listened to the speech, Lincoln's parody tells us much about the thought behind his definition of human nature. Falstaff speaks at the climax of the scene in which he and Hal compete for precedence. The young prince is the rising embodiment of a kind of kingly justice, and his immensely humorous yet menacing friend Falstaff is Shakespeare's complicated representation of a self-interest from which Hal can hardly separate himself. The mock trial in which each man plays at being king provides a mythic base for Lincoln's understanding that human nature is an unchangeable yet volatile (and perhaps perfectible) compound of opposites.

Of course, the nature of Lincoln's allusion draws the entire question into a realm of dramatic conflict not unlike the one he condemns Douglas for introducing into American politics. But Lincoln is expropriating Falstaff's melodramatic plea to argue that human nature itself—the *compound* of interest and the love of justice—cannot be abolished, and that the neglected half of that compound, contrary to Falstaff's self-promoting desires, is the heart's love of justice, which must eventually declare itself, as it does in the outburst here. As Shakespeare's Hal grows in his princely power to govern justly, he banishes Falstaff; but his measures, like Lincoln's in the speech, are incomplete. In the *Henry IV* plays it is only death that banishes Falstaff for good, if then. Without indulging in a learned allusion, Lincoln draws from this precedent by expressing his antislavery sentiment in the ironic frame of Falstaff's self-interested plea.

The biblical freight of Lincoln's outburst is carried in his reference to "the abundance of man's heart," which recalls some lines from the parable of the talents in Matthew 25.29: "For unto every one that hath shall be given, and he shall have abundance." In the Temperance Address, Lincoln had spoken of an abundance of heart expressed in the charity and sympathy that reformed drinkers can show for their fellow sufferers: "[O]ut of the abundance of their hearts, their tongues give utterance" (1.274). In the Gospel of Matthew, the faithful receive greater faith as a complement of their initial devotion. In both cases, a reservoir of goodwill, or something higher, overflows with replenishment as it encounters those who need charity. What the faithful have already, what they can call their own precisely because it is their faith, assures them of more. Their belief gives them a greater cause of belief. "The abundance of man's heart," as Lincoln puts it in the Peoria speech, rests upon the not dissimilar principle that something deep in human nature finds expression in speech and gesture directed against the extension of slavery. The free man knows or should know, in his self-interested way, his sympathy for the man who is enslaved.

This self-interested sympathy, even when it reaches beyond self-interest, is complex. The reformed drinker's sympathy is for the unreformed drunkard, who is his other self. In Lincoln's projection of this temperance principle into the debate over Nebraska, the abundance of what will become the Republican heart will have to be an expression of a compound human nature that includes self-interest and the recognition of self-interest, especially the power of one's own ambition to subdue the love of justice. In political terms, what seems to be merely a conflict between the Slave Power and the free farmer is therefore more fundamentally a struggle within the free man as well as the slaveholder. The greatest danger posed by Douglas's legislation is that it tempts the free North to neglect the complexity of its own nature, and the nature of the Union, by putting its faith in the deceptively simple mechanism of the territorial ballot box.

Lincoln's outburst establishes the deeper ground for his criticism that Douglas's legislation is malicious. The Kansas-Nebraska Act is wrong not merely because it appeals to the self-interest of northerners and southerners who are eager for land and willing to say they "don't care" about whether slavery expands or not. Douglas has seemed to act on a higher level, in the name of the principle of popular sovereignty. The deeper mischief of the Kansas-Nebraska Act is its *provocation* of a conflict between self-interest and the love of justice. The legislation was adventitious, surprising even the South (2.273). Between those antagonists, Lincoln says, the "genius of discord" has thrown an apple—territory open to the first-comer—asserting deceptively that their rivalry is at an end. Douglas's great mistake is to appeal to the principle of popular sovereignty as though it could harmonize interest and principle in the local ballot box, when in fact it brings self-interested slave owners and opponents of slavery into direct conflict. He has recklessly disturbed, in Lincoln's view, the problematic and volatile complementarity of principle and self-interest that exists within all sections of the country and within all human beings, a complementarity that must be guided by something more than Douglas's misleading faith in popular sovereignty. As part of human nature, the love of justice and the love of one's own interest must somehow be acknowledged and accommodated without forcing Americans to war against themselves.

The density of Shakespearean references in this section of the speech is remarkable. Besides the evocation of Falstaff and Hal, we are given allusions that link slavery to Claudius's guilty pleasures ("It hath no relish of salvation in it"[23]) (2.270), Macbeth's bloody hand (2.276), and the allegation that Douglas has mischievously turned peace into war—the latter couched in vocabulary and phrasing that invite comparison with Richard III, another of Lincoln's favorite Shakespearean figures. (We know Lincoln could recite Richard's speech by heart, and to great effect, in the presidential years.) As we noted in an earlier chapter, Richard's opening soliloquy is an apt expression of the kind of political ambition Lincoln (who was not blind to the impulse in himself) thought most dangerous and most characteristic of the Caesar-like men who might arise when the Founders' generation had expired. That Lincoln has this collateral thought in mind is evident in his reference to Charles Phillips's *The Character of Napoleon* to illustrate the destructive power of Douglas's legislation: "As Phillips say of Napoleon, the Nebraska act is 'grand, gloomy, and peculiar; wrapped in the solitude of its own originality; without a model, and without a shadow upon the earth'" (2.281). The essence of the Caesarian, Napoleonic hero is the desire to destroy what others have built well, if only because there is no opportunity to add something of self-distinguishing value to the edifice. In his first lines, Richard III declares himself the destroyer of peace par excellence: he will create dissension where there is harmony, wintry war in place of summer. Referring to the "naked FRONT and ASPECT" of the Kansas-Nebraska Act, Lincoln may be using emphatic capitalizations to register a connection with the vocabulary and themes of Richard's introductory speeches, in which war's "smooth-visaged front" is allied with Richard's "ugly and unnatural aspect" and "naked villainy" (2.271).[24] The argument with which he surrounds these allusions draws Douglas into Richard's world. The Kansas-Nebraska Act shows its own menace, if those around Douglas have the courage to see it. The bill's explicit repeal of the Missouri Comprise is what it seems to be—an ugly abrogation of the old consensus, whatever Douglas might say, Richard-like, to assure his audiences that its effects will be benign. Despite Douglas's pleasing speeches, the law says what it says. Its "front and aspect" declare what it is. Douglas's sequent arguments are "lullabies," much like the saccharine speeches of the crooked-back Richard, by which he seduces victims who cannot see menace in his ugliness.

* * *

How could Lincoln insinuate and accuse along these lines without having his gestures turn back upon himself? How could he escape the charge of hypocrisy? It helps to remember that the Peoria crowd and the readers of the newspaper were of a sort that relished the privilege of observing two shrewd lawyers thrust and parry with the instruments of legal argument. Rather than look for hypocrisy with the expectation of finding it, they were more likely than modern audiences to appreciate the speeches as wrestling holds and displays of bravado—attempts to convince the audience, of course, but carried off in ways that modern audiences are supposedly conditioned to dismiss as querulous grandstanding and devious persuasion. The crowd's interest in the exchange of speeches no doubt derived partly from the contest itself, the way in which each partisan wielded his available means of defeating his opponent and winning the assent, or at least the respect, of the audience. The nature of the contest promoted a form of posturing, which an unsympathetic, overly detached modern auditor would be bound to identify as merely hypocritical.

In its use of principles and close readings of legal language, Lincoln's posturing is almost a mirror of Douglas's. Whereas Douglas contends that the idea of popular sovereignty informs the early territorial legislation, he interprets the laws as embodiments of that principle: when they are not explicit about their sanctioning idea, he finds them to be implicit indicators of its influence. Conversely, when he draws evidence from the Constitution and the laws, he finds no sanction for the notion that the axioms of the Declaration control or sway laws that do not explicitly cite them. Lincoln, in his dueling reply, insists that popular sovereignty be substantiated by specific language in the founding documents and, finding none, notes instead the ubiquitous power of the spirit of compromise, the persistence of the Jeffersonian axiom of equality, and the endurance of the Founders' expectation that slavery would be controlled and gradually eliminated. That we know so much about the shape of Douglas's oratorical argument by reading Lincoln's speech is a tribute to Lincoln's sagacity in mastering his opponent's ideas. The formal symmetry of both men's views, as it is revealed in Lincoln's analytic argument, suggests that they are locked in a kind of oratorical parity—unless, of course, we discern something more in the nuances of the two positions that will distinguish each man's cause.

We see something of this difference when we read closely Lincoln's last sentences, which show him analyzing the shape of Douglas's argument with a humor that urges his audience to look beyond the agonistic formalities and fireworks of the debate:

> A word now as to the Judge's desperate assumption that the compromises of '50 had no connection with one another; that Illinois came into the Union as a slave state, and some other similar ones. This is no other than a bold denial of the history of the country. If we do not know that the Compromises of '50

were dependent on each other; if we do not know that Illinois came into the Union as a free state—we do not know any thing. If we do not know these things we do not know that we ever had a revolutionary war, or such a chief as Washington. To deny these things is to deny our national axioms, or dogmas, at least; and it puts an end to all argument. If a man will stand up and assert, and repeat, and re-assert, that two and two do not make four, I know nothing in the power of argument that can stop him. I think I can answer the Judge so long as he sticks to the premises; but when he flies from them, I can not work an argument into the consistency of a maternal gag, and actually close his mouth with it. In such a case I can only commend him to the seventy thousand answers just in from Pennsylvania, Ohio and Indiana. (3.282–283)

The idea that Douglas is a master of anesthesia is central to the purpose of Lincoln's conclusion. The Napoleonic anti-hero thrives when the great masses of moderate citizens are no longer vigilant. If the Kansas-Nebraska Act is a soporific that lulls the moderates while setting the armed extremists from both sides against each other, the moderates who oppose the extension of slavery will lose their hold—unless a new sense of the justice of their cause invigorates them. Lincoln's final paragraph is designed to supply that bracing tonic, but in a humorous vessel. It affirms the antislavery principle in language appealing to self-respect and pugilistic pride.

It may be that in the form and substance of Lincoln's 1854 duel with Douglas, self-interest and principle are fundamentally incompatible. But here as elsewhere, Lincoln's humorous Euclidian logic cannot operate without bringing principle and interest into proximity with one another. We can see this movement most clearly when we have heard Lincoln through. His appeal to axioms and revolutionary sentiment blend into an appeal to partisan energies, and his partisan claims draw attention to something beyond self-interest. Douglas is guilty of political impiety and must be gagged. But the self-effacing humor of Lincoln's imperative blunts the desire to gag him. Lincoln fails, he says, in the attempt. His evocation of geometrical reasoning, with the reminder that political argumentation depends on an acceptance of certain axioms, is not enough. The vital axioms of revolutionary faith are "dogmas, at least," necessary but insufficient means of preserving the Founders' hopes or triumphing over Douglas. This seems to be a way of saying that although Douglas may be a danger to self-government and a threat to sacred political memories, he is a formidable, refractory opponent

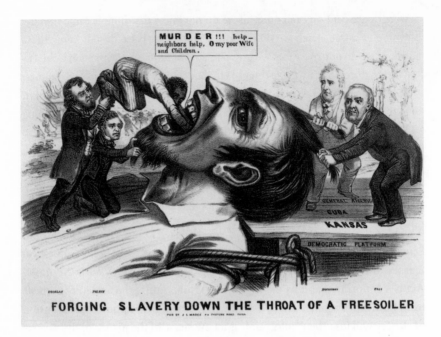

FORCING SLAVERY DOWN THE THROAT OF A FREESOILER

"Forcing Slavery Down the Throat of a Freesoiler" (1856), Anonymous, in the Library of Congress collection of reproductions: Stern Collection, portfolio 4, no. 25 (Rare Book Collection), Reproduction # LC USZ62-92043.

This 1856 depiction of the struggle over the slavery in the territories attempts to expose an aggressive tenor within Douglas's doctrine of "popular sovereignty," and to defend the bearded Free-Soiler's abhorrence of the black man whose company Douglas and members of his party are forcing upon him by means of the Kansas-Nebraska Act of 1854. In a scene imitating the everyman Gulliver's capture in *Gulliver's Travels*, the Free-Soiler is a giant pinned down by the tiny figures of prominent Democrats James Buchanan (the 1856 nominee for President), Lewis Cass, Stephen Douglas, and President Pierce. The cartoon is another instructive example of an approach Lincoln does not take. In the Kansas-Nebraska Speech of 1854 and his later prepresidential efforts to confront Douglas, Lincoln consistently appealed to principle over fear, and to the prospect of ending slavery gradually rather than acceding to indifference, violence, or revulsion—whether it was the unprincipled revulsion of the Free-Soilers or the abolitionists' vehement rejection of all delays in ending slavery. He did not stoke negrophobia, and he maintained that the enslaved man was yet a man.

whom Lincoln, his partner in the ring of partisan debate, cannot presume to control by preaching conviction into his audience, even as his speech reaches its triumphant close. Douglas does not threaten reason and memory so much as conviction—the deeper sense of what memories mean. For Lincoln, the threat is subtle and immensely appealing in its use of reasoning and appeals to the passions of free citizens. The entertaining close of the Peoria speech thus pointedly leaves it up to Lincoln's audience, particularly those who feel the pull of Douglas's lulling arguments, to recognize the threat those arguments pose to the capacity for self-government. It's time to join the seventy thousand voters who rejected him—to snap awake.

7

The "House Divided" Speech

The Logic of Hopeful Resolve

Either the *opponents* of slavery, will arrest the further spread of it, and place it where the public mind shall rest in the belief that it is in the course of ultimate extinction; or its *advocates* will push it forward, till it shall become alike lawful in *all* the States, *old* as well as *new*—*North* as well as *South.* (2.461)

The peculiar character and striking consistency of Lincoln's conservatism becomes increasingly evident in his most unsettling and influential political speeches: the famous addresses of 1858 and early 1860 that set the tone for his senatorial and presidential campaigns. Amid the wreckage of the Great Compromise and the Kansas-Nebraska Act, as the Republican Party began to rise out of the disarray of Whig loyalists and the increasingly vehement clash of abolitionists and defenders of southern prerogatives regarding slavery, Lincoln helped bring forth that new organization with even-tempered yet incendiary rhetorical performances that discovered deep-seated, logical foundations for the claims of the new party. Each address, explosive yet adamant in its organization and argument, was a revolutionary disclosure of venerable grounds for maintaining and pursuing Republican principles.

In April 1858 Lincoln delivered an early version of his Lecture on Discoveries and Inventions, in which he dwelt upon the sometimes slow and yet often remarkable development of man-made improvements in the human condition. Fundamental innovation, according to his examples, was extremely difficult to commence because it typically depended upon inventors' ability to see what many others had missed. True invention brought something laboriously to the light where, once uncovered, it could be employed for the sake of other innovations. Discovery was in this sense for Lincoln an assertion of venerable truths that men might have known but had missed. It was by definition a conservative force that worked in a revolutionary manner once its findings came into use.

The same could be said for the two powerful inventions that animate these pivotal speeches. In the "House Divided" Speech of June 16, 1858, Lincoln's argument from necessity becomes a lever to force to the surface an almost unbroachable topic—the possibility of civil war—in a manner that allows for consideration of a deeper, more dangerous and pressing alternative that might not entail violence at all: the government's inability to endure indefinitely as half slave and half free. His device reveals what he calls the sinister, novel "machinery" of Democratic maneuvers to close off the option of restricting slavery in the territories (2.462). In the Cooper Union Address of 1860, Lincoln returns to the old records of the Founders' votes on slavery legislation to test empirically, in response to Douglas's challenge, his contention that the Founders favored restriction of slavery in the territories. His collection and interpretation of their less-than-unanimous votes on various questions creates a compelling but inherently risky basis for Republican resistance to Douglas's argument for territorial plebiscites.

Upon his nomination as the Republican candidate for the Senate in 1858, Lincoln spoke before the state convention. Herndon contends that Lincoln's speech was not novel, that he had ventured similar arguments, including the contention that a house divided against itself would not stand, at the party's inaugural meeting in Bloomington two years before.[1] But there is no surviving record of that effort, except for a brief summary in the Bloomington press (2.375). The unrecorded speech came to be known as the famous "Lost Speech." Much like the famous 1812 oration Lincoln had called Clay's greatest performance, the Bloomington speech was supposed to have been so passionate and impressive that no one thought to record it.

Herndon's own account of the lost speech contains evidence that the lack of a printed record of the 1856 speech was no accident: "[I]n obedience to the emphatic protest of Judge T. Lyle Dickey and others, who conceived the idea that its 'delivery would make abolitionists of all the North and slavery propagandists of all the South, and thereby precipitate a struggle which might end in disunion,' he [Lincoln] consented to suspend its repetition, but only for that campaign."[2] Characteristically, Lincoln conceded the point for strategic, not philosophical, reasons. The agreement entailed the assumption that he might use the arguments again.

The time for repetition and publication came in 1858, after two more years of slavery "agitation" from all sides (2.461). From remarks made by Herndon and others, we gather that Lincoln composed his presentation from notes on various scraps of paper he held in his hat. He took pains to keep the draft secret, and then arranged to read it to friends (first to Herndon, then to a group of friends) before he delivered it to the Republican convention. In the notes from Herndon's interview of Jesse Dubois, a Republican state official in the late 1850s, we have the intriguing if fanciful recollection of Lincoln expressing some hesitation about going through with his plans:

> One day—just before Lincoln delivered his house divided against Speech—Dubois Came into Lincolns office & found L writing—Dubois said—L. what are you writing. I am writing something which you may or may never see [.]—Said Dubois—Let me see it now—No Sir Said Mr Lincoln I have said I will not. The conversation between L & Dubois then changed to a subject of business. In a few days after this his house divided against itself speech Mr Dub & L met. Mr. L said now Dubois I will tell you what I was doing when you Came into my office and why I would not show you what I was doing. You need not say what you were writing says Dubois—because I now Know. Mr Lincoln then said let me Explain why I would not read that Speech to you. This passage in the Speech about the house divided against itself I would not read it to you because I Knew you would make me Change it—modify & mollify. & I was determined to read it—had willed it so, and was willing to perish with it, if necessary.[3]

The recreated dialogue conveys some of the complexity of Lincoln's motives and circumstances. Whether or not Dubois recollected the event with complete accuracy, his story intimates that Lincoln's efforts to conceal his work from his doubtful friend are somewhat transparent: they reveal a determination to follow through. There is a measure of Lincolnian self-dramatization in Dubois's portrait that overlaps with Herndon's more detailed story of events leading up to the formal delivery of the speech. Supported by testimony from John Armstrong, a prominent fellow Republican, Herndon gives the impression that Lincoln expected his words to be unpopular but was still intent upon delivering them to the public. In several private meetings with his friends before he gave the speech, he informed them of his purpose and tested his resolve by reading from his text. He then underwent their almost unanimous criticism, based on their displeasure with the timing of the speech as much its substance. It is worth quoting at length from Herndon's texturing of the moment:

> Before delivering his speech he invited a dozen or so of his friends over to the library of the State House, where he read and submitted it to them. After the reading he asked each man for his opinion. Some condemned and not one endorsed it. One man, more forcible than elegant, characterized it as a "d—d fool utterance;" another said the doctrine was "ahead of its time;" and still another contended that it would drive away a good many voters fresh from the Democrats ranks. Each man attacked it in his criticism. I was the last to respond. Although the doctrine announced was rather rank, yet it suited my views, and I said, "Lincoln, deliver that speech as read and it will make you President." At the time I hardly realized the force of my prophecy. Having patiently listened to these various criticisms from his friends—all of which with a single exception were adverse—he rose from his chair, and after alluding to the careful study and intense thought he had given the question, he answered all their objections substantially as follows: "Friends, this thing has been retarded long enough. The time has come when these sentiments should be uttered; and if it is decreed that I should go down because of this speech, then let me go down linked to the truth—let me die in the advocacy of what is just and right."[4]

Douglas L. Wilson has demonstrated how modern readers, prone to detect an air of self-promotion in Herndon's recollections, unfairly discount their substance.[5] Although we cannot know whether Lincoln spoke these words, we know they harmonize with the written reports of Dubois, Swett, and Armstrong, the latter being Herndon's source for the quotation.[6] A more important question bears upon the *manner* of Lincoln's argumentation. What precisely is the innovation they articulate? Is Lincoln's famous introduction more forceful, complex, or ambiguous than what contemporary witnesses have so far told us?

The "House Divided" Speech distinguishes itself in the *way* it renders a familiar theme: the impending threat of civil war between slave and free sections of the Union. As in the Cooper Union Address of early 1860, when Lincoln drew attention to the "mode" of his use of largely familiar evidence, the language of the 1858 speech takes up his issue in a highly distinctive way. In his introduction especially, he makes a series of declarations that clarify and complicate the general sense of danger: a crisis is inevitable, and it will transform the Union, making it either all free or all slave:

> If we could first know *where* we are, and *whither* we are tending, we could then better judge *what* to do, and *how* to do it.
>
> We are now far into the *fifth* year, since a policy was initiated, with the *avowed* object, and *confident* promise, of putting an end to slavery agitation.
>
> Under the operation of that policy, that agitation has not only, *not ceased,* but has *constantly augmented.*
>
> In *my* opinion, it *will* not cease, until a *crisis* shall have been reached, and passed. (2.461)

The Union's distress is the symptom of an already advanced disease that must be undergone to its finish. After the crisis, the end will be either a new level of health—of general freedom from slavery—or death: the extinction of the spirit of liberty and equality throughout the organism of the republic. The next line draws the argument into a biblical context that enforces the notion of disease: "A house divided against itself cannot stand."

As a prophetic maxim in Lincoln's Euclidean formula, Jesus' words in Matthew 12.25 help Lincoln explain the nature of the Union's disease. The Union is, in a word, possessed. When Jesus is accused of doing the work of the devil when he casts out demons, he invokes the maxim about the house divided in order to show his detractors that their charge is illogical: if the devil did such things against himself, the devil's house would not stand. By parabolic implication, Jesus is saying *he* can cast them out and preserve the house precisely because he is not the devil. Jesus is the healer; Satan would destroy the house if he attempted to cast out devils, for he cannot cure himself.

Lincoln of course uses the maxim out of context by identifying the house with the Union. But it is unlikely that, speaking among his Bible-reading neighbors, he could have cleanly detached such a well-known passage from its source, or that he would have wanted to. There is a sense in which the devil's house resembles the Union possessed of slavery, a union unable to cure itself in its present political circumstances. Lincoln for his part does not easily escape imitating the prophet accused of hypocrisy. In fact, his speech anticipates that inevitable charge from the opposition: by predicting what will happen to the Union he is stirring up the "slavery agitation" he claims he wants to calm. He devotes the "House Divided" Speech to the effecting of a kind of cure, urging his audience to organize its support to resist Douglas's contradictory demonic plan to enlarge popular sovereignty by spreading slavery to the territories. In Lincoln's argument there is an element of resignation to logical necessity that dovetails with the biblical hope that the cycle of self-infection can be broken, this time with a new political frankness that forces the issue in the context of a reasoned weighing of alternatives.

Historians have noted that Lincoln begins with phrasing that evokes Daniel Webster's famous Second Reply to Hayne, which that formidable Whig had delivered and published in many thousands of copies a generation before. But whereas Webster was introducing an argument for preserving the Union against a southern spirit of secession, Lincoln's introduction assumed that the nature of the Union, not its existence, was the issue. Webster dedicated his remarks to preserving the Union as it was. He implicitly condemned Hayne's speech as a stormy agitation that had clouded the Senate's judgment and "driven" the debate "from its true course."

Webster directs his eyes toward constitutional precedents and the perpetuation of things as they are. More lawyer-like and daring than the Great Compromiser Henry Clay in his readiness to confront a particular opponent's point of view, he is here more like Clay than Lincoln in his evocation of the fearful consequences of change, particularly when that change is driven by explicit political disagreements on fundamental issues. His conclusion, which was a favorite passage for the northern schoolboy's recitations, melodramatically avoids speculation about what might lie "beyond the Union"—beyond the familiar bonds that had managed to balance slavery and freedom: "I have not allowed myself, Sir, to look beyond the Union, to see what might lie hidden in the dark recess behind. . . . I have not accustomed myself to hang over the precipice of disunion, to see whether, with my short sight, I can fathom the depth of the abyss below; nor could I regard him as a safe counsellor in the affairs of this government, whose thoughts should be mainly bent on considering, not how the Union may be best preserved, but how tolerable might be the condition of the people when it should be broken up and destroyed."[7] Facing Hayne, Webster speaks as though nothing were more immediately dangerous than dissolution. Turning at the end of the speech to his preferred vision of the Union, he sees no alternative but unity for the sake of "the gorgeous ensign of the republic . . .

still full advanced," which must be preserved by a fusion of principles that are now in troubling competition. What is needed more than ever is "that other sentiment, dear to every true American heart,—Liberty *and* Union, now and for ever, one and inseparable!"[8]

In contrast to Webster's ceremonial hyperbole, the words of Lincoln's introduction are spare and forensic, and his conclusion is directed toward building a Republican Party that will resist the false attractions of its rivals. Webster had begun his speech with an eighty-nine-word sentence. Lincoln's first sentence consists of twenty-six words, almost all of them monosyllables. Instead of offering a glimpse of the apocalypse, Lincoln's conclusion calls his audience toward the principle of freedom. It appeals to his political friends to stand against "a disciplined, proud, and pampered enemy" (2.468).

The lean, combative spirit of Lincoln's introduction becomes clearer when we compare it to the quietism of an editorial that appeared in a major Democratic newspaper the week before Lincoln spoke: "The slavery agitation may be considered as suspended for some time to come. Without the interposition of some new 'aggression' of the 'slave oligarchy,' no disturbing breeze of sectional excitement can be raised upon slavery and the 'slave power' in the approaching general campaign."[9] The *New York Herald*'s confident prediction followed a period of relative calm in the territory of Kansas, where raids and ambushes seemed to be giving way to electoral politics. John Brown's attack on Harpers Ferry would not be news for another year and a half. Disunity among Democrats in the Senate, not sectional conflict, was the *Herald*'s concern. It condemned, in another article on the same date, the "squabbling cliques and factions" that were hurting the party by illustrating the old proverb about "a house divided against itself." In these lines the danger of conflict was thought to come, if anywhere, from a northern indulgence in faction—the assumption being that the only legitimate cause for concern about the slavery question would be an unlikely and patently aggressive action on the part of the South.

Whether Lincoln's long-considered choice of words was influenced by the *Herald* (a paper the omnivorous reader could have seen in its train-delivered issue several days before he spoke), his speech amounted to a rejection of the *Herald*'s general outlook. By declaring that "slavery agitation" continued unabated and that it would go on until the country passed through a crisis, he interpreted the relative quiet in Kansas as a lull in a larger pattern of conflict. He called his party to unity on precisely the issue that the New York Democratic press was attempting to remove from view.

We would be mistaken, however, to assume that Lincoln was simply adopting a more aggressive tone than the one in Webster's Reply to Hayne. The phrasing of the "House Divided" Speech is meticulously controlled, especially in comparison to the antislavery vehemence Seward had exhibited in his oratory of the late 1850s. It is more accurate to say that Lincoln had found a way to take a principled position on middle ground that enabled him to make strong antislavery arguments. This seems to be why Herndon, writing after Lincoln's death, claimed that the "House Divided" Speech "drove the nail into Seward's political coffin."[10] Years before, it was Seward who had separated himself from Clay and Webster when he had condemned the 1850 compromise—which Lincoln had supported in his eulogies for Taylor and Clay—as an "insidious" violation of a "higher law" than the Constitution. In 1858, four months after the "House Divided" Speech roiled the waters of the Illinois Senate campaign, Seward would pack years of abolitionist argumentation into the famous prophecy of "collision" and "irrepressible conflict." Lincoln had by contrast adapted and refocused—not rejected—his favorite old Whigs' views and had refrained from converting their apocalyptic warnings into talk of war and apparent disregard for the Constitution.

It is safe to assume that Lincoln was more than casually acquainted with the militant direction of Seward's thought, and that in June 1858 he was attempting to formulate a Republican position that would consolidate and redirect Republican energies in the upcoming campaign. When Seward did speak, he famously declared that conflict was inevitable, that the only question was whether the defenders of freedom could direct their wills toward meeting the foe that history had created. His anticipation of moral victory blurred into an expectation of military conquest over "all the fields and all the castles which have been lost." Viewing the enemy from afar as though it could only be alien and noxious, he made his goal a crusade "to confound and overthrow, by one decisive blow, the betrayers of the Constitution and Freedom forever. . . . Either the cotton and rice fields of South Carolina and the sugar plantations of Louisiana will ultimately be filled by free labor, and the Charleston and New Orleans become marts for legitimate merchandise alone, or else the rye-fields and wheat-fields of Massachusetts and New York must again be surrendered by their farmers to slave culture and to the production of slaves, and Boston and New York become once more markets for trade in the bodies and souls of men."[11] Given the lurid alternative, there seems to be no doubt in Seward's mind that the North will prevail in this war of sections, in which it will overcome the enemy by invading the South.

Lincoln's featured argument also disturbs the settled view of things; but in contrast to Seward's approach it is a chiseled statement of resolve and restraint. It is helpful to read it again with these comparisons in mind:

> If we could first know *where* we are, and *whither* we are tending, we could then better judge *what* to do, and *how* to do it.
>
> We are now far into the *fifth* year, since a policy was initiated, with the *avowed* object, and *confident* promise, of putting an end to the slavery agitation.
>
> Under the operation of that policy, that agitation has not only, *not ceased,* but has *constantly augmented.*
>
> In *my* opinion, it *will* not cease, until a *crisis* shall have been reached, and passed.
>
> "A house divided against itself cannot stand."
>
> I believe this government cannot endure, permanently half *slave* and half *free.*
>
> I do not expect the union to be *dissolved*—I do not expect the house to fall—but I *do* expect it will cease to be divided.
>
> It will become *all* one thing, or *all* the other.
>
> Either the *opponents* of slavery, will arrest the further spread of it, and place it where the public mind shall rest in the belief that it is in the course of ultimate extinction; or its *advocates* will push it forward, till it shall become alike lawful in *all* the States, *old* as well as *new*—*North* as well as *South.* (2.461–462)

Between Webster's fear of dissolution and Seward's certainty of moral victory over an evil occupying power, Lincoln is deliberate, cautious, inquisitive, and daring. He describes a threat to the Union that is less nightmarish and more insidious than the ones Webster and Seward see. The house divided against itself is more precisely "this government," not the Union per se. He is very sparing in his use of the latter term, even though the Union, defined as a Union worth keeping, would follow the fate of the government. Lincoln wants to keep the immediate and difficult challenge to the government in view without leaping to apocalyptic possibilities no matter how threatening. He speaks with disarming decisiveness while hinting at complexities. Relying on complex double negatives ("A house divided against itself cannot stand"; "it will cease to be divided"), he points toward a positive prediction of the outcome but does not say exactly what it is. His prediction that the house will face unavoidable danger is couched in more double negatives: "I do not expect the Union to be *dissolved*—I do not expect the house to fall." Yet the Union will be transformed: it "cannot stand" as it is.

In the ensuing debates with Douglas, Lincoln heard the charges that his words in the "House Divided" Speech had, in a Seward-like spirit, implicitly threatened the South, if not with military action, then with the prospect of new laws restricting slavery in the southern states. A passage from his Springfield speech a month later illustrates the difficulty of Lincoln's position as he defended his "House Divided" prediction and prepared to meet Douglas in seven formal debates:

> [Douglas] charges, in substance, that I invite a war of sections; that I propose all the local institutions of the different States shall become consolidated and uniform. What is there in the language of that speech which expresses such purpose, or bears such construction? I have again and again said that I would not enter into any of the States to disturb the institution of slavery. Judge Douglas said, at Bloomington, that I used language most able and ingenious for concealing what I really meant: and that while I had protested against entering into the Slave states, I nevertheless did mean to go on the banks of Ohio and throw missiles into Kentucky to disturb them in their domestic institutions. (2.513)

He then quotes from the offending passage of the "House Divided" Speech and concludes:

> Now you all see, from that quotation, I did not express my *wish* on anything. In that passage I indicated no wish or purpose of my own; I simply expressed my *expectation*. Cannot the Judge perceive the distinction between a *purpose* and an *expectation*[?] I have often expressed an expectation to die, but I have never expressed a *wish* to die. (2.514)

The deeper argument of the "House Divided" Speech, which Douglas never directly engages in the debates, is that the process of transformation is unstoppable and already underway, and that citizens are in a crucial position to influence its outcome whether it leads to an embrace of slavery or freedom. The entire question, in other words, must be understood in terms of tendency rather than the desire to maintain a fractured status quo or declare open war. The potential for violence is thereby more prominent; but Lincoln's focus on tendency points out that there are threats to the peace that other understandings of the Union's condition are in danger of ignoring until it is too late. A few months later, Seward's speech on the impending crisis would not address the subtlety of these threats as Lincoln saw them. Seward's melodramatic vision of Massachusetts farmers being forced to turn over their fields to slave laborers and their masters, and of Boston becoming a thriving market for slaves, enflamed the issue and yet did not depict the true danger as Lincoln had seen it.

Seward's views and those of his supporters aside, the venerable and more general unionist position was particularly insufficient because it did not engage the territorial question. Sharing the sentiments of Webster's old apostrophe to the Union in his Reply to Hayne, an unreflective unionist would so recoil from the prospect of disunion that he would not be inclined to analyze the slavery question as a national question. Webster's notorious address on the Compromise of 1850, in which he vehemently refused to consider the status of slavery in the territories, offered no help. Douglas's more robust unionism, which displaced the slavery debate with the doctrine of "popular sovereignty," threatened to neutralize the old unionists as Douglas had done to Webster when he pushed Clay's compromises through Congress in 1850.

Viewed on the level of electoral rhetoric, Lincoln's speech is about resolve: it supplies a rhetorical technology, including an operative conception of the crisis, so as to resist the Democratic diffusion and absorption of Republican principles in the upcoming campaign. Without pronouncing upon the fate of the union, endorsing radical abolitionism, or attacking the slaveholding interests, it attempts to concentrate on the causes and remedies of the union's drift from the goal of ending that agitation. Its four parts follow Lincoln's opening sentence to articulate a practical, unflinching plan: "If we could first know *where* we are, and *whither* we are tending, we could then better judge *what* to do, and *how* to do it" (2.461).

In his movement to question two—the crucial question of tendency—Lincoln shifts attention to what he calls a "piece of machinery, so to speak—compounded of the Nebraska doctrine, and the Dred Scott Decision" (2.462). To establish his claims that Douglas and his allies are moving toward universalizing slavery, the speech must go beyond the facts to show that a conspiratorial tendency exists, in the use and design of that machinery, to make that universalization a fact. Such a tendency cannot be a simple movement in a particular direction. It must be understood in terms of various instrumentalities: the "work [it] is adapted to do, and how well adapted" as well as its "history" and its "evidences of design." Doubters of conspiracy should "carefully contemplate that piece of machinery" in all these respects in order to understand the danger of Douglas's machinations.

Though complicated by some measures, Lincoln's spare and meticulous approach is calculated to appeal to those who agree with him that the air is full of (as he calls it) Douglas's "loose declamation" (2.462). Lincoln's address gives the impression of being an assemblage of chiseled stones, a Euclidean proof, and as it grows in complication, its lines of argument seem to be absorbed into the larger structure like a frieze on a Greek temple. The industrious care of Lincoln's discovery and careful ordering of proofs makes the clean lines possible. Henry Clay Whitney, a longtime companion on the central Illinois circuit, reported that Lincoln used a similar method when he examined farm machinery during moments of leisure. The approach he used for developing an understanding of moral questions was similar:

> While we were traveling in ante-railway days, on the circuit, and would stop at a farm-house for dinner, Lincoln would improve the leisure in hunting up some farming implement, machine or tool, and he would carefully examine it all over, first generally and then critically; he would "sight" it to determine if it was straight or warped: if he could make a practical test of it, he would do that; he would turn it over or around and stoop down, or lie down, if necessary, to look under it; he would examine it closely, then stand off and examine it at a little distance; he would shake it, lift it, roll it about, up-end it, overset it, and thus ascertain every quality and utility which inhered in it, so far as acute and patient investigation could do it. He was equally inquisitive in regard to matters which obtruded on his attention in the moral world; he would bore to the center of any moral proposition, and carefully analyse and dissect every layer and every atom of which it was composed, nor would he give over the search till completely satisfied that there was nothing more to know, or be learned about it.[12]

Analysis and presentation are distinctive operations, and they pursue generally divergent ends. But in the "House Divided" Speech Lincoln's inquisitive thoroughness, and the impression of finality it gives when his presentation emerges freed from the detritus of his excavations, is especially persuasive to those he wins over, challenging to those he does not.

In his discussion of the protean topic of tendency, Lincoln takes care to exploit the resources at his command to make daring and far-reaching charges. The political and judicial judgments of a number of the highest politicians, not just those of Douglas, are at issue: Pierce, Taney, and Buchanan share in the political indictment. The full list of charges is long and complex. The rival politicians are accused of acting in concert to create, or threaten to create, a public indifference to the question of slavery in the territories and the states, by means of the Nebraska act, the Dred Scott Decision, and measures Lincoln believes are being contemplated to remove the last barriers to the spread of legally protected slavery throughout the country. The relation of all these things to the public's attitude toward slavery—to the *tendency* of the public mind—at times seems more important than the certainty of slavery's spread; but the precise connection between tendency and legislation is difficult to sort out. In Lincoln's presentation, these priorities are mixed because moral apathy is both the cause and the effect of the conspiracy's success. To judge the speech on the questionable accuracy of its most daring predication—that slavery would spread into states such as Illinois and Ohio if the Democrats remained in power—is to miss the full complexity of Lincoln's argument. He presents the relation between moral tendency and legislation in terms of their unpredictable, dangerous potential for combination. Legislation and court decisions have the capacity to reflect public attitudes or transform them utterly, just as tendencies in popular opinion can drive legislation and provoke court decisions that legislators and judges might not have anticipated.[13]

The effects of the "machinery" that Douglas and his associates are allegedly fashioning are multiple and difficult to trace because the disease they insinuate into the body politic deprives the Union of its means of resistance (2.462). Stealth, design, and cooperation—acting allegedly in conspiracy—have not only constructed an almost complete legal framework for preventing the northern states and territories from keeping slavery outside their borders. They have persuaded many followers to accept these changes and pay unthinking homage to the principle of "popular sovereignty," to which all Republicans as well as Democrats at least nominally subscribe. Lincoln must therefore address an audience with a physician's skill. His patient, he believes, is in danger of a fatal infection. It is infected already, by a disease whose symptoms it does not feel. He must craft his words to address an audience that needs frank talk and perhaps curative intervention because it might not be in its right mind.

This double challenge—the demand to speak plainly in response to the threat of internal and external derangement—helps to explain another aspect of Lincoln's organization: the stairstep quality of the argument, which helps him demonstrate logical rigor while finding license for intervening with helpful oversimplifications. First, he explains, the Kansas-Nebraska Act disrupted the various federal prohibitions on slavery in most of the territories and states. Next came a campaign to win public approval of that congressional action, effectuated by Douglas's new doctrine of "popular sovereignty." (Here Lincoln breaks from his austere logic to satirize that doctrine as "'squatter sovereignty,' otherwise called [the] 'sacred right of self government'" [2.462]). After these undermining operations, which contributed to the election of a Democratic president, came the decision on the Dred Scott case, its announcement carefully timed to avoid the election. The court's commentary on the slavery issue, embedded in its decision, was designed, first, to "deprive the negro, in every possible event, of the benefit of this provision of the United States Constitution, which declares that—'The citizens of each State shall be entitled to all privileges and immunities of citizens in the several States.'" The decision worked to prevent Congress and territorial legislatures from keeping slavery out of "any United States territory." Legislative ambition and public opinion were combining to spread slavery simply for the sake of preserving the peculiar institution, not necessarily for immediate gain:

> This point is made in order that individual men may *fill up* the territories with slaves, without danger of losing them as property, and thus to enhance the chances of *permanency* to the institution through all the future. (2.464)

Finally, Lincoln charges, there arose a choreographed dispute between fellow Democrats—Douglas and President Buchanan—over the constitution that was voted on by the people of Kansas—a confrontation without substance, but appealing, with misleading friendliness, to Republican support for the uncontroversial "right of a people to make their own constitution" (2.464). The goal was to deflect attention from the conspiracy and toward Douglas's leadership as a bipartisan champion who would feel no moral compunctions if slavery were extended:

[I]n that squabble . . . [Douglas] declares that all he wants is a fair vote for the people, and that he cares not whether slavery be voted down or voted up. I do not understand his declaration that he *cares* not whether slavery be voted *down* or voted *up*, to be intended by him other than as an *apt definition* of the *policy* he would impress upon the public mind—the *principle* for which he declares he has suffered much, and is ready to suffer to the end. (2.463–464)

Students of the Lincoln-Douglas debates know that this charge—in the form of Lincoln's taunting repetition of Douglas's words—will be used to dog the opposition throughout the upcoming senatorial campaign: "These things *look* like the cautious *patting* and *petting* a spirited horse, preparatory to mounting him, when it is dreaded that he may give the rider a fall" (2.465).

Douglas's attitude of indifference, purportedly for the sake of honoring the people's freedom to choose "subject only to the Constitution," hides the tendency of this combination of political and judicial actions. With just one more step, Lincoln argues, the Supreme Court could take advantage of Douglas's teaching of indifference to conform the Constitution to a national policy prohibiting the states from excluding slavery. The court would thereby perfect the conspiratorial machinery's tendency to make the Union all slave in moral outlook and, in stages, all slave in fact:

We shall *lie down* pleasantly dreaming that the people of Missouri are on the verge of making their State *free;* and we shall *awake* to the *reality,* instead, that the *Supreme* Court has made *Illinois* a *slave* State. (2.467)

The high stakes of the conflict with Douglas remind Lincoln of Ecclesiastes:

They [the followers of Douglas] remind us that *he* is a very *great man,* and that the largest of *us* are very small ones. Let this be granted. But "a *living dog* is better than a *dead* lion." Judge Douglas, if not a *dead* lion for *this work,* is at least a *caged* and *toothless* one. How can he oppose the advances of slavery? He don't *care* anything about it. His avowed *mission is impressing* the "public heart" to *care* nothing about it. (2.467)

Lincoln is thinking of a passage in Ecclesiastes that expands the contrast between the dog and the lion by connecting the dead lion to ignorance and ignominy:

For to him that is joined to all the living there is hope: for the living dog is better than a dead lion.

For the living know that they shall die: but the dead know not any thing, neither have they any more a reward; for the memory of them is forgotten.[14]

The line Lincoln takes from Scripture becomes the particular criticism that he will make an essential element of his campaign against Douglas for the Senate: Douglas and his allies are attempting to form a "don't care" party of moral apathy and death.

The people, Lincoln visibly assumes, are capable of the vigilance they will need to resist such a party; but so is the conspiracy a powerful means of clouding their judgment. To awaken the people's vigilance under these circumstances, Lincoln makes a point of conceding his inability to see what is warily hidden, or to foretell the future; but he does so in a way that increases the likelihood that the hidden conspiracy will be revealed by close attention to the *tendency* of seemingly nonconspiratorial acts:

We cannot absolutely *know* that all these exact adaptations are the result of preconcert. But when we see a lot of framed timbers, different portions of which we know have been gotten out at different times and places and by different workmen . . . and when we see these timbers joined together, and see they exactly make the frame of a house or a mill, all the tenons and mortices exactly fitting, and all the lengths and proportions of the different pieces exactly fitting, and all the lengths and proportions of the different pieces exactly adapted to their respective places, and not a piece too many or too few—not omitting even scaffolding—or, if a single piece be lacking, we can see the place in the frame exactly fitted and prepared to yet bring such piece in—in *such* a case, we find it impossible to not believe that Stephen and Franklin and Roger and James all understood one another from the beginning, and all worked upon a common plan or draft drawn up before the first lick was struck. (2.465–466)

David Donald, writing about Lincoln's motives in framing the "House Divided" Speech in such startling terms, argues that the conspiracy charge "was not based on fact" and that its specific claims were "less important than its general import," which was to show that Douglas "could not be trusted and must be defeated."[15] Certainly, Lincoln's charges strain our credulity. They must have met resistance within his immediate audience, large portions of which held Douglas in high esteem. But Lincoln anticipates those doubts with his interesting qualification ("We can not absolutely *know*"), followed by extensive evidence of the conspiratorial form and direction—the tendency—of the evidence. Circumstantial evidence, when it is developed with insight and skill, is capable of revealing the shape and tendency of condemnable activities. Lincoln identifies compelling grounds for belief based on what he later writes were "incontestable facts" (2.548). Douglas and others were acting upon a shared idea: "[A]ll understood one another." They had a "common plan" they may or may not have written down in a "draft." Whether they cooperated in one another's secret company is not at issue, although Lincoln leaves this possibility open. The core of his case is that the facts point toward a cooperative effort to create a public indifference to the expansion of slavery.

In his private outline of ideas prepared for his upcoming debate with Douglas, Lincoln freely labels this cooperation a "conspiracy," though he concedes that the evidence is "circumstantial only." The case is circumstantial in the sense that all forensic arguments, at least the great majority that do not rely on confessions (confessions being themselves problematic when there is a chance they are coerced or self-serving), are circumstantial. Intent must be inferred. Adopting a courtroom method of negative definition imitated by modern science, Lincoln says he has tested his theory and found it "inconsistent with every hypothesis, save that of the existence of such conspiracy" (2.548–549).

The "House Divided" Speech attempts to alert its audience to the remarkable complementarity and success of these tactics as evidence of a concerted, subtle design—a conspiracy in *effect*, if not in origin, designed to "educate and mould public opinion" (2.465). In the fifth debate Lincoln insists that his charge does not assume that Douglas *means* to make slavery national. But he adds that, even if Douglas is not part of a conscious conspiracy toward this end, he is the ideal "instrument" to complete the design:

> I do not charge that he means so; but I call upon your minds to inquire, if you were going to get the best instrument you could, and then set it to work in the most ingenious way, to prepare the public mind for this movement, operating in the free States, where there is now an abhorrence of the institution of Slavery, could you find an instrument so capable of doing it as Judge Douglas? (3.233)

Whether by proven or hypothesized design, Douglas's popularity, political abilities, and apparent neutrality make him the best means of lulling northern public opinion into indifference. He is in this sense unworthy of election, not because of criminal intent but because he has made himself the wrong man to elect.

If the danger of failing to detect Douglas's subtlety is so great and the facts so difficult to establish, the threat might have to be met with a contrary insinuation of suspicion to ensure the public is alert. Pure deliberation is not enough; some form of preemption, rightly considered, might be indispensable if the union is to be saved as more than a shell. There must be a counteragitation that alarms the public's capacity to see the danger before the public can see it. Otherwise the threat might not be apprehended in time to be resisted. The dilemma as Lincoln frames it is reminiscent of Brutus's, as Shakespeare dramatized it in *Julius Caesar*. One must act against a great danger when the threat has hardly shown itself, in order to anticipate the deadly manifestation of that danger. But what if the apprehension is wrong? As Lincoln sets for himself the task of being vigilant and high-minded, like Brutus, he moves dangerously close to the role of Antony, the famous demagogue in Shakespeare and Plutarch who, after Caesar's death, will stop at nothing to turn the crowd against "honorable men."

During the 1858 campaign, Douglas accused Lincoln of engaging in his own conspiracy within the Republican Party to overthrow a constitutional government the Founders made part slave and part free. But the groundwork for Douglas's case consisted almost entirely of insinuations of collusion among leading Illinois Republicans. He had almost no other evidence, except for his quotations from Lincoln's carefully wrought speeches and from political platforms Lincoln did not endorse. He depended on establishing Lincoln's guilt by loose lines of association: those who were alleged to be "Black Republicans" were tainted by association with abolitionists, who in turn were associated with black men. What was distinctive about Lincoln's charge in the "House Divided" Speech was its apparent forensic clarity—its gesture of submission to public opinion. It assembled public facts about the dates and qualities of legislative acts and judicial decisions, placed them in an accessible logical framework, invoked principles of judgment, and then asked whether there could be any plausible explanation for this sequence of decisions other than the one he had ventured. If those acts and decisions

were not assembled by conspirators to detach public opinion from its venerable expectation that slavery was in the course of extinction, what could their
purpose be?

The careful aggressiveness of Lincoln's rhetoric in the "House Divided"
Speech was crucial to his framing of the issue in terms of ideas, which his audience could not entertain so well *as ideas* without the particular sense of
alarm raised by Lincoln's words. The charge that there was a hidden conspiracy undermining the public's judgment depended on the audience's paradoxical ability to respond to the *idea* that its powers of judgment were in
danger of being undermined. A belief in "popular sovereignty" was not
enough. The danger of apathy, or of making the wrong decision while being
enamored merely of the liberty to make decisions as citizens equal in the
franchise, was too great. The audience had to deliberate, but it might not do
so unless it could be subjected to a shock of recognition. It somehow had to
take into account the fragility and indispensability of its political inheritance,
and act upon what it found. Lincoln's logic and his hypothesis of conspiracy
were attempts to encourage—and provoke, if necessary—that sort of thinking. If he had to become a rhetorical conspirator to do this, the speech he
created managed to affirm and depend upon his audience's active sense of
that fragility and that debt. If the audience could see that in his ideas of conspiracy and resistance there were principles and imperatives more fundamental than individual voters' right to choose, those who heard him might
regain their stature as inheritors of the American republic.

The success of the "House Divided" Speech depended on its treatment
of this paradoxical capacity in Lincoln's audience. Anticipating a debate
with Douglas "on *principle*" in the upcoming Senate campaign (2.468), Lincoln appealed to his audience's ability to apprehend, amid increasing per-
plexity and obfuscation, what was already known but not effectively recognized: "The result is not doubtful. We shall not fail—if we stand firm, we
shall not fail" (2.468). In the context of the entire speech, this simple line
richly suggests the power and limitation of just principle. There is something everlasting about a just principle, at least as it inspires those who remember it and stand by it. For Lincoln that "something" makes victory inevitable and perhaps providential when the audience is moved to recognize
what it somehow knows in its heart and deeper thoughts is the case. The encouragement he offers at the end of the speech seems wholly superficial and

unnecessary unless we appreciate the subtlety of his effort to draw permanent principles closer to the world of deeds, where his audience might find in them a strangely familiar source of moral and political strength:

> *Wise councils* may accelerate or *mistakes delay* it, but, sooner or later the victory is sure to come. (2.469)

Lecture on Discoveries and Inventions

Self-Government and Arts of Literacy

The great difference between Young America and Old Fogy, is the result of *Discoveries, Inventions,* and *Improvements.* These, in turn, are
the result of *observation, reflection* and *experiment.* For instance, it is
quite certain that ever since water has been boiled in covered vessels,
men have seen the lids of the vessels rise and fall a little, with a sort of
fluttering motion, by force of the steam; But as long as this was not spe-
cially observed, and reflected and experimented upon, it came to nothing. At length, however, after many thousand years, some man observes
this long-known effect of hot water lifting a pot-lid, and begins a train of
reflection upon it. . . . But was this first inventor of the application of
steam, wiser or more ingenious than those who had gone before him?
Not at all. Had he not learned much of them, he never would have succeeded—probably, never would have thought of making the attempt.
(3.358)

At its inception in the first decades of the nineteenth century, public
lecturing in America was a means of education that found eager audiences in
thousands of local churches, libraries, and lyceum halls. By the 1840s and
'50s, local organizing committees could draw from a stream of professional
lecturers, many of them provided by eastern agents. Lawrence Buell's survey
indicates that half the major authors of the day (and a third of all the authors
on his voluminous list) participated, some of them for healthy fees.[1] The
number of lecture societies across the northern states in the 1850s has been
estimated at three to four thousand, and their total weekly audiences at four
hundred thousand.[2] The lyceum's traditional purpose was the edification of
large and varied audiences seeking general knowledge and practical advice.

Commercialization and democratization, which characterized the lyceum circuit of the 1850s, did not fundamentally alter that goal. Speakers with political purposes tended to embed their messages in quasi-academic topics.

In the winter months of 1859, the *Illinois State Register* of Springfield announced a lecture by the educational reformer Horace Mann, a presentation by a specialist on "The Brain, the Organ of the Mind," and a plea from a local poet on the need for more forceful American statesmanship.[3] An eminent Lincoln friend, Orville Browning, recorded in his diary the parade of lecturers and performers through central Illinois in the same year. In Quincy, his hometown near Springfield, he heard Herman Melville speak on the South Sea Islands ("Erratic but interesting").[4] A candidate for Democratic governor read his poetry,[5] and a friend, possibly the man who spoke in Springfield on the same subject, delivered a lecture on "American statesmanship."[6] Another speaker entertained his audience with a lecture about France.[7] In Chicago that year, Browning heard what he called a "lecture" on "the character and public services of Clay," an eminently political subject adapted for the lyceum. Unfortunately, the speaker was drunk.[8] Returning to Quincy, he heard John Gough, the famous reformed drinker who delivered three hundred lectures a year, urging his audience to take up the cause of temperance. Browning himself lectured in a Springfield church "for the benefit of the poor" and dined afterward at the Lincolns'.[9]

Although our knowledge of Lincoln's career as a lecturer is incomplete, we have a good deal of evidence, most of it in his own writings and speeches, for ascertaining its general outline and some of its purposes. The primary texts are extremely interesting. Of course, we have the Lyceum Address, which he delivered in Springfield in 1838. The Temperance Address of 1842 is, as we have seen, an occasional endorsement of the Washingtonian Society that often depends upon lecture-like exposition and argumentation to reassess traditional views. We also have two brief fragments or preliminary notes that Lincoln might have intended to elaborate in formal lectures. The first is a description of Niagara Falls. The second is a compact essay of advice about the practical and ethical challenges that await all lawyers, whether they are novices or old hands.

The fragment on Niagara Falls was perhaps written around 1848, during Lincoln's return trip to Illinois at the end of his lone congressional term. Its dense mixture of facts and expressions of wonder might have been a response to Tom Paine's suggestion, published in *The Age of Reason,* that if a

man were placed in the proper situation he might "behold at one view, and
. . . contemplate deliberately, the structure of the universe." He would then
"know the system of laws established by the Creator" that "teach him the
power, the wisdom, the vastness, the munificence" of God.[10] Whatever the
case, an attempt to contemplate and analyze the falls in their largest dimensions would have given Lincoln opportunity to turn his attention away from
his time in Congress and toward a new life outside of public office. The fragment documents an attempt to take in the entire phenomenon, to fix his attention not on the sound, color, or form of the falls but on their manifestation
of the history of creation, the magnitude of the created world's operations,
and the contrast between those operations' relentless power and the mortality of their human observer:

> Niagara-Falls! By what mysterious power is it that millions and millions, are
> drawn from all parts of the world, to gaze upon Niagara Falls? There is no
> mystery about the thing itself. Every effect is just such as an intelligent man
> knowing the causes, would anticipate, without [seeing] it. If the water moving
> onward in a great river, reaches a point where there is a perpendicular jog, of
> a hundred feet in descent, in the bottom of the river,—it is plain the water will
> have a violent and continuous plunge at that point. It is also plain the water,
> thus plunging, will foam, and roar, and send up a mist, continuously, in which
> last, during sunshine, there will be perpetual rain-bows. The mere physical of
> Niagara Falls is only this. Yet this is really a very small part of that world's
> wonder. It's power to excite reflection, and emotion, is it's great charm. The
> geologist will demonstrate that the plunge, or fall, was once at Lake Ontario,
> and has worn it's way back to it's present position; he will ascertain how *fast*
> it is wearing now, and so get a basis of determining how *long* it has been wear-
> ing back from Lake Ontario, and finally demonstrate by it that this world is at
> least fourteen thousand years old. A philosopher of a slightly different turn
> will say Niagara Falls is only the lip of the basin out of which pours all the sur-
> plus water which rains down on two or three hundred thousand square miles
> of the earth's surface. He will estim[ate with] approximate accuracy, that five
> hundred thousand [to]ns of water, falls with it's full weight, a distance of a
> hundred feet each minute—thus exerting a force equal to the lifting of the
> same weight, through the same space, in the same time. And then the further
> reflection comes that this vast amount of water, constantly pouring *down,* is
> supplied by an equal amount constantly *lifted up,* by the sun; and still he

says, "If this much is lifted up, for *this one* space of two or three hundred thousand square miles, an equal amount must be lifted for every other equal space; and he is overwhelmed in the contemplation of the vast power the sun is constantly exerting in quiet, noiseless opperation of lifting water *up* to be rained *down* again.

But still there is more. It calls up the indefinite past. When Columbus first sought this continent—when Christ suffered on the cross—when Moses led Israel through the Red-sea—nay, even, when Adam first came from the hand of his Maker—then as now, Niagara was roaring here. The eyes of that species of extinct giants, whose bones fill the mounds of America, have gazed on Niagara, as ours do now. Co[n]temporary with the whole race of men, and older than the first man, Niagara is strong, and fresh to-day as ten thousand years ago. The Mammoth and Mastadon—now so long dead, that fragments of their monstrous bones, alone testify, that they ever lived, have gazed on Niagara. In that long—long time, never still for a single moment. Never dried, never froze, never slept, never rested . . . (2.10–11)

Many years later, Nicolay and Hay speculated that Lincoln had intended to expand his observations into a lecture;[11] but no record has been found of an attempt to do so. Herndon argues that after his own trip to Niagara, ten years after Lincoln's return from Washington, Lincoln spoke of the falls as though he possessed no sensitivity to nature. In the eyes of the transcendentalist, he had nothing much to say.[12] Still, the fragment on Niagara is full of suggestions for an extended treatment of themes that transcend natural philosophy. Fashioning himself as a natural philosopher, Lincoln discovers, analyzes, and removes successive layers in observers' understanding of the falls. Pondering the operation of this natural wonder, he touches on the global operations of nature through natural history, then through the full sweep of human history. By the end of the fragment, he is taking on the garb of the metaphysician. Before breaking off, he is in the process of refocusing his speculation on the metaphysical consideration of unchanging motion: What is to be made of the falls' constancy that outlasts everything, including the ancient animals that viewed the falls just as he does? If the living witnesses, Lincoln included, leave only their bones while Niagara Falls never rests, what conclusions should be drawn from this wondrous sight?

The power of this fragment to intimate the shape and substance of Lincoln's thought should alert us to the depth of those public lectures we know he delivered. Here, associating himself with the mammoth as a temporary bystander contemplating a power that would outlast him, Lincoln writes of the falls' triumph over time and space as though it were something so vast it reduced everything else to a few skeletal fragments, except for persistent human wonder at the magnitude of that power's operations. Whether or not Lincoln observed the falls on his return to Springfield in 1848, his vision of their power would have embodied and offered a melancholy insight—and the consolation—that they would always flow.

The fragment on Niagara exemplifies Lincoln's twin tendency to analyze his subjects with an aggressive energy that touches on contemplative themes. The falls offer access, in his deliberate contemplation, to an enormous yet "quiet, noiseless operation" in the action of the sun. In the presidential years, he would write of the "mere quiet power" of Providence. Time scatters the bones of beast and man, but the sun's hidden operation, which is partially manifested in the enormous power of the falling water, is also strangely mild: "quiet" rather than silent, sustaining the falls' constant motion and striking man with wonder once he begins to glimpse their ever larger significance.

Lincoln presents these speculations as though addressing an audience: either himself, or an imagined mixture of auditors. Rather than setting out a dry exposition, he expresses amazement at the spectacle and then analyzes it by addressing himself as though to be overheard. Yet in setting out the problem in a manner that enables him to speak clearly to others, he draws from currents of thought that are not explicit. The falls elicit a wonder, he says, that cannot be explained with obvious evidence. The incompleteness of the fragment is testimony to the ambiguity of his effort to speak plainly about profundities. He propels the argument toward increasingly comprehensive conclusions until it breaks off, as though he had made the case or perhaps saw that he could not make it in the lecture-like forms of speech he had chosen.

In the fragment on the practice of law, possibly from the same period, there is a somewhat similar pattern of outward clarity and internal complication. Lincoln refers to the possibility of composing a lecture on the subject by noting that his shortcomings as a lawyer are "quite as much material for a lecture" as other points in which he has been "moderately successful" (2.81). Whatever authority he can claim as a lecturer on the subject would have to be qualified by his own history of error, which should caution any audience keen on hearing simple advice about how to succeed. He predicates his positive advice on the assumption that precautions must be taken against one's tendency to err.

On one level, Lincoln's advice is simple. The lawyer's knowledge of detail is essential to his practice. No matter how skilled as a speaker a lawyer might be, the good lawyer must be methodical, not only in mastering the facts of the case but also in his habits of work. But methodical habits have a deeper purpose. The good lawyer's methods recognize and resist the general human tendency to err (which he identifies in himself) and in particular the temptation to choose dishonest means. As he learns the practice of law the lawyer needs to maintain his own precautionary methods so that he remains accountable. He must not be drawn to abuse his power even in petty matters:

> As a general rule never take your whole fee in advance, nor any more than a small retainer. When fully paid beforehand, you are more than a common mortal if you can feel the same interest in the case, as if something was still in prospect for you, as well as for your client. And when you lack interest in the case the job will very likely lack skill and diligence in the performance. Settle the amount of fee and take a note in advance. Then you will feel that you are working faithfully and well. (2.82)

An understanding of human weakness helps enforce virtue, and the satisfaction gained from that enforcement draws strength from knowing what it has overcome.

In the business of persuasion and making peace without litigation, "the lawyer has a superior opportunity of being a good man." But peacemaking is unfortunately not always possible: "There will still be business enough" (2.81). Is it then possible to be a good man and a lawyer? Lincoln answers affirmatively, but with a caveat. An ordinary resolve to be honest will not be enough; the influence of public opinion on a lawyer's conception of the law must be taken into account. The lawyer must recognize the power of "a vague popular belief that lawyers are necessarily dishonest." He must find an honest way to be worthy of the public's opposite tendency to believe that lawyers are worthy of "confidence and honors."

> Let no young man choosing the law for a calling for a moment yield to the popular belief—resolve to be honest at all events; and if in your own judgment you cannot be an honest lawyer, resolve to be honest without being a

lawyer. Choose some other occupation, rather than one in the choosing of which you do, in advance, consent to be a knave. (2.82)

After almost discarding his initial topic, Lincoln recovers it in this turn of logic and his repeated call to "resolve to be honest . . . resolve to be honest." Choice is not enough. The greater task is summoning one's resolve, in the face of the attraction of consenting to one's own undoing. Recognition of that human weakness means that it might not be possible for some aspirants to be honest lawyers. All must develop the resolve to choose another path— in a sense, to risk their security—if the alternative is to be trapped in their own device. In these lines of argument, Lincoln presents miniature variations on themes he developed in the Lyceum Address, the Temperance Address, the Kansas-Nebraska Speech, and other speeches throughout his career.

* * *

Readers commonly encounter one of Lincoln's more complete efforts, his Lecture on Discoveries and Inventions, in Basler's edition of Lincoln's collected works. It appears there in what have long been thought to be two versions: the first delivered in Bloomington in 1858, and the second in Jacksonville on February 11, 1859. Wayne Temple has plausibly argued that both texts are in fact parts of a single work, which Lincoln delivered, probably with variations and embellishments, in a number of central Illinois towns between February 1858 and April 1860. There were at least four, and perhaps as many as six or more presentations. We are reasonably certain that Lincoln delivered the lecture in Bloomington (April 6, 1858), Jacksonville (February 4, 1859 [not the 11th, as Temple points out]), Springfield (twice: February 21, 1859, and April 26, 1860), and probably Decatur (March 1859). A repeat performance in Bloomington (scheduled for April 8, 1859) was canceled at the last minute for lack of sufficient attendance. Still another performance might have occurred in Pontiac, Illinois, on January 27, 1860.[13] If Lincoln did not always fill the hall when he spoke on the subject of inventions, the popularity of the lecture was sufficient to elicit invitations that he had to turn down for the sake of other obligations.[14]

The account of the 1858 lecture in the Bloomington *Pantagraph* gives us strong evidence that Lincoln used material from both the texts that Basler places in separate sections of the complete works. When we read the two segments of the work together (Temple notes that the manuscripts were reported to be connected by tape when Lincoln handed them to a friend for safekeeping in February 1861),[15] we see not only the consistency of their general subject matters but also the evidence that each fragment contains particular elements of the other, sometimes in what looks like revised form. According to an 1858 report, Lincoln discussed "Young America," a subject we now find only in the 1859 version in Basler's collection. He called writing "the greatest of all inventions," an idea that is missing from the first version but carefully developed in the second. He discussed music, a topic missing from both surviving texts. The *Pantagraph*'s 1858 summary picks up the gist of the second text, which the reporter could not have gleaned from the fragment now ascribed to 1858: "We have all *heard* of Young America. . . . Still, we must not be forgetful of the Old Fogeys. Without them Young America would be comparatively helpless."[16] Conversely, the 1859 text incorporates the lead sentence of the 1858 version and reworks the earlier discussion of steam power into a more extended narrative.[17]

It is likely that Lincoln's lecture on both occasions was partly written and partly extemporized, and that it made use of the ideas available in both drafts. John Nicolay's description of the lecture's 1860 rendition in Springfield tells us that Lincoln embroidered his script with comments that were not preserved in print. Writing in the *Century Magazine* thirty-five years after the fact, he says the performed lecture was "much longer than the present one, and contained several fine passages."[18] One was "a reference to the importance and value of laughter, and a characterization of it as the 'joyous, beautiful, universal evergreen of life.'"[19] The humorous material must have contributed significantly to the "much longer" version of the lecture Nicolay remembered. His description recalls the Bloomington paper's 1858 account, which Herndon quotes in his life of Lincoln, of how the lecture "treated of and illustrated" laughter in Lincoln's "own inimitable way," presumably with the help of his distinctive facility for telling jokes.[20]

The earlier speech, if it was indeed based primarily on what is called the 1858 text, was more of a success than we might assume if we based our opinion on the undeveloped fragments that survive. The Bloomington newspaper reports that Lincoln's large audience was "appreciative" of the speech's "searching analytic process" of argument. The speaker, the reporter concludes, was "an able and original thinker," one who "in the department of literature fully sustains the reputation he has so justly earned at the bar."[21] If we put the two fragments in juxtaposition, they suggest that Lincoln had composed, or was composing, a substantial statement about human nature and human progress, one that resonated with, and elaborated, his philosophical and political views.

* * *

Over the past century and a half, critical opinion of the Lecture on Discoveries and Inventions has been mostly negative. In the era in which idolatry for the assassinated president reached its apogee, Lincoln's old secretary John Nicolay wrote that the lecture was a "literary experiment" to which it would be "unjust to devote any serious criticism." It "must be regarded," he wrote, "in the light of mere recreation to satisfy the craving for a change from the monotony of law and politics."[22] Roy P. Basler called the speech "somewhat colorless," Lincoln having "never thought much of it."[23] Despite the publication of Temple's industrious research in 1983, the recent American Library Edition of Lincoln's writings printed only the second fragment—the presumably authoritative version Basler thought had been delivered in Jacksonville in 1859. In his recent book on the Gettysburg Address, Garry Wills mines that text for ideas that illuminate the great speech; but his citations of passages from the lecture are accompanied by only one line of commentary.[24] Even Temple's groundbreaking essay does not include an extensive analysis of the speech.

Herndon's verdict is negative and complex. He says he is certain that Lincoln's heart was not in the lecturing business, that the discoveries lecture seemed to expose a lack of seriousness—or, worse, an awkward attempt to enter a world for which Lincoln's greatness was not suited:

> Political business being off his hands, [Lincoln] now conceived the idea of entering the lecture field. He began preparations in the usual way by noting down ideas on stray pieces of paper, which found a lodgement inside his hat, and finally brought forth in connected form a lecture on "Inventions." He recounted the wonderful improvements in machinery, the arts, and sciences. Now and then he indulged in a humorous paragraph, and witticisms were freely sprinkled throughout the lecture. During the winter he delivered it at several towns in the central part of the State, but it was so commonplace, and met with such indifferent success, that he soon dropped it altogether. The effort met with the disapproval of his friends, and he himself was filled with disgust. If his address in 1852, over the death of Clay, proved he was no eulogist, then his last effort demonstrated that he was no lecturer.[25]

Writing years after the fact, Herndon does not acknowledge that Lincoln delivered the lecture to an approving audience in Bloomington just before the campaign against Douglas for the Senate. He does not refer to Lincoln's extension of his argument in the address to the Wisconsin State Fair at the end of 1859. Nor does he note the prominent delivery of the discoveries lecture to an audience in Springfield just a few weeks after the Cooper Union Address had propelled the speaker onto the national stage.[26]

In Herndon's view, Lincoln's "unpretentious" manner made him vulnerable to "fashionable" audiences whenever he made formal speeches out of the courtroom and off the political platform.[27] Lincoln was "not qualified in any way to deliver a lecture to our people who are intelligent."[28] Herndon probably heard the unscripted jokes in Jacksonville and, unlike Nicolay, judged them an embarrassment. Replying in 1891 to a correspondent who apparently questioned his earlier impressions, Herndon's verdict was unequivocal, this time not mentioning what he once said about the speech's occasional wit and humor: "I know that Mr. L. was not fitted, qualified, read, and well educated. I was not mistaken in the lecture which Mr. L. read; it was a lifeless thing, a dull dead thing, 'died aborning.' It fell on the ears of the audience a cold flat thing. There was no life, imagination, or fancy in it, no spirit and no life. The whole thing was a kind of farce and injured Mr. L's reputation as a man of sense among his friends and enemies."[29] The judgment of Lincoln's friend Ward Hill Lamon echoes Herndon's.[30] Henry Clay Whitney, who accompanied Lincoln for years on the Illinois circuit, partly confirms Herndon's opinion that the lecture was not an entirely pleasant memory for Lincoln himself: "I once read in a newspaper, that Lincoln went to Clinton to deliver a lecture on 'Man, his Progress, etc.,' and that nobody came to hear him, and that he went home with his lecture undelivered, and the paper added, 'That don't look much like his being President.' So I joked with him about it when I saw him. He said, laughingly: 'Don't mention that, for it plagues me some.'"[31]

Perhaps Herndon's own lack of success on the lecture platform colored his judgment. His lyceum efforts in 1857 and early 1859, a month before Lincoln's appearance in Jacksonville, had met with a tepid response, or had been overshadowed by the popularity of entertainments that had drawn much larger crowds.[32] In 1866 his lectures on Lincoln's life stirred resentment as well as respectful interest. In later years, his attempt to give a series of lectures on that still-popular topic was a failure.[33] Still, the assumption that

Herndon's judgment might have been controlled by his resentment does not address the considerable evidence of his reliability in other important observations about Lincoln's life.[34] The likelihood that he was biased in some of his judgments does not tell us that he was biased in this one. It seems more likely that for him as perhaps for many others the fundamental difficulty of evaluating Lincoln as a lecturer was the gap between Lincoln's persona as a lecturer and his presence as the politician of his age. The fact that in 1859 Lincoln delivered the ostensibly apolitical, problematic discoveries lecture to a small audience at Jacksonville College, the abolitionist alma mater of his law partner, would have highlighted this contrast all the more.[35]

There is reason to believe that Lincoln himself had mixed feelings about lecturing. He does not appear to have invested himself in the discoveries lecture with unalloyed enthusiasm. He told one correspondent that he coordinated its delivery with his other work in several towns so that it was "a waste of no time whatever" (3.374). He rejected some invitations to lecture, saying he had other engagements (3.377). And he revealed no high opinion of his lecturing efforts, calling his work on discoveries "a sort of lecture" (3.374), and indicating in a conversation with Louis Agassiz that the presentation was not fully developed.[36] In turning down, in 1860, F. C. Herbruger's request that he give a lecture, he wrote, "I am not a professional lecturer—have never got up but one lecture, and that, I think, rather a poor one" (4.40).

We know that Lincoln's lecture audiences were not as large as they tended to be for his political speeches. His 1858 Bloomington lecture had to be moved from a hall seating almost one thousand to a room with space for just three hundred, and his 1859 reading of the lecture in Jacksonville attracted a meager two dozen.[37] Delivered mainly between campaigns, the lectures did not have an obvious political attraction. Lincoln was risking his reputation for drawing crowds, sometimes helping local committees and associations raise money for purposes that were not explicitly political. Unlike a political candidate, he was accepting money for his pains—when there was enough for him to be paid.

It is worth noticing, however, that in the period between the first and last performances of the discoveries lecture Lincoln's political activity was especially intense. Two months after his Bloomington appearance, he accepted the Republican nomination to the Senate and gave his defining speech on the "house divided against itself" (June 16, 1858). Bloomington was not merely a stop on the national lecture circuit. It was a home of strong support for Lincoln's political ambitions, and the site of the 1856 Republican meeting in which Lincoln delivered the famous "Lost Speech" that cemented his leadership role in the Illinois Republican Party.[38] The senatorial campaign that followed involved the seven famous debates with Stephen Douglas (August 21–October 15) and many separate speeches. In defeat, Lincoln resumed his legal practice and his lecturing in 1859, when he delivered the discoveries lecture in at least three towns and declined several invitations. By April of that year, his friends in Illinois were contemplating nominating him for the presidency at the Republican convention to be held in Chicago. In the last half of 1859, he gave political speeches in Dayton, Indianapolis, Columbus, Cincinnati, Beloit, and Janesville.

Amid these commitments, Lincoln gave a lecture-like address at the Wisconsin State Fair in Milwaukee. Speaking on September 30, 1859, he joked about expectations that as a politician he would give a political speech, then set out to show that he had a respectable knowledge of farming. The lecture was ostensibly apolitical and yet deeply thoughtful about issues related to the upcoming campaign. Its most important argument (the subject of next chapter) had to do with the responsible use of land, a topic with connections to the controversy over slavery in the territories. Lincoln presented his views as a response to the farmers' desire that he "give some general interest to the occasion" and "make some general suggestions, on practical matters" (3.473). But he used the occasion to discuss the implicitly political effects of good farming at a time when the responsible use of land in the territories was becoming an issue for the next presidential campaign.

The address in Milwaukee should make us wonder whether the discoveries lecture was merely a passing whimsy. The Milwaukee address referred explicitly to the earlier lecture's title, and applied and extended its ideas with regard to agriculture. Echoing language in the discoveries speech, Lincoln said that state fairs were occasions for bringing together "all which is supposed to not be generally known, because of recent discovery, or invention" (3.472). He then discussed the application of recent discoveries and inventions to the task of using farmland more thoroughly with free labor. In both speeches, we begin to see, the language is dense with political meanings.

Lectures and political speeches were in fact often complementary performances. The month before the Milwaukee address, Lincoln had received an invitation to lecture at Plymouth Church in Brooklyn, on the platform of the famous Republican lecturer and churchman, Henry Ward Beecher. In

December, before embarking for New York, he made a political speaking tour in Kansas, giving speeches immediately before and after the hanging of John Brown. He turned immediately to the composition of what later became known as the Cooper Union Address (the subject of chapter 11)—a unique mixture of historical lecture and political speech that propelled him toward the presidential nomination. Amid the whirl of political activity and speechmaking that followed that address, he was again thinking of the discoveries lecture. His friend Henry C. Whitney recalled that during the eastern tour that immediately followed the Cooper Union Address, Lincoln met the eminent Harvard scientist and lecturer Louis Agassiz, mentioned his earlier effort at academic lecturing, and asked Agassiz "about how he studied—how he composed—how he delivered his lectures—how he found different tastes in his audiences, in different parts of the country, etc."[39] A few weeks after his triumphant return from New York, he was asked to deliver the discoveries lecture one more time, to an audience that probably included many people who had heard it before.

Lincoln publicly recalled the discoveries lecture again in 1865, after four years of exhausting war and political controversy. Noah Brooks reports that when Lincoln resumed his conversation with Agassiz, he said, "When I get out of this place . . . I'll finish it [the discoveries lecture] up, perhaps, and get my friend [perhaps Noah Brooks] to print it somewhere"[40] What was it about Lincoln's humble attempt at lecturing on discoveries and inventions that kept him thinking about elaborating what he had said? The discoveries lecture seems to have supplied a balancing countermovement during a period of personal defeat and triumph—an opportunity to delve into philosophical issues not bound by immediate political imperatives, yet containing deep political ramifications in a time of crisis.

* * *

Lincoln formed the Lecture on Discoveries and Inventions from a dense array of familiar yet interesting materials—from the Bible, a series of encyclopedia articles, and other sources familiar to lyceum audiences—in order to reach unconventional conclusions about a topic of common interest. The probing, relatively exploratory nature of the talk was consistent with Edward Channing's description of lecturing style, whereby the best speakers "hold a sort of conversation with men upon what they are already to some extent acquainted with, in order that they may compare their ideas with those of a fellow-inquirer, and be assisted to take comprehensive views of subjects which they had examined by themselves very much in detail."[41] A similar characterization appeared in the 1865 issue of the *Atlantic Monthly:*

> American life is crowded with facts, to which the newspapers give daily record and diffusion. Ideas, motives, thoughts, these are always in demand. Men wish for nothing more than to know how to classify their facts, what to do with them, how to govern them, and how far to be governed by them; and the man who takes the facts with which the popular life has come into contact and association, and draws from them their nutritive and motive power, and points out their relations to individual and universal good, and organizes around them the popular thought, and uses them to give direction to the popular life, and does all this with masterly skill, is the man whose houses are never large enough to contain those who throng to hear him. This is the popular lecturer, *par excellence.*[42]

In general form, Lincoln's multileveled approach conforms to an expectation of the day, which put a premium on public lectures that worked on several levels at once. A contemporary commentator praised performances that could hide "the soundest sense under the most brilliant and humorous rhetoric."[43] Lincoln rose to the occasion in a variety of ways. He used jokes to make implicit connections between his apolitical topic and contemporary issues, for example by referring sarcastically to the "invention of negroes, or, of the present mode of using them in 1434" (3.362). He took advantage of analogies, and of intersections between the history of inventions and self-government to take up philosophical elements in his political thought, and then to treat those elements in ways that illuminated his political thinking.

The discoveries lecture was an opportunity to present the history of technology and exploration primarily in terms of the verbal arts—literacy being, paradoxically, the cause and effect of the emancipation of the mind. The story of the emergence of literacy in America became, in Lincoln's formulation, a commentary on the strengths and fallibilities of technological revolutions that needed, and helped to secure, the institutions and attitudes that led to self-government. It also suggested analogies between slavery and illiterate ignorance, and between the emancipation of the mind and the freeing of those held in bondage. Rather than construct a reductive allegory, Lincoln made use of the genre and substance of the lecture so that each topic qualified and deepened the other.

In a parallel motion, the lecture also provided Lincoln with an opportunity to comment on Young America's sense of "Manifest Destiny," which threatened to replace the struggle for literate self-government with a drive for conquest and self-aggrandizement. His sentence, "We have all heard of Young America," refers to a vague but significant current of opinion that had from time to time favored Stephen Douglas and the rapid expansion of American territory. Although Young America's political influence as a focused point of view had dissipated after Douglas's failure to win the Democratic nomination in 1852, in 1859 the label still represented a strain of ambitious idealism in the American electorate. As M. E. Curti has observed, "Young America, as a slogan, meant something long after the movement, as such, was dead—its influence was registered in the national self-consciousness" as a desire to expand American democracy, whether by encouraging revolution abroad or by annexation of new lands and promotion of trade.[44] The enthusiasms aroused by the Mexican War, the westward movement of pioneers, and the occasional call for annexation of Cuba all floated within Young America's nimbus, drawing attention away from the question of slavery's moral status and the issue of slavery in the territories. With humor and academic inquiry, Lincoln was able to argue indirectly for Republican principles against Young America and other rival views.

It is likely that in the late 1850s Lincoln's interest in such subjects was quickened by current events, including the news in 1857 that Justin Morrill, a Whig-Republican in the House of Representatives, had introduced legislation to found a system of land-grant colleges devoted to the agricultural and mechanical arts and "not excluding" the liberal arts, which included the study of language and hence the means of propagating literacy—a key theme in the discoveries lecture.[45] The proposal was an adaptation of a favorite Whig notion that the maintenance of liberty depended most of all upon an educated citizenry. It was also a plan that engaged the Democrats over the crucial issue of the extent of the federal role in the states and the emerging territories. As a means of expanding liberal learning as well as the mechanical arts in the new lands, it was a symbolic precursor to Republican initiatives to expand the range of free farmers responsibly, while simultaneously limiting the range of slavery. (President Buchanan was to veto the bill in 1859, and President Lincoln was to sign it into law, with modifications, in 1862.)[46]

In the context of the public lecture circuit, the discoveries lecture was also a literary and rhetorical response to the sweeping historical surveys that the historian George Bancroft, the abolitionist Wendell Phillips, and others were delivering in lecture form during the 1850s.[47] It is likely that Lincoln had Bancroft and Phillips particularly in mind. He told Whitney that he intended to write a lecture on a subject similar to Bancroft's, and he could hardly have avoided responding to Phillips's lecture on inventions, which for many years had been the most popular presentation on the northern lecture circuit.

A sympathetic summary of Lincoln's ambitious plan comes down to us from Henry C. Whitney, who heard Lincoln describe it while they rode the circuit in 1855: "[H]is purpose was to analyze invention and discoveries— 'to get at the bottom of things'; and to show when, where, how, and why such things were invented or discovered; and, so far as possible, to find where the first mention is made of some of the common things. The Bible, he said, he found to be the richest store-house for such knowledge."[48] This description of Lincoln's method of preparation is consistent with Whitney's account of Lincoln's habit of focused, thorough analysis: "He had the faculty of patient and continuous reflection in a wonderful degree; he held a subject in the focus of his mental vision with the grip of a vise. He would pursue a complicated problem through its various sinuosities, nor would he release it till he understood it in all its parts. He never had a superior in this nation in resolving a complex subject into its simple elements."[49] When Whitney read to him George Bancroft's lecture on the progress of man (titled "The Necessity, the Reality, and the Promise of the Progress of the Human Race"),[50] Lincoln informed him "that he had for some time been contemplating the writing of a lecture on *man*." Lincoln "proposed to review man from his earliest primeval state to his present high development, and he detailed at length the views and opinions he designed to incorporate in his lecture."[51] Herndon recalls that Lincoln "was surprised to find his investigations in that direction so interesting and instructive to himself."[52]

Lincoln's interest in Bancroft's lecture, which had been delivered before the New York Historical Society in 1854, brought him into contact with an ambitious attempt to define human nature according to the supposed inevitability of human progress and "the sovereignty of the common people's intelligence."[53] Bancroft contended that by "the necessity of the case" history moves "always toward something better." In this Americanization of Hegel's grand optimism, "[e]ach successive generation is wiser than its predecessor" thanks to the progress of "the totality of contemporary intelligence."[54] Class interests may temporarily block man's progress toward truth, but Providence reconciles imperfect strivings with "the perfect idea" in the "drama" of history.[55]

Bancroft's powerful optimism, for all its attractions, ran counter to Lincoln's worries about territorial expansion that paid no attention to the issue of slavery. It assumed that the movement toward personal independence and freedom was unstoppable and that Christianity would provide the impetus for the progressive emancipation of slaves and women. Literacy and publication would play their roles: the modern press would be "the controlling agency in renovating civilization."[56] Science would clarify human perceptions "each successive year," and the general progress of truth would even renovate theology: the old conundrums of religion would be dispelled. Somehow, religion would be saved by science. So would government. The "science of government" would promote freedom by confronting the problem of "private selfishness" and showing that "it is a common instinct that man is responsible for man."

Lincoln would have encountered Bancroft's optimism about the time he had publicly concluded that Douglas's 1854 Kansas-Nebraska Act was an irruption of ambition that endangered the cause of self-government. Bancroft looked the other way. A "better science of distribution," he argued, will bring "social equality."[57] The truth, once it is known in this "new era in the history of the race," will free mankind from superstition and pride.[58] Professions of sincere truthfulness will dissolve the specter of civil war. "Equality and freedom" must come, and not by violence. The gradual progress of "internal activity" will make the change. The movement will be slow, but certain and inevitable. The transcendental truth of things will be borne out of its own accord: "The subtle and irresistible movement of mind, silently but thoroughly correcting opinion and changing society, brings liberty both to the soul and to the world. All the despotisms on earth cannot stay its coming."[59] Henry Ward Beecher's lecture on "man and his institutions," published in 1856, made a somewhat similar case for the power of genius over material limits and for the progress of history;[60] but Bancroft is far more adamant about the force of the aspiring mind, which he consistently describes in terms of the universalizing power of science and religion. Neither political persuasion nor "external philosophy" is for him the real power in the world. The "irresistible . . . movement of mind" is. Political parties and the problem of mastering individual ambition, choice, and restraint recede into history. Somehow the "imperishable groundwork of universal freedom" will persist and prevail thanks to that force, which carries forth "the principles of justice and philosophy" to build a better society.[61]

The upshot of this philosophy, which sometimes rings with Emersonian sentiments, is hardly Emersonian in its practical application. The inevitable expansion of freedom requires aggressive political expansion: "The area of our land has been so extended that a similar increase, twice repeated, would carry THE STARS AND STRIPES to the polar ice and to the isthmus."[62] The triumph of the liberated mind manifests itself in America's unstoppable enlargement of its terrestrial domain. The unreflective acquisition of new territory—for Lincoln, one of the most troubling causes of the impending crisis—is for Bancroft yet more evidence of America's self-realization.

Bancroft's idea of progress found its most famous competitor in Wendell Phillips's lecture on the lost arts, what has been called "the most popular and the most charming lecture ever delivered from an American platform."[63] Phillips's view was more pessimistic, though he too believed that progress was inevitable. The difference between the two notions of progress rested in each man's treatment of slavery. For Bancroft, slavery was an obsolete, benighted institution that had no place—and merited no mention—in his optimistic predictions. Phillips assumed that the destruction of slavery was inevitable, but that abolition—meaning the confrontation and defeat of the Slave Power, or the radical separation from it—was necessary to bring that destruction about.

It is difficult to imagine that Lincoln would not have been familiar with Phillips's famous and subtle treatment of these issues in his well-known lecture. He certainly would have known Phillips's explicit arguments in favor of abolition in his more controversial speeches, which make it more likely that one would detect the antislavery strains in the popular presentation. There was a good chance he was aware that the speech had earned the abolitionist and his cause an extraordinary sum of money.[64] Phillips had presented the lecture on the lost arts thousands of times since 1838, sometimes pairing it with an abolitionist speech he delivered on an adjacent night.[65] Although Phillips retained control of the lecture by keeping it out of publication for over twenty years, its ubiquity on the lecture circuit ensured that his performances were familiar all over the North.

Paired with Bancroft's lecture, Phillips's discussion of the lost arts provided a remarkable foil for Lincoln's words on discoveries and inventions. Lincoln's lecture established itself between the opposing extremes mapped out by these prominent predecessors. Whereas Bancroft hyperbolically praised Americans' highest aspirations, Phillips disparaged their materialistic self-centeredness. Phillips did not doubt that enlightenment would prevail; but he devoted his introduction to humbling that pride so that the real cause of progress (the inventions created by the common people though the ages) could be honored and rewarded. "The most objectionable feature of our national character," he argued, is "self-conceit,—an undue appreciation of ourselves, an exaggerated estimate of our achievements, of our inventions, of our contributions to popular comfort, and of our place, in fact, in the great procession of the ages. We seem to imagine, that whether knowledge will die with us, or not, it certainly began with us. We have a pitying estimate, a tender pity, for the narrowness, ignorance, and darkness of bygone ages. We seem to ourselves not only to monopolize, but to have begun, the era of light. In other words, we are all running over with a fourth-day-of-July spirit of self-content."[66] Phillips implicitly compares Americans' self-conceit with the pride of kings and priests who in earlier ages oppressed the true inventors, many of them slaves, by stealing their works and suppressing their ingenuity, thereby dooming their civilizations to decay. He does not entirely dismiss American ingenuity or its capacity to respond to his critique; but his catalog of fascinating, mysterious technologies, which must have contained the lecture's most popular passages, is full of illustrations of wondrous arts now lost to oppressive pride.

Phillips titillates his audience with tales of secret arts and near-magical accomplishments no longer understood. We hear of clothing that seemed invisible, sculpture so small one needed a magnifying glass to see it, and exquisite arts of glassmaking lost to the modern world. Exaggeration takes on the respectability of scientific utterance: "The railroad dates back to Egypt," we hear, since in that land of pharaohs and slaves there were those who experimented with steam and made paintings of what looks like railroad equipment.[67] Phillips uses an impressive and vague statistic to humble and fascinate modern Americans' love of innovation: "[O]f the hundreds of things we know, I can show you ninety-nine of them which have been anticipated."[68]

Despite his criticism of American pride, Phillips assumes that American civilization is the most likely place for the revival of such arts, since the advancement of American civilization is "the divine will." But Bancroft's optimism is not a guide. Progress will come but not in the way one would think. America must honor a principle that is distinct from the oppressive suppositions of dead and dying civilizations—a principle that "should govern every land. . . . [I]t is one [principle] which this nation needs to practise this day. It is the human property: it is the divine will that any man has the right to know any thing which he knows will be serviceable to himself and to his fellow-man, and that will make art immortal if God means that it shall last."[69] Access to the knowledge of discovery and invention is a right that law and government must protect. The contingencies and vagaries of the history of discovery and invention are the result of unjust rulers' interference with that right: the "right to know any thing."

Beneath this argument seems to be the assumption that literacy is all-important, particularly for those now forbidden to learn the art of reading, and who therefore have no access to the records of discovery and invention throughout the history of the world. In order to honor a universal "right to know," it would seem that nothing short of a technological and social revolution would be necessary. Phillips indirectly sustains the possibility of violence if that principle is denied. Because God will enforce the human being's right to know the arts he needs, all persons will be justified in discovering and inventing what will be useful to themselves, as well as to others. Nothing should stand in their way. Ominously praising the ruthless conqueror Cambyses, who as champion of the common man "came down from Persia, and by his genius and intellect opened the gates of knowledge, thundering across Egypt," Phillips implicitly compares the Persian conqueror's triumph with a northern abolitionist campaign to bring knowledge, including the technology of revolution, to the slaves of the American South.[70] Genius makes good weapons for slaying slave masters: amid his entertaining examples, Phillips praises the inventive powers of "the irrepressible negro," who is "coming up in science as in politics" by making razors sharper than those of the Europeans.[71]

* * *

Lincoln's Lecture on Discoveries and Inventions deftly adapts and deflects lines of argument in the speeches of Bancroft and Phillips. The result is a competing conception of history, human nature, and political institutions. One is struck immediately by the lecture's heavy reliance on illustrations from the Bible, by its humor, and by its synthesis of Bancroft's optimism and Phillips's mockery of American pretensions. In place of Bancroft's aggressive transcendentalism and Phillips's thinly veiled abolitionism, Lincoln reintroduces and adapts old Whig ideas about the development of individuals and institutions by means of enlightened legislation and personal effort. Whiggish Republican concerns about territorial expansion and universal moral reform take on new dimensions in his discussion of innovation and the foundations of American liberty. The history of language, print, and literacy unifies these ideas and directs them toward a higher understanding of the connection between literacy and self-government.

Abstaining almost completely from mentioning slavery by name, Lincoln redefines slavery as a combination of institutional and psychological conditions mitigating against discovery and invention—conditions such as the lack of patent laws and the predominance of the illiterate mind's "false and under estimate of itself," which can make the achievement of literacy seem so remote as to be virtually impossible. Self-interest is another important factor. Without the incentive of a reward for inventing something others can copy and use, innovative genius languishes because it is subject to the theft of its labors (3.362-363). Without access to the fruits of discovery and invention, or even amid such benefits but without an adequate sense of what the history of discovery and invention means for the liberation and self-government of human beings, the illiterate person is in danger of remaining enslaved to ignorance and the conviction that lettered persons are his permanent masters.

The history of discoveries and inventions reveals what Lincoln calls human and political "susceptibilities" as well as the virtues of genius and cooperation (2.437). His view in this sense resembles David Hume's much more than Bancroft's or Phillips's, though we have no direct evidence that he read the philosopher's most relevant essay, "Of the Rise of Progress of the Arts and Sciences." Hume drew attention to the delicacy of true progress in all the arts and sciences because progress depended on "free government" based on the security of laws that encourage and sustain productive "emulation." Although scientific accomplishments that were "profitable to every mortal" were not easily lost, they would eventually disappear if the laws that cultivated the spirit of emulation were neglected. Law and the spirit of emulation needed one another: if the law failed, the spirit that invented it would decline. The will to invent had developed the laws over time; but it could not by itself sustain the progress of the arts and sciences, or even itself, without free institutions and enlightened laws that the progress of discovery and other inventors had bequeathed to later generations for safekeeping. Like Lincoln, Hume noted the importance of an additional factor that the human will alone could not produce: "fresh soil." The great benefit of new lands for renewing the spirit of invention had to do with good fortune: they had to exist. The will to explore and, if necessary, to conquer might not be enough if there was no new land. But even with new land an unexamined faith in the force of history, the perfectibility of human nature, or the unaided power of the laws might not be sufficient.[72]

Developing these and other ideas, Lincoln departed from Bancroft and Phillips by arguing from accessible evidence, particularly evidence he drew from the Bible and the history of particular discoveries and inventions known to his audience. In this approach he also distanced himself from the old charges that he was an infidel, and he provided the partisan *Bloomington Pantagraph* with a good lead. Lincoln's "great research and . . . careful study of the Bible," the newspaper reported, was evidence that "the lawyer is not by any means unfamiliar with the Booke of the Great Law-Giver."[73] Lincoln was conforming to the principle for successful lecturing that J. G. Holland was to detect and summarize some years later: the pubic lecturer should primarily select and interpret facts for an audience that is generally familiar with those facts, not focus his efforts on introducing new ones.[74] Thus Lincoln drew from the most widely known and respected record of human achievement, which among stories of transgression and dependence on God made available a history of inventions and discoveries that he could use to present his complex theme with simple force.

Given the complexity and political force of the lectures by Lincoln's two intellectual rivals, it is not hard to imagine Herndon's recoil at the almost childish simplicity of his partner's reliance on biblical evidence. But Lincoln's language is devoted to the complex idea that discoveries and inventions depend on human beings' origins and "nature," their moral and physical qualities as well as their intellectual beings, and the additional idea that progress in discovery and invention depends on the enlightened action of flawed human beings who are themselves dependent upon the accomplishments of their predecessors, good fortune, and perhaps even divine gifts. Human beings discover and invent, or fail to do so, as a result of their choices and dispositions with regard to these factors. Beginning with the Genesis story, Lincoln is also able to suggest that even Adam and Eve, the first discoverers and inventors, were not self-sufficient—that much like later inventors they depended upon their own nature, one another, and a legacy of creation they could claim only cautiously as their own. The first lines of the 1858 fragment begin to set out these ideas with a simplicity that is authoritative yet full of speculative possibilities:

> All creation is a mine, and every man, a miner.
>
> The whole earth, and all *within* it, *upon* it, and *round about* it, including *himself,* in his physical, moral, and intellectual nature, and his susceptibilities, are the infinitely various "leads" from which, man, from the first, was to dig out his destiny.
>
> In the beginning, the mine was unopened, and the miner stood *naked,* and *knowledgeless,* upon it. (2.437)

Lincoln's Bible-reading audience would have detected in these lines much of the direction of his thought. "Knowledgeless," Adam and Even were given the earth; but they did not explore the mine until they gained knowledge that had—to say the least—mixed consequences. When they did discover with their new knowledge what had previously been hidden from them, their first discovery was of their nakedness. Then followed, Lincoln reminds his audience, the first invention: clothing, "the one thing," Lincoln says, for which nearly half of the toil and care of the human race has ever since been expended" (2.437–438). On the one hand, the summary of the story in Genesis is selective and optimistic. Adam and Eve sat down (as Lincoln elaborates the event in the 1859 fragment) to make clothing, thereby bringing about the first world's fair:

> [T]he very first invention was a joint operation, Eve having shared with Adam in the getting up of the apron. And, indeed, judging from the fact that sewing has come down to our times as "woman's work" it is very probable she took the leading part; he, perhaps, doing no more than to stand by and thread the needle. That proceeding may be reckoned as the mother of all "Sewing societies"; and the first and most perfect "world's fair" all inventions and all inventors then in the world, being on the spot. (3.360)

The omitted information, which Lincoln did not have to summarize because everyone knew it, he includes by way of allusion: it was the Fall that set the parents of humankind to work on what still takes up, he notes, half its working hours. Their nakedness is an inconvenience and discomfort they must work to remedy; but it is also a condition they recognize in shame because of their deeper inadequacies. Invention and joint efforts are not in themselves a guarantee of the progress of discovery and invention. The cooperation that helped Adam and Eve invent the first clothing was not entirely unlike the joint effort that led to their fall. Lincoln later jokes that the inventive genius, strengthened by the assistance of others, was later responsible for inventing "negroes, or, of the present mode of using them [i.e., slavery]" (3.362).

It is worth noting how many of Lincoln's examples in the first fragment are connected with error, misfortune, and divine favor. We hear of the sons' covering of the drunken Noah (the invention of other forms of clothing), Abraham's use of thread (evidence that spinning originated during the captivity in Egypt), the appearance of chariots under Pharaoh's command (just before their destruction as the Jews' escaped across the Red Sea), the creation of the Ark (what Lincoln calls a "miraculous" instance outside the history of human inventions), and Job's mention of the "weaver's shuttle" (evidence that weaving had been invented by the time the book of Job, "a very old book," was written). An audience generally familiar with the Bible would have remembered Job's suffering. Readers might have recalled the full, despairing phrase in Job 7.6 to which Lincoln alludes: "My life runs swifter than a weaver's shuttle . . . without hope" (2.438–442). The allusive force of the entire sequence engages the literate audience's understanding of both interpretations, the comic and the tragic, without Lincoln's needing to explicate the well-known pattern of transgression, suffering, and divine intervention that parallels his accounts of humankind's creation of helpful innovations.

The larger point Lincoln is gradually bringing into view is the "strange" slowness of the process of discovery and invention. The first appearance of thread, in the story of Abraham, takes place halfway through the biblical history of the world and is marked in a passage Lincoln cites but does not quote (Genesis 14.23) in which Abraham explicitly refuses to take "a thread or a shoelachet" in exchange for the persons he has just freed from captivity (2.438). Wind power remains unharnessed on land, despite its long employment on water (2.441). Steam power, though it was observed ages past, did not come into use until the modern era (2.442). And agriculture, the oldest labor of humankind, "stands at the head of all branches of human industry" yet "has derived less direct advantage from Discovery and Invention, than almost any other " (2.440).

Given that, as Lincoln notes, labor "was imposed on the race, as a *penalty* —a *curse,*" the lack of progress in the labor of agriculture is a powerful reminder of the Fall. Innovation, he is arguing, is possible and desirable, but ought not to proceed in ignorance of the conditions that have made discovery and invention difficult over the ages. When Lincoln turns to the contemporary scene, he praises American innovation in a tone of humorous admonishment:

> We have all heard of Young America. He is the most *current* youth of the age. Some think him conceited, and arrogant; but has he not reason to entertain a rather extensive opinion of himself? Is he not the inventor and owner of the *present,* the sole hope of the *future?* Men, and things, everywhere, are ministering unto him. (3.356)

The problem is that Young America "owns a large part of the world, by right of possessing it; and all the rest by right of *wanting* it, and *intending* to have it" (3.357). Territorial expansion and the progress of invention flow together under the power of ambition, which is capable of doing great wrong as well as good things.

When Bancroft listed the exotic goods that Americans enjoy from all over the world, he connected their prosperity with the virtues of the American republic. He assumed that the American acquisition of territory would enlighten the world.[75] A distortion or frustration of that impulse seemed out of the question. Lincoln's pointed humor sets out a far more complex and guarded view of the future. Young America is justly proud, but that pride indicates that he is a bit of a dandy, susceptible to his baser passions: "The whale of the Pacific furnishes his candle-light; he has a diamond-ring from Brazil; a gold-watch from California, and a spanish cigar from Havanna" (3.357).

More than a show of prosperity, Young America's accoutrements are signs of an ambition to grasp and control that might easily exceed the world's capacity to supply: "As Plato had for the immortality of the soul, so Young America has 'a pleasing hope—a fond desire—a longing after' ter[r]itory. He has a great passion—a perfect rage—for the '*new*'; particularly new men for office, and the new earth mentioned in the revelations, in which, being no more sea, there must be about three times as much land as in the present." Lincoln's phrasing ensured that the word *territory* thudded in the scholars' ears, for the quotation is from Joseph Addison's play *Cato,* in which the line reads "longing after *immortality.*"[76] In his identification of Young America's ambition for land and wealth with Cato's speech contemplating suicide and immortality, Lincoln turns the force of the solemn reference outward. The excess of American overreaching, in contrast to the courage of the Roman hero who died defying Julius Caesar, is his point.

By touching on a crucial moment in Cato's resonant history, Lincoln's joking allusion plants the idea that there is a heroic alternative to the tyrannical ambition for territory. Addison's play, held in high esteem by George Washington and performed at Valley Forge, depicts a heroic resistance to an imperial, Caesar-like ambition that sought to destroy republican government. In defeat, Cato was the paradigmatic preserver of Roman virtues whose example helped stimulate the political invention of America. Lincoln's struggle with Douglas and the lure of "popular sovereignty" would have made the allusion all the more appropriate: Addison had resuscitated those virtues in writing and print, and Washington enacted them with the help of Addison's text. Cato's precedent, brought by these means into modern America, would have offered powerful confirmation of the role of writing and print in Lincoln's theory of discovery and invention.

Lincoln's allusion to Revelations 21.1–2 expands upon his suggestion that Young America's territorial expectations are in danger of becoming tyrannical. His point is that America's passion for "the new earth mentioned in the revelations" is a hunger for more land than the earth can supply—at least until the Day of Judgment dries up the seas. Even with "three times as much land as the present," Young America will have barely enough land to satisfy its ambition. Its excessive territorial ambitions distort its highmindedness with acquisitive appetite: "[Young America] is a great friend of humanity, and his desire for the land is not selfish, but merely an impulse to extend the area of freedom. He is very anxious to fight for the liberation of enslaved nations and colonies, provided, always, they *have* land, and have *not* any liking for his interference." Expansion in the name of freedom is not necessarily a bad thing; but when it is exercised to liberate others who "have *not* any liking for his interference" (in Mexico, for example, or Cuba), the appetite for land overrules the liberating impulse. Lincoln had argued elsewhere that such enthusiasms paradoxically dimmed interest in condemning slavery, not just in the slave states but in the territories.[77] Without criticizing the aspiration to move west, he questions Young America's lack of interest in those who "have no land, and would be glad of help from any quarter" to get it. The heedless liberators ignore the landless as though they were slaves: they "can afford to wait a few hundred years longer" (3.357).

Here Lincoln's indirect methods of making his point remind us of Phillips's roundabout argument for abolition. But as we move to the lecture's core, Lincoln shows that he is primarily interested in the history of language, communication, and literacy, which he says make possible the emancipation of all human beings. Instead of developing Phillips's idea that superior arts have been lost to oppression, and that inventions will prosper in an era in which slaves are emancipated, Lincoln examines those currently prospering arts of literacy that are the greatest of all inventions, and suggests that the emancipation of all mankind comes gradually—by means of insight, good fortune, the development of free institutions, and the struggle to overcome the belief that literacy is beyond one's reach. The productive habits, inner resources, and political heritage of the inventor make the difference. First there must be "a habit of observation," something Lincoln says is "no doubt" acquired from previous generations who passed the art of mining the world on to their successors (3.358). Next there must be a trained capacity for "reflection," which connects that habit to an application the inventor understands as the fulfillment of a need long neglected. The inventor detects a pattern of action in what has been closely observed, and then considers the way in which that principle might be used to assist "hard laboring" men. Finally comes experimentation or "trial," as Lincoln calls it, suggesting an analogy between all three phases of mechanical invention and the lawyer's work, in which the inventor discovers and applies facts and principles to cases for the discovery of truth. Both reflection and trial are, in the early history of invention, extraordinary operations undertaken by rare individuals who somehow prevail over a poverty of expectations and social resources. Their gradually accruing successes, when those successes are not lost to the indifference that marks almost all the ages of history, contributes to the impressive yet delicate articulation of human inventive powers in the current era, when the inventors become "old fogies" hardly appreciated by their beneficiaries.

As a political movement within the Democratic Party, Young America was indeed aligned against the "old fogies" of the Democratic establishment, with whom Lincoln humorously aligns himself.[78] The scope of Lincoln's argument is clearly broader than a pronouncement on controversy within the rival party; he identifies himself with the most out-of-date yet canonical model of the discoverer and inventor: Adam himself, "the first of old fogies." Countering Young America's disdain for its predecessors, he bases his argument on an exemplar who is too simple to be taken seriously as a type for the modern American, yet too venerable and too strangely familiar to the

Adamic American pioneer to be dismissed. Lincoln presents him as an apparently sorry yet formidable type: the uneducated backwoodsman trying to make his way:

> If the said Young American really is, as he claims to be, the owner of all present, it must be admitted that he has considerable advantage of Old Fogy. Take, for instance, the first of all fogies, father Adam. There he stood, a very perfect physical man, as poets and painters inform us; but he must have been very ignorant, and simple in his habits. He had no sufficient time to learn much by observation; and he had no near neighbors to teach him anything. . . . [T]he most that can be said is, that *according to his chance* he may have been quite as much of a man as his very self-complaisant descendant. Little as was what he knew, let the Youngster discard all he has learned from others, and then show, if he can, any advantage on his side. In the way of *land,* and *live stock,* Adam was quite in the ascendant. He had dominion over all the earth, and all the living things upon, and round about it. (3.357–358)

Examined in the light of truth, the rube outshines the dandy. Here Phillips's praise of the genius of the oppressed has been displaced by Lincoln's problematic picture of the original human ruler of the earth, who despite (or because of) his initial awkwardness—and, indeed, his profound error—becomes and remains an exemplary parent of the human race.

As Lincoln's greatest of all examples of the inventor, Adam does not threaten. He is "very ignorant," without the fancy geographical and scientific knowledge of Young America. But he is also the first and greatest owner of territories and livestock, and the beneficiary of gifts from his Maker that are so magnificent they must dwarf those that later generations have tried to gain by conquest. If Young Americans should seek to be Adam's equals, they would have to take the ludicrous course of conquering the entire world, proving their inferiority all the more: "The land has been sadly divided out since; but never fret, Young American will *re-annex* it" (3.358). Unlike Phillips's image of the common man as an obscure, heroic, secretive slave whose mastery of invention humbles, fascinates, and threatens selfish oppressors, Lincoln's Adam represents the flawed and admirable common man of all ages, whose shortcomings and strengths question and instruct Young America's modern self-satisfaction.[79]

Lincoln's Adam is a particularly intricate exemplar of the "habit of observation and reflection" that he claims is crucial to technological progress. The origin of that habit is ancient, apparently a mystery. We cannot be certain that the first man invented it, though it would seem he needed the habit of observation in order to invent. The modern man who invented steam power learned observation from "old fogies," perhaps going back to Adam. Yet Adam's first recorded invention, "*the fig-leaf apron,*" apparently did not result from a habit of observation, since "as might be expected he seems not to have been a very observing man at first; for it appears he went about naked a considerable length of time, before he even noticed that *obvious* fact" (3.358–359). How was this possible? Lincoln's account humorously skirts (and so acknowledges) the answer: the habit of observation somehow derived from Adam's shame over his transgression and the labor that came to him as a result.

Compactly and suggestively, the lecture cautions and encourages its audience to remember that Adam in his fallen state saw his nakedness and, out of that realization, which derived partly from his shame and partly from his aboriginal powers, saw his habit of observation develop. He cooperated with Eve, and their joint effort to repair their fallen condition (as Lincoln reminds his listeners) led to the invention of clothing, the first technological innovation,[80] and the first "world's fair." Lincoln jokes at Adam's expense: "[H]e, perhaps, [did] nothing more than to stand by and thread the needle." But the gist of the argument is more serious (3.360). In the Milwaukee Address, which Lincoln delivered in the fall of 1859, we learn that fairs are civilizing institutions of great moment—seedbeds of invention because they draw isolated laborers together peacefully to compare their ideas and innovations. Such avid cooperation magnifies the individual's inventive powers while demonstrating his dependence upon the assistance of others. In the discoveries lecture, Lincoln tries to explain how it draws out the individual's "impulse" to express aspirations and needs:

> The inclination to exchange thoughts with one another is probably an original impulse of our nature. If I be in pain I wish to let you know it, and to ask your sympathy and assistance; and my pleasurable emotions also, I wish to communicate to, and share with you. (3.359)

> What one observes, and would himself infer nothing from, he tells to another, and that other at once sees a valuable hint in it. A result is thus reached which neither *alone* would have arrived at. (3.360)

Thus language, Lincoln argues, is the most prominent *"instrumentality"* by which communication takes place. Whether it is an invention or a gift, it is now an inherited and manipulable facility of such expressive power and complexity that it wonderfully articulates the meticulous generosity of a deity. Even as a human invention, language depends on "the superior adaptation" of the tongue and the "organs of speech" to the ends of articulate speech—a correspondence for which neither Adam nor his descendants can take credit. The evidence of design in this process is so impressive that it proves that speech, if it was not a divine gift, had to be the first of all human inventions:

> [W]hether Divine gift, or invention, it is still plain that if a mode of communication had been left to invention, *speech* must have been the first, from the superior adaptation to the end, of the organs of speech, over every other means within the whole range of nature. (3.359)

As the world's most articulate organ, the tongue is a lowly thing. But since its facilitation of speech is unmatched by any relation of means to ends in all of nature, the tongue's humble virtues are "absolutely wonderful."[81] Compared on the basis of instrumentality—on its adaptation to its end—writing is relatively cumbersome and inconvenient, dependent upon other inventions. By contrast, "one always has his tongue with him, and the breath of his life is the ever-ready material with which it works." Whereas writing sets down mere signs, the tongue ingeniously molds the gift of life into 283 "distinct sounds or syllables" at a speed of seven syllables per second (3.359).

This mixture of invention with gift, and gift with invention, disperses the tendency to attribute the power and fruits of invention to human ingenuity; yet it does so without attributing invention wholly to chance or the will of God. The same pattern is evident in music and humor, which the newspaper account claims were two of Lincoln's topics in his Bloomington performance. Speaking extemporaneously or from additional pages of draft lost to us, Lincoln apparently spoke about music as though it resembled "flowers . . . a gift of pure benevolence." He "paid a feeling tribute" to "plaintive songs," mentioning "the triumphal exultation" of "Miriam"—possibly the well-known "Magnificat" of Luke 1.46–55 in which Mary praises God after hearing she would bear the Christ child.[82] The lecture seems to have provided a density of examples in which invention and gift, language and the applications of language, are intertwined. In the encyclopedia that Herndon claimed was Lincoln's primary source, the article on "voice" treats language in terms of musical tones, which are formed and ornamented by man's inherited vocal apparatus in cooperation with his expressive purpose: "[T]he tones . . . convey the ideas and emotions of rational man, and furnish his noblest music"[83] When Lincoln brought up the topic of laughter (a curious subject for a lecture on invention yet appropriate to Lincoln's conception of invention as a fusion of gift and ingenuity), he is said to have "treated of and illustrated" laughter "in his own inimitable way," exercising his wit by drawing from his proverbial trove of funny stories.[84]

* * *

Revising Bancroft's view of history as well as Phillips's, Lincoln argues that the real history of invention is full of false starts, gaps, near miracles, and contingencies. He sets out the rarity of the inventive temperament, the gradual and by no means inevitable development of institutions that encourage and protect that temperament's accomplishments, and the certainty that humble origins can manifest inventive powers just as they display the inventor's dependence upon others. Thus even speech, despite its distinction as the "indispensable" and first of inventions, needs another invention (writing) and the favorable developments of history to perpetuate itself beyond the hearing of its immediate audience. And the power of invention is in some ways accessible to all who can read.

Progress is evident but is not clearly the rule. In comparison with speech, writing is much more artificial, yet "[s]peech alone, valuable as it ever has been, and is, has not advanced the condition of the world much." It is "abundantly evident," that societies without writing's "considerable additional means of communicating thoughts" are in a "degraded condition" (3.360). Whether or not he directly consulted the popular Hugh Blair's *Lectures on Rhetoric and Belles Lettres,* Lincoln would have found in the sixth lecture a parallel set of arguments about writing's paradoxical relation to speech: "Speech without Writing, would have been very inadequate for the instruction of mankind; yet we must not forget to observe, that spoken Language has a great superiority over written Language, in point of energy or force. The voice of the living Speaker, makes an impression on the mind, much stronger than can be made by the perusal of any Writing."[85] Speech, like the original invention, comes first, but it cannot realize itself unless it joins with writing. What Lincoln had said earlier about Adam's dependence on

Eve and the nimbleness of the tongue is duplicated in speech's dependence on writing. Writing, so understood, becomes the inferior yet—in point of effect—the superior embodiment of speech: its transliteration and actualization.

The perpetuation of the invention of writing is itself reliant on other inventions and other circumstances conducive to innovation. Writing is crucial to civilized progress: Lincoln calls it the "greatest help, to all other inventions." But the inventors of writing "were very old fogies" whose connections with the present era are as delicate as they are continuous: "[W]e may readily suppose that the idea was conceived, and lost, and reproduced, and dropped, and taken up again and again." The intermittent history of writing raises a profound doubt about Young America's self-sufficiency: "Take [writing] from us, and the Bible, all history, all science, all government, all commerce, and nearly all social intercourse go with it" (3.361). Extraordinary skill, native virtue, and good fortune are not enough to recover it with reliable speed: "Suppose the art, with all conception of it, were this day lost to the world, how long, think you, would it be, before even Young America could get up a letter A. with any adequate notion of using it to advantage?" (3.360).

We can understand this half-humorous argument better in the light of an old encyclopedia's article on writing, the text that Herndon reports Lincoln mined for his lecture. The *Encyclopedia Americana,* published in 1831, treats the idea of writing in terms that generally harmonize with Lincoln's approach: "The art of writing, especially when reduced to simply phonetic alphabets like ours, has, perhaps, done more than any other invention for the improvement of the human race. . . . It has been the most efficient means of raising mankind from barbarism to civilization. Without its aid the experience of each generation would have been almost entirely lost to succeeding ages, and only a faint glimmer of truth could have been discerned through the mists of tradition."[86] Herndon had ridiculed Lincoln's lecturing career in part because his friend used such a mundane source for the discoveries lecture.[87] But we see in this comparison of texts how Lincoln refocuses and elaborates the encyclopedia's learning so that it contributes to his explanation of the interdependence of new inventions, previous innovations, genius, the institutions of self-government, and the habit of observation. In the discoveries lecture, writing is the supreme invention, but its dependence on other inventions and other sources of support make its supremacy an indica-

tor of the importance of self-government, a sense of humility, and other factors separate from as well as conducive to the individual's inventive spirit.

Perhaps the most revealing example of Lincoln's revisionary approach is
his treatment of the commonplaces clustered in the *Encyclopedia Americana*'s article called "Invention." Like Lincoln, the encyclopedia asserts that
the history of discovery and inventions is worth studying because it is a bell-
wether of the rise and fall of civilizations: it exhibits "the stages of progress
and decline of human activity, and the great variety of motives which have ac-
tivated different ages." But the encyclopedia does not discuss two of Lincoln's most important topics: the habit of observation and technical and
political innovations that encourage and protect it. Nor does it link, in its
brevity, one set of inventions to another:

> Inventions owe their origins, as discoveries do, either to chance, to some
> happy idea suddenly striking the mind, or to patient reflection and experi-
> ment. . . . As man, in modern times, is always inclined to consider that which
> is nearest him the most important, he generally considers the inventions of
> his age as far surpassing those of other times; but the study of history teaches
> us more modesty. The invention of the screw, of the wheel, of the rudder, of
> the double pulley, may be compared with any modern inventions in mech-
> anical science, and could not, moreover, have been struck off at once by
> chance.[88]

Here, as in Phillips's lecture, the inventions stand primarily as instances of
ingenuity—not, as Lincoln renders them, as the result of interactions between a host of factors that include good fortune or grace. The "habit of observation," which Lincoln considers to be of such importance, is not a subject that the encyclopedic writer, or Phillips, considers of interest. For them
the inventive spirit is a given; their concern is that it be given its due. In Lincoln's lecture, as we have seen, it is one of the distinguishing attributes of an
inventive being. Why, he asks, did "yankees" discover gold with such alacrity
in California, which had been inhabited by others "for centuries" (3.358)?
Their habit of observation was fostered and protected by literacy and free institutions as well as by their aspiration to invent.

Expanding this pattern of argument, Lincoln repeatedly distinguishes between the *origins* of literacy and the inventions that have been integral to its
spread, while making a point of emphasizing their need for one another, and
drawing attention to some of the problems that arise from that interdepend-

ence. Printing, the discovery of America, and the patent laws are successive inventions that all have provided "great efficiency in facilitating . . . other inventions." But if printing is "but the other half—and in real utility, the *better* half—of writing," the educational system it fosters is not enough to establish literacy. Yet another innovation is necessary, one that human effort cannot command into being. A new land—which like a gift can only be discovered, not invented—makes the difference: "It is, in this connection, a curious fact that a new country is most favorable—almost necessary—to the immancipation of thought, and the consequent advancement of civilization and the arts" (3.363). At each level of accomplishment, the inventor and his circumstances, no matter how effective their interaction might seem, rely on forms of ingenuity and external support that further ennoble and qualify the inventor's accomplishments.

Lincoln is being consistent, then, when he adds that even the discovery of a new country is not enough. The lines of causation move up and down the ladder of determining factors. Those persons who find themselves in the New World need patent laws from an innovative country in the Old World so that America's inventive thinkers can have their ideas protected and so they can be rewarded for their work. In a stagnant old country (like China, in which "the dust of ages" stifles initiative), invention dies, despite the literacy of its inventors, without enlightened laws and access to new lands (3.363). The same might have happened in the New World if certain key inventions from the Old had not taken root or, conversely, if "the dust of ages" (read: slavery) had been allowed to spread indiscriminately and thereby corrupt the prospects of invention in America's territories.

Lincoln carefully describes the inspired solitude of the inventors who made phonetic writing and harnessed steam power, but he consistently connects the individual genius to a web of social bonds. He uses the word *genius* only once in his lecture, in his last sentence, and carefully downplays its role in the discovery of steam power: "But was this first inventor of the application of steam, wiser or more ingenious than those who had gone before him? Not at all. Had he not learned much of them [the old fogeys], he never would have succeeded—probably, never would have thought of making the attempt" (3.358). This argument is not only an answer to Bancroft and Phillips. It also seems to be a purposeful reversal of Edwin De Leon's famous 1845 lecture to Young America, in which he had taken a view of the inventor not unlike Phillips's: the inventor is a romantic genius, he said, one of those "uncouth, wayward, sullen men of study and reflection." De Leon insisted that "the greatest benefits conferred on society have ever come from the isolated thinker, not the busy actor; and solitude ever has proved the fostering nurse of great inventions and daring deeds."[89]

For Lincoln the success of discoveries and inventions is not only contingent on other things; it must pursue the Good if it is not to be defined by a will to power. He humorously reminds his audience that the great age of invention, not the unenlightened past, brought slavery—what he bitingly defines as "the invention of negroes, or, of the present mode of using them"—in 1434. The danger of misusing the power of invention is as great as the danger of misunderstanding the opportunities it presents: "The *capacity* to read," he argues, "could not be multiplied as fast as the *means* of reading," not only because there were not enough teachers and spelling books, but because "the great mass of men . . . were utterly unconscious, that their *conditions,* or their *minds* were capable of improvement" (3.362). This strange inhibition—not an external oppression—was until recently an almost universal "slavery of the mind," a condition that presumably still threatens those who seek to *become* literate, including (as Lincoln's terminology suggests) those who might eventually be freed from chattel slavery (3.363).

Even when the technology of literacy has been perfected, a conviction of one's own profound inferiority as an illiterate person impedes the growth of literacy. Throughout history, illiterate men have "looked upon the educated few as superior beings" (3.362). Literacy brings freedom; but, like invention, it depends on a "habit"—in this case, the "habit of freedom of thought." We come back to the legacy of the "old fogies," the discoverers of America, the makers of the patent laws, the cultivators of a habit of observation and the institutions that foster a disposition toward self-government. To achieve an emancipation of thought, one must discover that kind of freedom on one's own; but the habit of mind that makes that discovery likely and sustainable arises out of a host of interconnected emancipatory precedents, things beyond the aspiring slave's (or freedman's) personal control.

* * *

During the period in which he delivered his discoveries speech, Lincoln put these principles into effect by industriously preparing for the publication of his 1858 debates with Stephen Douglas. According to Don Fehrenbacher, he entered into negotiations for publication within a month of delivering the

Jacksonville address.[90] He had come to identify his own success in law and politics with the power of printed language to reach future ages—a major theme of his presentation.[91] His legacy would therefore be a fusion of his own ingenuity with those many interconnected and sometimes adventitious innovations he knew he depended upon for his political success. Exercising his faculty of speech, working from and augmenting his own and others' written texts, arranging for publication for a much wider audience, and drawing on the literate capacities of a people who had inherited the legacy of slavery, the Reformation, and the fortunate discovery of a new country, he sought to escape the temporal bonds of his electoral defeat by giving to future audiences a chance to understand the vulnerability as well as the virtue of the invention called America.

For a time, Lincoln would have a patent on these ideas as the work of his hand alone. If they proved to be true and useful political inventions, they would show, according to his general argument, that they were indeed the work of genius. As he said of other inventions protected by a patent, his publication of the debates would add "the fuel of *interest* to the *fire* of genius, in the discovery and production of new and useful things" (3.363). He might receive credit for his ideas by being elected, and then implement them to keep slavery out of the territories, thus transforming Young America's "Manifest Destiny" into a method for expanding the range of free institutions.

Lincoln's return to the topic of self-interest in these last lines of the lecture is the culmination of his redefinition of the history of discoveries and inventions. With an almost biting humor, he begins and ends by restrainedly praising a Young America that is a paradigm of self-interest, a country that believes, in accordance with Tocqueville's famous observation, that it has rightly understood its interests and has acted rightly upon them to its advantage. Following the course of Lincoln's remarks, we see many of the grounds of that self-assurance must be ceded to chance, acts of genius, the influence of institutions, habits of mind, and the work of what might be Providence in the discovery of the New World.

We detect in Lincoln's words a tightly rationed sarcasm that occasionally draws attention to innovation's baleful effects. In its prevalent temper, however, the lecture is a remarkable blend of humbling humor and frank admiration. It takes a middle path, between Bancroft's transcendental chauvinism and Phillips's subtle denigration of modern aspirations. Lincoln's Adam is "very ignorant, and simple in his habits" yet capable of "dominion over the earth." The first man, "*according to his chance*" and his capacity to act on it, is the remarkable peer, in fact the superior version, of "self-complaisant" Young America. He shows the challengers of Old Fogey their own greater promise as well as their more dangerous limitations. Here it is no leap of the imagination to see Lincoln as an ingenious political inventor helping to lead America by recollecting his debt to the assistance of others and fashioning himself in the form of a humbly derivative, yet ambitious and inventive Adam worthy of higher office: "The effects [of discovery and invention] could not come, all at once. It required time to bring them out; and they are still coming" (3.362).

Seven months after speaking of these things in Jacksonville, Lincoln extended the themes of the discoveries lecture in a speech delivered at the Wisconsin State Fair. The Milwaukee Address was an extended application of the principles he had outlined in the discoveries lecture. On the verge of the 1860 campaign, he proposed—with similar indirection, complexity, and firm simplicity—a reflective, deliberate way for Young America and his general audience to temper themselves and expand freedom's garden. It would be necessary, Lincoln suggested, to reflect on the limits as well as the opportunities inherent in agricultural innovation and the pursuit of political happiness in a self-governing republic. Acquiring new territory might be a good thing, but only if "thoroughness" in farming—governed by the liberal and practical arts and by farmers' recognition of their debts to free institutions and habits of observation—became the watchword of agricultural labor. Otherwise land hunger would make free farmers indifferent to the spread of slavery, neglectful of the very discoveries and inventions that sustained life.

The Lecture on Discoveries and Inventions and the Milwaukee Address elaborate upon each other, each using its own peculiar mixture of humor and analysis, and its own telling avoidance of direct political argument. Their cumulative preoccupation, even though they are separate lectures on distinctive subjects of great intrinsic interest, is the subject of the next chapter.

9

The Milwaukee Address

Thorough Farming and Self-Government

One must guard against obscuring this idea [free will], for it is a question of elevating souls and not completing their prostration.
—Alexis de Tocqueville, *Democracy in America*

The effect of thorough cultivation upon the farmer's own mind, and, in reaction through his mind, back upon his business, is perhaps quite equal to any other of its effects. Every man is proud of what he does *well;* and no man is proud of what he does *not* do well. With the former, his heart is in his work; and he will do twice as much of it with less fatigue. The latter performs a little imperfectly, looks at it in disgust, turns from it, and imagines himself exceedingly tired. The little he has done, comes to nothing, for want of finishing. (3.475)

Delivered seven months after the Lecture on Discoveries and Inventions at Jacksonville College, Lincoln's address to the Wisconsin State Agricultural Society on September 30, 1859, drew praise from the *Illinois State Journal,* which called it "dignified and impressive."[1] The address was an opportunity for Lincoln to elaborate and apply the earlier lecture's leading ideas. The link between the two speeches is most obvious in the latter's praise for agricultural fairs. In Jacksonville, Lincoln had half-humorously described the first world's fair as a sewing society meeting in which Adam and Eve made the first clothing. In the Milwaukee Address, he begins by approving of fairs as civilizing events, thanks largely to their educational and scientific value. They are designed "to bring together especially all which is supposed to not be generally known, because of recent discovery, or invention"

(3.472). The patent laws, which Lincoln described in Jacksonville as pivotal constitutional innovations that stimulate and protect the American genius for innovation, are here described as "kindred" to the state fair. Both kinds of innovation combine interest with genius for the propagation of discoveries and inventions: "[T]hese Fairs are kindred to the patent clause in the Constitution of the United States, and to the department, and practical system based upon that clause" because they excite "emulation, for premiums, and for the pride and honor of success—of triumph, in some sort—to stimulate that discovery and invention into extraordinary activity" (3.472).

The "department" Lincoln refers to is the U.S. Patent Office, to which he had applied for a patent in 1849, just before completing his single term in the House of Representatives. (His invention, a method of enabling steamboats to navigate shallow waters, was devoted to agriculture: the problem of opening access to markets for farmers in remote regions [2.32–36].) In that year, the Patent Office became a branch of the new Department of the Interior, which was charged with many responsibilities vitally related to the application of discoveries and inventions for the common welfare. The new department also supervised the public lands, including the territories. Its powers extended to areas Lincoln discussed or alluded to in the Lecture on Discoveries and Inventions: it regulated the mines on those lands and was responsible for the storage and circulation of public documents. In sum, it was the federal office that linked inventions, as Lincoln broadly defined them, to the federal government's prerogatives and responsibilities associated with internal improvements. Most importantly, as the federal agency that supervised public lands, it brought discoveries and inventions into contact with the most controversial political questions then vexing the country—questions involving territorial expansion and statehood. Indicative of the importance Lincoln attached to its responsibilities was his attempt in 1849 to put himself forward for a position in the General Land Office. He was disappointed when the Taylor administration appointed someone else.[2]

The Wisconsin State Fair was an invention in the service of goals related to the Department of Interior. It not only imitated the Patent Office by giving awards for the best innovations in agriculture in order to encourage invention; it provided an occasion for "a regular *address*," which in Lincoln's hands clarified and directed some of the fair's activities, and thus contributed to its inventive operations (3.472). Not incidentally, the fair also created a space for *strangers* to meet peacefully to exchange ideas and compete for prizes. The occasion, Lincoln argued, was a necessary means of joining recreation with "virtue and advantage" (that is, genius and interest). Civilized laws and admirable development of personal virtue were by themselves insufficient. Americans needed healthy and edifying opportunities to turn their minds away from their immediate labors and meet one another in a fair field of friendly competition. Otherwise they would be like their primordial ancestors, fighting among themselves and exercising passions particularly dangerous to a self-governing union.

In the first sentences of the address, Lincoln is startlingly frank about the dangers such occasions allay:

> From the first appearance of man upon the earth, down to very recent times, the words "*stranger*" and "*enemy*" were *quite* or *almost,* synonymous. Long after civilized nations had defined robbery and murder as high crimes, and had affixed severe punishments to them, when practiced among and upon their own people respectively, it was deemed no offence, but even meritorious, to rob, and murder, and enslave *strangers,* whether as nations or as individuals. Even yet, this has not totally disappeared. The man of the highest moral cultivation, in spite of all which abstract principle can do, likes him whom he *does* know, much better than him whom he does *not* know. To correct the evils, great and small, which spring from want of sympathy, or positive enmity, among *strangers,* as nations, or as individuals, is one of the highest functions of civilization. To this end our Agricultural Fairs contribute in no small degree. They make more pleasant, and more strong, and more durable, the bond of social and political union among us. (3.472)

The vocabulary of recent events seeps into Lincoln's global history: strangers "enslave" one another; highly cultivated men fail to overcome prejudices, as with sectional feelings spawned by unfamiliarity. "Political union" suffers. A bit like local wrestling matches (with which Lincoln was familiar both as a participant and a judge), the fairs promote forms of emulation and rivalry that strengthen political ties.

Fairs answer a "positive need" for such "occasional recreation." Milwaukee's celebration is a "present pleasure," which, if it is "associated with virtue and advantage," and "followed by no pain," is capable of "making the future more pleasant" (3.472). Lincoln also has in mind the fair's deeper functions as a recreation that makes room for the sharing of knowledge about the "great calling of *agriculture,*" which he implies is the enterprise most conducive to peaceful, happy union if it is pursued with a necessary "thorough-ness." Properly developed, the agricultural life cultivates a habit of responsibility that tempers the rapacious hunger for land: "The ambition for broad acres leads to poor farming, even with men of energy" (3.475). The challenge is to grow at least as much produce on farms half the normal wasteful size so that unprecedented increases in the farming population can be accommodated without reckless expansion (3.481).

Speaking just a year after the Lincoln-Douglas debates, Lincoln implies that wasteful farming and careless hunger for land undermine the farmer's pride in his work and dissipate the integrity of free institutions. Indiscriminate farming fuels war-breeding ambitions for new territory. Thorough cultivation not only minimizes needless competition for land as population grows; it enlarges the sphere of responsible freedom, turning back the "money kings" and the "land kings," including (Lincoln does not need to name them) the power of indiscriminate capital and southern interests that inadvertently or deliberately extend the reach of slavery. Lincoln adverts to this last danger in a number of ways, all governed by a maxim: "No community whose every member possesses this art [of thorough agriculture], can ever be the victim of oppression in any of its forms" (3.481).

Lincoln does not speak from the stump. Indeed he says he will not take the politician's role of flattering the farmers for their votes. But his manner has an unmistakable political edge, which we see him honing in his introduction and then wielding at crucial moments in the remainder of the speech. He is, after all, the farmers' chosen speaker because he is a politician. He points out that his knowledge of farming is not the reason why he has been invited to Milwaukee (3.473). But he abstains from making direct political appeals. Instead, he takes the middle ground, giving "some general suggestions, on the practical matters" regarding agriculture. He says he will discuss the connection between good agricultural practice and the cultivation of happiness.

Lincoln characteristically assumes that in both activities self-interest is at work. Indeed, one of the foundations of the Milwaukee Address is an elaborate appeal to the farmers' self-interest, which he implicitly and optimistically defines as self-interest rightly understood. Saying he will not address their narrow self-interest by means of flattery, he does not abstain from forms of flattery that raise expectations of what that self-interest *should* be. Farmers' true interests, he asserts, deserve to be defended if the defenders of other groups attack them:

I presume I am not expected to employ the time assigned me, in the mere flattery of the farmers, as a class. My opinion of them is that, in proportion to numbers, they are neither better nor worse than other people. In the nature of things they are more numerous than any other class; and I believe there really are more attempts at flattering them than any other; the reason of which I cannot perceive, unless it be that they can cast more votes than any other. On reflection, I am not quite sure that there is not cause of suspicion against you, in selecting me, in some sort a politician, and in no sort a farmer, to address you.

But farmers, being the most numerous class, it follows that their interest is the largest interest. It also follows that that interest is most worthy of all to be cherished and cultivated—that if there be inevitable conflict between that interest and any other, that other should yield. (3.472–473)

This is backhanded praise for a purpose: the farmers should not consider themselves superior, as individuals, to members of other classes. Their numbers make them more significant; but the greater power of their interest as a group needs to be understood as entailing political responsibility; it is not a simple political fact. There is something about their role in the union that should take precedence over the claims of those other interests; but that something is not their number.

What is valuable in the farmers' calling and labor is not detached from self-interest; it grows out of an aspiration for true prosperity and "happiness," which Lincoln defines upwardly by quoting from Pope's high-minded *Essay on Man:* "[H]appiness is our being's end and aim" (3.472). Pope has in mind the happiness of self-satisfaction when that pleasure looks upward to providential, natural, and moral constraints on human ambition that enable it to transcend mere self-interest—when virtue, not good fortune, makes for bliss and when "true self-love and social [love] are the same."[3] Lincoln takes up this general idea in his praise of agriculture as "the most valuable of all the arts," the most responsive to what its practitioners can learn about their powers and limitations by means of "cultivated thought"—that is, by tempered ambition that draws assiduously from observation and experiment, and from the thoughts and experiments of others:

This leads to the further reflection, that no other human occupation opens so wide a field for the profitable and agreeable combination of labor and cultivated thought, as agriculture. I know of nothing so pleasant to the mind, as the discovery of anything which is at once new and valuable—nothing which so lightens and sweetens toil, as the hopeful pursuit of such discovery. And how vast, and how varied a field is agriculture, for such discovery. The mind, already trained to thought, in the country school, or higher school, cannot fail to find there an exhaustless source of profitable enjoyment. Every blade of grass is a study; and to produce two, where there was but one, is both a profit and a pleasure.... In all this, book-learning is available. (3.480–481)

Lincoln's appropriation of Jeffersonian praise for the yeoman farmer is in this sense a somewhat un-Jeffersonian effort to reform farming, although it serves some Jeffersonian ends. He pointedly refrains from contrasting rural virtue with urban corruption, focusing instead on the insufficient (and falling) productivity of American farms, particularly in the northwest but not excluding the country as a whole. In the discoveries lecture he had observed that agriculture, in comparison to other arts, had progressed very little. Speaking in Milwaukee, he notes that farms in the region are producing less than they did in previous generations—at best about half of what the land seems to be capable of bringing forth. There is something in the nature of contemporary farming, in other words, that frustrates "thorough" cultivation, and which prevents it from "push[ing] the soil up to something near its full capacity" (3.474). Not just capital and slave interests but the yeoman's misunderstood interests feed land hunger, waste effort, and in turn menace rural virtue and happiness. A new agricultural art for smaller fields is necessary, one in which Americans learn to derive "a comfortable subsistence from the smallest area of soil" without seeking to own more land than they can productively tend. As the rural spaces fill with new arrivals, farmers must make the agricultural arts more efficient by making them more intellectual, perfecting them through study and experiment.

The Wisconsin State Fair provides Lincoln with an appropriate forum for praising the arts of peace while alluding to the prospect of war—or at least to the prospect of a conflict between interests and principles that are not amenable to indefinite compromise. His glancing reference to the possibility of an "inevitable" conflict recalls the central thought of the "House Divided" Speech of the previous year, and it probably signals an awareness of Seward's more emphatic statement, delivered just two weeks before the Milwaukee Address, that an "irrepressible conflict" was brewing between North and South (see also 3.408, 431). These phrases do not apply directly to the farmers' cause—unless one begins to think of their circumstances as linked to the fate of slavery's status in the territories. In Lincoln's estimate, the north-western farmers' support for the Republicans or their opponents depended on their conception of their agricultural calling's relation to true prosperity for themselves and their country.

The ease with which Lincoln introduces these complex ideas is not without a measure—probably a considerable measure—of calculation. But it seems wrong to assume that Lincoln's reckonings are necessarily deceptive. He does not seem to have composed the address merely to reveal himself to a sophisticated few or to shade his meaning for an ignorant general audience. Tempered by a pessimistic estimate of the pace of agricultural progress over the millennia, he takes the modern farmers' respectable but defective expertise as a given, then declares a desire to test his ideas against their greater experience. Read closely, his speech self-consciously manifests its dependence upon its audience's readiness to follow a detailed exposition, and to entertain general ideas that challenge current views. Lincoln therefore takes up familiar knowledge to suggest new ways his audience ought to perform its ancient and slowly perfected art. Not denying the power of the farmers' self-interest and preconceptions—indeed, by acknowledging their force—he draws them toward the higher pleasures of the fair, which he thinks derive from what they can learn about thorough farming. That this vision of thorough cultivation is harmonious with Republican principles is an inference he insinuates, or makes available, with persistence yet argumentative restraint.

Inefficient farming is not only more expensive because it drives farmers to purchase more land than they need; it undermines their pride in a job well done, in turn sapping their energy because they feel "disgust" for their imperfect work. The mutual influence of pride and self-interest redefines labor as something more than toil:

> The effect of thorough cultivation upon the farmer's own mind, and, in reaction through his mind, back upon his business, is perhaps quite equal to any other of its effects. Every man is proud of what he does *well;* and no man is proud of what he does *not* do well. With the former, his heart is in his work; and he will do twice as much of it with less fatigue. The latter performs a little imperfectly, looks at it in disgust, turns from it, and imagines himself exceedingly tired. The little he has done, comes to nothing, for want of finishing. (3.475)

The thorough farmer does more work than the wasteful one, and his burden is lighter. Less perfect farming is not lazy farming; it entails more work on unproductive tasks, such as harvesting meager crops over large areas (3.474–475). The thorough farmer does more work overall because his self-interested toil enhances and draws from his self-respect. He has confidence in his power to improve his lot.

The importance Lincoln places on this reciprocating engine of pride and effort helps to explain the next sections of the address, which tend to be baffling to modern readers because they are devoted to the technical and seemingly tangential topics of the steam plow and the differences between free labor and slavery. In fact, both subjects expand Lincoln's complex consideration of thorough labor.

The steam plow, the age's the most impressive example of a labor-saving device in agriculture, stands ready to strengthen *or undermine* thorough effort. Lincoln praises mechanical progress, and carefully considers how the new plow might best be used to increase yields on relatively small plots of ground. But he says nothing directly about its more obvious power to expand the farmer's rule over larger fields. Instead, he likens "mammoth farms" to unmanageable machinery: "The ambition for broad acres leads to poor farming, even with men of energy. . . . Mammoth farms are like tools or weapons, which are too heavy to handle. Ere long they are thrown aside, at a great loss" (3.475–476). The cumbersome yet immensely promising steam plow is the paradigmatic test case. Will it encourage more thorough farming without stoking the sheer ambition for territory or, conversely, without encouraging a stereotypically southern-style disdain for labor, which leads to a desire to live off the labor of others? Because each of these perverse ambitions amplifies and supports the other, the plow—which might satisfy them both—must be understood and employed with great care.

Readers familiar with Lincoln's earlier life are bound to notice the difference between his advocacy of farming and his own abandonment of agricultural labor once he came of age. Stories of his aversion to physical labor abound, accompanied by many accounts of his physical strength and assiduous study. His fragmentary lecture notes on the practice of law put the matter into perspective. There, too, thoroughness is his watchword, and the means to that end are intellectual and ethical, as well as laborious. Labor is leavened by a sense of accomplishment. Legal practice requires careful rationing and timely action so that details receive effective attention. Lincoln's lawyer toils like a mindful gardener, concentrating on hourly tasks yet watchful over the longer-term interests of clients, the lawyer's own self-respect, and the demands of the law (2.81–82).

As in law, thoroughness in agriculture is labor governed by thought, and thought disciplined by labor. Lincoln argues that work on limited acreage concentrates the mind. The farmer is more likely to give his attention to the causes of poor harvests because he identifies the fate of his land more directly with himself and his knowledge of good farming. If he is thorough, he does not compensate for inefficient farming by simply buying and seeding more land (3.474). The steam plow might help him—if he uses it to achieve greater efficiency in cultivating "a small quantity of ground" (3.477). But how could Lincoln's argument about the steam plow be persuasive, given the magnitude of the machine's projected power? How could he seriously influence the use of an innovation that promised to transform agriculture?

Without meeting this challenge directly, the Milwaukee Address raises questions the farmer should ask about the precise configuration and use of the new technology. Lincoln takes advantage of the fact that the precise course of the agricultural revolution was unclear. Self-powered plows (stationary engines or moving tractors and their trains) had hardly begun to make their way onto the American farm at the time Lincoln was speaking. Even by 1859 he had not seen one (3.476). Ten years later Horace Greeley was still looking forward to an efficient design.[4] The apparent advantages of the new plow did not clearly outweigh the novel burdens it seemed likely to impose, especially with regard to the goal of thorough farming (3.476–477). The point of Lincoln's discussion was therefore not only to identify the variety of the plow's possible applications. On a deeper level, he sought to demonstrate the degree of deliberation and experiment that would be necessary to design and implement the steam-plow technology for the best, most-thorough cultivation, the only application in Lincoln's opinion worth making. Thus he gives his audience a compact and detailed set of questions about the various possible methods of locomotion, the machine's endurance between refuelings, the expense and accessibility of fuel, and the prospects for discoveries and inventions that might facilitate the new plow's most beneficial application. Describing several experimental applications, Lincoln points out a number of problems that remain to be solved:

The successful application of *steam power,* to farm work is a *desideratum*—especially a Steam Plow. It is not enough, that a machine operated by steam, will really plow. To be successful, it must, all things considered, plow *better* than can be done with animal power. I must do all the work as well, and *cheaper;* or more *rapidly,* so as to get through more perfectly *in season;* or in some way afford an advantage over plowing with animals, else it is no success. I have never seen a machine intended for a Steam Plow. Much praise, and admiration, are bestowed upon some of them; and they may be, for aught I know, already successful, but I have not perceived the demonstration of it. I have thought a good deal, in an abstract way, about a Steam Plow. (3.476)

Lincoln carefully configures his questions so as to challenge complacency while tempering land-hungry ambitions: "I have not pointed out difficulties, in order to discourage, but in order that being seen, they may be the more readily overcome" (3.477).

If the steam plow needs a reflective farmer to put it to work thoroughly, so does the laboring man who works for the farmer. The determination of the precise method of guidance or control is controversial; but the challenge of thinking about the best kind of control must be acknowledged so that the land is cultivated well: "Much disputation is maintained as to the best way of applying and controlling the labor element." The laborer's work, like the farmer's, is much more than muscular toil. Just as the most advanced labor-saving technology requires cerebration and experiment to be employed effectively, so must human labor, whether it is work of the hired hand or of the one who hires him. Technology will not soon change the fact that "*labor* is the source from which human wants are mainly supplied" (3.477). How then should that labor be directed and used? Lincoln's audience would have known that factory owners and workers in American cities had clashed with increasing frequency in recent years, and that the recession of 1857 had led to high unemployment and violence not only in the east but in Cincinnati and Chicago.

What was labor? Was it closer to freedom than to slavery? If hired laborers and slaves amounted to the same thing, what grounds would the North have to employ one and exclude the other? What would be the eventual treatment of immigrants who made up a high and increasing proportion of those laborers? If all enterprise had to be divided between labor and capital, and the two were inevitable enemies, how long would the struggling independent farmer with little or no capital be able to rationalize his position—or the position of those working for him—as any better than a slave's?

How could the North defend its labor practices against southerners' charges that laborers were in fact worse off than slaves? The general argument sounds strained to modern ears, but it was well developed in the writings of two authors whose work Lincoln is likely to have read: Frances Wayland for the North (in *The Elements of Political Economy*) and George Fitzhugh for the South (in his *Sociology for the South*). Wayland had seen virtue in the traditional philosophy of Whig self-sufficiency. He was optimistic about the future of the laborer, including the laborer who was a recent immigrant: "The common laborer, if industrious, virtuous, and frugal, may not only support himself, but also, in a few years, accumulate a valuable little capital. And notwithstanding the great immigration of foreigners, the wages of labor are annually rising. Hence, it is evident, that the increase of capital more than keeps pace with the natural and imported increase of the human race."[5] Fitzhugh's strident defense of slavery, which appeared in 1854 (the same year as the Kansas-Nebraska Act), attacked views like Wayland's and expressed disdain for the Declaration's equalizing axiom. Fitzhugh threw down the gauntlet before those who argued that northern labor was free and clearly superior to slavery: "The issue is made throughout the world on the general subject of slavery in the abstract. The argument has commenced. One set of ideas will govern and control after a while the civilized world. Slavery will everywhere be abolished, or everywhere re-instituted." Because "Nature has made [men] slaves," freedom is for those born to rule them. The notion that labor tends to liberate, that it leads to independence, ownership of property, and the exercise of self-government, must bow to necessity.[6]

In an article published in a Springfield newspaper the year of Lincoln's Milwaukee Address, The Reverend F. Springer had taken a position that anticipated Lincoln's, but without Lincoln's emphasis on the power of the farmer's literacy and his capacity to rise by his own efforts. For Springer, the problems of agricultural labor stemmed from "the odious distinctions of caste." He argued as though the crimes of the oppressors were more important than the prospect of reform. The ancient antagonism between capital and labor, he wrote, had created a scandalous degradation of agricultural effort and a low opinion of the farmer's capacity to benefit from education. Education was "the one most effectual remedy" for securing "the rational equality with which all men are regarded in the eyes of God." But the consequence of millennia of oppression was a legacy of injustice and brutalization:

> The legislation of the world has always been partial to capital and neglectful of labor, hence but little favor has been shown to the workers whose hardy toil cultivated the fields and made them remunerative to the owners.
>
> False views regarding education have had no small share in retarding the progress of agriculture, and depressing the rank of those laboring in it. Learning has been regarded as useful, chiefly to acquire shining distinctions of office and power. . . . For the laborer that tilled the ground, knowledge was held to be useless. As the only service required of him was that of the body, of course it was a matter of no concern whether he possessed a mind. The more brute-like he could be rendered in activity, strength and endurance of body, the more valuable would he be to his employer. . . . I tell you my friends, that to make beasts of burden, pack horses and draught horses of the million masses of mankind, was the procedure of the ancients, and in most countries of Europe and Asia, the same brutalizing inhumanity still prevails.[7]

Speaking in Milwaukee, Lincoln assiduously avoids appealing to farmers' resentments. He flatters them by respecting their calling in the way he carefully demonstrates his knowledge of what they do, and of what they might do if they used the learning already available to them. He challenges them to live up to their potential and their opportunities.

Of course, Lincoln had famously declared his position on slavery and free labor the year before, in his pivotal "House Divided" Speech. Seward, speaking soon afterward in somewhat similar terms, had projected an impending "irrepressible conflict" between slavery and liberty, applying to America Napoleon's sentiment that Europe would eventually be "all Cossack or all Republican."[8] But unless we look carefully at all these rival arguments, we miss much of what Lincoln is doing in the prewar speeches, especially his effort in Milwaukee. Wayland, Fitzhugh, Springer, Seward, and even Napoleon all frame the greatest question of the age in terms of the freedom or enslavement of all men, without regard for race. So does Lincoln. As we have seen in his previous oratory, the larger argument running through the "House Divided" and Milwaukee speeches makes chattel slavery an example of a larger pattern of conflict over the power of men to govern themselves. But Lincoln is unique in maintaining interest in the self-governing individual amid the larger conflict, not as that individual is a victim or oppressor but as he is a microcosm of the whole, and a contributor to the outcome.

Lincoln's linkage of the free-labor question to the matter of slavery carried risks. Labor unrest in the North had aggravated divisions within his audiences. Two months before the Milwaukee Address, when he had delivered a version of his remarks on labor to an audience in Cincinnati (one of the afflicted cities), the local newspaper had apparently replaced his statements on free labor with a bland summarizing sentence (3.459). On the basis of newspaper accounts of Lincoln's speeches in other cities, Basler has argued that Lincoln did not reinstate (or did not succeed in reinstating) the missing paragraphs when he proofread the Cincinnati paper's transcription.[9] He contends that the missing passage is the intriguing Fragment on Free Labor, which includes sentences that explicitly bridge the gap between the white laborer and the black slave:

> As Labor is the common *burthen* of our race, so the effort of *some* to shift their share of the burthen on to the shoulders of *others,* is the great, durable curse of the race. Originally a curse for transgression upon the whole race, when, as by slavery, it is concentrated on a part only, it becomes the double-refined curse of God upon his creatures." (3.462)

Here the ruling paradigm is the good of free labor, not the evil of slavery. Slaves work harder, Lincoln contends, when they receive pay for higher production rather than corporal punishment for low output—that is, when slaveholders adopt what Lincoln considers free-labor practices (3.463).[10] In the Milwaukee Address, he goes on to contend that hired laborers can find ways to save enough to become employers of others and that labor in a free country tends to ascend toward economic independence. A majority of citizens, he concedes, neither work for nor hire others. But many of them employ, in effect, their own family members, and many others find independence. Lincoln dares to say it is "the general rule" that they will do so, even though the majority do not. In other words, the deeper tendency is what matters: "Many independent men, in this assembly, doubtless a few years ago were hired laborers. And their case is almost if not quite the general rule" (3.478):

This, say its advocates, is *free* labor—the just and generous, and prosperous system, which opens the way for all—gives hope to all, and energy, and progress, and improvement of condition to all. If any continue through life in the condition of the hired laborer, it is not the fault of the system, but because of either a dependent nature which prefers it, or improvidence, folly, or singular misfortune. (3.479)

The prospect of slavery for all laborers would have to be the result of a kind of moral suicide. Because all men have two hands and a head, those hands were "probably intended" to feed that head's mouth, not someone else's. The aspirations of free labor are therefore extensions of what is "probably" a divine plan. The circumstances of free labor "insist on universal education," because each set of laboring hands is matched with a mouth that it must learn to feed on its own. In a half-humorous jibe, Lincoln hints that the ingenious and enterprising North might go along with the opponents of free labor if the rewards were great enough: "A Yankee who could invent a strong *handed* man without a head would receive the everlasting gratitude of the 'mud-sill [anti–free labor] advocates'" (3.479). Northern help had already been given to create political inventions—the Dred Scott Decision, the Kansas-Nebraska Act, and the endorsement of Stephen Douglas for the presidency—that had in Lincoln's view made the slave's rise toward free labor, and the hired laborer's rise toward independence in the new lands, seem increasingly remote.

The job ahead, as Lincoln presents it, is bracing but reassuring. The farm that is thoroughly cultivated is bound to be more valuable per acre, and hence a larger source of capital. The thorough farmer's study of crops, climate, and soils will be challenging, but it will also, by its nature as a seasonal activity, take advantage of the farmer's seasonal leisure, and restore his energy for greater exertions (3.480-481). The pleasures of study will mix with the satisfaction of self-interested and highly physical toil: "The mind, already trained to thought, in the country school, or higher school, cannot fail to find there an exhaustless source of profitable enjoyment" (3.480).

There follows a list of thirty-six topics for pleasant and profitable study, all "specimens" of thousands of other avenues of inquiry, "each a world of study within itself." The thorough farmer's intellectual task is liberal as well as practical: "book-learning" is not only a way to learn about what others have discovered, but a preparation and strengthening of that habit of observation and experimental spirit that Lincoln had outlined in his previous lecture. Beyond information, reading gives "a relish, and facility, for successfully pursuing the yet unsolved" problems. It facilitates "cultivated thought," opening the mind to disciplines that are studied at least partly for their own sakes—botany, chemistry, and the "mechanical branches of Natural Philosophy" (i.e., physics) (3.480–481).

As he did in the Lecture on Discoveries and Inventions, Lincoln makes literacy the crucial attainment for the largest class of Americans. Northern farmers are already literate, but they need a higher, more thorough literacy to prosper as conditions change. As does the discoveries lecture, the Milwaukee Address presents that attainment as a complex achievement (3.480). There must be a habit of study, and circumstances that favor the mixing of self-interest with the hope of success. But in Milwaukee only, as we have seen, Lincoln adds a substantial new challenge for effective literacy: the necessity of thoroughness, without which even the fortunate confluence of the other factors cannot stop the decline in harvests or head off the prospect of war over land or liberty. The violent Hobbesian world he describes in his introduction (a world that existed "down to very recent times" [3.471]) lurks figuratively just beyond the edge of the fairground and literally on the border of the northern farmers' prosperous region—in the South and in the territories—from where it can invade their lands and intellect if thoroughness is not achieved in time.

Without turning his audience's full attention toward these unsettling possibilities, Lincoln approaches the topic with characteristic indirection. He ends the address by confronting the prospect of failure in the state fair's competition for "premiums," and so invites those in his audience to acknowledge the certainty that they will continue to know failure despite their best efforts. In this motion, Lincoln prepares them to consider how even failure teaches resolve. He detains them "but a moment longer" to give them some "philosophy" about facing defeat.

Implicitly drawing upon and adapting the spirit of Pope's *Essay on Man* that he invoked in his introduction, Lincoln defines the farmer's happiness in terms of virtue rather than success and links self-interest to higher ends. Pope had argued, "Self-love but serves the virtuous mind to wake, / As the small pebble stirs the peaceful lake." Without attempting to maintain Pope's vision of earthly and heavenly happiness,[11] Lincoln pairs the "successful" farmer with the "unsuccessful" one: he warns the victor and encourages the loser according to the principle of thorough exertion. Simply understood as ambition, one gathers, exertion is not enough. Ambition finds its reward, but rewards are fleeting. Victorious ambition is vulnerable to self-satisfaction. But the disappointed and still hopeful farmer can learn from defeat and rise to victory at the next fair. The seesaw of ambition's fortunes suggests that there is something higher: wise resignation, which will paradoxically renew the farmer's effort. The fair brings "sober and durable benefits" more lasting than the ephemeral "exultations and mortifications" of one year's quest for awards (3.481). Even the fair's durable benefits are unsteady in comparison with the eternities: "[T]his too shall pass away" (3.482). But Lincoln does not end on this note. It takes no leap of the imagination to place him amid his own audience in the light of this advice, October 1859 being a time of heart-sinking, inspiring crisis and Lincoln's own incipient rise from defeat in his senatorial campaign against Stephen Douglas.

Coming at the end of an address urging thorough effort, Lincoln's call for acquiescence to the limits on worldly ambition is the apparent capstone of his argument's ascent. The call is not for simple resignation. The biblical origin of the idea of earthly resignation would seem to give the peroration a conclusive authority; but then Lincoln almost prayerfully questions the biblical meaning of the passage he has cited: "And yet let us hope it is not *quite* true." A second conclusion follows, one that incorporates and modifies the first:

> Let us hope, rather, that by the best cultivation of the physical world, beneath and around us, and the intellectual and moral world within us, we shall secure an individual, social and political prosperity and happiness, whose course shall be onward and upward, and which, while the earth endures, shall not pass away. (3.482)

Again, thoroughness ("best cultivation") is the key, this time carefully placed in the context of the apocalypse so that the goal on earth is reachable, though incomplete, by means of thorough effort "while the earth endures."

Self-government, which makes that thoroughness possible, remains the speech's first and last concern. Like all worldly things, and especially like all things political that need recurrent renewal, it will not last. But it will not perish, Lincoln vows for himself and his audience, as long as there is earth.

10

The Cooper Union Address

The Empirical Wager

The facts with which I shall deal this evening are mainly old and familiar; nor is there anything new in the general use I shall make of them. If there shall be any novelty, it will be in the mode of presenting the facts, and the inferences and observations following that presentation. (3.522)

In the months after he delivered his speech on the "house divided," Lincoln engaged Stephen Douglas in the seven famous debates that gave their race for the Senate its distinctive national prominence. The campaign was the turning point of Lincoln's political career. Although his victory in the popular vote was not enough to prevail over the balloting in the state legislature, his grueling loss to a leading national figure won him respect in circles beyond Illinois and gave his arguments wide circulation in numerous newspapers. Eventually taking the form of a book that included the "House Divided" Speech with transcripts of the seven debates, Lincoln's 1858 oratory put him in a position to be considered for the Republican presidential nomination.

Before that book was assured of publication, Lincoln experimented, as we have seen, with delivering lectures that broadened the philosophical reach of his political ideas. When the invitation came for him to speak in New York, he used his lecturing experience to deepen the intellectual basis of his arguments for resisting the expansion of slavery into the territories. The speech he delivered at the Cooper Union on February 27, 1860, was a political lecture, all the more powerful as Republican political rhetoric because of its reliance on mathematical evidence and archival research into the Founders' intentions. Its hybrid mode helped him establish the moral authority of the Republican position without relying on abolitionist fervor. He could appeal to his immediate audience's interest in the mind of the Founders, and he could condemn slavery, repeatedly questioning the South's claims against the North without treating the South as a reprobate. Un-Seward-like in his interrogation, he addressed the South as though it were still an opponent in a civil debate, an erring and perhaps wrongheaded brother who might still be persuaded even though Lincoln did not expect a civil reply. Anticipating failure in that effort, he addressed the South as though it were a compatriot deserving Lincoln's frank declaration of the reasons for Republicans' opposition. And so he spoke in order to be overheard by an audience more open to public debate though not yet settled in its views of the territorial question.

Delivered in New York City three months before the Republican Party's nominating convention, the Cooper Union Address was in this sense a carefully prepared and impressive gamble. It called upon the intellectual powers of a relatively mixed political audience to move them toward endorsing or more resolutely embracing Republican principles. And it attempted to make that appeal without stigmatizing southern affiliations or identifying the Republican position with abolitionism. Just as important, it tried to do all this without presuming to own a nomination Lincoln could not ask for.

What we know of the history of Lincoln's preparation tells us something about the intricacy of its form, audience, and objective. There had been an invitation to give a lecture. A telegram from an agent experienced in arranging such events invited Lincoln to speak at Henry Ward Beecher's Plymouth Church. It offered two hundred dollars for a speech "on any subject," presumably a lecture. According to Herndon, when Lincoln told him he had been invited to give a "lecture," his law partner advised him to "lecture on politics" rather than the general topics he had toyed with unsuccessfully (at least by Herndon's estimate) on the local lecture circuit in 1859.[1] In the negotiations that followed, Lincoln said he preferred to deliver a "political speech," but added he was willing to "speak, or lecture," on a second evening, presumably on another topic, if his sponsors invited him to do so (3.494). Referring to the upcoming event, Horace Greeley's *Tribune* muddled the distinction by announcing that Lincoln would deliver a "lecture" that would be an "exposition and defense of the Republican faith."[2] The speaker and his sponsors were attempting to maintain a terminological distinction between lecturing and making a political speech. But they were also maneuvering to make the two modes overlap in performance so that the occasion gave Lincoln an opportunity to make his case before a wide and influential audience.

A second organizing committee took over the arrangements and communicated more explicitly to Lincoln the need for a fusion of lecture and political oratory. In a letter to the prospective speaker, the committee frankly stated that its goal was to gather a large crowd, including prominent citizens who might not have been drawn to a political rally, to hear what Lincoln had to say about views favored by those "in the ranks" of the Republican cause: "Of the audience I should add that it is not that of an ordinary political meeting. These lectures have been *contrived* to call out our better, but busier citizens, who never attend political meetings. A large part of the audience would also consist of ladies . . . . Those of us who are 'in the ranks' would regard your presence as very material aid."[3] The design to attract prominent citizens had complex ramifications, because the "busier citizens" and "ladies" it would draw to the event would not necessarily appreciate discovering themselves in "an ordinary political meeting." The oratory for the occasion needed to make the Republican case without relying upon partisan support.

Made aware of the organizers' purposes, Lincoln continued to assume that he would deliver his speech in Beecher's church, a setting that—despite and because of that minister's support for the Republican cause—would have allowed for a broad range of partisan as well as apolitical reference. In his biography of Lincoln, Herndon recalled his friend's four months of effort preparing a performance that would be very different—in method and impact—from the "House Divided" Speech:

> [H]e spent the intervening time [between accepting the invitation and delivering the speech] in careful preparation. He searched through the dusty volumes of congressional proceedings in the State library, and dug deeply into political history. He was painstaking and thorough in the study of this subject . . . . [The result was a speech] devoid of all rhetorical imagery, with a marked suppression of the pyrotechnics of stump oratory. It was constructed with a view to accuracy of statement, simplicity of language, and unity of thought. No former effort in the line of speechmaking had cost Lincoln so much time and thought as this one. It is said by one of his biographers, that those after-

wards engaged in getting out the speech as a campaign document were three weeks in verifying the statements and finding the historical records referred to and consulted by him.[4]

When he arrived in New York, Lincoln was told that the main address would be given not at the Plymouth Church but at the Cooper Union. The possibility of a second performance at Beecher's church was apparently left open but never brought to fruition. According to Herndon, Lincoln reacted to this news by quickly modifying the speech—in ways we do not know. It is possible he changed or eliminated material specifically directed toward a fully partisan audience, or that he excised overly academic passages, or both. In any event, he had to adjust the speech quickly to meet an even more differentiated, hence more difficult, audience with a wider range of political affiliations and levels of resolve.

Taking the stage at the Cooper Union with other prominent politicians, Lincoln also had the opportunity to show himself as a candidate for nomination to the presidency. He needed to be persuasive to various kinds of Republicans without presuming to be a designated favorite, and without ignoring Democrats and potential Republicans who had not alienated the South from their sympathies. True to Herndon's recommendation, the final version of the speech was a remarkable fusion of lecture-circuit oratory and impressive political appeal, its first half reviewing in empirical, dramatic detail the antislavery voting records of the signers of the Constitution, its second half coolly setting out the basis for the Republican repudiation of Douglas's democracy and southern threats of secession.

In the "House Divided" Speech of 1858, Lincoln had shocked his friends with a starkly deductive, disturbing argument that a crisis would inevitably transform the union into a slave society or a free nation. In the Cooper Union Address twenty months later he was at first meticulously inductive. The address's analysis of the Founders' voting records created an almost neutral space within which he ventured to show, with gradual disclosures and carefully limited declamations, the unavoidable incompatibility of the Founders' principles with southern and Douglasite representations of the Founders' ideas. In the process he hardly drew attention to the Declaration's axiom about human equality. He avoided reference to the prerogatives of the states and did not use the word *crisis*. He focused on the Founders' views, arguing for conservation of their precedents. When he spoke about slavery he based his argument not on doctrine or moral imperatives but on the premise that an abhorrence of slavery was part of human nature, which was God's work and could not be changed. He drew attention to established principles of deliberation and framed the central question in definite terms that did not force the slavery issue:

> Let us now inquire whether the "thirty-nine," or any of them, ever acted upon this question [of slavery in the territories]; and if they did, how they acted upon it—how they expressed that better understanding. (3.523)

Stephen Douglas had recently defined the question differently, though like Lincoln he had used the season after the 1858 election to approach these volatile topics by means of quasi-academic deliberation and calibrated partisan appeals. In September 1859, five months prior to Lincoln's speech, he had published a defense of popular sovereignty in *Harper's Monthly*. He had also undertaken a speaking tour in Ohio to popularize his arguments. In that article he made use of intricate legal arguments and a century and a half of court cases to argue that popular sovereignty, not congressional prerogative, should determine whether slavery entered the territories. In a speech he delivered in Columbus, he boiled down his elaborate legal case to a defense of the local voters' will against the encroachment of congressional power. His argument further codified his position in the 1858 debates: "Our fathers, when they framed this Government under which we live, understood this question [of popular sovereignty] just as well, and even better, than we do now. They knew when they made this Republic that a country so broad as ours, with such a variety of climate, soil, and productions, must have a variety of interests, requiring different laws adapted to each locality."[5] The real founders were the various citizens and officeholders who represented those interests over the generations. By implication, the signers of the Constitution were recorders and codifiers of these long-standing trends. They were "fathers" but not Founders.

At the Cooper Union, Lincoln quoted Douglas's sentence and made it his starting point. He had outlined his intention to confront Douglas on these terms when he had spoken in Ohio, a few months before he took the stage in New York. Douglas had created a wall, Lincoln had argued in Ohio, within which he was trying to hold Republicans prisoner. The correct response was not to imitate a mouse trying to find its way through a crack in the edifice.

Lincoln preferred to "clear it at a bound" as though he were a horse, by questioning Douglas's fundamental axiom (3.413). If a means could be found to show that the Founders' definitive legislative actions did not support Douglas's case for popular sovereignty, he could defeat Douglas's argument. He could demonstrate that federal prerogatives, not local elections, should determine the disposition of slavery in the territories.

Douglas had built his *Harper's* essay as though it were a legal brief, using documents unfamiliar to a general audience. He had omitted what Lincoln thought were key documents. The esoteric detail and selectivity of his project permitted him to omit the history of the Founders' legislative acts, even though he had claimed their authoritative support for his conclusions. In response, Lincoln contended that a study of the Founders' record would settle the matter. Douglas's edifice would become irrelevant because the votes of the Founders were actions that spoke louder than words:

> If . . . we can show that these very men took hold of that subject, and dealt with it, we can see for ourselves *how* they dealt with it. It is not a matter of argument or inference, but we know what they thought about it. (3.413)

In Ohio Lincoln had supplied some of this evidence. In the New York speech, he is much more systematic. He speaks as though delivering a summation before a jury, reenacting the legislative drama of the Founders' sovereignty in order to effect "a change in the public mind" (3.424). The thirty-nine signers of the Constitution step forward individually and in groups to submit their votes. The tally gradually mounts, and Lincoln discovers a majority vote for federal control. Acts rather than words are used to establish the Republican view as something plainly seen, above ordinary "argument or inference."

Visual evidence is, of course, not enough. A record of actions and numbers may be more convincing than an argument based on words, but its meaning can be even more difficult to establish and secure. Its accuracy and significance must be buttressed by words. Lincoln's tally of the Founders' votes introduces complexities in his use of evidence that he needs to justify or elide. What precisely were the Founders' actions in those votes that spoke louder than any argument? Was a consensus vote, without a tally, the same as a "yay"? Did everyone favor such a vote if no one objected? Were the signers of the Constitution the same as the body of delegates to the convention? Was the action of voting on a law for the territories more authoritative than the practice of owning slaves?

In one sense, Lincoln risks everything on the credibility of an extremely limited body of evidence. He is back on the Illinois circuit, conceding almost his entire case to the prosecution except for the authority of an almanac, by which he shows his client is innocent because there was no moon the night he is alleged to have been seen committing the crime. The famous proof works precariously: the witness must mistakenly claim the authority of moonlight and the almanac must be correct in revealing the moon's true phase. In the Cooper Union Address, Lincoln does not go this far. His argument draws strength from its statistical findings, but it does not ultimately rely on them to make his case. He indeed risks being wrong in his empirical facts (which investigators checked afterward, as we have seen, to prepare the speech for publication); but the greatest weight of his argument rests in his many logocentric axioms and proofs, which run throughout the address and are indispensable to his arithmetic calculations.

In his apparent simplicity Lincoln is not naive. He does not claim to have found information that no one else knows. He tells his audience that it is the *pattern* and *significance* of his data, and the way he presents them, that forms the essence of his case. In his introduction he directs attention not simply to the facts but to his "mode" of imparting his information, the "inferences" he will make from that presentation, and the "observations" that will follow (3.522). His "general use" of his evidence might resemble, he concedes, a familiar story. The value of his presentation will be in subtleties of nuance and in *what he draws out of* his analysis of the numbers:

> The facts with which I shall deal this evening are mainly old and familiar; nor is there anything new in the general use I shall make of them. If there shall be any novelty, it will be in the mode of presenting the facts, and the inferences and observations following that presentation. (3.522)

Herndon's biography preserves the account of a newspaper reporter who witnessed the audience's reaction to these novelties. The speech, the reporter said, was one of " 'great fairness,' delivered with 'apparent candor and great interest. For the first half hour his opponents would agree with every word he uttered; and from that point he would lead them off little by little until it seemed as if he had got them all into his fold.' "[6] Allowing for the likely partisanship of the newspaper account, one gets the sense that the reception of the address proceeded through the two stages Lincoln outlined in his introduction. The reviewer sees more: the impression of candor was accompanied by an argument of "great interest." The numbers, mixed with Lincoln's supporting proofs, were familiar but new. The second part of the speech, based on what Lincoln called his "inferences and observations" drawn from his tally, was taken to be more important and persuasive. It was the culmination of a speech that had to be much more than its statistics.

Beginning with an air of magnanimity, the address quotes and endorses Douglas's 1859 statement about the Founders knowing best how to resolve the issue of slavery in the territories:

> *Our fathers, when they framed the government under which we live, understood this question just as well, and even better, than we do now.* (3.522)

As we have noted, Douglas had assumed that the fathers were all those citizens of the seventeenth and eighteenth centuries who expressed their disapproval of the king's resolve to impose laws (including laws promoting slavery) upon unwilling colonial assemblies. His examples supported the impression that local control might prohibit slavery in the territories if the federal government did not interfere; but they also appealed to those segments of the electorate who promoted or ignored slavery, or who disliked it but did not favor federal control of the issue in the territories. He omitted from his detailed history of the issue any mention of the Northwest Ordinance or its prohibition of slavery in the territories, and he welcomed the Dred Scott Decision as a confirmation of settlers' right to take slaves into all the territories when they so desired.[7] The Constitution, he argued, "does not authorize Congress to control or interfere with the domestic institutions and internal polity of the people (either in the States or the Territories)." Such a principle "blots out the dividing line between Federal and local authority."[8]

By taking advantage of Douglas's initial deference to the Founders, Lincoln shifted attention to the task of discovering their views. He began with the radically conservative assumption that the Founders were the thirty-nine signers of the Constitution, not the much larger body of colonial and post-colonial citizens that Douglas had made his authority. Lincoln made Douglas's confident assertion into a question of fact. Is it true, Lincoln asked, that local liberty had traditionally trumped federal authority regarding slavery in the territories? It is worth looking again at the question at issue:

Does the proper division of local from federal authority, or anything in the Constitution, forbid *our Federal Government* to control as to slavery in *our Federal Territories?* (3.523)

Lincoln's formulation of the issue is meticulously nonpartisan, yet aggressively analytic. His embedded double negative (Does division forbid?) gives him latitude to ask whether any explicit provision prohibits Congress from determining the status of slavery in the territories. The question places the burden of proof on those who doubt that Congress has such a power.

Of course, the Constitution does not give a direct answer. Douglas had based his principle of noninterference on the idea that the Constitution's silence meant prohibition. To make this notion his point, he had to reject the possibility that the absence of a declaration of Congress's power in the territories did not prohibit Congress from acting there constitutionally according to powers implicit in its constitutional role. But Lincoln likewise had to make a crucial assumption: that the Founders' actions manifested a constitutional prerogative, and that the thirty-nine signers, not the homogenized authority of the earlier generations, were the authoritative actors in the drama.

The compact argument in Lincoln's first paragraphs takes another seemingly simple yet momentous step. It asserts that the votes of the Founders on particular questions of policy, not their published opinions or private practices, should determine the issue. In their legislative actions, according to Lincoln, they "expressed that better understanding" to which Douglas referred (3.523). Their deliberate deeds in the legislative assembly were the decisive factor because "actions speak louder than words," and "speak all the louder" because they were taken "under such responsibility" as attended the founding and the knowledge that their actions were setting decisive precedents (3.530).

Lincoln charged that Douglas's review of history had ignored the essential facts: "I have the impression that" Douglas's statements "are inaccurate in a great many instances" yet rely upon "the suppression of statements that really belong to the history" (3.413). On the occasion of the Cooper Union Address, Lincoln gave this charge a new bite:

If any man at this day sincerely believes that a proper division of local from federal authority, or any part of the Constitution, forbids the Federal Government to control as to slavery in the territories, he is right to say so, and to enforce his position by all truthful evidence and fair argument which he can. But he has no right to mislead others, who have less access to history, and less leisure to study it, into the false belief that "our fathers, who framed the government under which we live," were of the same opinion—thus substituting falsehood and deception for truthful evidence and fair argument. (3.535)

As we have seen, in reducing the historical record to the firm stratum of the Founders' voting records, Lincoln's daring argument shifted the controversy to authorial intent as well as numbers. If, as he argued, twenty-one out of the thirty-nine signers were on record as favoring the prohibition of slavery in the territories, then by extension they supported the principle that federal authority could be used to enforce that prohibition:

The sum of the whole is, that of our thirty-nine fathers who framed the original Constitution, twenty-one—a clear majority of the whole—certainly understood that no proper division of local from federal authority, nor any part of the Constitution, forbade the Federal Government to control slavery in the federal territories, while all the rest probably had the same understanding. Such, unquestionably, was the understanding of our fathers who framed the original Constitution; and the text affirms that they understood the question "better than we." (3.532)

In limiting his sample to the signers of the Constitution and discovering that a narrow majority fulfilled his initial criteria for establishing an authoritative precedent, Lincoln needed to omit those delegates who attended the convention but did not sign the document. The footnotes Lincoln's supporters added to the printed version of the speech mention that some of those men gave reasons for not signing and put those reasons in print. We know that others were summoned to the convention but did not attend, possibly because they disapproved of what the new document might do. The wider controversy after the signing, in which state legislatures were bypassed in favor of the votes of fractious state conventions, Lincoln did not mention.

The manner in which the Founders voted—in some cases by consensus without a polling of individual members—raised further questions. Referring to the first Constitutional Congress's approval of the Northwest Ordinance "without yays and nays," Lincoln interpreted the vote as "equivalent to an unanimous passage" (3.527). Since sixteen of the Founders were sitting in the first Constitutional Congress—by far the most important bloc in his calculations—this argument for unanimity was crucial to the success of the entire mathematical argument. (Three more votes are added on the basis of another untabulated vote in 1798.) Was the absence of yays and nays a sign of the body's unanimity or only an indication that a substantial majority would carry the measure? If the latter, would all sixteen members have voted in favor if polled separately? In Lincoln's view, the Founders were principled men who would have objected to the vote by consensus if they disagreed over the issue: "Certainly they would have placed their opposition to [the Ordinance] on record, if, in their understanding, any line dividing local and federal authority, or anything in the Constitution, properly forbade the federal government to control as to slavery in federal territory" (3.528). Those who voted in favor of the Ordinance and related measures must have approved of their constitutionality because as signers of the Constitution they would have been "guilty of gross impropriety and willful perjury, if, in their understanding" they thought these laws were unconstitutional (3.530).

The narrowness of Lincoln's ultimate tally, just one vote more than needed, is a severe test of this principle. Elsewhere in the address he himself casts doubt on the significance of a "bare majority" in the Supreme Court's Dred Scott Decision (3.543). Artificial proofs in support of his marginal numbers assume even greater importance when one notices that the majority includes five votes in favor of federal control of slavery—not prohibition (the result of the Northwest Ordinance)—and one vote for the Missouri Compromise, which allowed slavery into Missouri as well as certain territories south of the Mason-Dixon line. The address anticipates this complexity in its initial framing of the proposition in terms of federal control in the territories, not necessarily federal preference for slave-free territories. But the thrust of Lincoln's argumentation is clearly more ambitious: he wants to establish a case for the Founders' careful attention to prohibition, not merely federal control. How then does he proceed, given the limitations of his statistical evidence? A more powerful kind of argumentation is at work.

The challenge Lincoln faced in mounting such an argument is evident in his reluctance to use his favorite ways of speaking about the issue. Prior to speaking in New York, he had sometimes argued that no one, at least no prominent figure, had spoken against the Declaration's axiom about equality until after the Compromise of 1850. In the Cooper Union Address, he only insists that no evidence could be found that any of the signers had questioned federal control over slavery in the territories prior to 1800 (or parenthetically, that anyone had denied such authority prior to 1850). Instead of referring directly to the antislavery principles that stock the earlier speeches, he uses the double negative and avoids reference to the Declaration. He defines the issue in narrower terms, with more fervor:

> It is surely safe to assume that the thirty-nine framers of the original Constitution, and the seventy-six members of the Congress which framed the amendments thereto, taken together, do certainly include those who may be fairly called "our fathers who framed the Government under which we live." And so assuming, I defy any man to show that any one of them ever, in his whole life, declared that, in his understanding, any proper division of local from federal authority, or any part of the Constitution, forbade the Federal Government to control as to slavery in the federal territories. I go a step further. I defy anyone to show that any living man in the whole world ever did, prior to the beginning of the present century, (and I might almost say prior to the beginning of the last half of the present century,) declare that, in his understanding, any proper division of local from federal authority, or any part of the Constitution, forbade the Federal Government to control as to slavery in the federal territories. (3.534)

The repetition more than enforces his legal stand. It adds to his dare, which he screws to an almost comical height, "almost" saying that he defies anyone to discover contrary evidence in the history of the world. His meticulous repetition of the terms of his wager further limits and focuses the hyperbole. He indulges the exaggeration as a foil for a calculated claim: that before Douglas's machinations no one in prominence had publicly questioned the federal prerogative.

Lincoln's argument grounds the Founders' authority and consistency not only in terms of their voting records and their sense of honor. They have an intellectual seriousness, Lincoln says, that Douglas does not appreciate. Douglas's implicit charge that the Founders are inconsistent—in approving the Constitution and then passing the Tenth Amendment, which gives remaining powers to the states and the people—Lincoln calls "presumptuous." Such a position, Lincoln contends, defies Douglas's own declaration that they knew what they were doing:

> Is it not presumptuous in any one at this day to affirm that the two things which that Congress deliberately framed (the Bill of Rights as well as the

Northwest Ordinance), and carried to maturity at the same time, are absolutely inconsistent with each other? And does not such affirmation become impudently absurd when coupled with the other affirmation from the same mouth, that those who did the two things, alleged to be inconsistent, understood whether they really were inconsistent better than we—better than he who affirms that they are inconsistent? (3.534)

To support this logic, Lincoln makes a lawyer's case for intention. Congress, including those signers of the Constitution who were members of that body, deliberated over the first ten amendments both before and after they passed the Northwest Ordinance. The consistency of their intentions coincided with their material identities as actors in a single scene. It was their purpose to direct both deeds to the same end:

> Not only was it the same Congress, but they were the identical, same individual men who, at the same session, and at the same time within the session, had under consideration, and in progress toward maturity, these Constitutional amendments, and this act prohibiting slavery in all the territory the nation then owned. (3.533)

Lincoln's solution to the deeper problem of establishing the Founders' intentions is to amass evidence of an antislavery *tendency*—a moral disapproval of slavery—in their votes and deliberations. He signals this turn in his abrupt transition from numerical calculations to complex allusive proofs in the middle of the speech:

> But enough! *Let all who believe that "our fathers, who framed the Government under which we live, understood this question just as well, and even better, than we do now," speak as they spoke, and act as they acted upon it. This is all Republicans ask—all Republicans desire—in relation to slavery. As those fathers marked it, so let it again be marked, as an evil not to be extended, but to be tolerated and protected only because of and so far as its actual presence among us makes that toleration and protection a necessity.* (3.535)

The italicized passage, which in Lincoln's characteristic calligraphy would have been underlined for emphatic delivery, articulates the assiduous fervor that drove his empirical calculations. But more essentially, it decisively turns attention away from the intricacies of the tally, toward the substantial word-centered arguments that Lincoln had almost always used to set out the Republican case.

Lincoln assumes that the Founders' *ideas* about freedom in the territories, not their record of holding slaves or their supposed accommodations of southern interests in the Constitution, were the decisive formative influence on their deeds and sentiments. He presents what he contends are their implicit and explicit ideas about slavery as passionately held and interlocking principles. They are fusions of reason and conviction embedded in the larger argument of their public records. It is worth the attempt to paraphrase these ideas in a compact list:

1. The men who made the Constitution and who deliberated the Northwest Ordinance (and related legislation) acted consistently with their highest principles, not only in making the frame of the new government but also on the matter of limiting slavery in new territorial acquisitions.

2. They performed these tasks guided by ideas, in a crucial moment of the Union's history informed by the ideas of the Declaration, the Constitution, and the unique circumstances that enabled them to determine the future of all territories the country then possessed.

3. Their creation and endorsement of the Constitution and later acts of legislation were their definitive public actions.

4. They had such a strong conviction of their own honor, the importance of the Constitution, and the gravity of their legislative work that they would have spoken or published their objections to any votes on territorial control that they thought were unconstitutional or contrary to general principles of republican government.

5. They believed slavery was wrong, and they acted in the understanding that the status of slavery in the territories would eventually determine the fate of slavery elsewhere in the Union.

If these arguments or something close to them are indeed crucial implicit components of Lincoln's speech in New York, the fact that they are only partially disclosed should give us pause when we try to characterize Lincoln's method and the nature of his argument. It is not obvious that the Cooper Union Address simply hides or implicitly projects what it does not make manifest of these ideas. It is too easy to be wrong about what we think is implicit in his oratory. But if we take Lincoln at his word, he did not conceive of himself as a manipulator of words or—as even some of those close to him believed—a trimmer. Surely he was a master of rhetorical judgment, and that mastery had to do with choosing to present one argument or one part of an argument more prominently than another. Certainly, his choices provoked or drew him into controversies in which he was not believed to be expressing his deeper thoughts. Granting all this, it is striking how consistently his proofs connect his complex apparatus of assumptions with commonplace understandings, accessibly logical inferences, and established principles. And when he uses the historical record, as we have seen, he differs from Douglas by using definite and testable information.

In the New York address, we see Lincoln drawing from such commonplaces as the audience's understanding of traditional rules and freedoms of fair debate; from the general abhorrence of slavery, variously expressed, in all sections of the country; from the idea of the presumed innocence of the accused (the northern states), and thus the illegitimacy of threats of secession that do not muster decisive evidence of alleged northern depredations. He repeatedly attempts to point to what is already the case, whether it is in plain view or resident in tacit understandings of what seems right and true. He speaks as though his audience's opinions and beliefs are the substratum and incipient form of whatever develops in his own arguments. Thus he spends almost as much time articulating and responding to the opinions of the South as he does to the assumptions of his immediate audience.

Lincoln liked to say "Opinion is everything"—not because he thought it was a manipulable shell of arbitrary ideas but because he conceived of it as the basis for public deliberation, the prize that unscrupulous as well as principled speakers fought to influence. A public speech that moved opinion had to draw out what truth it had to offer in public debate, weighing it against other, sometimes more reliable, opinions and then ordering it within the audience's understanding. Lincoln's engagement with opinion and belief was what made it possible for him to encourage audiences to act in the light of what was being discovered—not because it appeared to be new, but because it reflected what the audience already knew, or knew it should have known, or would know to be sensible once it came to light. He made this his endeavor in the Cooper Union Address with an energy and concision that distinguishes that work of oratory from all his other antebellum speeches.

To the extent that Lincoln's public speech depends upon received opinion, it is an almost circular endeavor. But this method of persuasion calls upon the audience to defend the Founders' principles as Lincoln understands them. The argument is from necessity, though it draws the audience closer to its own sense of obligation, and toward the possibility, perhaps the inevitability, of conflict over what the audience believes. The argument does not rule out military conflict; on the other hand, it does not dwell upon the prospect of war as Seward had done. Lincoln hardly discusses it. What matters is the political and moral necessity—entailed by the Founders' deeds and pressed upon the audience by the continuing territorial controversy—to assume what is already the audience's responsibility: to reserve for federal determination the status of slavery in the territories, and presumably to prevent thereby the expansion of slavery.

The South, Lincoln now ventures to assert, is contemptuous of opinions not its own. It "denounce[s] us as reptiles, or, at the best, as no better than outlaws," and will not enter into a discussion of the rightness or wrongness of Republican principles:

> If we do repel you by any wrong principle or practice, the fault is ours; but this brings you to where you ought to have started—to the discussion of the right or wrong of our principle. If our principle, put in practice, would wrong your section for the benefit of ours, or for any other object, then our principle, and we with it, are sectional, and are justly opposed and denounced as such. Meet us, then, on the question of whether our principle, put in practice, would wrong your section; and so meet us as if it were possible that something might be said on our side. (3.536)

In the absence of a reply, Lincoln means to be overheard by his northern audience as a defender of principles *they* would defend. He means to be seen as the temperate yet immovable representation of what they are and what they must become as reasonable, devoted citizens:

> Again, you [the South] say we have made the slavery question more prominent than it formerly was. We deny it. We admit that it is more prominent, but we deny that we made it so. It was not we, but you, who discarded the old policy of the fathers. We resisted, and still resist, your innovation; and thence comes the greater prominence of the question. Would you have that question reduced to its former proportions? Go back to that old policy. What has been will be again, under the same conditions. If you would have the peace of the old times, readopt the precepts and policy of the old times. (3.538)

Slavery will be protected where it exists because the Constitution's protection of that institution is a "necessity," entailed by the power of another form of necessity in the fact of inheritance. It is "*to be tolerated and protected only because of and so far as its actual presence among us makes that toleration and protection a necessity*" (3.535). That presence will fade, as Lincoln's language implies it must. The *impermanence* of this necessity means that slavery has no deep foundation in the Founders' legacy that protects it. Slavery will live securely, on borrowed time.

What is permanent is a conviction, somehow rooted in human nature, that slavery is wrong. Lincoln describes that judgment concessively, in almost neutral terms, as "a feeling against" slavery. He does not give reasons why it is wrong. But he implies that the voting sentiment that opposes slavery is national (though not yet clearly in the majority), and that because it is embedded in human nature, it "cannot be changed":

> Human action can be modified to some extent, but human nature cannot be changed. There is a judgment and a feeling against slavery in this nation, which cast at least a million and a half votes. You cannot destroy that judgment and feeling—that sentiment—by breaking up the political organization which rallies around it. You can scarcely scatter and disperse an army which has been formed into order in the face of your heaviest fire. (3.541–542)

The military language is more than a pose but less than a threat. The point is not that the North abhors the South's peculiar institution, though indeed in Lincoln's aside he seems to indicate it would not be wrong or unnatural to do so. What matters is that a potential majority in the North will not abandon what it cannot, in recognition of its own nature, give up, in the face of the South's insistence that the North universalize its toleration of slavery.

This insistent humility characterizes the remainder of the speech. When Lincoln refers to slavery as "wrong," he pairs his charge with his claim that the South's defense of slavery and its extension should be respected as a consistent moral position. His point is not to abandon his axiom but to increase adherence to the Republican view as the moral alternative to what he concedes and asserts is the South's attempt to make its own universal claim:

> Holding, as they do, that slavery is morally right, and socially elevating, they cannot cease to demand a full national recognition of it, as a legal right, and a social blessing.
>
> Nor can we justifiably withhold this, on any ground save our conviction that slavery is wrong.... [T]hinking it right, as they do, they are not to blame

for desiring its full recognition, as being right; but thinking it wrong, as we do, can we yield to them? (3.549–550)

The point is to forbear, even though (and because) the dispute cannot be resolved by compromise. The Republicans will proceed with even temper in the face of severe disagreement. They will concede as much as possible without giving up claims that must, if necessary, be maintained in the face of war. Lincoln's appeal for peace does not make peace its highest aim:

> *It is exceedingly desirable that all parts of this Confederacy shall be at peace, and in harmony, with one another. Let us Republicans do our part to have it so. Even though much provoked, let us do nothing through passion and ill temper. Even though the southern people will not so much as listen to us, let us calmly consider their demands, and yield to them if, in our deliberate view of our duty, we possibly can.* Judging by all they say and do, and by the subject and nature of their controversy with us, let us determine, if we can, what will satisfy them. (3.547)

There should be concessions, but only "if" they are consistent with duty, and only if that sense of duty is "deliberate." In this nesting of compromise within principle, and principle within compromise (and in the preceding passage, union within "confederacy"), Lincoln holds out the olive branch while wearing a sword. Slavery must be held out of the territories "while our votes will prevent it" (3.550); the concession to electoral decorum is a call to organize electoral, not military, resistance. The contest will be over how well the Republicans can hold and expand their ground to attract voters' natural aversion to slavery and, if necessary, place themselves in the way of secession. Lincoln belittles the idea that the Republicans can embrace "some middle ground between right and wrong." Yet his emphasis on the political contest and the need to build the Republican Party veers from armed confrontation.

By submitting to the laborious drama of tallying the Founders' votes, and then by mortifying Republican fervor to condemn the South, Lincoln's mode of insisting on federal control in the territories presents his audience with a compelling model of principled compromise. More precisely, he draws his fellow and prospective Republicans into the ordeal by presuming to speak for them and their incipient desire to follow through. In this rhetoric of identification, the Cooper Union Address invites those in the audience to do something of great consequence—as though they had no alternative if they remembered who they were.

* * *

The Cooper Union Address helped to lay the groundwork for Lincoln's nomination the following summer—and New York's favor in the election. In partisan yet revealingly detailed reports, the speech was pronounced a rhetorical success as a hybrid of academic and political ideas. In the next day's *New York Daily Tribune,* the speech was said to have "excited frequent and irrepressible applause. [Lincoln's] occasional repetition of his text never failed to provoke a burst of cheers and audible smiles."[9] Horace Greeley, whose political influence as a newspaper editor helped promote the event, praised the address for its lecture-like qualities as well as its political incisiveness.[10] He claimed that Lincoln showed a "clearness and candor of statement, a chivalrous courtesy to opponents, and a broad, genial humor."[11] The *Tribune* pronounced the speech a worthy rival of the performances of Clay and Webster. In its power to address a cultivated audience more interested in intellectual stimulation and reasonable argument than partisan brimstone, it built, said the *Tribune,* upon the heritage of Lincoln's old Whig heroes: "The speech of Abraham Lincoln at the Cooper Institute last evening was one of the happiest and most convincing political arguments ever made in this City, and was addressed to a crowded and appreciating audience. Since the days of Clay and Webster, no man has spoken to a larger assemblage of the intellect and mental culture of our City. Mr. Lincoln is one of Nature's orators, using his rare powers solely and effectively to elucidate and to convince, though their inevitable effect is to delight and electrify as well."[12]

A minor but revealing controversy arose regarding Lincoln's fee. Its outcome highlighted his rhetorical success in a risky venture. Was he a lecturer, and so entitled to be paid, or was he a political speaker whose cause and character would be compromised by the appearance of a desire for gain? When Lincoln received two hundred dollars for his effort, the payment became an issue in the Democratic press. He was accused of embarking on a "financial tour," taking money for a political speech that was advertised as a lecture, by implication concealing political sentiments ignobly in a quasi-academic presentation: "[I]n return for the most unmitigated trash interlarded with coarse and clumsy jokes," one paper alleged, "he filled his empty pockets with dollars coined out of Republican fanaticism."[13] Even if the charges were campaign fustian, they carried a sting. A few months later, Lincoln gave a somewhat pained reply to a friendly editor's questions:

> It is not true that I ever *charged* anything for a political speech in my life—but this much is true: Last October I was requested, by letter, to deliver some sort of speech in Mr. Beechers church, in Brooklyn, $200 being offered in the first letter. . . . I made the speech . . . neither asking for pay nor having any offered me. Three days after, a check for $200—was sent to me . . . and I took it, *and did not know it was wrong.* My understanding now is, though I knew nothing of it at the time, that they did charge for admittance, at the Cooper Institute, and that they took in more than twice $200. I have made this explanation to you as a friend; but I wish no explanation made to our enemies. What they want is a squabble and a fuss; and that they can have if we explain; and they can not have if we don't. (4.38)

Lincoln had acknowledged receipt of the lecture agent's check for two hundred dollars on March 4 (3.554) and deposited it in a Springfield bank immediately upon his return from his eastern trip. Having presented himself credibly as a lecturer in a highly political setting, he passed through the controversy over his fee in public silence. Antagonistic Democrats had detected an anomaly, but they could not erase Lincoln's achievement. The Cooper Union Address had passed beyond the strictures of ordinary lectures and conventional political discourse. It had taken Lincoln's self-effacing and profoundly assertive rhetoric to the frontier of civil speech and to the verge of his nomination as a Republican candidate for president.

Presidential Eloquence and Political Religion

Governing "in the Providence of God"

In telling this tale I attempt no compliment to my own sagacity. I claim not to have controlled events, but confess plainly that events have controlled me. Now, at the end of three years struggle the nation's condition is not what either party, or any man devised, or expected. God alone can claim it. (7.282)

In this cautious yet logically insistent allusion to providential sanction, Lincoln defended his policy of emancipation following his issuing of the Emancipation Proclamation. He knew that his letter, written to Albert G. Hodges on April 4, 1864, seven months before the election, would be circulated among political friends and their fellow Kentuckians. It was a public act, an evocation of political religion in which he found in the will of God a means of defending his controversial position without needing to claim that his own actions had determined events.

According to his friend Orville Browning, Lincoln had presented the arguments initially in the form of "a little speech."[1] In the letter that he wrote at the request of his small audience, he was venturing to explicate, through the more permanent medium of writing and publication, a subtle idea that could easily lose him the support he sought to gain. How could one be assured of understanding God's will, particularly when it seemed to favor the course of events Lincoln seemed intent upon influencing amid opposition in the border states and in the North? What he wrote to Hodges in an effort to meet such questions was a version of the haunting argument that would become the core of the Second Inaugural Address.

Yet the passage comes almost as an afterthought, or a benediction upon much more concrete and controversial proofs of the need to use apparently unconstitutional means to save the Constitution. Lincoln sought to secure the support of friends from the border states that had refused his earlier proposal for compensated emancipation, friends who continued to question the constitutionality of his prerogative, especially his decision to free slaves and use them to enlarge the Union army in the border region. He therefore first appealed to their understanding of constitutional powers, justice, and military necessity—principles he had used to justify the Emancipation Proclamation. But then he asked them to consider higher sources of authority—what the proclamation called "the considerate judgment of mankind, and the gracious favor of Almighty God." Such things by their nature could not be claimed as one's own. One had to *appeal* to or at least hope for favor from "considerate judgment" and "gracious favor," not merely invoke them. In the letter to Hodges, as in the proclamation itself, Lincoln was thereby acknowledging a rhetorical and political dependence on things beyond the power to claim.

Was this gesture merely conventional, of form without substance? The fact that much of the religious language of the proclamation's crucial sentence was contributed in draft by Salmon Chase, a rivalrous member of a fractious cabinet, lends support to this possibility. Had Lincoln simply accepted Chase's wording to win his cabinet's support? Because the proclamation's appeal to divine favor appears in the most convoluted sentence of the proclamation, it is tempting to dismiss it without further ado. But is it possible that Lincoln was simultaneously indebted to and constrained by what he might have wished not to say?[2]

Consulted over the draft proclamation in late December, 1862, Chase had asked the president to recognize the gravity of the occasion by adding a conclusion that was "a solemn recognition of responsibility before men and before God" (6.25). He suggested inclusion of a sentence much like the one Lincoln finally wrote. The official copy of the proclamation, in the president's handwriting, incorporated Chase's suggestion with a few small but significant modifications:

> Chase: And upon this act, sincerely believed to be an act of justice warranted by the Constitution,

Lincoln: And upon this act, sincerely believed to be an act of justice, warranted by the Constitution,

Chase: and of duty demanded by the circumstances of the country,
Lincoln: upon military necessity,

Chase: I invoke the considerate judgment of Mankind and the gracious favor of Almighty God.
Lincoln: I invoke the considerate judgment of mankind, and the gracious favor of Almighty God. (6.25, 30)

Chase's choice of words and punctuation shows that he wanted a relatively simple declaration of sincerity backed by the Constitution and the general circumstances. So armed, the president could then call upon the opinion of "Mankind" and divine favor. But Lincoln's signed copy, although it accepted most of Chase's diction and phrasing, did not adopt his idea. It modified the meaning of the act of petition, first with the insertion of a crucial comma after "justice" to distinguish the expression of sincerity from the constitutional warrant, and then by narrowing Chase's open-ended circumstantial argument to the specific assertion of military necessity. The overall effect was to sharpen and diffuse responsibility into personal, constitutional, necessary, universally human, and divine causes (the last two separated and individually emphasized with another inserted comma). Lincoln's official document therefore made the appeal to mankind's judgment and divine grace more contingent and more urgent, less a quid pro quo:

And upon this act, sincerely believed to be an act of justice, warranted by the Constitution, upon military necessity, I invoke the considerate judgment of mankind, and the gracious favor of Almighty God. (6.30)

Lincoln subtly proclaimed his own policy after all, in his own name, yet in submission to universal human judgment and the sanction of a higher power. He could not proudly petition for that power's approval, yet he had to solicit its favor—and credibly, too—if the proclamation was to do its work. The evidence of the phrasing suggests that Lincoln judged Chase's suggestion to be correct but his addition in need of these crucial improvements.

How serious was Lincoln about such ideas? What did they mean? What significance do they hold for his readers now? How do they contribute to the persuasive force of Lincoln's words? When we attempt to interpret the role of providential reasoning in such texts, we are at a disadvantage. Modern American political sensibilities tend either to stigmatize political oratory's references to divine favor or to assume that they are always more or less legitimate in purely religious or tactical terms. Our interpretation of Lincoln's references to Providence thereby suffers from a general lack of curiosity about the substance of his claims. In either case, we tend to assume we know the dangers of false confidence, and so we are less likely to be awake to legitimate claims that arguments from Providence might make on the American imagination.

Lincoln's practice of artfully deferring, in speech or writing, to some form of providential guidance runs throughout his life. The habit is evident in his younger days, in one of his letters to his friend Joshua Speed:

> The truth is, I am not sure there was any merit, with me, in the part I took in your difficulty [Speed's courtship and marriage]; I was drawn to it as by fate; if I would, I could not have done less than I did. I always was superstitious; and as part of my superstition, I believe God made me one of the instruments of bringing your [new wife] and you together, which union, I have no doubt He had fore-ordained. Whatever he designs, he will do for *me* yet. "Stand still and see the salvation of the Lord" is my text just now. (1.289)

The records of private correspondence are easily misused, and it is good that one feels a reluctance to draw conclusions from confidences that in their intimate detail might reflect too much or too little of the complete man. But here we can at least take note of the resonances of this form of thinking with Lincoln's later discussions of Providence. Writing to celebrate his friend's recent marriage, yet in despondence over his own isolation, he judges himself as a superstitious man, one whose superstition adjoins belief in a form of providential favor. That favor uses him without making him the essential cause of what, under its favorable influence, he helps bring about almost against his will. He is but one of many instruments, and the limitations of his position are evident in his need to wait for favor in his own case. He waits; he does not seek. His passivity, which he says helped him become an instrument for his friend's marital union, is now an ambiguous form of patience: it might yield something similar for himself, but it is difficult to distinguish from overconfidence or inertia. During this period Lincoln's friends were especially concerned about his mental balance.[3]

It is not purely coincidental that Lincoln's mention of his friend's "union" should resonate with his later thinking about Providence and Union. For him, the word *union* could be rich in matrimonial and providential meaning, entailing an original and yet unbroken, "perpetual" condition of unity among the states—sustained, as he says in the First Inaugural, by "a firm reliance on Him, who has never yet forsaken this favored land" (4.271). True, he conceded, the political union of the states gives the states constitutional protections and is itself subject to the "*revolutionary* right to dismember" and reconstitute its political order. But an act of separation, by states declaring themselves divorced from the others, he rejected as impossible in a geographic, political, and constitutional sense. First, it would violate "the vital element of perpetuity" (4.265), which he associated with the idea of union and the persistence of divine favor. Second, it would defy the fact that the union is a more permanent, political version of human matrimony, which in the common language of the wedding ceremony is something only God (and a miraculous change in geography) can put asunder:

> Physically speaking, we cannot separate. We cannot remove our respective sections from each other, nor build an impassable wall between them. A husband and wife may be divorced, and go out of the presence, and beyond the reach of each other; but the different parts of our country cannot do this. (4.269)

In the First Inaugural the union is a *confirmation* of the promise of perpetuity—a preordained union brought into being by human assistance in a process of birth. It is a *forming,* as Lincoln says, rather than a creation. It brings into being something already inchoately present. In this rendering of the preordained as well as invented birth of the Union, Lincoln introduces language and ideas he will develop in the opening of the Gettysburg Address:

> The Union is much older than the Constitution. It was formed in fact, by the Articles of Association in 1774. It was matured and continued by the Declaration of Independence in 1776. It was further matured and the faith of all the then thirteen States expressly plighted and engaged that it should be perpetual, by the Articles of Confederation in 1778. (4.265)

Finally, in 1787, one of the declared objects of ordaining and establishing the Constitution was "to form a more perfect union."

But if destruction of the Union, by one, or by a part only, of the States, be law-fully possible, the Union is less perfect than before the Constitution, having lost the vital element of perpetuity. (4.265)

Such a change, Lincoln argues, is inconceivable if the Union is to exist as perpetual—as it is now, as it was before the Constitution, and as in a sense it has always been—in the providential scheme of things. In both the political and matrimonial sense, the union's indissoluble bonds therefore predate the Constitution and the Articles of Confederation—bonds that have apparently come into being through instrumentalities that are both human and provi-dential.

It is worth wondering, at this juncture, whether any high oratory can be persuasive, especially under difficult circumstances that test the endurance of a political union, without invoking the authority and influence of some-thing beyond human reach, in Lincoln's case something that transcends the Union. If abstaining from such invocation is difficult to avoid, can we say that high oratory depends on a form of political metaphysics—or, in Lincoln's case, political religion—because it is an organic part of such rhetoric? If we assume that the highest priority of such speech is simply the precedence or survival of citizens, leaders, or any particular order of government, the ques-tion is answered before we begin. We have to conclude that political oratory is a cover for Machiavellian and Darwinian imperatives, which we can either accept as realists or reject as idealists. Such imperatives are means of getting one's way and gaining another day, to be justified or excused by grim circum-stance. But such a view does not seem to do Lincoln the courtesy of taking his words seriously. At a minimum, we should ask whether his high oratory can have purchase over time if it has nothing to do with appeals to something transcendent. How else does such a high orator move an audience beyond its concern for survival, and toward an idea of its own persistence in the light of an animating principle or proposition?

It is a commonplace (one out of harmony with Lincoln's proverbial wis-dom about attempts to fool the people) that audiences can be easily and thor-oughly deceived, and that, conversely, once an audience detects or suspects deception, persuasion fails, or succeeds only because audiences have mo-tives of their own that compete with the speaker's intentions. Yet, to draw a cynical conclusion from this observation is to make the rhetorical analysis inoperable. The phenomenon of persuasion disappears. Better to consider

Lincoln's proverbial warning: you can't always fool everyone. If we begin reading the speeches of Lincoln's career in sequence, the presidential eloquence of the later speeches forces several questions upon us: Is his rhetoric's appeal to transcendent or semitranscendent sources organic to his purposes, and, if so, what is its significance? Is it possible for at least great political oratory to invoke what is beyond ordinary ideas and beliefs in such a way that it purposely and legitimately draws listeners toward better versions of themselves and wiser understandings of their predicament? Even a tentative answer to these questions would tell us something interesting about political rhetoric and its relation to political religion. The questions at least draw us back, with new questions, to Lincoln's presidential oratory.

But first, and paradoxically, we must prepare to read the canonized speeches anew by reviewing a few more examples of Lincoln's language of political religion. If we can sufficiently remind ourselves of the ubiquity and frequent subtlety of the political-religious language he uses in a wide range of his writings, we will be in a better position to detect and appreciate the resonances of his appeals to a higher power in the Gettysburg Address and the Second Inaugural.

* * *

The first stage of Lincoln's letter to Hodges begins with an emphatic and complex disclaimer:

> I am naturally anti-slavery. If slavery is not wrong, nothing is wrong. I cannot remember when I did not so think, and feel. And yet I have never understood that the Presidency conferred upon me an unrestricted right to act officially upon this judgment and feeling. It was in the oath I took that I would, to the best of my ability, preserve, protect, and defend the Constitution of the United States. I could not take the office without taking the oath. Nor was it my view that I might take an oath to get power, and break the oath in using the power. I understood, too, that in ordinary civil administration this oath even forbade me to practically indulge my primary abstract judgment on the moral question of slavery. I had publicly declared this many times, and in many ways. And I aver that, to this day, I have done no official act in mere deference to my abstract judgment and feeling on slavery. (7.281)

The disclaimer extends, ostensibly, to religion; but considerations of religion gradually reenter Lincoln's words. To be "naturally" against slavery is not merely to register a disposition. The natural aversion, which Lincoln in his previous speeches had attributed to mankind, if not to all individuals, stems from a moral universal from which he cannot recall ever wavering. These justifications introduce important qualifications. Rather than declare that slavery is an abomination condemned by God, the letter connects Lincoln's rejection of slavery to his humanity, and his history of thoughts and feelings about it. Human nature and logic, rather than a fixed revelation, order his words. As part of mankind, he "naturally" shares mankind's aversion. Thus he relies on his not infallible memory, not the Bible or an unalloyed moral axiom, to confirm that he has felt and thought so all his life. The moral absolute is thus couched in flesh: his God-given or at least "natural" and flawed humanity, which through its imperfections somehow has gained access to the grounds of truth. Lincoln guards against overinterpretation by framing these sentences with a series of negatives. He depends on a hypothetical series of negatives to set out an *implicit* positive doctrine: "I am naturally *anti*-slavery. *If* slavery is *not* wrong, *nothing* is wrong. I can *not* remember when I did *not* so think, and feel." All this instead of saying "Slavery is wrong."

Lincoln's oath and office, he goes on, do not give him the "unrestricted right to act officially upon this judgment and feeling." Thus even here, four months after issuing the proclamation, he does not condemn slavery outright and on moral grounds as an act of office. The oath of office has trumped all. He took it freely as an inevitable requirement for assuming office, which entailed making a promise that could not by its nature be taken "to get power, and break the oath in using the power." It was a pledge, he notes, to "preserve, protect, and defend" the Constitution.

Within these assertions Lincoln's qualifications mount up; but the moral urgency of the argument, which is linked to broader considerations of human beings' moral nature and Providence he will make explicit in his last paragraph, remains. At each step he nests practicalities within more general considerations of what the Constitution *is* outside of time, and what history is doing beyond the fog of daily events to shape his response. In the same movement, he embeds and limits the transcendental within the practical.

To fulfill his promise to leave the Constitution undisturbed, Lincoln notes, the oath-taking president must promise to defend it. This means that he must take into consideration circumstances that might jeopardize its very existence as the "organic law" of the nation:

I did understand however, that my oath to preserve the constitution to the best of my ability, imposed upon me the duty of preserving, by every indispensable means, that government—that nation—of which that constitution was the organic law. Was it possible to lose the nation, and yet preserve the constitution? (7.281)

To honor his oath he must attend to the Union, and so save the body that the Constitution organizes and animates—likewise saving the Constitution in its practical effect. As he works up to this idea, Lincoln has already indicated his willingness to frame the problem in terms of embodied, animate things: the "natural" and fallible human being and now the Constitution, which cannot meaningfully persist except as it is the "organic law" of the government and the nation it has constituted. In putting aside any desire of his own to act as president upon his "abstract" judgment on the question of slavery, he treats his scruples the same way: they cannot exist, for all practical purposes, separated from actions governed by his oath.

Of course, this does not reduce the Constitution to a merely material, malleable entity, nor does it fully dismiss Lincoln's moral aversion to slavery. But it assumes that the Constitution has taken on the body of the nation in having formed it: if the nation goes, so does the law that has organized it. And, by implication, so goes the practical influence of the Declaration's proposition about self-evident truths, which (as Lincoln had maintained for years) animates the Constitution and his own antislavery scruples.

These things persist, Lincoln lets his readers know, in the simple and subtle way he has fulfilled his oath. "In ordinary civil administration," he maintains, he would not have the right even to speak of his aversion to slavery in the abstract. But under the extraordinary circumstances of a civil administration, we gather, he might very well have it. When he finally avers that he has never acted upon his personal judgment and feeling about slavery, he more precisely means that he has never acted "in mere deference" to them. Although judgment and feeling have never controlled his actions, they have not been excluded from influencing and helping to guide them. As ordinary civil administration has given way to extraordinary times, he has implicitly modified his reticence to "indulge" his "primary abstract judgment on the moral question of slavery." The way is open for a consideration of conditions not wholly restricted to civil affairs under which he might act on the basis of an extraordinary right to do something he seems bound not to do:

By general law life *and* limb must be protected; yet often a limb must be amputated to save a life; but a life is never wisely given to save a limb. I felt that measures, otherwise unconstitutional, might become lawful, by becoming indispensable to the preservation of the constitution, through the preservation of the nation. Right or wrong, I assumed this ground, and now avow it. I could not feel that, to the best of my ability, I had even tried to preserve the constitution, if, to save slavery, or any minor matter, I should permit the wreck of government, country, and Constitution all together. (7.281)

All these points in the second phase of the argument seem to draw as much from feeling and emphatic avowal as from their connection to understanding ("I felt . . . and now avow;" "I could not feel . . . [that] I had even tried to preserve the constitution, if . . . I should permit the wreck of the government").

Some aspects of the organic law are more vital than others when the patient's life is in danger. To save the whole (the organism's life, not its every appendage), a limb might have to be sacrificed. Lincoln manages to intimate the additional, unspoken suggestion that the dispensable part of the Constitution, if not an accidental, "minor part," resembles a gangrenous limb, which according to contemporary medical practice had to be amputated to save the wounded patient. By 1864 the war had supplied enough examples of such surgery to make it a sanguinary commonplace.

So had the Bible, if one takes into account its presentation of a providential commentary on the history of what Lincoln had called an almost chosen people. In the passage from chapter 18 of the Gospel of Matthew that Lincoln would make central to his Second Inaugural a year later, the gospel writer links divine judgment with amputation: "Woe unto the world because of offences! For it must needs be that offences come; but woe to the man by whom the offence cometh! Wherefore if thy hand or thy foot offend thee: cut them off, and cast them from thee: it is better to enter into life halt or maimed, rather than having two hands or two feet to be cast into everlasting fire."[4] The physician who saves the political union of the states is not unconnected to the divine judge who, as Lincoln's last paragraph makes clear, he associates with the war-willing prerogatives of the Creator. Circumstances have denied Lincoln alternatives to this now indispensable means: the sacrifice of part for the whole to save the organic law that sustains the Union:

When, early in the war, Gen. Fremont attempted military emancipation, I forbade it, because I did not think it an indispensable necessity. When a little later, Gen. Cameron, then Secretary of War, suggested the arming of the blacks, I objected, because I did not yet think it an indispensable necessity. ... When ... I made earnest, and successive appeals to the border states to favor compensated emancipation, I believed the indispensable necessity for military emancipation, and arming the blacks would come, unless averted by that measure. They declined the proposition; and I was, in my best judgment, driven to the alternative of either surrendering the Union, and with it, the Constitution, or of laying strong hand upon the colored element. (7.281–282)

Lincoln is willing to admit that without his extraordinary reasons for carrying it out, his action was "otherwise unconstitutional." Was he not saying, then, that he was like a demigod, above the law? Does the surviving nation continue to be governed by the organic law, or is it a maimed remnant, alive yet hardly its old self? To address such questions, the argument turns again upon what he *has not* done, and upon what circumstances have *forced* him to do, even as he imitates and redirects the forces acting upon him. The emancipatory act described in the last line takes the form of another shackling, this one directed by events and his instrumental will. Given that the presidential vow upon his taking office, which "imposed" upon him "the duty of preserving, by every indispensable means, that government—that nation—of which that constitution was the organic law," the war president *in extremis* has generalized his own condition and the circumstances of the nation so that they apply to those held in bondage. He is therefore "laying strong hand" on the "colored element," whom he pulls from its linguistic designation as slaves and prepares to call "men." Their evil bondage, now broken, has been replaced by their justifiable duty (and, at Lincoln's hand, an imperative task like the one required by his oath) to save the embattled nation by laboring and fighting for the Union forces. For those observing these developments, he argues, the "palpable facts" best prove the justice of his action. The size of the freedmen's contingent—150,000—just a few months after the proclamation, and the absence of demands that they be replaced by white troops, has foreshortened public debate over the proclamation. Lincoln reduces the question to military necessity—*and* the sort of fait accompli normally attributed to God: under circumstances winnowed by the providential hand, facts prevail, and alternatives "otherwise unconstitutional" become the presidential prerogative: "[A]bout which, as facts, there can be no cavilling" (7.282).

Of course, unquestionable facts raise questions when we ask how unquestionable they are. The letter reaches for a more explicit justification for emancipation, in a paragraph Lincoln says he is adding to his original speech:

> In telling this tale I attempt no compliment to my own sagacity. I claim not to have controlled events, but confess plainly that events have controlled me. Now, at the end of three years struggle the nation's condition is not what either party, or any man devised, or expected. God alone can claim it. Whither it is tending seems plain. If God now wills the removal of a great wrong, and wills also that we of the North as well as you of the South, shall pay fairly for our complicity in that wrong, impartial history will find therein new cause to attest and revere the justice and goodness of God. Yours truly
>
> A. Lincoln (7.282)

Rather than an afterthought, this deliberate addition presides over the entire letter. Its supple concessions and unyielding assertions reorient and draw out the quasi-providential implications of the preceding paragraphs.

The added passage can be read as an ostensibly conventional bow to God's will. If such were indeed the will of God, then Lincoln's fundamental, personal objection to slavery would have been finally put into action by an unknowable yet somehow eminently accessible, just, and divine policy. Characteristically, however, Lincoln subtly shapes these general notions to a different end. God's role in events is not clear; yet it is the only role that explains what is happening and why: "God alone can claim it." In one sense, it is not for a mere man to invoke the influence of Providence. In another, a mere man must speak of it, if only to consider the possibility of its operation, because his absolute silence would exhibit his uncommon ignorance. The nature of providential influence is beyond human understanding, but the direction of its emancipatory "tendency," in this particular case, is certain *if* God so wills it. Lincoln implies that the end of that tendency is full emancipation, but he does not name or claim it.

Knowledge of God's will is hard to come by even if one believes. But the very fact that one does not know the Divine's precise intentions is cause, in this part of Lincoln's argument, to believe the divine justice and goodness are at work. Because the contest of civil war inflicts such a terrible retributive suffering on both sides, neither can claim providential favor. The war is not a conquest or a crusade, but a "struggle" that "impartial history" can judge better than those undergoing the ordeal. If Providence exists (and again it seems unwise, at least in the way Lincoln presents the idea, for anyone to dismiss that possibility), it molds and judges these events. By its evenhanded retribution, it turns back individual claims of justice while affirming a higher judgment of justice and goodness that is at once "plain" in its tendency and hidden to the vainly certain mind. Lincoln revolves these thoughts as though they existed in a time and place beyond his power, while in the same words laying "strong hold" on the idea that the human being, amid politics and war, can be Providence's instrument.

* * *

Lincoln's presidential rhetoric is of course famous for its blending of religious and political ideas. There is a greater density of religious or quasi-religious ideas in the presidential speeches than in the prepresidential rhetoric, though Lincoln did not simply turn to religious rhetoric when he arrived in Washington. His antebellum speeches, as we have seen, use abbreviated, suggestive allusions to religious ideas in support of a variety of arguments, including those resisting slavery. Sometimes he indulged in what modern readers tend to assume is hyperbole, as when he preached "reverence for the laws" in the 1838 Lyceum Address. That reverence needed to become, he said, "the political religion of the nation," so that Americans would "sacrifice unceasingly" upon the "altars" of the new faith to overcome the tyrannical threats posed by the mob and the homegrown tyrant (1.112). He characterized that danger as an almost Satanic potential for destruction within the body politic, and he described the nation's "proud fabric of freedom" as though it were a lesser version of "that only greater institution," presumably Saint Peter's church. If the nation could be placed on the firm foundation of the "rock" of Reason, it would resemble that greater institution all the more. On his own day of judgment, George Washington would return to discover how well Americans had perpetuated the institutions of liberty and self-government:

> [T]that we improved to the last; that we remained free to the last; that we revered his name to the last, that during his long sleep, we permitted no hostile foot to pass over or desecrate his resting place; shall be that which to learn the last trump shall waken our WASHINGTON. (1.115)

As the law-abiding man in Lincoln's hall of heroes, Washington might not be a biblical judge (when he awakens, he will "learn" of the outcome, not necessarily cast wrongdoers into the pit). But Lincoln's unsettlingly vivid imagery presents his transcendental role in the national drama as something real, as extending his reason and self-command beyond the grave to discover how well succeeding generations have preserved his trust. The hyperbole establishes something that plain prose or another rhetorical figure could not have so well secured: Washington is the living standard of self-government by which the American experiment is to be judged in its own best eyes. Political piety not only supports that vision; it draws from it the necessary inspiration and strength that free citizens need in order to do battle against their own tyrannical predilections. Without it, the mob will rule, and then the tyrant—unless the people's attachment to the laws transcends a merely civil obedience. In Lincoln's oratorical understanding, the republic must recognize and undergo such forms of commemoration and sacrifice in order to know itself, in order to *be* itself.

Of course, Lincoln's blending of religion and politics entails the general risk of being understood as reducing politics to religious belief, an outcome some of the abolitionists and southern defenders of slavery championed but which moderate Democrats and Republicans (and the Whigs before them) had long sought to avoid. At the same time, Lincoln's invocation of religious ideas helps him overcome the danger of seeming to ignore what he considers to be the long-standing convictions of mankind, and the possibility that potentially credible claims—such as those regarding the existence and power of Providence—are true. The Temperance Address provides us with a particularly illustrative example of his early thinking about the oratorical and philosophical problem of determining how far such a claim could go. In an almost parenthetical yet illustrative passage, he refers to the general belief in Providence in order to make a simple point about the daunting task of ending the intemperate consumption of alcohol:

> The universal *sense* of mankind, on any subject, is an argument, or at least an *influence,* not easily overcome. The success of the argument in favor of the existence of an over-ruling Providence, mainly depends upon that sense; and men ought not, in justice, be denounced for yielding to it, in any case, or for giving it up slowly, especially where they are backed by interest, fixed habits, or burning appetites. (1.275)

A long-accepted attachment to drink, supported by the general sense of mankind for many generations, is not to be dismissed if a similarly universal, long-standing sense of mankind has supported the belief in Providence.

The universal sense of Providence, as Lincoln frames it, is similar to the toleration of drink because it too "is an argument, or at least an *influence,* not easily overcome." Belief in Providence might therefore slowly change as arguments change, along with attitudes toward alcohol. Is this what Lincoln means to intimate? Without explicitly pursuing the matter, he uses the juxtaposition of the two types of universal sense to characterize the belief in Providence as an argument, a politically accessible formulation that can enter into the discussion of political and moral ideas. If that idea is relativized in some sense by the transformation, Lincoln treats it as an axiom or article of faith capable of condescending to the needs of plausible political argumentation. The universal sense of mankind is "mainly" responsible for the success of arguments for the existence of Providence. Lincoln's phrasing preserves the notion that something beyond common wisdom and experience or the power of rhetoric might determine whether Providence is real.

Throughout his career, Lincoln seems to have framed his allusions to Providence carefully, as though it were dangerously easy to say too much or too little, either by overestimating its bearing on particular events, or by underestimating the possibility of its influence. The former error was one he attributed to Douglas during the debates. Competing with Lincoln to define a prevailing vision of America's future, the Little Giant had called upon God's favor to justify his policy of popular sovereignty—by which he hoped the territories would be settled without federal control with regard to slavery. America's prosperity, Douglas argued, had always stemmed from its capacity to include slave and free states, and by its ability to accept new states into the Union without regard for whether they made slavery legal. That prosperity was protected, Douglas said, by divine favor: "During the whole period of our existence [under conditions that divided the nation into regions that were slave or free] Divine Providence has smiled upon us, and showered upon our nation richer and more abundant blessings than have ever been conferred on any other" (3.178). America's "destiny," he insisted, is evident in the fact that "Providence has marked out for us" a future of prosperity, with no need for Americans to agonize over the status of slavery in the new lands (3.274–275). He went on to express a powerful rhetorical confidence in Providence's favoring influence on the country's westward expansion.

America had "a great mission to perform": to "go on as we have done, increasing in wealth, in population, in power, and in all the elements of greatness, until we shall be the admiration and terror of the world" (3.321).

Douglas's certainties about providential favor had drawn Lincoln's fire years before, when he had half-humorously accused Douglas of welcoming President Zachary Taylor's death as an act of divine favor for the Democratic cause. In a highly partisan speech supporting General Scott's run for the presidency, Lincoln had wondered aloud whether Douglas was ready to defend his contention that Providence had intervened in partisan politics by ending Taylor's life. Douglas's faith in the voice of the people, Lincoln sarcastically concluded, "seems to go no farther than this, that they may be safely trusted with their own affairs, provided Providence retains, and exercises a sort of veto upon their acts, whenever they fall into the 'marvelous hallucination,' . . . of electing some one to office contrary to the dictation of a democratic convention" (2.150).

Lincoln's persistent rejoinder to Douglas during the debates was to question the notion that westward expansion was somehow so manifestly favored by God that the morality of slavery was irrelevant. By invoking Providence, Douglas had not only justified the tide of westward settlement; he had tried to argue that popular sovereignty was blessed. Lincoln avoided making such claims of providential favor in his own cause. He concentrated on the foundational texts and detailed historical inquiries. In the 1858 debates, *Providence* was not a word in his lexicon. He dwelt on the hazards of heedless expansion: its power to forget its origins, destroy the prospects for deliberate political choices, and allow slavery to permeate, in influence if not by presence, the entire country. For him, the apparently providential inheritance of the land called forth the responsibility to choose well, to draw the good things forward, and to subdue what would harm the good. He made it his purpose to probe and, when the occasion warranted, disclose what he thought were the good and sinister possibilities of that more gradual expansion so that Americans might choose the good.

Lincoln would have found contemporary support for his position in the writing of Alexis de Tocqueville, who in summing up his observation of American society defers to a providential power when he grants that "Providence has not created the human race either entirely independent or perfectly slave. It traces, it is true, a fatal circle around each man that he cannot leave; but within its vast limits man is powerful and free; so too with peoples.

... [I]t depends on [nations] whether equality leads them to servitude or freedom, to enlightenment or barbarism, to prosperity or misery." The authors of the *Federalist Papers* had similarly combined the notion of providential favor with a manifest sensitivity to the problem of judgment and the assessment of limits: "This country and this people," they had argued, "seem to have been made for each other," not merely for the sake of expansion or the exercise of choice, but for the development of a self-governing polity. Neither authority says that God compels Americans to be free, or that their westward movement obviates the question of what to do about slavery. Both are full of warnings and advice about how to adjust and guide a force of democratic expansion by means of reflective choice, through change that might otherwise destroy the republic that makes liberty possible.[5]

There is a Miltonic strain in Lincoln's approach to the providential gift, which formulates the relation between choice and providential influence in terms of a crucial passage of *Paradise Lost*. In the Lecture on Discoveries and Inventions of 1859 he had referred to Eve as God's "best present" to Adam (3.359), echoing John Milton's description of Eve as God's "last best gift" to Adam.[6] Joshua Speed reported to Herndon in 1866 that Lincoln read, among others, "Burns Byron Milton or Shakespeare—the news papers of the day—and retained them all as well as any ordinary man would any one of them—who made only one at a time his study."[7] The echo of Milton's text in Lincoln's lecture seems to be one result of that habit of reading and remembering.

In Milton's poem, the result of Adam's receiving that "last best gift" is not simply the fall of Man. In that poetical universe, the free, devoted companionship of the first parents is meant to prove or disprove, for all time, that self-government under God is possible. Eve is precariously and providentially joined with Adam in part because she is the first object of Satan's tyrannical ambition, and when she and then Adam succumb to his powers of seduction, they go out into the world with an awareness not only of their fallen condition but also of their Edenic history. They remember (more immediately, readers of Milton remember) their God-given powers of self-government as well as their ruination. In Milton's poetical treatment of Genesis, the persistence of that memory, assisted by the poem and its ardent readers, means that those powers of self-government are not beyond repair. In his political writings the poet famously and repeatedly reminds his readers of another possible fall—the descent into political tyranny—if the Edenic precedent and promise are forgotten. In the postlapserian history of disaster and redemption that Adam glimpses before his expulsion from the garden, he does not see only more disasters; he catches sight of a providential history enlivened by human choice. Lincoln seems to have had Milton's phrasing of these ideas in mind when he referred to the American republic, in his Second Annual Message to Congress, as "the last best, hope of earth" (5.537). The republic is a type of Milton's Eve—or rather, a type of the union in which Eve and Adam govern themselves and the land of their stewardship, depending on their choices and yet deferring to the possibility that history is being formed by a higher power.

Evidence that suggests Lincoln thought deeply about these aspects of Milton's biblical history can be found in the 1842 Temperance Address. There he set out his idea that human nature was unchangeable, using language that he seems to have taken from *Paradise Lost:* human nature, he wrote, is "God's decree, and never can be reversed" (1.273). The idea, as well as the phrasing of Lincoln's sentence, echoes the famous Miltonic lines in which the poet makes God decree that human beings, whatever their flaws, will be free. In the world of *Paradise Lost,* which lived in the imagination of many mid-nineteenth-century Americans, the rule of Providence somehow permits and encourages fallen human begins to shoulder the responsibility and risk of self-government:

> I [God] formd them [angels and men] free, and free they must remain,
> Till they enthrall themselves: I else must change
> Thir nature, and revoke the high Decree
>
> Unchangeable, Eternal, which ordain'd
> Thir freedom, they themselves ordain'd thir fall.
> The first sort [the fallen angels] by thir own suggestion fell,
> Self-tempted, self-deprav'd: Man falls deceiv'd
> By the other first: Man therefore shall find grace,
> The other none.[8]

In lines that strangely harmonize in tone and substance with parts of the most elevated oratory of Lincoln's presidency, Milton expresses a divine confidence in the power of free will, which is capable of wise government (and perdition) under God's providential rule.

There are of course two doctrines here, famously juxtaposed by Milton's version of Christian theology. The first involves the free will of angels and human beings: "Man" like the angels remains free in his power to choose and is therefore complex—capable of escaping sin and susceptible to a slavery he can bring upon himself. The second doctrine is a division of this principle: Satan and his angels fell on their own, "by thir own suggestion," whereas Man fell tempted by others, and so is offered grace. The division is not clean. Man is in some sense like Satan: both "themselves ordained thir fall." Yet the temptation by Satan mitigates Man's fall, though it does not exempt him from responsibility for collapsing under the pressure of Satan's power. In other words, Man is somehow free to fall or to reject a temptation that is in a sense beyond his powers to deflect. Likewise, he is free to transcend his condition by recognizing and choosing to accept his need for a greater power to save him. Choice ennobles submission while accession to a higher power reveals the urgency of choice. Providence presides over choices capable of swerving from and affirming providential rule.

* * *

Lincoln hardly used the word *Providence* in the antebellum period, avoiding it as he avoided joining a church. In an early stage of his political career, however, he set out a philosophy of "Necessity." Accused of infidelity (of being an "open scoffer at Christianity") during the 1846 congressional campaign, he replied in a handbill that he had been misunderstood. He ventured no doctrinal argument, except to say that the one controversial doctrine he had defended "in early life" was the quasi-providential view that a higher power moved and constrained the mind. The plainness and subtlety with which he makes his statement frame the question in civil and religious terms not unlike the ones he uses in later texts:

> A charge having got into circulation in some of the neighborhoods of this District, in substance that I am an open scoffer at Christianity, I have by the advice of some friends concluded to notice the subject in this form. That I am not a member of any Christian Church, is true; but I have never denied the truth of the Scriptures; and I have never spoken with intentional disrespect of religion in general, or of any denomination of Christians in particular. It is true that in early life I was inclined to believe in what I understand is called the "Doctrine of Necessity"—that is, that the human mind is impelled to action, or held in rest by some power, over which the mind itself has no control;

and I have sometimes (with one, two or three, but never publicly) tried to maintain this opinion in argument. The habit of arguing thus however, I have, entirely left off for more than five years. And I add here, I have always understood this same opinion to be held by several of the Christian denominations. The foregoing is the whole truth, briefly stated, in relation to myself, upon this subject. (1.382)

Here the idea of necessity overlaps and competes with conventional ideas of Providence. It also approaches, but does not embrace, the Calvinist idea of predestination. Lincoln's declarations of respect for conventional religion and Scripture are couched in double negatives that leave him room to articulate an unconventional view that is not strictly bound by doctrine. His definition of necessity as a power "over which the mind itself has no control" preserves a role for freedom of the will. As something that impels the mind "to action," or holds it "in rest," the force of necessity would seem to be absolute, and—as he implies in his conclusion—tantamount to a predetermining power over all things. But Lincoln's deliberate concision indicates that although necessity moves the mind to act, or keeps the mind at rest, it does not dictate *how* the mind acts—its *mode* of expression. In the very act of being kept at rest, the mind exhibits a self-moving power that necessity holds in check but does not eradicate. Even if it were inferred from this language that necessity directed the mind toward a particular kind of action, Lincoln's choice of *impel* rather than *compel* distinguishes the action from an exercise of raw power.

In the collected works, *compel* is a relatively common verb appearing twenty-six times, usually to describe the workings of the law or military force, and almost always signifying coercion.[9] *Impel,* appearing just five times, always has to do with complementary influences: one is impelled by respect for an admired friend (1.341), by an inclination to do the right thing (4.250), by natural causes of the desire for freedom (4.8), and by justified grievances (4.257). According to the handbill's definition of necessity, in other words, the mind is impelled—not determined in a wholly impersonal sense—by a power that leaves it to choose its direction, or the way it proceeds in a direction, or at least the way it responds to something that might be compatible with its moral being. The power to impel, thus understood, entails the influence of a just or admirable principle on the chooser: the person being impelled is typically drawn toward something solid, persistent, and worth choosing, even though it is something by definition he does not control.

In the process of defending his position, Lincoln distances himself from the doctrine of necessity without saying it is wrong. He admits, even declares, that he once defended it in argument, though he has now "left off" the "habit" of doing so. The handbill concedes, even specifies, much of the substance of the accusation; but it does not apologize for Lincoln's having held a belief in a complex doctrine of necessity: a belief in a power that somehow rules over all without reducing the mind to slavery. Having separated himself from an interpretation that would label him an infidel or a fatalist, this new turn in the argument draws necessity into the orbit of Providence. Lincoln turns back the accusation with an almost backhanded profession of faith that is not quite a profession because he says he no longer ventures such an opinion in public. The handbill's conclusion notes that this deeper doctrine of necessity is not unlike a Christian orthodoxy, presumably the Miltonic strain for which, as we have seen, Lincoln's thinking about necessity has a certain affinity. In fact his definition of necessity in 1846 is not wholly different from his later references to Providence as a largely undefined yet sovereign power, perhaps ruling all yet somehow not dictating or determining obedience. In the handbill Lincoln refrains from converting his crucial term into Calvinistic predestination, a conventional Christian idea of Providence, or a doctrine of his own. We learn his thoughts by means of his omissions and implications as much as by his declarations.

It is not surprising that Lincoln hardly mentioned Providence in the surviving record of his antebellum career. He likewise avoided the term *Necessity*, after elucidating its meaning in the 1846 handbill as a term with potentially religious connotations. During the 1858 campaign, he vehemently and repeatedly criticized the argument from necessity that was employed by Senator Preston Brooks, who contended that the expansion of slavery had become "a necessity" with the invention of the cotton gin (2.515, 3.87, 3.117, 3.277). The idea that necessity could be misused as a principle of political action was, of course, a rhetorical commonplace. An observant politician and orator did not need to know literary precedents; but powerful and lucid versions of the idea were in the air. Speaking before the House of Commons, William Pitt had famously called necessity "the argument of tyrants," "the creed of slaves," and "the plea of every infringement of human freedom."[10] In the first book of *Paradise Lost*, Milton had similarly characterized Satan's plea from necessity as a sign of tyranny: "So spake the Fiend, and with necessity, / The tyrant's plea, excus'd his devilish deeds."[11] In his own time of civil conflict, Milton's contemporary and sometime patron Oliver Cromwell anticipated Milton's condemnation of Satan by arguing that the false argument from necessity was akin to an impious invocation of Providence: "Necessity hath no law. Feigned necessities, imaginary necessities . . . are the greatest cozenage that men can put upon the Providence of God, and make pretences to break known rules by."[12]

Lincoln's Shakespeare offered sentiments about necessity that were famously sunny, as in an exiled Duke's contention that "Sweet are the uses of adversity," and Gaunt's effort to steel his exiled son with the idea that "There is no virtue like necessity" (quoted, at Stephen Douglas's expense, by Lincoln in the sixth debate [3.282]).[13] But in *King Lear*, there was the sinister Edmund's notorious critique of his father's hypocritical use of the word: "This is the excellent foppery of the world, that, when we are sick in fortune,—often the surfeit of our own behavior,—we make guilty of our own disasters the sun, the moon, and the stars; as if we were villains by necessity, fools by heavenly compulsion."[14] Edmund is the unsettling sort of Shakespearean villain who speaks as well as embodies truths that other characters do not know or understand. He uses his own arguments from necessity to carry out his murderous transgression of all familial and human connections.

Among such memorable rhetorical commonplaces, the misuse of the argument from necessity does not mean that necessity is never to be invoked for what might be just purposes. Cromwell qualifies his ringing condemnation of tyrannical uses of necessity with a vehement declaration that "manifest necessities" must be acknowledged. There must sometimes be subtle arguments from necessity to show the real force of manifest necessities when doubt dismisses them: "[I]t is deceitful and as carnal and as stupid, to think that they are no necessities, that are manifest necessities, because necessities may be abused or feigned. And truly I should be so, if I should think so; and I hope none of you think so."[15] Cromwell was a dictator, of course. Did Lincoln ever use arguments from necessity in this way, and, if so, for the cause of truth?

Lincoln's speeches show that he took up and elaborated arguments from necessity in the years just before and after the beginning of the Civil War. He spoke, for instance, of the imperative to accede to the power of necessity when it was the constitutional presence of slavery in the country's midst. He managed to avoid Webster's fate as a defender of the necessity of the Fugitive Slave Law and other measures by placing further conditions on his concession, some of which he connected to a higher necessity. Respect for the constitutional protections of slavery did not for him efface the Founders' expectation, which was embedded in the Declaration and the Northwest Ordinance, that slavery would become extinct. In the Cooper Union Address he strove to show that that expectation was a moral and political necessity because it informed the Constitution and could be demonstrated to exist in the undeniable mathematics of the Founders' votes. There were thus at least two kinds of necessity. One, the constitutional protection of slavery, "drove [the Founders] so far, and farther, they would not go" (2.274). They left later generations with the imperative "of necessity" to "manage" that state of affairs "as best we can" (2.266). Slavery could then be "hedged and hemmed in to the narrowest limits of necessity" (2.274). The second kind of necessity was moral and political. Slavery would be gradually extinguished in order to manifest the legacy that informed the Constitution and Declaration, and which defined the (seemingly providential) promise of American freedom. The first necessity would serve the second if it could somehow permit territorial expansion to be stopped on a moral as well as a political basis.

Lincoln used this complexity in the term's meaning to justify patience as well as aggressive political action, especially after he became president. "*To the extent* a necessity is imposed upon a man," he said in an 1858 speech in Chicago, "he must submit to it" (2.501; emphasis added). Conceding the legality of the slave laws was a sacrifice to the demands of the Constitution. Yet because that concession did not, in Lincoln's view, dislodge the Declaration's principles of equality and freedom that he assumed informed the Constitution, it might justify an interpretation of the Constitution in time of war that set the protection of constitutional principle above the meticulous adherence to all constitutional provisions. "[H]aving by necessity submitted to that much [protection of slavery where it exists], . . . does not destroy the principle that is the charter of our liberties" (2.501).

The policy Lincoln advocated toward slavery therefore mirrored his most characteristic rhetorical gesture, which compounded submission with a more prevailing resistance, the latter being arguably a higher form of submission to vital principle. The first form of necessity required submission; the second called for a resolve not to see that submission destroy what he considered to be the indispensable instruments of free government. The will submitted, and then a shrewder and finer resolve, operating under the influence or authority of a higher sanction, began to work. As though without will, in the way Lincoln expresses it, it worked in an almost neutral yet profoundly stubborn adherence to that principle, acceding to the possibility of defeat while seeking vindication in the fullness of time. All depended upon a combination of humility and virtue that would overcome necessity with necessity, neither presuming upon Providence nor disregarding the possibility of providential design.

12

The Farewell Address

"Let us confidently hope"

> In the present civil war it is quite possible that God's purpose is something different from the purpose of either party—and yet the human instrumentalities, working as they do, are the best adaptation to effect His purpose. (5.404)

The epigraph, drawn from Lincoln's wartime Meditation on the Divine Will, illuminates retrospectively the speech he made just before departing Springfield for the White House. Standing by the tracks that led to Washington, he implicitly characterized himself as an instrumentality: a man severely determined by circumstances that propelled him forward. Yet he was also showing himself, through the modalities of his speech, a free human being, one who could envisage the choices and sacrifices of his past and future converging on the present, a present in which he touched the strings that bound him to his fellow citizens and petitioned for the aid of a higher power. If we simply give close attention to his choice of verbs in the Farewell Address, we begin to appreciate how his words reflect and enact his instrumental condition:

> My friends—No one, not in my situation, can appreciate my feeling of sadness at this parting. To this place, and the kindness of these people, I owe every thing. Here I have lived a quarter of a century, and have passed from a young to an old man. Here my children have been born, and one is buried. I now leave, not knowing when, or whether ever, I may return, with a task before me greater than that which rested upon Washington. Without the assistance of that Divine Being, who ever attended him, I cannot succeed. With

that assistance I cannot fail. Trusting in Him, who can go with me, and remain with you and be every where for good, let us confidently hope that all will yet be well. To His care commending you, as I hope in your prayers you will commend me, I bid you an affectionate farewell. (4.190)

The speech begins with a Lincolnian double negative, an expression of the speaker's sad conviction that no one will understand his sadness. But the statement is, to a degree, a commonplace sentiment that allows him to express a special kind of melancholy that seems inexpressible. It is his "situation" that is beyond the reach of others; no one else stands where he stands, not because he is an individual leaving his home but because his great personal and public sadnesses, as yet undescribed, are by their nature not others' to know. The words indicate that it cannot be otherwise. And now, his gesture implies, the two sadnesses are entwined. To go on seems impossible. Yet he goes on, with a weighty yet simple concession of his debt to those he has just said cannot know his grief. He is not, he says, merely indebted to them; he owes all to them. What does this mean? He expresses a sense of his own fixity profoundly beyond his control yet somehow *his* to attribute to others: what he owes to others is "everything," which cannot be all theirs because it is more than they can know—beyond a brief speech's power to count and describe, perhaps beyond any speech. The clichés of speech in parting give way, in these sentences, to Lincolnian depth. His time in Springfield has covered the complete cycle: from youth to age, from seeing children born to seeing one buried. What comes next will be another life, or death: "I now leave, not knowing when, or whether ever, I may return." How then can that future be described? Lincoln faces his friends on the platform as though he has nothing and everything to say to them. In this sense he owes them an attempt to say "every thing" necessary for the circumstances of his parting. His reticent eloquence denies him the role he takes, and it makes that role archetypal.

The new life and possible death comprise a "task" that is "before me." His destination is inevitable, self-evident in some ways for a president elected in that time and place, but undescribed in any specific detail and therefore obscure. What he will do is not the matter. *Where he is*—his situation, which no one can know and yet which he adumbrates in every phrase— is the subject of the speech. It is here that a notion of Providence enters in, through an invocation of Washington but more specifically by means of Lincoln's assertion that "the task before me [is] greater than that which rested upon Washington." The speaker's immobility increases, if that is possible, in his reference to a burden surpassing Washington's. Paradoxically, when he speaks of Providence, he speaks for the first time as one who acts. He means that he will act with the "assistance" of Providence, perhaps in this way surpassing Washington's actions under a previous dispensation of heavenly favor. Here Lincoln's verbs are more forceful, though tasked with negation: "Without the assistance of that Divine Being . . . I cannot succeed. With that assistance, I cannot fail."

Emerging from the syntax of these negations is a commanding sense of resolution. Lincoln will not say that he will succeed, but he can express an almost breathtaking conviction that he "cannot fail." The "C" version of the speech, which seems to be a transcription not of Lincoln's authorship, overlays this subtle certainty with an awkward assertion:

> Unless the great God who assisted him, shall be with and aid me, I must fail. But if the same omniscient mind, and Almighty arm that directed and protected him, shall guide and support me, I shall not fail, I shall succeed. (4.191)

The "A" version in Basler's edition, which seems more likely to be Lincoln's, is much more suggestive in its simplicity. Washington was not merely "directed and protected." Providence "ever attended" him, although the great precursor's relation to divine favor was complicated as well as constant. Providence did not guard and command him; it accompanied him. Neither of the other versions (including Basler's "B," what is probably a reported version appearing in *Harper's Weekly* the next day) grasps this crucial subtlety.[1]

In the final two sentences, Lincoln uses active verbs to describe what God does and what it means to pray for others. He does not use them to express his independent action:

> Trusting in Him, who can go with me, and remain with you and be every where for good, let us confidently hope that all will yet be well. To His care commending you, as I hope in your prayers you will commend me, I bid you an affectionate farewell. (4.190)

Again it is instructive to see the other versions get this artful reticence wrong. The "B" version forces the lines with its use of active verbs at every opportunity:

> [O]n the same Almighty Being I place my reliance for support, and I hope you, my friends, will all pray that I may receive that Divine assistance without which I cannot succeed, but with which success is certain. Again I bid you an affectionate farewell. (4.190)

The "C" version (which, interestingly, Herndon preferred) does much the same thing, but with an air of false gentility:

> Let us all pray that the God of our fathers may not forsake us now. To him I commend you all—permit me to ask that with equal security and faith, you all will invoke His wisdom and guidance for me. With these few words I must leave you—for how long I know not. Friends, one and all, I must now bid you an affectionate farewell. (4.190)[2]

The far more lucid and complex "A" version contains the unique and nuanced ideas that God's action is threefold (going, staying, being), hence capable of influencing events and interacting with human volition, with a complexity associated with the divine attendance upon Washington.

In asking that he himself, as well as his audience, "confidently hope" for success, Lincoln again resorts to paradox. The success he hopes for is not what one might think: the speech is firm but haunting in its hope "that all might yet be well." It is not about *his* success. The nature of what is hoped for is indistinct. With his use of "yet," Lincoln extends the hope with a concession to what does *not* seem hopeful: all will be well despite what we may fear. The danger hangs in the air, unarticulated. Lincoln's words enforce the impression of stasis: his "situation" is beyond words, and in a sense it will remain with him when he departs. Thus the appropriateness of his request to his friends to commend him in their prayers. He articulates the thought in a sentence that bears repeating because it subtly affirms his consubstantiality, as he leaves, with all those staying behind, in imitation of the divine action he described in his previous sentence:

> Trusting in Him, who can go with me, and remain with you and be every where for good, let us confidently hope that all will yet be well. To His care commending you, as I hope in your prayers you will commend me, I bid you an affectionate farewell.

It is difficult to imagine a better, more compact example of Lincoln's moving ability to shape ideas about the relation between Providence and human will.

* * *

We can get a better sense of the remarkable persistence of these ideas of Providence and necessity into the presidential period if we examine several statements Lincoln is reported to have made to religious delegations. In late 1862, when he met with clergymen who asked him to abolish slavery, he seized upon their central argument: that Providence willed abolition. According to the report of his remarks, he at first rejected their reasoning, then accepted it with an important qualification. The reliability of men's reports of revelation, he began, did not seem to prevent wide disagreement among believers. One man found in revelation a favor toward the South, while another detected favor for the North. Some religious spokesmen favored immediate abolition on the basis of Scripture; others were not so sure. Lincoln could not accept the clergymen's contention that a decision to emancipate the slaves, carried out immediately and universally, was either God's will or prudent policy. The age of miracles, he was reported to have said, had passed. He did not expect to resolve the matter by way of a "direct revelation" when men who are "equally certain that they represent the divine will" took opposing positions. Still, it was his "earnest desire to know the will of Providence in this matter. . . . *And if I can learn what it is,"* he added, *"I will do it!"* In the absence of revelation he would have to study "the plain physical facts of the case, ascertain what is possible and learn what appears to be wise and right" (5.420). Yet he did not rule out, according to the clergymen's account, discerning the providential will: "Whatever shall appear to be God's will, that I will do" (5.425).

The nature of the facts of the case, which Lincoln made a point of listing for his visitors, is the key. Their report focuses on the facts too. (The clergymen's own account of the interview assumes but does not mention Lincoln's moral sympathy for the cause of emancipation, a sympathy he had seemed to express freely to another group of churchmen two months before [5.327]). Lincoln's leading consideration during the interview, in careful deference to the religious arguments advanced for emancipation, was about whether the facts to date—September 12, 1862—had a clear providential meaning. Given that the news from the army had been almost unrelievably bad for many months, the providential meaning of the facts was obscure. Lincoln said he seemed to be powerless to enforce an order of emancipation in rebel territory, and that if he were, he was not certain what to do with the freedmen, or how to prevent border-state soldiers from joining the Confederacy in protest. He could, he said, constitutionally issue the order as a military necessity, thus invoking his powers as commander in chief, but the benefits of such an action remained unclear: "[T]ell me, if you please, what possible result of good would follow the issuing of such a proclamation as you desire?" (5.421). All his reported remarks turn on the question of whether God's will *appears* to be at work in the immediate circumstances ("Whatever shall appear to be God's will, that I will do").

With the battle at Antietam approaching, Lincoln was leaving the providential question open just enough to keep it in view, as though the facts might indeed yield providential guidance as well as military news. His suggestive hesitation turned away ambitious piety; and yet it invited the clergymen to join with their friends in considering how emancipation might be understood by a wider audience, one without the clergymen's enthusiasm, as an advantageous *political* as well as moral good. The clergymen had already interpreted the long sequence of Union defeats as a providential proof that the Union cause would not prevail without its taking the high moral ground of emancipation (5.422). Now, to further their own ends they needed to see and endorse Lincoln's immediate political reasons for holding back and (if possible) moving ahead.

Lincoln had of course introduced a draft proclamation of emancipation to his cabinet long before he met with the clergymen from Chicago. In a cabinet meeting on July 22, 1862, he had proposed compensated emancipation in the border states and the liberation of slaves held in rebel areas. But many members of his own cabinet, and numerous congressmen he had met two weeks before, had objected. He omitted the offending passages before releasing the order on July 25. The result was a general order to seize rebel property, without reference to compensated emancipation or forced abolition in rebellious districts (5.336–37, 341). But the existence of Lincoln's draft had made clear that a presidential order involving emancipation—in the absence of support for legislation—could go into effect at any time. The public knew, through the *New York Tribune's* publication of congressmen's replies to Lincoln's proposal, that his administration was considering such an action (5.319). What was missing was the right moment. Lincoln needed general support, if not formal congressional approval, for the proclamation. And general support, at home and abroad, would not be forthcoming without a change in the facts and their interpretation.

The event that changed the facts was, of course, the Union victory in the sanguinary struggle at Antietam on September 17, just five days after Lincoln's reticent meeting with the clergymen from Chicago. The Preliminary Emancipation Proclamation, using phrasing Lincoln had employed in previous drafts but almost disavowed in the September 12 meeting, was issued five days later. Was the idea of Providence a factor in Lincoln's speech and thought? It is difficult to exclude it from Seward's advice that he wait for a victory so that he could show the world that the order was not his last resort in a failing cause (5.337). Whether Lincoln wished to invoke Providence or not, his previous refusal to claim providential favor paradoxically amplified the occasion as potentially providential. The facts, which had seemed to circumscribe him, now appeared to speak for themselves, without the need to claim them for justification. In issuing the preliminary proclamation when he did, he was able to deny himself the direct use of them, and yet speak in their light. In the final document issued January 1, 1863, which incorporated almost unchanged a concluding sentence crafted by Salmon Chase (6.25), Lincoln did *not* claim direct providential sanction. But he invoked "the gracious favor of Almighty God" to bless what he first characterized as a moral, legal, and tactical decision in the face of compelling circumstances (6.30). The almost bland opacity of the final proclamation's language did not fail to convey its earthshaking implications—as attested by the perhaps apocryphal but fitting story about Lincoln's trembling hand as he signed the document.

If there was a possibility for critics to interpret Lincoln's timing as opportunistic (and there was, and continues to be), the extent of the horrific losses on both sides at Antietam, as well as the Union victory, allowed him to make the proclamation an outcome of the battle in a way that almost defied criticism. Something of what he articulated in similar circumstances at Gettysburg and on the steps of the Capitol in March 1865 he used tacitly here, by his actions and his refusal to commit himself explicitly. The Union victory at Antietam had displayed, in its terrible facts, a willingness to sacrifice that shifted attention toward a higher cause and the Union's apparent willingness—confirmed, at least, in retrospect—to pay a high price for that cause.

* * *

There is other, more specific preliminary evidence to indicate that Lincoln's idea of Providence during the presidential years should not be dismissed as a merely rhetorical gesture. In a conversation with Presbyterian ministers visiting the White House in October 1863, he reportedly articulated his thinking in a manner that is consistent with the hints we have been gleaning from his presidential writings and speeches. The encounter with the Presbyterians is doubly interesting because we have two newspaper versions of what Lincoln said, each apparently formulated by a different writer. In the crucial portion of the interview when Lincoln ventured to speak about divine favor and Providence, the different papers give us a conventional and an unconventional version of his ideas. In the first, published in the *National Republican,* Lincoln is quoted as saying that providential guidance is close at hand, its promise assured:

> [U]pon taking my position here . . . I was early brought to a living reflection that nothing in my power whatever, in others to rely upon, would succeed without the direct assistance of the Almighty, but all must fail.
>
> I have often wished that I was a more devout man than I am. Nevertheless, amid the greatest difficulties of my Administration, when I could not see any other resort, I would place my whole reliance in God, knowing that all would go well, and that He would decide for the right.
>
> I thank you, gentlemen, in the name of the religious bodies which you represent, and in the name of the Common Father, for this expression of your respect. I cannot say more. (6.535–536)

In the second, published in the *National Intelligencer,* Lincoln says he is hopeful but much less certain:

> I was early [in my administration] brought to the living reflection that there was nothing in the arms of this man, however there might be in others, to rely upon for difficulties, and that without the direct assistance of the Almighty I was certain of failing. I sincerely wish that I was a more devoted man than I am. Sometimes in my difficulties I have been driven to the last resort to say God is still my only hope. It is still all the world to me. (6.536)

In each passage, the pivotal sentences are those in which Lincoln describes his turn to God's assistance. In both, the gesture is a last resort; but only in the first is there an assured assertion of Providence's power to guide events toward the outcome Lincoln wishes. The second version is much more tentative, yet more definite about Lincoln's distress. It has the ring of authenticity. He says he has "been driven" to his last resort, compelled or impelled "to say God is my only hope." Rather than simply embrace the divine power and see its providential favor supporting his efforts, he speaks about his hope for God's help. That is, he reports, on the basis of a devotion that falls short of his wishes, that such help must be forthcoming if he is not to fail. Although he does not explicitly say, as he is reported to in the first version, that he prays for that help, he is reported here to have said—in concise phrasing whose characteristically enigmatic eloquence could easily be his—that God is his last resort. Whether his language takes the form of prayer or an assertion, or both, we do not know. What he does say is that he needs that help and hopes it will be given. His conclusion, "It is still all the world to me," attributes everything to a vague pronoun. Is it God's help that is everything? Hope for that help? The meaning of such nuances becomes clearer and more complex the more we examine the written and oratorical record of his last years.

Perhaps the richest source of evidence for Lincoln's thoughts about Providence and political religion is what is now called the Meditation on the Divine Will, which Nicolay and Hay thought was written a few weeks before Antietam. Found in Lincoln's desk after the assassination, the meditation dwells on the meaning of military stalemate, and prepares a conceptual setting for the Gettysburg Address that looks ahead to the language of the Second Inaugural:

> The will of God prevails. In great contests each party claims to act in accordance with the will of God. Both *may* be, and one *must* be wrong. God cannot be *for,* and *against* the same thing at the same time. In the present civil war it is quite possible that God's purpose is something different from the purpose of either party—and yet the human instrumentalities, working just as they do, are of the best adaptation to effect His purpose. I am almost ready to say this is probably true—that God wills this contest, and wills that it shall not end yet. By his mere quiet power, on the minds of the now contestants, He could have either *saved* or *destroyed* the Union without a human contest. Yet the contest began. And having begun He could give the final victory to either side any day. Yet the contest proceeds. (5.403–404)

Here God's rule over all things has a purpose. He is "for" some things. He is not "for" and "against" the same thing. Second, and in consequence of the first, we cannot assume that we know what God's will is. Third, also an unfolding of the first, we can speculate reasonably about that will. The will of God is not simply unknown. Although it is "quite possible" that the divine purpose differs from the human one or the wishes of either side in the war, it is not a certainty that God's will is alien to human purposes and human understanding. Fourth, the very idea of divine purpose, despite and because of its problematic anthropomorphism in the religious traditions from which Lincoln draws his terms, tentatively connects the human with the divine. We can at least know something about what God's will is *not,* and we can assume that in great contests there is a chance that God's will is or will be at work, and that we might understand something about what its work is. Fifth, in the absence of evidence of God's shaping intention to end the war directly, there may be evidence of divine purpose in human purposes. If God acts through intermediaries, "the human instrumentalities" are the best of them for this purpose, not simply because they are human, but because of the ways in which they act. God could easily have extended the peace by commanding the inner beings of these intermediaries through "his mere quiet power," or by acting alone. Their "adaptation" or response to that power or to great and violent contests involves human freedom, and thus, for Lincoln, a capacity to act in the light of higher and lower purposes. The war that the divine power could have averted and could stop at any moment goes on, with the agony of the conflict being enacted by human beings whose actions and sufferings embody the war, human beings who have joined it by performing in a certain *way*—"working just as they do." If God's will prevails and does not stop the war without human help, the contest seems to be largely in the hands of human beings who are the choosing, suffering instrumentalities of that will. As God chooses to withhold divine might, the human actors, "working just as they do," choose to take up their burden and carry it for the sake of a good they can discern beyond their suffering.

The meditation ends suspended between God's choice to withhold that power, a choice that is by nature changeable, and the human effort to persist despite the danger of losing heart or choosing the wrong side. Lincoln's words temper and offer strength to that persistence. If both sides are wrong, as he thinks possible, there is at least the prospect that the human instrumentalities will respond well to the presence—and purposeful absence—of direct providential guidance. Lincoln proposes to himself that Providence, properly understood, is a double motion toward the good, an action that engenders humility while it deepens resolve.

God's overarching will therefore seems to use human instrumentalities, *as though they were needed,* in two ways: to express a divine will that might not need them after all, and to manifest human and political volition in ways that are necessary for the survival and prosperity of self-governing political associations. In Lincoln's lexicon, instrumentality has an important political meaning that helps us understand that second function. The linguistic association of *law* and *instrument,* still common in legal language, invests several of the devices of the law—the means of its enforcement—with a significance that transcends their mere efficiency. As instruments, the Constitution, the government, the elected officeholder all serve as intermediaries between higher and lower causes.[3] Modern legal language still refers to juries, which mediate the will of citizens and the forms of legislated law, as instrumentalities. Rightly convened, such bodies have a will and a purpose to refine and express the purposes of those they represent, in accordance with legislative precedent and the power to judge. They are intermediaries between what is relatively fragmentary and what can be more judicious, complete, or just. In many of these relatively concrete operations they mirror or shadow the providential mediation Lincoln contemplated in his Meditation.

* * *

The testimony of contemporaries who claim to have revealed Lincoln's religious convictions is unreliable. But to reject all such evidence, especially while inquiring into Lincoln's political religion, is to ignore the possible contributions of opinions more directly informed than our own. Relying upon skepticism is not enough to guard against the ways that skepticism arbitrarily limits the search for truth by choosing what it expects not to see. For one thing, the vernacular records offer insight into the power of Lincoln's humor, which seems to have been one of his ways to keep the question open. He had, in particular, a capacity to take advantage of a rhetorical situation to make fun of his own pretenses without conceding that his use of political religion was preposterous. Elton Trueblood retells a story printed in numerous papers during the war: two pious women discussing the chances of Confederate and Union victory disagreed, the first concluding that Jefferson Davis would prevail because he was "a praying man," the second saying Lincoln prayed too. The reply from Davis's defender settled the matter: "Yes, . . . but the Lord will think Abraham is joking." Lincoln, the butt of the joke rather than its author, is reported to have thought it a very good story indeed. For him and for his audience it somehow held a strange charm. It exposed doubts about his piety while indicating that he resorted to prayer, and it could be heard as a general indictment of the assumption that either side's dedication to prayer guaranteed victory.[4]

James F. Wilson wrote a detailed account, published in 1896, of Lincoln's reply to the argument that God's Providence was clearly on the side of the righteous. An observer of the first Union defeat at Bull Run had declared in Lincoln's presence that a divine judgment would befall all those who did not support the Union. Despite its flowery expressions and its remoteness from the event, Wilson's recollection of Lincoln's words suggests, in some of its mannerisms, how Lincoln might well have checked and transformed that bitterly righteous remark. According to the report, he begins by agreeing, then ends by refocusing the exchange on the idea that Providence is profoundly coactive with human volition:

> "My faith is greater than yours. I not only believe that Providence is not unmindful of the struggle in which his nation is engaged; that if we do not right God will let us go our own way to our ruin; and that if we do right He will lead us safely out of this wilderness, crown our arms with victory, and restore our dissevered union, as you have expressed your belief; but I also believe that He will compel us to do right in order that He may do these things, not so much because we desire them as that they accord with His plans of dealing with the nation, in the midst of which He means to establish Justice. I think He means that we shall do more than we have yet done in furtherance of His plans, and he will open the way for our doing it. I have felt His hand upon me in great trials and submitted to His guidance, and I trust that as He shall further open the way I will be ready to walk therein, relying on His help and trusting in His goodness and wisdom."

The manner of Lincoln's delivery [Wilson continues] was most impressive, and as Mr. Lincoln resumed his seat he seemed to have recovered from the dejection so apparent when we entered the room. With a reassured tone and manner, he remarked: "The Army of the Potomac is necessary to our success; and though the case at this moment looks dark, I can but hope and believe that we will soon have news from it relieving our current anxiety. Sometimes it seems necessary that we should be confronted with perils which threaten disaster in order that we may not get puffed up and forget Him who has much work for us yet to do. I hope our present case is no more than this, and that a bright morning will follow the dark hour that now fills us with alarm. Indeed, my faith tells me it will be so."[5]

Wilson's crafted recollection is full of subtleties that instructively distinguish the first speaker's righteous certainty from Lincoln's complicated, corrective insistence upon Providence's interaction with human desire and free will. The first speaker threatens divine punishment for all disloyal citizens. Lincoln then stands, and speaks as though *anyone* might be capable of embracing wrong and suffering a consequent, hence chosen punishment. God would preside over the punishment by permitting it, not inflicting it: "If we do not do right God will let us go our own way to our ruin." Once the country is on the righteous path, the goal will not be heaven (the first speaker's implied reward for the loyal heart) but the certainty that God will lend a hand to lead the Union "out of this wilderness." The goal will be blessed yet earthly, effected by divine influence rather than unmediated command. God will not create victory but "Crown our arms" with it. He will not create the Union but "restore" it. The war does not obey, and might disappoint loyal unionists' desires. In fact the threat of defeat might very well be a fitting means for God to work through the unionists' self-deceptions.

There will indeed be divine compulsion: "He will compel us to do right." But as Lincoln wrote in the 1846 handbill's argument about Necessity's power to compel the mind, the coercion will not fully displace the motion of the mind or its obligation to choose. Rather than crossing the human desire to do right, it will take a form that "open[s] the way for our doing" the divine will. For this reason the precise action God wills is not clear and, by its nature, will not be clear to those who are ambitious to claim it as their own. Lincoln hedges Providence about with double negatives: "Providence is not unmindful of the struggle . . .; if we do not right. God will let us go our way to our ruin." Lincoln says that it must be human "work," a war-making labor (following one traditional meaning of the word) that arduously merges with divine direction. God wills it, and so the human actors must suffer to do it. But the work is not so arduous, at least not yet, that it defies all attempts to understand it. And its rigors do not extinguish all active anticipation of relief: "I hope our present case is not more than this." Characteristically, the reported conclusion of Lincoln's remarks qualifies the hope of relief: his anticipation of the Union army's success might be misdirected. More trials might indeed come, and thus he inserts the idea that the hope of relief is not the same as a broader faith in divine guidance.

In Wilson's version of Lincoln's statement, these ideas are embedded in Lincoln's effort to discern providential influence as it works through human beings. Without taking on a preacherly voice, Lincoln alludes to a providential influence that depends on human understanding and choice, as well as submission. The gist of Wilson's recollection attains further definition when we contrast it with the sentiments expressed in a contemporaneous sermon by Horace Bushnell, who preached his apocalyptic message within a week of the Bull Run defeat:

> God is pressing us on the apprehending of that for which we are apprehended. Our passion must be stiffened and made a fixed sentiment as it can be only when it is penetrated and fastened by moral ideas. And this requires adversity. As the dyers use mordants to set in their colors, so adversity is the mordant for all sentiments and morality. The true loyalty is never reached till the laws and the nation are made to appear sacred or somewhat more than human. And that will not be done till we have made long, weary, terrible sacrifices to it. Without shedding of blood, there is no such grace prepared.[6]

Bushnell's biblical reasoning draws from wellsprings Lincoln would later channel into the Gettysburg Address and the Second Inaugural. But the spirit of Wilson's rendition of Lincoln, which was likely to have been colored by his recollection of the Gettysburg Address and the Second Inaugural, is very different. Bushnell rationalizes suffering in the war as though it had a purely religious cause and end; and yet in the way he asserts these ideas he politicizes the act of sacrifice as though it were a mechanically compelled worship of the laws and the nation. He describes God as a tactician whose calculated hammer blows have clear causes and unequivocal effects, whereas Wilson's recollection of Lincoln frames providential action in terms of its influence upon human choice as well as divine prerogative. His Lincoln takes up the political challenge of encouraging adherence to an embattled, perhaps losing, but honorable cause—without resorting to misconceived threats, even though the situation is so dire it lends itself to fanaticism.

In the context of these comparisons, it is instructive to recall that Lincoln frequently quoted Hamlet's speech about "a divinity that shapes our ends, / Rough-hew them how we will."[7] Even out of context, these lines give us a glimpse of the depth of his idea of Providence as a divine power molding rather than absolutely dictating the human ends that Lincoln and others try to set out for themselves. In the context of the fifth act in Shakespeare's play, the meaning of the passage is instructively complicated. It is his "rashness," Hamlet says, that in a moment of desperation has somehow been guided by a divine power.[8] As he tells Horatio, he rose from his sleep on the ship that was taking him ominously toward England with the realization that his powers of reason and his vague fears of Claudius's intentions were insufficient guides. He had to rise from his bed in the middle of the night to discover his fate by stealing and opening his stepfather's letter to the English king. In that moment he saved himself from being executed, and he sent the messengers to their deaths instead. Divinity's shaping power seems to have guided Hamlet's rashness, but not in all ways. It does not tell him that he is in danger, or what the danger is. It stirs him and sends him forth to find out the danger. And it exposes him to the possibility of error. It does not clearly sanction his idea to send Rosencrantz and Guildenstern to *their* execution. It shapes his ends in ways he cannot master, while enabling and tempting him to second its power for his own ends.

The conversation between Hamlet and Horatio that surrounds these lines is made up of ideas that remind us of Lincoln's complicated understanding of Providence. Hamlet assumes that a divine power moves him toward a certain end—the saving of his life. Because it is Prince Hamlet's life he preserves, he may also mean that the shaping divinity saves his claim to his father's throne; hence there might be a providential blessing on his actions and his cause. Horatio at first agrees with him in his general principle (that there is "a divinity that shapes our ends," he says, is "most certain")[9] but he wonders about the outcome. In his silence Horatio does not subscribe to Hamlet's enthusiasm in sending the king's messengers to their deaths, and he indeed eventually denies, when he defends his dead friend, that Hamlet did any such thing.

Hamlet's general attitude toward Providence enlarges and focuses in the last act. The crucial moment of this change is his dramatic distinction between "augury" and "special providence"—between vague misgivings or prognostications, and the greater assurance of divine guidance promised in Matthew 10.29. Troubled by the sense that the proposed duel with Laertes might be a dangerous foolishness, he suddenly rejects his anxieties and settles upon the biblical teaching of providential dominion: "[W]e defy augury. There is special providence in the fall of a sparrow. If it be [now], tis not to come; if it be not to come, it will be now; if it be not now, yet it [will] come—the readiness is all."[10] Providential power is not to be taken for granted, for it neither ensures victory nor keeps the sparrow from falling. Hamlet might fall. But the idea of the sparrow's providential end settles Hamlet's resolve.

Being saved from death is not, in this sense, the point. Indeed Hamlet's interpretation of the scriptural passage, if we look closely at his behavior in the following events, might be construed as a combination of stoicism and militant resolve that leaves little to providential design in Christian terms. One could argue that what matters most to Hamlet in this moment and in the rest of the play is readiness for death, and for the chance to live and fight on to preserve his honor and reputation.

Of course, Shakespeare does not resolve the matter entirely in this way. For good reason, Hamlet remains the most famous riddle in literature. The last lines of the play are haunted by a sense that providential favor means more than assistance in preparing for death, and that the hero might still be wondering whether he will be vindicated in life and in death by a higher power. His dying request that Horatio tell his story is quite possibly an effort to solicit a providential blessing. And indeed, Horatio petitions for "flights of angels" to "sing thee to thy rest."[11]

Insofar as Lincoln was cognizant of these deeper contexts surrounding Hamlet's statement about divinity shaping our ends—which seems likely, given his lifelong reading of the plays—these complexities would have colored his use of that quotation with a precedent that should cast doubt on conventional interpretations of his reasoning about Providence. His strong sympathy for Claudius, which we have noted in previous chapters, might well have suppressed his outward identification with the melancholy prince who slays him. We know he was more admittedly fascinated with the sublimation of the providential question in the obviously condemnable witchcraft of *Macbeth,* in which a false understanding of mischievous but true prophecies spectacularly destroys an overly credulous, evildoing hero. *Hamlet* and its immensely appealing hero must have remained for him, however, an attractive trove of dramatic material. It would have offered him rich means of understanding how providential reasoning could save or condemn a strong and sensitive political imagination in a noble man attempting to avenge a great wrong. It certainly offers Lincoln's modern readers a probe for understanding the many dimensions of his idea of Providence.

13

The First Inaugural, the Gettysburg Address, and the Second Inaugural

Providence and Persuasion

The prayers of both could not be answered; that of neither has been answered fully. (8.333)

How then did these ideas take form in the great presidential speeches? The pressures of impending war and civil conflict were eminently capable of changing, distorting, and misdirecting them, or redefining them on a level transcending their previous applications. In the four months between the 1860 election and the inauguration, silence was the rule. As Lincoln prepared for his First Inaugural Address, he avoided public speech. Relying on the printed record to speak for itself, he immersed himself in the private negotiations that were necessary to form the new administration. When he ventured to insert, with careful maneuvering, a few anonymous paragraphs in the speech of his friend Lyman Trumbull, his effort to reassure the South of his peaceful and law-abiding intentions failed. The language he added to his friend's speech could not say enough, and Trumbull for his own part said too much. Their explanations were interpreted as innovations. Lincoln concluded that the gesture had been counterproductive.[1]

Before assuming office the president-elect found himself in circumstances in which he could not add to the record, even to clarify it, without risking the appearance of announcing what would have amounted to a new policy—a platform upon which he had not been elected. His promise to take office as the candidate elected under the Constitution, presumably on the basis of his carefully articulated, published views, was the substance of his policy and could not be overturned. Yet the expectations of many of his supporters, like the suspicions of detractors, were high. The credible impression that he could, with a few words, mold events almost providentially or throw the country into an unnecessary conflict by misreading the signs of the times threatened to make all his speech problematic. Once he began to speak publicly again, he had to meet the expectation that he would hold to his principles *and* avoid war. To do so, he had to engage and allay apocalyptic hopes and fears, and draw out those embattled passions and convictions that would sustain the Union.

On his way to Washington, Lincoln made a few statements that combined basic facts with general principles. When he addressed the New Jersey legislature, his speech was brief and cautious. He managed to venture the claim that he was "the representative man of the nation" on the basis of his election. "As such," he said, he accepted their welcome "more gratefully than I could do did I believe it [the election] was tendered to me as an individual" (4.236). Because he and his audience were "united by a purpose to perpetuate the Union and liberties of the people," they were both dedicated to preserving "something more than common." In their struggle to save the Union, Lincoln implied, they all substantiated the legacy of Washington, the Declaration, and "the original idea for which the [revolutionary] struggle was made" (4.236). He did not attempt to state explicitly what that idea was.

The First Inaugural was, of course, Lincoln's first opportunity to speak as president. When he delivered the address, he could for the first time make rhetorical concessions to the South as an expression of presidential magnanimity. At the same time, he could invoke the quasi-religious sanction of his presidential vow to preserve the Constitution and hence—as he saw his duty—to block secession. The two motives became bound up with each other:

> In *your* hands, my dissatisfied fellow countrymen, and not in *mine,* is the momentous issue of civil war. The government will not assail *you.* You can have no conflict, without being yourselves the aggressors. *You* have no oath registered in heaven to destroy the government, while *I* have the most solemn one to "preserve, protect and defend it." (4.271)

Without directly claiming the sanction of heaven for himself, Lincoln explicitly denies the secessionists its authority, then declares his resolve to act upon a vow that is "most solemn"—a religio-political invocation of presidential authority that protects the status quo even as it intimates a resolve to go to war if necessary.

This variation on a life-long pattern of yielding and resisting, of deferring to other views yet refusing to abandon principle, is at work throughout the speech. It is most memorably embodied in its final paragraph. Lincoln's conclusion relies heavily upon Seward's suggestions, which were offered to replace the dangerously awkward ending of the prior draft. The extreme concision of that version alluded to Jesus' statement about bringing judgment to all the earth (Matthew 10.34): "With you, and not with me, is the solemn question, 'Will it be Peace, or a Sword?'" Taking a different tack, Seward recommended a conciliatory conclusion, which Lincoln sculpted into his own notable utterance.[2] In syntax that is both elliptical and frank, Lincoln softens and focuses the prospect of conflict, repeatedly inviting his dissatisfied audience to choose the peaceful path: "I am loth to close. We are not enemies, but friends. We must not be enemies." He had similarly refrained, in the prior paragraph, from referring to civil conflict directly, in a positive sentence; he wanted the South to see the dangerous proximity of war, not to interpret his words as a challenge to a duel or an empty threat: "In *your* hands, my dissatisfied fellow countrymen, and not in *mine,* is the momentous issue of civil war" (4.271).

The First Inaugural's final paragraph is the culmination of this complex gesture of conciliation and confrontation. When we compare Seward's vague phrasing to the supple gravity of Lincoln's final revision, we see more clearly how Lincoln's concessive tone skillfully sheathes a resolute blade.

> Seward: I close. We are not we must not be aliens or enemies but fellow countrymen and brethren. (4.261)
> Lincoln: I am loth to close. We are not enemies, but friends. We must not be enemies. (4.271)

Seward directly signals the end of the speech; in syntax and thought, Lincoln expresses a desire not to end, not to curtail his appeal for conciliation. He retains the core of Seward's declaration: he will close. But the meaning is different. His regret is all the more real because he is recognizing that the end of the speech will necessarily conclude its oratorical effort to achieve reconciliation. He wants to continue for the sake of peace, but he lets it be known he must stop. He defers to the decorum that demands all speeches end but in a

way that intimates and rehearses preparation for war. In the next line he goes
farther than Seward in referring to his dissatisfied countrymen as friends, but
then characteristically adds an almost intimate, insistent, negative imperative: "We must not be enemies." There must be reconciliation because the
sections are really friends; there must be reconciliation because the South
must not risk war. Lincoln's lines appeal to his listeners' powers of choice.
He gives them almost unsettling access to his divided thought. Reluctant, re-
gretful, almost self-dramatizing in his repetitive assertion of friendship, he is
affectionate yet adamant. In contrast to Seward's matter-of-factness, Lincoln's high oratorical tenderness penetrates, and is penetrated by, his terse
commands:

> Seward: Although passion has strained our bonds of affection too hardly they
> must not ["be broken they will not" deleted], I am sure they will not be bro-
> ken. (4.261)
> Lincoln: Though passion may have strained, it must not break our bonds of
> affection. (4.271)

Seward wants to reassure. Lincoln pares the sentence down to its ambiguously commanding, self-expressive core, appealing to the South's power to
choose conciliation, within the shadow of a demand to abandon the opposite
course.

Seward's final sentence, like Lincoln's, attempts to move the argument
into a religio-political sphere.

> Seward: The mystic chords which proceeding from so many battle fields and
> so many patriot graves pass through all our hearts and all the hearths in this
> broad continent of ours will yet again harmonize in their ancient music when
> ["touched as they surely" deleted] breathed upon by the ["better angel"
> deleted] guardian angel of the nation. (4.261–62)
> Lincoln: The mystic chords of memory, stretching from every battle-field,
> and patriot grave, to every living heart and hearthstone, all over this broad
> land, will yet swell the chorus of the Union, when again touched, as surely
> they will be, by the better angels of our nature. (4.271)[3]

Seward's imagination is more literal and airy than Lincoln's. He formulates
but rejects the more imaginative phrasing ("touched as they surely . . . ") that
Lincoln will adopt. Most importantly, he does not develop the possibility
that the audience might choose the proper path. He does not powerfully ar-

ticulate the possibility that the divided nation might reconcile with itself, or that individual citizens might listen to their own better natures. His angel is at once more concrete and ineffectual. If he has in mind Milton's famous guardian angel in *Lycidas*—a Saint Michael that stands watch on the frontier—he describes it as a vague power.[4] It animates his audience's connections to an ancient, common past, but there is no distinct indication of what that animation would be, or what it would be for.

Lincoln's famous emendations animate Seward's sentences with greater firmness, and attention to the audience's power to choose. They anchor Seward's mystic chords internally, in memory, and anticipate that their music will be a particular song shared by all: "the chorus of the Union." The overarching guardian angel becomes a more psychologically compelling (and religio-political) angel in each person: the "better angels of our nature." The animating force that plays the "mystic chords of memory" is not a general breath but each angel's touch, a force that works in company, repeating and renewing prior harmonies. The music revivifies the Union chorus *of* as well as *for* the Union.[5] Lincoln's Shakespearean and Miltonic rendering of "the better angels of our nature" reminds his audience of their choice, which is informed by a better version of themselves though by implication not free of the danger posed by an angel that is worse.[6] Lincoln's words claim power to speak within his audience's memory as reminders of that audience's capacity to renew that chorus of union.

Here it is worth pausing to consider this passage's harmony with Lincoln's broader pattern of oratorical thought. The intimacy and impersonality of Lincoln's revisions of Seward's notes are the presidential version of his lifelong oratorical pattern of concession and assertion. If, as Richard Weaver has argued, Lincoln's presidential style is to be understood in terms of its impersonal "oracularity, opacity, and distance,"[7] it is also strangely familiar. In such moments, Lincoln seems to speak from within his audience as well as from on high. How is this possible? Is it philosophically as well as politically credible?

When David Donald comes to the conclusion that an understanding of Lincoln's passivity is crucial to our interpretation of his life, he speaks to the suspicion that there is something more than natural in that passivity.[8] It is indeed something that works upon us. Donald refers to Keats's famous definition of "Negative Capability," which the poet called the leading attribute of the "Man of Achievement." It is a characteristic Keats said he found most amply demonstrated in Shakespeare. We see that attribute, Keats wrote, "when a man is capable of being in uncertainties, Mysteries, doubts, without any irritable reaching after fact & reason." Shakespeare in Keats's view was a master of masterlessness: "It is . . . a very fact that not one word I ever utter can be taken for granted as an opinion growing out of my identical nature—how can it, when I have no nature? When I am in a room with People if I ever am free from speculating on creations of my own brain, then not myself goes home to myself: but the identity of everyone in the room begins . . . to press upon me that, I am in a very little time an[ni]hilated."⁹ The fact is that Lincoln achieved oracularity not by naive sympathy but by thinking in speech about basic principles, and by selectively anticipating and so gaining useful access to his audience's intellectual imaginations of those principles and their significance.

The strange mingling of his resolute energy with an almost alarming passivity allowed Lincoln to persuade while withdrawing into his audiences' world, like a profound dramatist who spoke elliptically through others. In that world he enunciated principles and challenged his hearers to act; but his method was predominantly elliptical and indirect, punctuated by unsettling assertions. He drew out and animated (or subdued) the passions, axioms, and habitual inferences that moved his audiences. Allowing himself to be absorbed into his audiences' world did not mean that he became Keats's sparrow, the bird the poet identified with. Lincoln moved audiences for the sake of principles he detected in their aspirations as well as in their self-interest. By appealing to those ideas and the passions that pursued them, he worked to enlarge the ground of civil speech not only, he argued, to preserve the Union but to make it worth saving.

We see this animating principle at work in the famous conclusion to Lincoln's 1862 Message to Congress, in which he advocated compensated emancipation. As was the tradition for such messages, the document was read by a clerk, not delivered by the president. Still, the combination of assertion and submission in its concluding periods must have impressed its audience with Lincoln' fusion of negative capability and resolve:

> We can succeed only by concert. It is not "can *any* of us *imagine* better?" but "can we *all* do better?" Object whatsoever is possible, still the question recurs "can we do better?" The dogmas of the quiet past, are inadequate to the stormy present. The occasion is piled high with difficulty, and we must rise

with the occasion. As our case is new, so we must think anew, and act anew. We must disenthrall our selves, and then we shall save our country. (5.537)

First is the call to unity that leaves no alternative, then the imagined retorts of opponents and supporters that lead up to the recurring, ineradicable question that is also an invitation: Can we do better? Then comes an oratorical submission to the storm of circumstances, and next the imperative and/or choice to "rise with the occasion" and "act anew" with and against those circumstances. To "disenthrall" is not the same as to liberate. Lincoln's verb renders the idea of rising as the negation of a kind of slavery, an arduous disentanglement from an involvement that has captured the mind as well as the body. The final argument invokes Providence in the context of these disparate, somehow unified motives as Lincoln takes on—confronts and inhabits—the thinking of his audience:

> Fellow-citizens, *we* cannot escape history. We of this Congress and this administration, will be remembered in spite of ourselves. No personal significance, or insignificance, can spare one or another of us. The fiery trial through which we pass, will light us down, in honor or dishonor, to the latest generation. We *say* we are for the Union, The world will not forget that we say this. We know how to save the Union. The world knows we do know how to save it. We—even *we here*—hold the power, and bear the responsibility. In *giving* freedom to the *slave*, we *assure* freedom to the *free*—honorable alike in what we give, and what we preserve. We shall nobly save, or meanly lose, the last best, hope of earth. Other means may succeed; this could not fail. The way is plain, peaceful, generous, just—a way which, if followed, the world will forever applaud, and God must forever bless. (5.537)

* * *

Throughout his early oratorical career, Lincoln used such powerful phrasing sparingly, most often to introduce and close his prewar speeches. He embedded his most powerful rhetorical effects in plain speaking. Yet he strove for a level of rhetorical honesty that required a habit and art of expressive restraint that left him vulnerable to the distrust of those who were not sufficiently moved by his efforts. The direct invocation of providential favor was by his standards something easily misdirected or overwrought. But he did not eschew oracular utterance. His plain speaking had a way of projecting eloquence, and of providing a space for flights that briefly demonstrated the power of oratory that he held in reserve. We see this happening on an almost routine basis in the greatest of the presidential speeches.

Passages that dilate upon the ways of Providence are more frequent in the presidential years, though still spare even when they are among the most memorable. In the concise and beautiful Thanksgiving proclamations whose authorship Lincoln seems to have shared with Seward, providential reasoning is both sanctioned and confined by the ceremonial occasion. In the First Inaugural and the 1862 Message to Congress, as we have seen, he pours out eloquence in his last sentences, in passages that incorporate and lift the rest of the performance. His two most famous speeches rely upon providential reasoning throughout. All are distillations of an oratorical power that enlarges the significance of the florid language it rations for strategic passages.

Perhaps the greatest tests of that power took place at Gettysburg in November 1863 and on the inaugural platform on March 4, 1865. In the first case, the occasion dictated a brief address. The letter that David Wills, the leader of the dedication committee, wrote to Lincoln asked for "a few appropriate remarks" to be delivered "after the oration," so as "to perform this last solemn act" of dedication. Unlike Everett's oration, Lincoln's address was expected *not* to be an oration (Everetts's was "the" oration). His role was almost entirely ceremonial: to provide a culminating act of consecration rather than a continuation or elaboration of the long disquisition that was expected to go before.[10] Contrary to the popular lore of the past 140 years, Lincoln did not merely decide to write a brief address; he was aware of the expectation that he would deliver a short speech. The day after the dedication, he wrote Edward Everett, "In our respective parts yesterday you could not have been excused to make a short address, or I a long one" (7.24).

We begin with the version of the Gettysburg Address that Basler calls the "final text" (7.22). Although there is controversy over the precise wording of the authoritative version, and indeed over whether an authoritative version exists or can be redacted,[11] the task remains to apprehend the form and meaning of what Lincoln said. The point is to come upon it, as much as possible, with a readiness to see it anew.

> Four score and seven years ago our fathers brought forth on this continent, a new nation, conceived in Liberty, and dedicated to the proposition that all men are created equal.

Now we are engaged in a great civil war, testing whether that nation, or any nation so conceived and so dedicated, can long endure. We are met on a great battle-field of that war. We have come to dedicate a portion of that field, as a final resting place for those who here gave their lives that that nation might live. It is altogether fitting and proper that we should do this.

But, in a larger sense, we can not dedicate—we can not consecrate—we can not hallow—this ground. The brave men, living and dead, who struggled here, have consecrated it, far above our poor power to add or detract. The world will little note, nor long remember what we say here, but it can never forget what they did here. It is for us the living, rather, to be dedicated here to the unfinished work which they who fought here have thus far so nobly advanced. It is rather for us to be here dedicated to the great task remaining before us—that from these honored dead we take increased devotion to that cause for which they gave the last full measure of devotion—that we here highly resolve that these dead shall not have died in vain—that this nation, under God, shall have a new birth of freedom—and that government of the people, by the people, for the people, shall not perish from the earth. (7.22–23)

The fierceness of the battle that marked the culmination of Lee's thrust into the North had manifested the Union's resolve. But it had also exposed that resolve to the uncertainties of pursuing Lee's wounded yet still substantial and dangerous army before it recrossed the Potomac. Meade's hesitation in pursuing Lee was not only a military demonstration of the difficulty of pushing a battered, victorious army to pursue final victory without rest. It also exemplified the challenge of carrying on when the hallowing price of victory had proved so terrible that victory seemed, to many in the North, almost indistinguishable from defeat. Lincoln found a way to speak over the honored dead, and the finality of their sacrifices, by directing attention to the campaign ahead. Conceding the decisive distance between the actions of those who fought at Gettysburg and the words he sought to deliver, he somehow drew from the occasion an animating power that enabled him to rededicate the Union cause.

To dedicate the cemetery in a ceremonial speech was, as Lincoln said in his address, "altogether fitting and proper," but wholly inadequate "in another sense" to the place and the moment. Another task besides the original dedication awaited the speaker and his audience. Our printed version of the address registers, in its remarkable internal commentary on what it is and what it is doing, the nature of that task: to rekindle devotion to the cause, and to issue a credible vow emanating from that devotion. The two actions sustain one another. Much has been written about the address's embedded Christian language by which much of this transformation is effected. But the formal cause or plot of the speech is more accurately understood in terms of these two central movements: Lincoln's gesture of rededication and his inclusive vow.[12] After Lincoln accepts the propriety of speaking at such a place, indeed by using the language of the invitation that the ceremonial committee had set for him, he almost surrenders his claim to speak. It is in this double gesture of rededication and oath-taking that he finds, in the residuum of that surrender, the grounds for renewing the Union's resolve.

> Four score and seven years ago our fathers brought forth on this continent, a new nation, conceived in Liberty, and dedicated to the proposition that all men are created equal.

For Lincoln, the cemetery at Gettysburg is to be understood within the frame of the American founding, which, like the battlefield and its legacy of valor and sacrifice, is an inheritance to be honored, even though in an important sense it is utterly beyond the power of the living to duplicate. The unique Declaration of '76, with its founding proposition, is his reference point—not the amendable Constitution of '87. His choice of phrasing sets out a pattern of similar paradoxes. First, the position of the fathers is similar to his own prominence and powerlessness. They "brought forth" the new nation on that date; they did not author it. As fathers they were founders, but the sense of that founding is in its specific character obscure. They assisted in the nation's birth but did not create it. Except for the date of the birth, Lincoln elides the details of the beginning. Certainly, if one presses the metaphor to its sensible limit, the nation had parentage; but the manner and precise timing of its conception, in Lincoln's phrasing, is hidden as well as enacted in Liberty. In 1774 the first Continental Congress's protest of the Intolerable Acts might have marked its origins. Or perhaps the next year's skirmishes at Lexington and Concord marked it. But Lincoln refrains from filling in such historical information. The point is that the nation was "conceived in [within or by means of] Liberty" and "brought forth upon this continent" in 1776. The land was the circumstance and occasion, the receiver, and the mother all together. The fathers presided over a process that was of their parentage but not of their manufacture. Liberty, as well as the circumstances and the fore-given processes of generation, preceded them.[13]

Lincoln's role at Gettysburg was not entirely different from that of the fathers at the beginning of the nation. The instructive obscurity of the birth resembled the paradox of Lincoln's task: he had to do what he knew and said he could not do. Eighty-seven years ago the nation was dedicated to something, not solely by means of the fathers and not *to* them. It was to be devoted to a thing beyond itself and its parentage: the proposition that all men are created equal. In being dedicated to that proposition the nation, conceived in freedom, had to submit to something beyond itself—had to, in some sense, give up its freedom. To the degree such a proposition could be proved in that nation's endurance, it would be confirmed beyond the authorship of those who brought it forth. And insofar as all men were then seen to be *created* equal, the Founders and their successors would be shown to be subordinate to the divine author in their proof. In the Gettysburg Address, Lincoln incorporates this story of the founding and its persistence in the humbling and exalting words of his dedication.

At each level of this apparently simple, complex chain of inferences, the introduction outlines the problem and intimates the solution of Lincoln's dilemma in dedicating the cemetery at Gettysburg. He is, like his audience, a ceremonial bystander; but he has also been given the opportunity to draw from the past a sustenance that can be embodied and renewed in his own and his nation's endurance. If he succeeds in that task, the process will help the inheriting generation (whose dilemma he first described in the Lyceum Address) see how they might help the nation endure—beyond the limited powers of the fathers to perpetuate it.

Lincoln's father of fathers, George Washington, had shown his awareness of the limits of the Founders' reach and of the need for a testing of later generations when he said in his Farewell Address that the new republic was an "experiment": "Is there a doubt whether a common government can embrace so large a sphere? Let experience solve it. To listen to mere speculation in such a case were criminal. . . . It is well worth a fair and full experiment."[14] Lincoln accepts the sanguinary ordeal of his generation as a given, a test of that government:

> Now we are engaged in a great civil war, testing whether that nation, or any
> nation so conceived and so dedicated, can long endure. We are met on a great

battle-field of that war. We have come to dedicate a portion of that field, as a final resting place for those who here gave their lives that that nation might live. It is altogether fitting and proper that we should do this. (7.23)

The proposition that all are created equal is, like a Euclidean proposition in Lincoln's proudly mastered book of geometry, in need of proof. Indeed it demands testing. And the demand for proof has come, in the form of a war that tests the nation's capacity to endure—not merely to survive but to persist as a nation "conceived in Liberty, and dedicated to the proposition that all men are created equal." The field at Gettysburg is the symbolic and literal site of that test: "We are met" at that place as we are "engaged in a great civil war," the parallel passives of Lincoln's syntax linking the two conditions of peaceful commemoration and war. The speakers and their audience gather themselves on a field of battle, now a resting place. They gather together and then gather themselves up in the place of sacrifice. Lincoln's oratorical goal is to bring these things together in words so as to help bring them to pass in deeds.

The deaths of the soldiers have in fact enabled the ceremony to go on, not only for the obvious reasons—that the battle ended in Union victory and called for commemoration—but because the nation continued to live, and to be "so conceived and dedicated" to the proposition that Lincoln implies has been tested in the battle. "It is altogether fitting and proper" to make such a dedication, though in the act of saying what is proper Lincoln signals the gesture's insufficiency. The cemetery is one corner of one place of struggle in a long, continuing war. The sacrifice of the fallen must somehow be incorporated into the living so that "that nation" might live.

What is "here" will be the persistent subject of the rest of the speech. (The word will be used seven more times.) It is supported by Lincoln's focus on "now," and his use of the present and future tense. The meaning of "here" unfolds: it will become the setting and the established marker for his renewed dedication and his vow, the place upon which it is witnessed and made. The source of resolve will be in the devotion spilled here, to be taken into one's being here, in a promise made here and now, in the presence of the living and dead.

But, in a larger sense, we can not dedicate—we can not consecrate—we can not hallow—this ground. The brave men, living and dead, who struggled here, have consecrated it, far above our poor power to add or detract. The world will little note, nor long remember what we say here, but it can never forget what they did here. It is for us the living, rather, to be dedicated here to the unfinished work which they who fought here have thus far so nobly advanced. (7.23)

The reduction and discovery of the task of dedication takes place through a series of negatives that turn the task back on itself, almost explicitly refusing to do what the letter of invitation had specifically requested: "These grounds will be consecrated and set apart to this sacred purpose, by appropriate ceremonies, on Thursday, the 19th instant." The president is asked to give "a few appropriate remarks" for this purpose.[15] In Lincoln's near refusal of this invitation, we have the densest array of negatives we find in the extent speeches:

> we can not dedicate—
> we can not consecrate—
> we can not hallow—this ground.

No speech can presume to magnify the place or the occasion, and yet it cannot detract from the occasion by failing in its task.

> The world will little note,
> nor long remember what we say here,
> but it can never forget what they did here.

The emphatic twinned negative of the last line ("never forget") incorporates Lincoln's rhetorical failure in the plainest possible—almost empty yet powerful—assertion of the value of the sacrifice, of "what they did here." Edward Everett's two-hour rendition of the causes and course of the battle is thus compressed into Lincoln's four words. The passage's movement from brief phrases of emphatic closure to the running admission "but it can never forget" winnows and then restores, submits and then reaches resolution.

Lincoln's use of "we" again includes the audience, the work of the speech being to move all who hear it toward this combination of ends. All must submit to their insufficiency and yet open themselves to a restorative test of an obligation given to the living. The consecutively *accented*, complexly en-jambed syllables at the end of the sentence simultaneously encumber and assert the thought:

> It is for us the living, rather, to be dedicated here to the unfinished work which they who fought here *have thus far so nobly advanced.*

The form of the phrasing opens deeper accesses of meaning. The passive voice ("to be dedicated") embodies an obligation to be undergone as it is taken up. We do not merely dedicate ourselves; we must become dedicated. The "unfinished work" tasks Lincoln and his audience; but it also makes the realization of what is needed more likely because the work has form and the prospect of completion. "It is for us." Understanding the work as an inheritance increases the burden as something unlooked for. Yet the task is lighter because it is given to us and is our rightful responsibility, as it has been the responsibility of previous generations. The work weighs upon yet frees the inheritors of the nation the more they understand its origins and purposes. The way is difficult, but the work "thus far" is an enlivening guide because it has been admirable—"nobly advanced."

> It is rather for us to be here dedicated to the great task remaining before us— that from these honored dead we take increased devotion to that cause for which they gave the last full measure of devotion—that we here highly resolve that these dead shall not have died in vain—that this nation, under God, shall have a new birth of freedom—and that government of the people, by the people, for the people, shall not perish from the earth.

Lincoln moves to a deeper level of dedication, this one taking "increased devotion" from the honored dead as though endurance could come from the substance of their sacrifice. In this second iteration of the idea of dedication, he places "here" before the participle "dedicated" to mark the vow with special emphasis. One devotion begets another. Those who "gave the last full measure of devotion" have gathered honor to themselves. Those who remember them somehow "take increased devotion" in turn. In referring to "the last full measure of devotion," the sentence draws from the rich meaning of *measure* in the Gospels where the word has to do with both giving and recompense: "With what measure ye mete, it shall be measured to you: and unto you that hear shall more be given" (Mark 4.24); and "with what measure ye mete, it shall be measured to you again" (Matthew 7.2). What returns is the Kingdom of Heaven. The mustard seed multiplies as the word of salvation is proclaimed and heard with a devoted heart (Mark 4.26–32; Matthew 7.7–8). In giving "the last full measure of devotion," the honored dead and those who honor them participate in a somewhat similar process of sacrifice and renewal.

The Gettysburg Address is, in this context, a resolution to do something of high political moment by undergoing and incorporating an exalted precedent, in a manner of submission and assertion that gives devotional force to its vow. This self-abnegating yet hallowing action is embodied in its next passages by means of matched clauses, which imitate and alter the *that*-clauses in the opening of the Declaration of Independence. Lincoln's *that*-clauses substantiate rhetorically the enumeration of Jefferson's self-evident truths by showing that the most important of those truths needs substantiation—that it is a proposition waiting to be proved, and in that sense capable of proof.[16]

The syntax of each clause echoes and expands upon Lincoln's line in the second paragraph, about those who "gave their lives that [*so that*] that nation might live." The series is introduced with the concessive assertion that "it is rather for us to be here dedicated to the great task remaining before us— that" (*so that*) four things may be accomplished:

   . . . that from these honored dead we take increased devotion to that cause for which they gave the last full measure of devotion

   . . . that we here highly resolve that these dead shall not have died in vain

   . . . that this nation, under God, shall have a new birth of freedom

   . . . and that government of the people, by the people, for the people, shall not perish from the earth.

Clause 1: The duty of dedicating the cemetery has been redirected, emphatically and in submission, to the task of upholding the cause for which the dead gave their lives. The mourning and exultation that would have been the dominant passions of a conventional dedicatory speech (as they were in the preceding oration by Edward Everett) are sublimated into a political sacrament, the blood of sacrifice turning into the sustenance of those rededicating themselves to the "great task." Their devotion to the task gives them access to a greater devotion shown by those who fought.

Clause 2: Lincoln's resolute immobility (his insistence that there be a form of dedication that at first seems impossible) transforms into his first and only direct and active vow, arising from an embedded double negative: "these honored dead shall *not* have *died* in vain." The compact locution rises above cliché as it confines and directs the force of his resolve. We do not exactly know what the vow makers will *do*; we hear only what they promise to *resist*. Yet the firmness and logical restraint of the double negative compresses its significance.

Clause 3: As Lincoln's briefest assertion in the series, this line compactly asserts and heavily qualifies itself with the phrase "under God," with its indication of the impersonality of the action the vow entails. Declaring that "this nation, under God, shall have a new birth of freedom," the vow maker looks forward to something he does not and cannot pledge to give. The idiomatic meaning of the clause resembles a promise, but it is really an anticipation of a form of regeneration the promiser can help effect but not claim as his own. The nation "shall have a new birth of freedom," as though it could be helped to give birth to a new, more comprehensive liberty while being itself born again.

Clause 4: The last component of the vow is another double negative. The new nation's government "shall *not perish* from the earth." Like the second clause, this resolution deepens and tempers itself by asserting what it will *prevent* from happening. The firmness of the declaration is enhanced by its emphatic concentration upon that sole, limited task. In Lincoln's phrasing, the vow distances itself from the vow maker as though it had its own working power. The task is strangely abstracted from human power. When we look closely, we see that Lincoln does not vow *to do* something we can concretely identify, or not to do it. Dedication to the task will somehow effect these ends. The ends themselves are removed from the particular effects of individual or even collective human effort. Lincoln links them to the vow as the necessary results of its fulfillment, which depends upon individual and collective effort assisted by gifts and powers beyond human control. The new birth will take place under God, dependent upon a higher power and yet in accordance with a promise that calls upon God as witness to the human resolve to bring that birth forth.

The preceding address at Gettysburg, by Edward Everett, was less ambiguously optimistic. For Everett, the battle marked a triumph of Union patriotism "under Providence."[17] He made no dramatic vow. Although his account of the battle was suspenseful and included a brief consideration of the calamity that would have befallen the Union if Meade's army had failed, he portrayed the Union as a durable thing. Hearkening back to the prewar sentiment of Lincoln's First Inaugural, he saw the Union's strength in the signs of growing Union support in several southern states: "[T]hese bonds of union are of perennial force and energy, while the causes of alienation are imaginary, factitious, and transient. The heart of the people, North and South, is for the Union. Indications, too plain to be mistaken, announce the fact, both in the East and West of the States in rebellion. In North Carolina and Arkansas the fatal charm at length is broken."[18]

Lincoln's strangely detached address is in comparison more assertive, though in a way more pessimistic. The Founders dedicated the new nation to a proposition—an idea to be proved—not to a geographical or fixed legal objective. The philosophical and biblical roots of the idea of equality had ennobled and inspired much of the Union's resistance to secession. But the persistence of the war, and the emergent Union aspiration to make it a war of emancipation, would test the limits not only of any residual fellow feeling between the sections but of all arguments based strictly on considerations of political necessity or seemingly transcendental truths. Intent upon directing Union energies toward a new level of sacrifice for the sake of preserving a nation that might prove a proposition true, Lincoln risked raising the stakes of defeat and enlarging the meaning of victory. In trying to affirm and *con*firm, at least in speech, the most compelling connection between winning the war and securing the principles of equality and self-government, his decision to include (in delivery or in a later draft, or in both) a reference to God was significant. The address's parenthetical yet all-qualifying phrase of reliance upon God ("that this nation, under God, shall have a new birth of freedom") serves as a last reminder that human effort will not be enough.[19]

The Gettysburg Address, of all Lincoln's speeches, is closest to a call to action. Whether or not it met with enthusiastic approval from its immediate audience, it seized the moment. Edward Everett, whose remarkable authority in matters of oratorical skill is today underappreciated, immediately wrote Lincoln to say, "I should be glad if I could flatter myself that I came as near to the central idea of the occasion in two hours as you did in two minutes." Everett admired Lincoln's conception of the whole in a brief space. So of course did Nicolay and Hay, whose praise of the speech tells us something about its power that should not be dismissed simply because they were invested witnesses. The speech, they concluded, was "an address of dedication so pertinent, so brief yet so comprehensive, so terse yet so eloquent, likening the deeds of the present to the thoughts of the future, with simple words, in such living, original, yet exquisitely molded, maxim-like phrases that the best critics have awarded it an unquestioned rank as one of the world's masterpieces of rhetorical art."[20] David Donald recounts how the opinions of newspaper editorials were divided along partisan lines that showed Lincoln had struck both a chord and a nerve. For the editor of the *Harper's Weekly* it was "as simple and felicitous and earnest a word as was ever spoken." For a leading paper of the Democratic press, its featuring of Jefferson's proposition rather than the precedence of the Union was "a perversion of history so flagrant that the most extended charity cannot regard it as otherwise than willful."[21]

For Lincoln, as we have seen, the idea that a proposition might characterize the nation was not a new thought. In the 1858 debates with Douglas, he had outlined the relation between the leading proposition of the Declaration, the political reverence that was needed to perpetuate it in the life of the Union, and the enduring democracy that would be the result:

> We hold this annual celebration [of Independence Day] to remind ourselves of all the good done in this process of time . . . and how we are historically connected with it . . . . But after we have done all this we have not yet reached the whole. There is something else connected with it. . . . [P]erhaps half our people . . . are not descendants at all of these men [the framers of the Declaration]. If they look back through this history to trace their connection with those days by blood, they find they have none, they cannot carry themselves back into that glorious epoch and make themselves feel that they are part of us, but when they look through that old Declaration of Independence they find that those old men say that "We hold these truths to be self-evident, that all men are created equal," and then they feel that that moral sentiment taught in that day evidences their relation to those men, that it is the father of all moral principle in them, and that they have a right to claim it as though they were blood of the blood, and flesh of the flesh of the men who wrote that Declaration, [loud and long continued applause] and so they are. That is the electric cord in that Declaration that links the hearts of patriotic and liberty-loving men together. (2.499–500)

For Lincoln in 1858, as before and after, the leading "self-evident" truth of the Declaration was a "moral sentiment" to be taught and incorporated into the body politic—not a disembodied principle.[22] The nature of the instruction to effect this embodiment therefore had to be "something more" than the commemoration of the original event or the reminder of inheritance. The nation, with all the variety of its citizens' histories and affiliations, could not be sustained by those means. Not just political necessity, but a thirst for some greater connection to the polity, called for recognition of something greater. The proposition that all are created equal had in this sense a reverential, almost religious function. It was the "father" of moral conviction in all who discovered it, "an electric cord" that joined hearts.

In the Gettysburg Address, the meaning of that proposition is found within a struggle that calls for "*increased* devotion" (emphasis added) to a particular national cause. A way of dedication, not just a ceremonial moment or a repetition of words, is necessary to bring that devotion about. The method of reaching this new stage of belief depends on a reverential identification, a renewed connection to the proposition that is slowly becoming embodied in the nation dedicated to it. By accident or design (or both), Lincoln's eloquent reverence and resolution in the Gettysburg Address elevate that possibility in speech so that it might be returned to and realized in acts of devotion. We could say in this regard that the address is Lincoln's way of surpassing the Founders by bringing forth the Declaration's leading proposition in a speech that makes it an honored regenerating parent, "the father of all moral principle" in the struggle of "that nation" to endure.

* * *

The Second Inaugural Address, which was delivered during the last months of the conflict, uses providential reasoning for a much different, though related, end. In a letter dated eleven days after he gave the speech, Lincoln provided a brief summary of his argument to Thurlow Weed:

> Men are not flattered by being shown that there has been a difference of purpose between the Almighty and them. To deny it, however, in this case, is to deny that there is a God governing the world. It is a truth which I thought needed to be told; and as whatever of humiliation there is in it, falls directly on myself, I thought others might afford for me to tell it. (8.356)

Amid cries for revenge that were amplified by the prospect of victory and the apparent assurance of providential favor, Lincoln's speech hardly acknowledged Union advances. It declared that God "has His own purposes," and called for "charity for all" (8.332–333). The very power of Providence, as Lincoln described it, was to be felt most directly not in victory but, for the foreseeable future, in the *continuation* of the war, under conditions that could have been expected to have ended it. The impressive progress of recent military campaigns, the removal of the war's fundamental cause through the Emancipation and the introduction of the Thirteenth Amendment for approval by Congress and the states, the growing conviction that the Union had been vindicated—all took subordinate positions to the "scourge" of war. The coincidence of this reasoning with the topic and circumstances of the Meditation on the Divine Will alerts us to Lincoln's preoccupation with human beings as instrumentalities acting within God's power, seeking to understand their relation to Providence, choosing, waiting, and suffering under seemingly illogical, almost unendurable circumstances, and somehow preserving in their minds and imaginations the possibility of knowing that divine will and finding a way to act freely in accordance with it.

The Second Inaugural, delivered at what seems to us a clear moment of penultimate triumph, predated Appomattox by more than a month. The culmination of Sheridan's pursuit of Lee's escaping army, followed by Johnston's surrender to Sherman's relentless advance, was a reasonable object of hope yet an uncertain prospect. Historians have noted the possibility that Lee could have escaped westward, perhaps protracting the conflict beyond the North's endurance and forcing an armistice rather than submitting to the terms of surrender. To the east, Johnston was buying time as well, pursued with unexpected ruthlessness by an incommunicado military operation more relentless than anyone but Sherman's forces could for the moment know. The presidential campaign of 1864 had weighed the goals of armistice and victory. By Lincoln's estimate in the late summer of 1864, the election had looked as though it was probably lost (7.514). His generals' decisive victories in Georgia and Virginia, the former just two months and the latter just three weeks before the election, turned the tide.[23] Despite his election victory, the war went on, and so extended the political and moral vulnerability of a weary and increasingly vindictive public.

Lincoln begins the speech, as he ends it, with "high hope" and caution concerning the war: "[N]o prediction in regard to it is ventured." Though the "progress of our arms" is evident, victory is unsecured. In the understated, abstract phrasing of these lines Lincoln's reflexive syntax removes himself from the act. The sentences convey remoteness—an almost inhuman distancing of the speaker from the few immediate facts he is citing—that paradoxically begins to refocus attention on the more distant, yet personally compelling question of how the course of battle is related to God's will:

At this second appearing to take the oath of the presidential office, there is less occasion for an extended address than there was at the first. Then a statement, somewhat in detail, of a course to be pursued, seemed fitting and proper. Now, at the expiration of four years, during which public declarations have been constantly called forth on every point and phase of the great contest which still absorbs the attention, and engrosses the enerergies [*sic*] of the nation, little that is new could be presented. The progress of our arms, upon which all else chiefly depends, is as well known to the public as to myself; and it is, I trust, reasonably satisfactory and encouraging to all. With high hope for the future, no prediction in regard to it is ventured. (8.332)

Lincoln's strangely exaggerated decorum allows him to refrain from directly taking credit for the course of the war. When he ventures an active predication, his sentence refers specifically to the war's unequivocal magnitude in the present moment, and what he hopes will be his audience's agreement that the course of Union arms has been "reasonably satisfactory." The double danger in using such rhetoric is that Lincoln might remove himself so far from responsibility that he either diminishes himself and the Union cause or conversely exaggerates his role, as though presuming to be a god. Instead the speech uses this distancing effect to make a more general, self-effacing argument about the nature of the war. Just how Lincoln accomplishes this feat has long been a subject for wonderment and controversy, and so is worthy of further analysis.

When Lincoln outlines the history of the war in his next lines, the combatants, like Lincoln himself, are strangely separated from the history they have made. The ensuing explanation of the war's origins reveals another pattern of intentions isolated from results. Out of each side's efforts to avoid war came the conflict no one wanted:

On the occasion corresponding to this four years ago, all thoughts were anxiously directed to an impending civil-war. All dreaded it—all sought to avert it. While the inaugural address was being delivered from this place, devoted altogether to *saving* the Union without war, insurgent agents were in the city seeking to *destroy* it without war— seeking to dissol[v]e the Union, and divide effects, by negotiation. Both parties deprecated war; but one of them would *make* war rather than let the nation survive; and the other would *accept* war rather than let it perish. And the war came. (8.332)

In this phase of the argument, Lincoln portrays the origin of the war almost as an accident contrary to everyone's intention. At first he seems to be saying the opposite—that one side, or the actions of both, decided the matter. The occasion of the first inaugural was "devoted altogether" to "saving the Union," whereas efforts elsewhere in Washington to avoid war, subject as they were to the influence of "insurgent agents," were by implication drawn into the work of secession. Damaging deeds were done, and the friends of the Union resisted them. But armed conflict was not originally the outward intention of anyone. On the one hand, Lincoln is arguing that even the insurgent agents—those who lured some leaders' attention away from the inaugural of a duly elected president—sought to avoid war, and that neither side entered the conflict as the sort of aggressive challenger one would expect. Even when he describes the insurgents' desire not "to let the nation survive," the phrasing of the speech on one level softens or shrewdly understates the impact of that intention with a euphemism, as though the enemies of the Union were remote from the true consequences of their deeds. All of this is consistent with one of the overarching themes of the speech: the importance of understanding the war as far more than a man-made event, more than a conflict in which one can fix blame for its origin.

On the other hand, Lincoln by no means forgets in his phrasing of these ideas the seriousness of the issue most responsible for causing the division or the mortal dangers of misguided attempts to use the peace. Even before he names that issue, he is using phrasing that suggests how the insurgents' pacific negotiations sought to end the nation's life in peace *or* war: they "would *make* war rather than let the nation survive." The euphemism takes on, in this context, an impassive, chilling significance.

No mention is made at this point of the political position of either side. The larger point is not only that both sides wished for peace, but that the insurgents tried to destroy the Union peacefully by negotiating a political divorce *in the absence of a contest over the issues behind the separation.* By referring to their activities at the moment he was delivering the First Inaugural, Lincoln implicitly reminds his audience that the insurgents did not accept the verdict of the 1860 election, which in Lincoln's view upheld the arguments for the restraint of slavery that he had championed for years. Thus they were attempting to negotiate peacefully for a settlement that would have ended the *political* life of the nation, not just its ostensible unity and territorial reach. It is remarkable to note that in Lincoln's otherwise subdued and unreproachful opening he frames the origins of the war with such chronological focus and, by initially *leaving out* the issue of slavery, with such implicitly political specificity. In this passage he defers and disperses consideration of blame while managing to set out the dire circumstances of early 1861 in terms that have a power to remind his audience of the Democrats' talk of armistice during the campaign of 1864.

In keeping with this ostensible characterization of the conflict, Lincoln describes the North's taking up the burden of war. It did not seize the occasion but met the threat that had been brought to it. The continuing conflict is more a matter of acceptance of what is the case than one might first appreciate. There is still no division into sections, only of "parties"—insurgents and unionists. The Union stays where it is. It copes with an internal disruption, not an end to its existence as the Union. Lincoln avoids naming the geographical sections at war, as he had refrained from recognizing them as regionally separate—hence divorced and independent—political entities throughout the conflict. When he speaks of the places where slaves lived in the Union, his draft shows that he seeks to frustrate any assumption of fixed regional divisions; he corrects his initial, geographical phrase "in the Southern half" to read more generally "in the Southern part." [24]

To conclude from these multiple inferences that Lincoln exculpates *or* settles blame on the South is to miss the force of his larger argument. One side stood unmoved until war came, while the other, like the democratic tyrant of the Lyceum Address, *equated* his own initially pacific ambitions with a willingness to undo the Union. But neither side made the war. They struggled in peace, and then "the war came." What Lincoln had written privately about his situation as president in the second year of the war has application here to the nature of divine judgment: "I shall do nothing in malice. What I deal with is too vast for malicious dealing" (5.346). All share the offense; all are subject to the obscure and unfailing purposes of the author of Providence.

Before the magisterial argument unfolds this far, Lincoln supplies an intermediate step:

> One eighth of the whole population were colored slaves, not distributed generally over the Union, but localized in the Southern part of it. These slaves constituted a peculiar and powerful interest. All knew that this interest was, somehow, the cause of the war. To strengthen, perpetuate, and extend this in-

terest was the object for which the insurgents would rend the Union, even by war; while the government claimed no right to do more than to restrict the territorial enlargement of it. (8.332)

These lines give a measure of philosophical substance to the insurgents' cause in the form of "interest," but that interest is not bounded by their possession of it, and it has no exclusively regional identification. It is self-existent, in principle ubiquitous, and strange. Lincoln is indirectly referring to the ownership of chattel slaves, but his syntax puts at the center the persons enslaved. The slaves—rather than the South or even the owners of slaves—"constitute" that interest, though they are not quite what it is. It is *peculiar* (as Ronald White has noted, the adjective the South traditionally attached to the institution of slavery).[25] Here it is like the looming, undefined shape in the foreground of Thomas Cole's antebellum painting of the ruin of empire.

Like the war, which overwhelms with a power that is undeniable yet obscure, the interest constituted by the slaves is known by all to be, "somehow, the cause of the war." Everyone senses its causative force but not the precise reason for, or origin of, its influence. It is not clear whether the insurgents "would rend the Union, even by war," by their own intent or as a result of the malevolent influence of that interest. Lincoln speaks as though from within his audience's power to remember its ability, before the hatred generated by war made its judgment vengeful, to see what was before its eyes while it wondered at what it saw. Indeed, the fact that the slaves made up an eighth of the total population meant that they were *part of* that population, kept in the shadows of thought yet counted, with a constitutional fraction, in the national census. It is understood that *somehow* this combination of interest and vague misgiving led to or became the object of the conflict.[26]

The point is doubly consistent with the argument so far, which ascribes responsibility in the context of a profound discontinuity of intentions and results that involved both sides. Lincoln will next say that both sides' expectations have dissolved in the course of the conflict, but not without wondering aloud why one side has *not* been favored over the other:

Neither party expected for the war, the magnitude, or the duration, which it has already attained. Neither anticipated that the *cause* of the conflict might cease with, or even before, the conflict itself should cease. Each looked for an easier triumph, and a result less fundamental and astounding. Both read the same Bible, and pray to the same God; and each invokes His aid against the other. It may seem strange that any men should dare to ask a just God's assistance in wringing their bread from the sweat of other men's faces; but let us judge not that we be not judged. The prayers of both could not be answered; that of neither has been answered fully. (8.332–333)

Rather than merely conclude that there is enough guilt to go around, Lincoln raises the moral question again: "It may seem strange . . ." begins his wondering sentence. Unlike the nonpartisan argument of the surrounding lines, this one offers a brief, forceful testimony to Lincoln's persistent support of the Union and the antislavery cause, though he elides the sentiment with a resolve not to judge. Beneath the grand placidity of the presentation, the conflict roils from paragraph to paragraph.

But Lincoln's temporary hint of anger is retrospective. As an "interest," slavery is a "cause" of the war that has ceased before the war has ended. Events have somehow overridden both sides' partisan interest in this regard, and Lincoln does not need to give those events names. The Emancipation Proclamation had for over a year worked its way into the rebellious regions. The North had gradually moved away from the limited antislavery policy outlined in the First Inaugural. Hundreds of thousands of freedmen were serving in the Union army. The Senate had approved the Thirteenth Amendment in April 1864. Lincoln's reelection had turned back the advocates of an armistice. Just a month prior to Lincoln's Second Inaugural, the Thirteenth Amendment had passed the House and had been sent to the states for approval. Not just the defense of slavery but toleration of the institution for a limited time had proved to be a temporary thing. But so had the hope for an emancipation that was not an ordeal.

"Neither party expected for the war, the magnitude, or the duration, which it has already attained." In that "already" Lincoln coolly posits another dissolving and bracing thought: even in this late stage of the conflict, after the ostensible cause of the war has begun to disappear, the war might wax in magnitude and duration to exceed everyone's expectations *again*. The hope of both sides for victory has already been replaced by a "result" more "fundamental and astounding" than they could have sought. Both sides continue to pursue victory (Lincoln still grants the possibility of a Union reversal and a triumph for the South) but now they must accept that victory will be an ordeal of change. The war's shaping agents include but go beyond those who make war. Just as "the war came," it will depart in a manner beyond the combatants' control and leave an unanticipated legacy.

Michael Leff has pointed out that Lincoln's shift from past to present tense in the next sentences of the paragraph—a change from history to religion—is the hinge connecting the historical and religious sides of his argument.[27] Once the shift is made, Lincoln can engage the general tendency of those in his audience to understand the history and course of the war through their biblical religion. He argues that a providential ordering of events has manifested itself in a more terrible, more sublime version of the war than the one he has so far described:

> The Almighty has His own purposes. "Woe unto the world because of offences! for it must needs be that offences come; but woe to that man by whom the offence cometh!" If we shall suppose that American Slavery is one of those offences which, in the providence of God, must needs come, but which, having continued through His appointed time, He now wills to remove, and that He gives to both North and South, this terrible war, as the woe due to those by whom the offence came, shall we discern therein any departure from those divine attributes which the believers in a Living God always ascribe to Him? (8.333)

The arguments circle around Lincoln's invocation of Matthew 7.1 and 18.17, along with the Nineteenth Psalm. These are texts that help him identify the war's destructive power, as well as its unanticipated length, with a divine judgment upon North and South for their mutual perpetuation of slavery over hundreds of years. Neither military necessity nor valor will determine the final outcome. The strange and familiar biblical patterns of one generation inheriting the sins of its fathers, of God's agents being punished for doing God's will, of God's judgments being paradoxically "true and righteous altogether" even when obscure and morally shocking to human interpreters—all point toward the possibility that the war will be prolonged until the price for ten generations of slavery is paid in wealth and suffering.

Here Lincoln is not merely ascribing the conflict to factors beyond human power. In his shaping of religio-political prophecy he recognizes and maintains the *instrumentality* of the human actors as self-reflective moral agents. The passage in Matthew 7 that begins "Judge not, that ye be not judged" immediately enjoins those who condemn their brothers to look into themselves: "And why beholdest thou the mote that is in thy brother's eye, but considerest not the beam that is in thine own eye?" (7.3). The words about God's righteousness in Matthew 18 are surrounded by Jesus' call to the disciples to acknowledge divine charity and judgment rather than to wonder about who is greatest in heaven. The chapter's concluding parable is about the servant whose debt is forgiven and who fails to forgive his own debtor: "Shouldest not thou also have had compassion on thy fellow servant, even as I had pity on thee?" (18.33). Judgment comes "if ye from your hearts forgive not every one his brother their trespasses" (18.35).

When Lincoln says God "wills to remove" slavery's curse, the human actors are assumed to be instruments of the scourge that punishes them. The war is not a hammer that obliterates the unworthy; it is *given* to the combatants, as though it were a responsibility to prosecute it as well as a punishment to endure: "[H]e gives to both North and South, this terrible war, as the woe due to those by whom the offence came." It may be supposed, Lincoln argues, that as instrumentalities of Providence, the North and the South together err and seek to act well again under a collective punishment for something imposed upon them. If so, they must persist in the sanguinary, terrible, strangely redeeming labors of war even as they prepare for the charitable labors of peace. Both responsibilities have been given to them to take up, as though in providential circumstances:

> Fondly do we hope—fervently do we pray—that this mighty scourge of war may speedily pass away. Yet, if God wills that it continue, until all the wealth piled by the bond-man's two hundred and fifty years of unrequited toil shall be sunk, and until every drop of blood drawn with the lash, shall be paid by another drawn with the sword, as was said three thousand years ago, so still it must be said "the judgments of the Lord, are true and righteous altogether." (8.333)

The war begins *and ends* by providential direction rather than by human fiat. A true armistice will not be declared unless the scourge has ceased. Conceivably, the scourge might continue during a false peace: the war is only one possible instrument for giving woe to those who have transgressed. What is left to the moral agents caught up in this process? To hope and pray for peace, do the charitable work of peace, consider the divine prerogatives for further punishment, praise divine justice, and prepare for more war.

As Garry Wills and others have noted, early March 1865 was not a time to celebrate the resolution of a national crisis.[28] New difficulties of effecting and adjudicating the end of hostilities, and of establishing "a just and lasting peace," were now piling atop the old. A few days before he delivered the Second Inaugural, Lincoln is supposed to have delivered the following brief remarks accepting his election as president for a second term. His first paragraph describes his circumstances as though he were a second Jonah:

> Having served four years in the depths of a great, and yet unended national peril, I can view this call to a second term, in nowise more flatteringly to myself, than as an expression of the public judgment, that I may better finish a difficult work, in which I have labored from the first, than could any one less severely schooled to the task. (8.326)

Like Jonah's, Lincoln's qualifications for the office are negative. He has endured in the depths of a peril far greater than any he could have made himself (after four years "unended," as though it were an unearthly storm), and yet a peril in its origin attributable at least partly to the nation and its people (Lincoln himself must be "severely schooled"). Like Jonah he is called to complete a task, but the goals are unclear. His preparation for the new phase of the ordeal has been his plummet into the depths of that compelling uncertainty. Now he must complete "a difficult work"—something unspecified of his own making, yet not his. It is not "my" difficult work. Still, it is for him to do, scourged by his strangely instructive circumstances. His language of immersion recalls the psalmist's cry from the deep: "Out of the depths have I cried unto thee, Lord, hear my voice" (Psalm 130), and Paul's lament, "[A] night and a day have I been in the deep; / In journeyings often, in perils of waters, in perils of robbers, in perils by mine own countrymen . . . " (2 Corinthians, 11.25–26).

The inaugural's analysis of the divine will is therefore a set of hypothetical propositions ("If," "If we shall suppose") that are to be further tested and proved by the actions as well as the sufferings of moral agents. In this regard, an automatic acceptance of the theological argument presented in the Second Inaugural would be as contrary to Lincoln's intentions as cynical rejection. In the terms in which it is framed, the speech manifests the possibility though not the certainty of finishing, by choice, resolution, and submission, a work of war and peace that implicates both sides and has more than human authorship.

In the Gettysburg Address, Lincoln had analyzed the legacy of the Declaration of Independence as "the proposition that all men are created equal"—something fundamental yet in need of being proved by those who would draw their dedication from those who had sacrificed before them. There is a version of this motion at the end of the Second Inaugural, where the explicit call to action begins:

> With malice toward none; with charity for all; with firmness in the right, as God gives us to see the right, let us strive on to finish the work we are in; to bind up the nation's wounds; to care for him who shall have borne the battle, and for his widow, and his orphan—to do all which may achieve and cherish a just, and a lasting peace, among ourselves, and with all nations. (8.333)

Here the call is for a universal magnanimity as though in deference to the Declaration's proposition; but in that proof of deference to all as equals there must be "firmness in the right," a resolve to continue the war, if necessary, as a cause in common with the defenders of the proposition. Charity braids with martial determination. In Lincoln's spare yet capacious phrasing, it ministers to the wounds of the entire country, not the North alone. It assists all who "have borne the battle" and the survivors, apparently without regard for region or the army for which the soldiers have fought. And it is supposed to love charitably—*cherish,* both words drawing from the same root—the peace that the end of the war will bring. Amid this call for charity, Lincoln urges on the work of war: charity will be given by those who rely upon "firmness in the right" to "achieve . . . a just, and lasting peace."

Lincoln draws charity and war-making closer together, without seeming to claim that they could be the same. Charity is the work of the victor, and victory is an unspoken, sublimated triumph to be manifested in a universal peace. Acting firmly in this way, "as God gives us to see the right," the human actors, as we have seen Lincoln describe them, do not know the right as God does. To repeat: Lincoln has framed his explanation of the divine will as a hypothesis ("If we shall suppose . . . Yet, if God wills"), rendering its conclusion in a negative: "[S]hall we discern therein any departure from those divine attributes which the believers in a Living God always ascribe to Him?" He captures the complexity of the human circumstance in common language: "with firmness in the right, *as God gives us to see the right,*" human beings are predisposed—*given* by God—to see in a certain way *insofar as* God gives and guides, and insofar as human beings are capable of seeing what God empowers them to see. To presume that one possesses divine knowledge of such things, even on the verge of a seemingly providential victory, is to err in the way that the North and South have done before.

Yet to ignore the hand of Providence in the Union's cause, or at least to neglect to wonder about its role in the costly war and the latest Union advances, is to risk the basis for the claim that the cause is just. Lincoln addresses this conundrum when he says the Union moves ahead "with firmness in the right," neither abandoning its moral claim nor presuming to have invented or seized it. In Lincoln's choice of words, the Union does not even assert that claim. It disposes itself to be strong, not so much to battle a foe as to be unmoved "in the right," where it already presumably is. The Union must act "with" charity and firmness, not strictly out of its own virtue. So must it prosecute the war "in" the right without claiming that right essentially for itself. Its effort to "strive on to finish the work we are in" combines, in Lincoln's syntax, the givenness of the task with the aspiring endeavor to take it up and complete it. The work of civil war and peace is already there, larger than the workers can know, yet somehow shaped so that it must be brought to a conclusion in their hands.

In the resonant simplicity of Lincoln's wording, God's help takes the form of a meditation: as divine assistance to the human *capacity* to see the right, which it would not see without God's aid but which it must see on its own, "as God gives us to see the right." Again, God's gift is not exactly a vision of the right, nor something to be taken by right. It helps human beings see the right, which then they must choose without presuming to possess it. Then they will be "in the right."

The impressive simplicity and depth of these ideas of human instrumentality in the Second Inaugural becomes more accessible as we read the speeches from 1837 to 1865 in sequence. Lincoln's oratorical efforts throughout his career can be read as a series of attempts to articulate the meaning of that instrumentality, beginning with his old and abandoned doctrine of necessity as the notion that "the human mind is impelled to action, or held in rest by some power, over which the mind itself has no control" (1.382). That old idea had proved to be a political liability for Lincoln in 1846, as it probably had been for years before. Despite his ingenious defense of it as a doctrine he no longer maintained in public, it seems to have presented him with an almost unworkable philosophical dilemma of little use in his personal troubles or his political responsibilities. It had depths, however, that his political opponents did not anticipate. It hardly reflected his later articulation of human instrumentality as a strange melding of choice and providential power. But it informed his later discussions of necessity, and it contained some of the seeds of his final oratorical arguments about the rigors and responsibilities of human action during the great national ordeal. Lincoln's ideas of necessity took on new life and form in his political religion, which comes to us most impressively through his final speeches.

When we read those speeches with the old ones, which connect Lincoln's early days with his last, the complex power and significance of his political religion become available to further inquiry. We have a chance to understand these aspects of Lincoln's thought in the light of his eloquence, and to ask how his eloquence might be influenced by his political religion. As we venture into territories opened by such literary and historical inquiry, we have an opportunity to ask ourselves, as Lincoln did, what we will do with them.

The Letter to Mrs. Bixby

Secular Scripture

I feel how weak and fruitless must be any words of mine . . . (8.116)

The consistency of Lincoln's idea of human instrumentality is evident, as we have seen, even in a marginal speech, such as the Lecture on Discoveries and Inventions. In one sense language is Adam's invention; in another it is a "Divine gift" that is available to the first man the moment tries to communicate his feelings. As the expression of what is "probably an original impulse of our nature," language is Adam's articulation of that impulse by means that are not assuredly his own. His language expresses his wishes in what might be the forms the divine power gave him to make them known.

These ideas and their variations, especially when they are effectively embedded in eloquent oratory on great occasions, give Lincoln's speeches a special force. But their elusive simplicity and strange depth put a severe strain on his imitators, and certainly test any commentary that claims to know exactly what those ideas mean or how they work. When we read Lincoln's earlier speeches in the shadow of the great presidential performances, his own oratory suffers in the comparison when we anticipate the wrong thing. In a case of now questionable authorship—the famous letter Lincoln is supposed to have written to Mrs. Bixby in 1864—humble and artful profundity is in danger of being read as cliché. If we measure everything by the standard of the Gettysburg Address and the Second Inaugural, and if we must be absolutely certain of Lincoln's authorship in order to appreciate the depth and range of texts attributed to him, we risk overlooking the power of careful reading to discover the astringency and richness of Lincolnian eloquence.

In the letter of November 21, 1864, to Lydia Bixby, we see how deeply some of Lincoln's ideas of instrumentality could inform an expression of national and personal grief, and the attempt to find credible reasons to persist in what he called, in his oracular language of passivity and resolve, "the work we are in." Lincoln knew that his general correspondence could at any time find its way into the newspapers.[1] The famous letter was phrased in language that could function in public as well as private, as a private message available to be overheard. It was in this sense the circulated record of a kind of private speech of condolence. (It is perhaps for this reason that it has served prominently since September 2001 as a national eulogy when other words have failed.) Its message to Mrs. Bixby, a bereaved mother of five sons reportedly killed in battle, has for generations been so well known it is difficult to apprehend with fresh eyes; but it is worth reading closely for what it says, and for its revealing and moving adaptation of several of the master tropes of Lincoln's speeches.

> Dear Madam,— I have been shown in the files of the War Department a statement of the Adjutant General of Massachusetts, that you are the mother of five sons who have died gloriously on the field of battle.
>
> I feel how weak and fruitless must be any words of mine which should attempt to beguile you from the grief of a loss so overwhelming. But I cannot refrain from tendering to you the consolation that may be found in the thanks of the Republic they died to save.
>
> I pray that our Heavenly Father may assuage the anguish of your bereavement, and leave you only the cherished memory of the loved and lost, and the solemn pride that must be yours, to have laid so costly a sacrifice upon the altar of Freedom. Yours, very sincerely and respectfully,
>
> A. Lincoln. (8.116–117)

Removed from the immediate struggle of the war and yet steeped in stories of carnage, modern readers have encountered the Bixby letter as an expression of grief beyond the reach of official condolences. It continues to move its readers; but as a historical artifact that was both an official as well as a private communication, it confronts us with the question of whether any political leader can console in speech the parents of those lost in war, or a country that has lost so many. Mrs. Bixby's supposed loss of all her many sons made her a symbol of that double bereavement. What, if anything, can any letter do to assuage such grief?

Our uncomfortable admiration for this famous work increases with the knowledge that controversy has attended the question of the letter's author-ship for generations. Those who attribute the letter to Lincoln have con-tended with those who see in its sculpted lines the hand of his secretary John Hay. It is "just a trifle over-written for Lincoln," says one doubter. Hay "had a tendency to overwrite his paragraphs," argued another, "and while it may seem lese majesty to say so it [h]as always seemed to me that the Bixby letter is a trifle overwritten."[2] When doubts are raised about Lincoln's imprimatur, the message becomes vulnerable to questions about its sincerity and origi-nality. The loss of the original letter, the secondhand but tantalizingly am-biguous accounts of Hay's alleged statements that the letter was his doing (supposedly passed from Hay to John Morley and then to Nicholas Butler, with the first two carriers of the secret asking that the news not be revealed until their deaths),[3] and finally the persistence in some quarters of doubts about the style of the work all conspire to keep the question alive, despite en-ergetic rejoinders over the years from many leading scholars.[4] Michael Burlingame's impressive recent gathering and sifting of the evidence in his recent book increase the chances of Hay's involvement, and present us with the strong possibility that Hay had a significant share in the writing unless it was entirely his own. Why else would a newspaper clipping of the letter be included in two surviving scrapbooks of Hay's writings?[5] Burlingame's evi-dence for reopening the question is substantial, and difficult to explain away.

The authorship question, however, should not end our interest in the Bixby letter as part of Lincoln's works. To assume that the letter is undeni-ably Lincoln's or an apotheosis of the letter-writing art is wrong. But so is re-jection of the letter as irrelevant to a study of Lincoln's writings and speeches simply because significant doubts have been raised about its authorship. It is worth returning to the text and its immediate context, which includes the challenge the writer faced in offering consolation, as a sympathetic citizen as well as the executive of a warring nation, to a bereaved parent and a mourn-ing nation.

Some brief comments on the style of the letter would be useful before going on to larger issues, for in questions of style we get a preview of larger uncertainties about the letter's sincerity, meaning, and moving power. Bur-lingame is right to discover and point out the many parallels between its phrasing and the habitual expressions found in Hay's collected works. The letter contains a number of word forms and phrases that occur more frequently in Hay's writings than in Lincoln's: *cherish, assuage, gloriously.* A few are apparently part of Hay's repertoire but not Lincoln's: the word *beguile* and the phrases *I cannot refrain from tendering* (which Hay used in a letter to a friend months before he allegedly authored the letter of Mrs. Bixby) and *I pray that our Heavenly Father,* which we do not find in Lincoln's writings outside of the letter in question. In another epistle Hay is said to have written the same day, we also find the echo of one of the Bixby letter's unusual and eloquent phrases. The syntactical shadow of "a loss so overwhelming" seems to appear in the next letter's phrase, "a citizen so venerable." We could add, apart from the comparison with Hay, that a number of the letter's phrases appear nowhere else in Lincoln's works: for example, *so costly, altar of freedom, the loved and lost, weak and fruitless, solemn pride.*

But these comparisons tend to ignore larger patterns, for example, the substantial number of unique usages in Lincoln's extant works. (In terms of vocabulary alone, an electronic concordance reveals scores of such instances just in the words that begin with an "a.") The number of unique phrases is much higher, of course. The more important point is literary rather than numerical: Lincoln, like Hay, was a reader of great examples of English prose. He may not have used *assuaged* but twice outside of the present tense form in the Bixby letter (once in the Temperance Address [1.279] and once in his brief Message on the Death of Van Buren [5.340]), but he would have known it in the book of Job, where it appears twice in adjacent verses highly suggestive of the context that generated the Bixby letter: "I would strengthen you with my mouth, and the moving of my lips should asswage your grief" (Job 16:5), after which Job answers, "My grief is not asswaged" (16:6). Lincoln's Shakespeare also uses the word a handful of times. The likelihood of its being called up from memory is arguably more significant than the frequency of its employment by Hay. The same might be said for *beguile,* which appears not at all in Lincoln's other works, but marks a crucial passage in Genesis: "The serpent beguiled me," Eve says. The word and its variations appear ten times in the King James Version, and in the New Testament with particularly resonant sentiment for someone writing a letter of condolence: "Let no man beguile you of your reward in a voluntary humility and worshipping of angels, intruding into those things which he hath not seen, vainly puffed up by his fleshly mind" (Colossians 2:18). Lincoln's Shakespeare uses the word or its variants dozens of times.

"I cannot refrain from tendering" is not far from Lincoln's "I cannot refrain," which appears twice in the works outside of the Bixby letter. *Tender* is used in this verbal form at least six times in Lincoln's works, and also in *Richard III* (one of Lincoln's favorite plays) and *Hamlet*.[6] *Gloriously* is not as common in Lincoln as in Hay, but he uses it nine times, in instances before and during his presidency. The use of *cherish* is even more common, the most famous instance being in the Second Inaugural. Finally, we have one possible exception: *I pray that our Heavenly Father*, a clause indeed characteristic of Hay and not Lincoln, to whom we attribute two uses of *Heavenly Father* he may have had nothing to do with: a proclamation authored by Seward (5.186), and Lincoln's famous note to Mrs. Gurney about God's will, which comes to us in another hand (5.478). Yet the letter's final reference to sacrifice and to the altar of freedom calls up Lincoln's line from the Lyceum Address about the need to "sacrifice unceasingly upon its [the law's] altars" (1.112). Also, the inverted syntax of *a loss so overwhelming* is paradigmatically developed in a clause of the Gettysburg Address ("a nation so conceived and so dedicated").

Beyond the intriguing vagaries of stylistic analysis, the internal arrangement and sequence of the Bixby letter's sentences flawlessly convey an unaffected sublimity that is consistent with the deep lines of development in the great presidential rhetoric. Given the difficulty of proving that Hay could do such a thing, it seems reasonable to continue to attribute the letter's artful yet simply powerful sentences to Lincoln, at least on stylistic grounds. If Hay is one day found to have indeed written the letter, then the evidence here points to the likelihood that he was engaged in a collaboration profoundly influenced by Lincoln's example if not his direct editorial intervention.

The letter had, unavoidably, a political purpose as well as a personal one. It would not have been written were it not for the specific request of the governor of Massachusetts, John A. Andrew. A mother's loss of five sons in the Union cause was "so remarkable," he asserted, "that I really wish a letter might be written her by the President of the United States."[7] It is certainly possible that Lincoln, under the pressure of his duties, passed the responsibility to Hay, who told Herndon in 1866 that Lincoln had responded personally to only a small fraction of the many letters he received and so "gave the whole thing over to me, and signed without reading them the letters I wrote in his name." But Hay then adds in his own memoir that Lincoln wrote many letters himself: "He wrote perhaps half-a-dozen a week himself—not more."[8] The "whole thing" is a hyperbole of a kind that might have colored what Hay said, or how his words were heard, when he later supposedly claimed the letter was entirely his own.

Lincoln would have had ample reason to write, or at least closely supervise the drafting of such a letter. It was not unlikely that it would be circulated in print, where it would provide him an opportunity to praise a host of sacrifices beyond what any form of conscription could request. Under circumstances that demanded massive levies of men, a public expression of grief could be a bracing means of purging sheer vengefulness and of directing attention to the need to carry on the fight. The need to levy more men had not disappeared with the election. Having won that contest after Sherman's taking of Atlanta and the fall of Mobile, Lincoln acted as though he assumed months of heavy fighting lay ahead. (As we have seen, the Second Inaugural, delivered four months later, spoke of the continuing struggle and did not venture to conclude that the war was almost won.) He had contemplated a tremendous draft of 500,000 men two months before, just prior to the election, if reenlistments did not increase.[9] Richmond was untaken. After a long series of levies, and perhaps more to come, the case of Mrs. Bixby's five sons, properly recognized, would have been one more way of fortifying the case for endurance. Old Union supporters who were tempted to embrace negotiations or revenge, along with those who were contemplating joining or rejoining the Union cause, would find in such a letter a reason to support Lincoln's efforts. One mother's "loss so overwhelming" for a just cause would have stood in admirable contrast to concerns that shrank by comparison.

Even if the letter was written as much for political as well as personal reasons (the foregoing in no way proving Lincoln's authorship or revealing the precise motives behind the letter's composition), its gesture of condolence is so impressive it calls out for interpretation. It is now apparent that Mrs. Bixby did not lose all her sons after all.[10] Should that fact remove the letter from consideration as a profoundly nuanced act of personal and political sympathy under circumstances that press down so hard on its originality it becomes something difficult for any author to claim? When we persist in reading closely, we can begin to notice how the Bixby letter offers a way, after almost surrendering to silence, to accede and appeal to the grieving parent's and nation's power to act instrumentally—by acting freely, in hope of a higher blessing, without a delusory denial of loss.

The surrender I have mentioned goes beyond a conventional concession to the limitations of words. Saying it will not "beguile" the mother from her

grief, as though the very offer of consolation were an act of magical deception, the letter falls back on a double negative that offers a strange comfort: "I
cannot refrain from tendering to you the consolation that may be found in
the thanks of the Republic they died to save." There are layers of consolation
in this denial of beguilement. In "tendering" comfort, the letter's gesture
gives consolation without giving it. Consolation, if it is there, is passed from
a source beyond the letter, to its recipient, who is invited to accept it. The letter's phrasing acknowledges that it cannot give that consolation in any ordinary sense. The consolation is already somewhere else: in "the thanks of the
Republic," which survives to extend such gratitude precisely because Mrs.
Bixby's sons died to save the Republic. The hard reality of this offer—that
the thanks are really there for the mother to accept because her sons lost their
lives saving the Republic—joins with the fact, which the letter need only
point to, that in her power is the choice to refuse or accept those thanks. Her
grief makes that choice as urgent as it is difficult, because her supposed loss,
as the letter acknowledges it, is so great.

The final paragraph of the letter begins with another near forfeit of the
power to persuade, in a prayer that asks for heavenly alleviation of the
mother's grief. The prayer is strangely limited. It asks for relief but not for an
end to the bereavement: "I pray that our Heavenly Father may assuage the
anguish of your bereavement." If the prayer were to be granted, it would
leave the mother with "only the cherished memory" of her sons. But it would
be a memory by its nature awake to them in their absence. It would recall
"the loved and lost," directing her grief toward love, not toward a forgetting
of her loss.

But a prayer is not a cure. The letter does not assume that by turning to
the forms of prayer that it is sufficient. The success of the prayer, if it comes,
would "leave" the grieving mother with "the solemn pride that must be
yours, to have laid so costly a sacrifice upon the altar of Freedom." Neither
the prayer nor the letter's other words would effect such a consolation. But if
the prayer were answered, it would at least remove enough of the pain for
Mrs. Bixby to know her own virtuous pride, which "must be" hers because
of the nature of her son's deaths. The cure, imperfect as it would be, would
be hers if she accepted it.

The pride the letter appeals to, if we look at it more closely, is a deeper
form of forfeiture: the mother's unrealized satisfaction that *she* gave up her
sons to a higher cause. The mother did not send them to die, nor did they

seek their deaths. Her true pride would be in her recognition that she had lost them as "a sacrifice upon the altar of Freedom." She might then rise to a pride that "must be" hers, not because the letter tells her so, and not even because her sons acted heroically to save the Union, but because she surrendered them to the deaths they found as they fought for the cause that made the Union worth saving. In this sense, the letter's assuaging of Lydia Bixby's grief offers her a choice to descend into a greater grief (of letting the sons go without help), but one that would free her to mourn, with that "solemn pride." Lincoln has signed a letter that invites her to make the sacrifice of one grief for the other.

It seems wrong to assign this gesture of consolation to anyone. The language of the letter has become a part of the liturgy of American political religion. But there is something in it that we can appropriately ascribe to Lincoln. Like the greatest of his writings and speeches, it teaches a kind of letting go, for the sake of leaving its audience resolved to do things that before it did not so clearly and fully apprehend. So might a book about Lincoln's wise eloquence approach its end.

NOTES

Introduction. The Mind of the Persuader

1. See Harvey Mansfield, "The Media World and Democratic Representation," in *Rhetoric and American Statesmanship,* ed. Glen E. Thurow and Jeffrey D. Wallin (Durham: Carolina Academic Press, 1984), 57–70.

2. Forrest McDonald, "The Rhetoric of Alexander Hamilton," in Thurow and Wallin, *Rhetoric and American Statesmanship,* 71.

3. Anonymous, "American Eloquence," *United States Magazine and Democratic Review* 34 (July 1854), 49.

4. "American Eloquence," 53, 42–45.

5. Joshua Speed, *Reminiscences of Abraham Lincoln and Notes of a Visit to California* (Louisville, Ky.: John T. Morton and Co., 1884), 23.

6. Henry C. Whitney, *Life on the Circuit with Lincoln* (Caldwell, Idaho: Caxton Printers, 1940), 136.

7. Whitney, 499.

8. Whitney, 138.

9. Isaac Arnold, *Abraham Lincoln: A Paper* (Chicago: Forgure Printing, 1881), 175.

10. William Herndon and Jesse Weik, *Herndon's Lincoln* (New York: Albert and Charles Boni, 1930), 332.

11. Herndon and Weik, 332.

12. *Edinburgh Review* 113 (1861), 557.

13. Joseph Gillespie, letter to William Herndon (December 1866), in *Herndon's Informants,* ed. Douglas L. Wilson and Rodney O. Davis (Urbana: University of Illinois Press, 1998), 508.

14. Charles N. Smiley, "Lincoln and Gorgias," *Classical Journal* 13 (1917), 125.

15. Edward L. Pierce, letter to William Herndon (December 1889), in Wilson and Davis, *Herndon's Informants,* 683.

16. Speed, 28.

17. Speed, 23.

18. John G. Nicolay and John Hay, *Abraham Lincoln: A History*, 10 vols. (New York: Century, 1909), 1.307.

19. See Albert Beveridge, *Abraham Lincoln, 1809–1858*, 2 vols. (Boston: Houghton Mifflin, 1928), 2.528. Herndon and Weik report the possibly apocryphal story of an Illinois Supreme Court case in which Lincoln said, "I have not been able to find any authority to sustain my side of the case, but I have found several cases directly in point on the other side. I will now give these authorities to the Court, and then submit the case" (Herndon and Weik, 260). What looks like a humorous fiction about Lincoln's honesty supports the firmer view that principle, not the legal precedents in a specific court action, was his priority. Herndon quotes Joshua Speed's report of an inadvertently telling incident in this regard: "I remember reading to him [Lincoln] one of Mr. Calhoun's speeches in reply to Mr. Clay in the Senate, in which Mr. Clay had quoted precedent. Mr. Calhoun replied (I quote from memory) that 'to legislate upon precedent is but to make the error of yesterday the law of today.' Lincoln thought that was a great truth and grandly uttered" (*Herndon's Lincoln*, 421).

20. Lord Charnwood, *Abraham Lincoln* (Garden City, N.Y.: Garden City Publishing, 1917), 133.

21. Arnold, 175.

22. Herndon and Weik, 331.

Chapter 1. Rhetorical Contexts

1. Harry Jaffa, *Crisis of the House Divided* (Chicago: University of Chicago Press, 1959).

2. Warren P. Edgarton, *The Western Orator: Comprising an introductory course of oratorical training, with a copious selection of pieces for practice* (Cleveland: Ingham and Bragg, 1860), viii.

3. James Engell, *The Committed Word: Literature and Public Values* (University Park: Pennsylvania State University Press, 1999), 4.

4. For accounts of Lincoln's reading, see Engell, 141–161; Douglas L. Wilson, *Honor's Voice: The Transformation of Abraham Lincoln* (New York: Alfred A. Knopf, 1998); and Douglas L. Wilson and Rodney O. Davis, *Herndon's Informants* (Urbana: University of Illinois Press), especially 807–808.

5. Testimony of John T. Stuart, Lincoln's first law partner. See Wilson and Davis, 519.

6. Alexis de Tocqueville, *Democracy in America*, trans. Harvey C. Mansfield and Delba Winthrop (Chicago: University of Chicago Press, 2000), 445 (vol. II, bk. 1, chap. 13).

7. One of the most popular textbook authors of the antebellum period, Charles

W. Sanders, defined elocution as "the art of delivering written or extemporaneous composition with force, propriety, and ease . . . giving each word, or combination of words, such a delivery as best expresses the meaning of the author." *Sanders' Union Fifth Reader, Number Five* (Chicago: Ivison, Blakeman, Taylor and Co., 1867), 13. Sanders's graded textbooks date back to the 1830s.

8. Tocqueville, 445–478 (vol. II, bk. 1, chaps. 13–21).

9. Tocqueville, 476 (vol. II, bk. 1, chap. 21).

10. Tocqueville, 403 (vol. II, bk. 1, chap. 1).

11. Tocqueville, 583–584 (vol. II, bk. 3, chap. 15).

12. Tocqueville, 198–199 (vol. I, bk. 2, chap. 5).

13. Tocqueville, 432 (vol. II, bk. 1, chap. 9).

14. Tocqueville, 584 (vol. II, bk. 3, chap. 15).

15. Tocqueville, 414 (vol. II, bk. 1, chap. 3).

16. Tocqueville, 434 (vol. II, bk. 1, chap. 10).

17. Tocqueville, 414–415 (vol. II, bk. 1, chap. 3).

18. Tocqueville, 438–439 (vol. II, bk. 1, chap. 10).

19. Tocqueville, 403 (vol. II, bk. 1, chap. 1).

20. Tocqueville, 414 (vol. II, bk. 1, chap. 3).

21. Tocqueville, 584 (vol. II, bk. 3, chap. 15).

22. Tocqueville, 410 (vol. II, bk. 1, chap. 2). See chaps. 1–3 for Tocqueville's elaboration of these ideas.

23. Tocqueville, 611, 615 (vol. II, bk. 3, chap. 21).

24. Edward Everett, "The Speeches of Henry Clay," *North American Review* 25 (1827), 437–438.

25. Everett, 439.

26. Tocqueville, 502–503 (vol. II, bk. 2, chap. 8).

27. Tocqueville, 502 (vol. II, bk. 2, chap. 8).

28. Edward Everett, "Webster's Speeches," *North American Review* 41 (1835), 231–251.

29. Daniel Webster, "A Discourse in Commemoration of the Lives and Services of John Adams and Thomas Jefferson," in *The Papers of Daniel Webster: Speeches and Formal Writings,* ed. Charles M. Wiltse, 2 vols. (Hanover, N.H.: University Press of New England, 1986), 1.270–271. For an informative introductory discussion of Lincoln's relation to Webster and his legacy, see Richard N. Current, *Speaking of Abraham Lincoln: The Man and His Meaning for Our Times* (Urbana: University of Illinois Press, 1983), 1–15.

30. In much of what follows I am indebted to Richard Weaver's seminal essay, "The Spaciousness of the Old Rhetoric," in *The Ethics of Rhetoric* (Chicago: Henry Regnary, 1953), 164–185. A modern audience, which typically absorbs political speech silently from the newspaper and hears it almost always in tiny bits, can range

more freely among sources of information. But that greater access comes at a price: a decline in affect, a desensitized, undifferentiated attitude toward exaggeration in political speech.

The interpenetration of literature and oratory, perpetuated through repetition and performance, seems to have supported hyperbolic speech. It led to a civil liturgy of public rhetoric that could be heard—not uncritically, but with a greater capacity for credulity, a greater willingness to listen. In that more spacious setting, even though it was vexed with controversies of great moment, speakers had more time to prepare their audiences and weave their arguments. Deception crawled in that garden; but audiences seem to have given speakers a license to exaggerate (literally, to draw out their subject matters) so that listeners could recognize whether the claim had been made good or not. The relatively habitual and ludic nature of the interchange—its repetitive and internalized processes enforced by many shared principles and the rules of a familiar occasion—made it more like the telling of a story and less of an appeal for support than we are habituated to expect. Flights of the imagination were in that space more likely to show themselves—and expected to show themselves—as credible and real.

31. From the speech "On the Slavery Question," March 4, 1850, in John C. Calhoun, *The Works,* ed. Richard K. Crallé, 6 vols. (New York: Russell and Russell, 1968), 4.559.

32. From the speech "On the 'Three Million Bill,'" February 9, 1847, in Calhoun, *The Works,* 4.316–317.

33. From the speech "On the Bill to Set Aside the Bank Bill Dividends," February 4, 1817, in Calhoun, *The Works,* 2.190–191.

Chapter 2. The Lyceum Address

1. Michael F. Holt, *The Rise and Fall of the American Whig Party* (Oxford: Oxford University Press, 1999), 29. For another helpful study of the history of the Whig Party, see Daniel Walker Howe, *The Political Culture of American Whigs* (Chicago: University of Chicago Press, 1979).

2. Holt, 64–65.

3. Holt, 28.

4. James D. Richardson, ed., *A Compilation of the Messages and Papers of the Presidents, 1789–1908,* 11 vols. (Washington: Bureau of National Literature and Art, 1909), 3.296–297 (hereafter *CMPP*).

5. *CMPP,* 3.296–297.

6. *CMPP,* 3.318.

7. *CMPP,* 3.298.

8. *CMPP,* 3.317–318.

9. Van Buren's view, however inadequate it might be, is consistent with the impression of Americans' law-abidingness that Tocqueville described just a few years before: "[I]n the United States everyone is personally interested in enforcing the obedience of the whole community to the law. . . . However irksome an enactment may be, the citizen of the United States complies with it, not only because it is the work of the majority, but because it is his own, and he regards it as a contract to which he is himself a party" (Alexis de Tocqueville, *Democracy in America,* 2 vols. [New York: Random House, 1990], 1: chap. 14, pp. 247–248.) But Lincoln, Jackson, and Van Buren all noted the sudden deterioration of this practice, which was signaled in the urban riots of 1835 and lynchings of the kind Lincoln will describe later in his speech.

10. Note how the Illinois Whigs' resolution tolerating slavery parallels the Mississippi law affirming the legality of the professional gamblers' activities. Lincoln makes sure his audience knows that the latter was passed, like the former, in the previous year.

11. Basler speculates that Lincoln was confident that his audience knew the story and that he could make use of their strong impressions simply by touching upon the fact: "[I]t seems possible that he chose a subtler way of pricking the conscience of his audience than by direct denunciation" (1.111).

12. Harry Jaffa, *Crisis of the House Divided* (Chicago: University of Chicago Press, 1959), 183–235.

13. Edward Beecher, *Narrative of Riots at Alton* (New York: E. P. Dutton, 1965), 55.

14. William Lee Miller, *Lincoln's Virtues* (New York: Knopf, 2002), 116–139.

15. Beecher, 51–60.

16. Beecher, 30.

17. *St. Louis Observer,* May 5, 1836.

18. Thomas Jefferson, *Writings,* ed. Merrill D. Peterson (New York: Library of America, 1984), 93.

19. Jeremiah 49.22; 2 Samuel 1.23. See also Ezekiel 1.10, 17.3.

20. *Macbeth* 1.1.33–35.

21. We know that Lincoln indeed used hyperbole with an almost aggressive abandon during this period of legislative apprenticeship. In an 1839 speech, again on the national bank, he wrote a paragraph of florid intensity in which he vowed to face death alone against "the evil [i.e., Democratic] spirit that reigns" in Washington. In that peroration his apocalyptic language verged on parody when he raised a specter of Satanic corruption and then resolved to offer a solitary, heroic resistance. It is difficult for modern ears to take his rhetorical overreaching seriously:

I know that the great volcano at Washington, aroused and directed by the evil spirit that reigns there, is belching forth the lava of political corruption, in a current broad and deep, which is sweeping with frightful velocity over the whole length and breadth of the land, bidding fair to leave unscathed no green spot or living thing, while on its bosom are riding like demons on the waves of Hell, the imps of that evil spirit, and fiendishly taunting all those who dare resist its destroying course, with the hopelessness of their effort; and knowing this, I cannot deny that all may be swept away. . . . If ever I feel the soul within me elevate and expand to those dimensions not wholly unworthy of its Almighty Architect, it is when I contemplate the cause of my country, deserted by all the world beside, and I standing up boldly and alone and hurling defiance at her victorious oppressor. (1.178)

Such language, embarrassing to commentators who measure Lincoln's achievement by the standard of his presidential rhetoric, would not seem foreign to an antebellum northern audience steeped in the sermonic language of judgment and redemption. The hyperbole illustrates substantially what might otherwise escape notice. Lincoln portrays his opponents' political corruption as a nearly overwhelming threat so powerful that it endangers the very basis of his own party's hopes. Despair is the prospect for the Whigs, not merely a political defeat. Is this an obvious untruth? Perhaps not, given the Whig Party's brief life, its desperate hold on its existence in the late 1830s, and its attempts to define itself in high-minded terms as the party of principle against the party of irresponsible passion. Lincoln's exaggerated projection of himself as the last resisting Whig is likewise interpretable as a reflection of the struggle within each powerless member of his party—not merely as the symptom of an unpracticed and overreaching orator. Here, as in the Lyceum Address, he conceives of the political struggle as a psychological test, not just a partisan battle. A hint of megalomania might be an appropriate means of depicting that struggle with a seemingly irresistible opponent. It enables Lincoln to embody momentarily a capacity within each Whig partisan to resist the inevitable tide by defying defeat.

22. Brackets signify Nicolay and Hay's interpolation of an obscurity in the manuscript.

23. The brackets at the end of the passage mark Nicolay and Hay's interpolations.

24. The brackets in these last lines are Nicolay and Hay's interpolations.

25. Hugh Blair, *Lectures on Rhetoric and Belles Lettres* (Philadelphia: T. Ellwood Zell, 1833), 263–264.

26. Alexander Hamilton, James Madison, and John Jay, *The Federalist Papers* (New York: Bantam Books, 1982), 255–256.

27. The scene Lincoln read several times from *Macbeth* was in act 2, scene 2, where the usurper contrasts Duncan's innocent sleep in death to his own tormented wakefulness. For a full description of the circumstances of Lincoln's reading aloud of this passage, see David Donald, *Lincoln* (London: Random House, 1995), 580.

Chapter 3. The Temperance Address

1. Eric Foner, *Free Soil, Free Labor, Free Men: The Ideology of the Republican Party before the Civil War* (Oxford: Oxford University Press, 1995), 237–242.

2. William Herndon and Jesse Weik, *Herndon's Lincoln* (New York: Albert and Charles Boni, 1930), 206– 207.

3. Mark 5.1–10.

4. An excellent and detailed study of the fault lines within one state's Washingtonian movement, as well as its complex relations with the old reformers, is Robert L. Hampel's *Temperance and Prohibition in Massachusetts: 1813–1852* (Ann Arbor, Mich.: UMI Research Press, 1982), especially chaps. 7 and 8. See also Ian R. Tyrrell, *Sobering Up: From Temperance to Prohibition in Antebellum America, 1800–1860* (Westport, Conn.: Greenwood Press, 1979).

5. Jesse W. Gooodrich, *A Second Declaration of Independence; or, The Manifesto of All the Washington Total Abstinence Societies of the United States of America* (Worcester: Spooner and Howland, 1841), 4.

6. Goodrich, 4–5.

7. Goodrich, 3.

8. Goodrich, 7.

9. Goodrich, 7–8.

10. Mason L.Weems, *The Life of Washington,* ed. Marcus Cunliffe (Cambridge, Mass.: Harvard University Press, 1962), 189. One of Washington's famous moments of self-conquest is his smoothing of a quarrel by offering wine instead of a case of dueling pistols.

11. Weems, 4.

12. Quoted in Tyrrell, 183.

13. Weems, 191.

14. *Macbeth* 1.3.64–69.

15. See Marvin Spevack, *The Harvard Concordance to Shakespeare* (Cambridge, Mass.: Harvard University Press, 1973).

16. *Macbeth* 4.3.67–68.

17. *Macbeth* 1.5.15–20.

18. *Macbeth* 2.1.31.

19. *Macbeth* 2.2.1.

20. *Macbeth* 5.2.14–16.

21. *Macbeth* 2.3.106, 5.5.27.

22. Frederick Douglass, *My Bondage and My Freedom* (New York: Miller, Orton and Mulligan, 1855), 408.

23. Douglas L. Wilson, *Honor's Voice: The Transformation of Abraham Lincoln* (New York: Alfred A. Knopf, 1998).

Chapter 4. The Speech on the War with Mexico
and the Eulogy for Zachary Taylor

1. A revealing instance of the history of tension between Lincoln and Hardin is documented in the letter Lincoln wrote Hardin on February 7, 1846, concerning the local Whig Party's process of nominating candidates for office (1.360–365).

2. G. S. Borit, "Lincoln's Opposition to the Mexican War," *Journal of the Illinois State Historical Society* 67 (1974), 89.

3. Borit, 79–100.

4. David Donald, *Lincoln* (London: Random House, 1995), 126.

5. Donald, 122.

6. Donald, 123–126.

7. Donald, 123.

8. Donald, 124.

9. Donald, 128.

10. Donald, 123. Fighting began in "a region claimed by both the United States and Mexico." Although the passage mentions that Lincoln's opinion (and that of his fellow Whigs) differed from Polk's view, as well as Mexico's, it treats that difference as a manifestation of partisan competition.

11. Donald, 126.

12. Donald, 128.

13. Donald, 124.

14. Donald, 129.

15. Borit, 79–100.

16. *Congressional Globe,* May 11, 1846, 788.

17. *Congressional Globe,* May 12, 1846, 800.

18. For background on the Whig Party and the Mexican War, I am indebted to Thomas Brown's *Politics and Statesmanship: Essays on the American Whig Party* (New York: Columbia University Press, 1985), Robert W. Johannsen's *To the Halls of the Montezumas: The Mexican War in the American Imagination* (Oxford: Oxford University Press, 1985), Daniel Walker Howe's *The Political Culture of the American Whigs* (Chicago: University of Chicago Press, 1979), and K. Jack Bauer's *Zachary Taylor: Soldier, Planter, Statesman of the Old Southwest* (Baton Rouge: Louisiana State University Press, 1985).

19. *Congressional Globe,* January 6, 1848, 125.

20. *Congressional Globe,* January 4, 1848, 97–98.

21. *American Review,* n.s., 1 (March 1848), 217–230.

22. *American Review,* n.s., 1 (February 1848), 175–177.

23. *American Review,* n.s., 1 (January 1848), 2.

24. *Congressional Globe,* December 20, 1847, 58.

25. *Congressional Globe,* December 21–22, 1847, 61–67. Lincoln's resolution is on page 64.

26. A highly popular pamphlet was written in 1847 by Albert Gallatin, "Peace with Mexico," reprinted in *The Writings of Albert Gallatin,* ed. Henry Adams, 3 vols. (New York: Antiquarian Press, 1960), 3.555–591. See also Henry Clay, "Speech in Lexington, Kentucky," in *The Papers of Henry Clay,* ed. Melba Porter Hay, 10 vols. (Lexington: University of Kentucky Press, 1991), 10.363.

27. Clay, 10.363, 375. The speech was delivered on November 13, 1847.

28. Clay, 10.376.

29. Clay, 10. 361.

30. Daniel Webster, *The Papers of Daniel Webster: Speeches and Formal Writings,* ed. Charles M. Wiltse, 2 vols. (Hanover, N.H.: University Press of New England, 1988), 2.436.

31. Webster, 2.436.

32. *Congressional Globe Appendix,* February 2, 1848, 159–163.

33. Richardson had been elected to the seat vacated by Stephen Douglas when Douglas was elected to the Senate. Lincoln's response to Richardson was no doubt electrically charged by his long-standing partisan rivalry with Douglas. It is not obvious, however, that such evidence makes Lincoln's position merely and essentially partisan. By 1848 that rivalry had already had much to do with substantial disagreements about the means and ends of government.

34. *Congressional Globe Appendix,* January 4, 1848, 171.

35. Lincoln is responding to Polk's second and third annual messages: December 8, 1846, and December 7, 1847. See James D. Richardson, ed., *A Compilation of the Messages and Papers of the Presidents, 1789–1908,* 11 vols. (Washington: Bureau of National Literature and Art, 1909), 4.471–506, 522–564 (hereafter *CMPP*).

36. *CMPP,* 4.485.

37. *CMPP,* 4.486.

38. *CMPP,* 4.487.

39. *CMPP,* 4.442.

40. *CMPP,* 4.440.

41. *Congressional Globe,* January 12, 1848, 146.

42. Here I take issue with one of the conclusions in Thomas J. Pressly's illuminating and thorough essay, "Bullets and Ballots: Lincoln and the 'Right of Revolution,'" *American Historical Review* 67 (April 1962), 647–662.

43. Borit, 91.

44. *Congressional Globe Appendix,* 161b.

45. *Congressional Globe,* January 3, 1848, 87.

46. T. B. Thorpe, *Our Army on the Rio Grande* (Philadelphia: Carey and Hart,

1846), 106. Lincoln may have creatively imitated the following passages or other reports upon which Thorpe based his narration:

> At a little before six, a confused rush of cavalry and straggling infantry towards the Rio Grande, announced the victory of the Americans, at the sight of which, an officer of the Seventh jumped upon the parapet, beside the regimental flag staff, and gave three cheers, which were responded to so loudly and heartily by all in the fort, that they silenced the enemy's batteries, for from that moment they ceased firing. . . . As our pursuing columns [emerged] . . . and saw the flag of our country still waving in triumph from its ramparts, they raised to the glory of its defenders, a shout that made the welkin ring, and it was sent back from the fort until cheer answering cheer, reverberated along the valley of the Rio Grande.

47. Lincoln does not name the poem, but on the basis of this letter and an earlier mention of what is apparently the same work in another letter written to his friend Andrew Johnson on February 24, 1846, Basler concludes that the poem is Knox's (1.378). Additional evidence is available in Herndon's collection of testimony about Lincoln's favorite poem from friends and acquaintants. See Douglas L. Wilson's *Lincoln's Informants* (Chicago: University of Illinois Press, 1998), 88–90, 343, 470n.

48. Donald, 48.

49. William Knox, "Oh, Why Should the Spirit of Mortal Be Proud?" in *One Hundred Choice Selections,* ed. Phineas Garrett (Philadelphia: Penn Publishing, 1897). The complete version is also available on the web: www.poetry-archive.com/k/oh_why_should_the_spirit.html.

Chapter 5. The Eulogy for Henry Clay

1. Edward Everett, "The Speeches of Henry Clay," *North American Review* 25 (1827), 443–444.

2. Mark E. Neely Jr., "American Nationalism in the Image of Henry Clay: Abraham Lincoln's Eulogy on Henry Clay in Context," *Register of the Kentucky Historical Society* 73 (January 1975), 31–60.

3. For graphic evidence of the persistence of the Democrats' charge that the Whigs did not support the American army in Mexico, see Lincoln's detailed 1858 letter to Joseph Medill (2.473–474).

4. Lord Charnwood, *Abraham Lincoln* (Garden City, N.Y.: Garden City Publishing, 1917), 102.

5. Henry Clay, *The Life, Correspondence, and Speeches of Henry Clay,* ed. Calvin Colton, 6 vols. (New York: A. S. Barnes, 1857), 5.330.

6. Clay, 5.339.

7. Clay, 5.339.

8. Henry Clay, "Speech on African Colonization," in Clay, 5.337.

9. In the antebellum period, Liberia's colonists never numbered more than a few tens of thousands. Yet in the time that Clay had presided over the colonization society, the settlers had successfully defended themselves against attack, had formed a sovereign government, and had grown geometrically in their numbers. The idea of colonization lived on, if only as a diplomatic means of softening the blow of military emancipation, into the first years of the Civil War. In the months before he signed the Emancipation Proclamation, President Lincoln convened a group of black freemen and asked for volunteers to establish an independent state in South America. See Lincoln's address of August 13, 1862, in 2.361–67.

10. Clay, "On Abolition," in Clay, 5.151, 155.

11. Kimberly C. Shankman, *Compromise and the Constitution: The Political Thought of Henry Clay* (New York: Lexington Books, 1999), 115. See also Glyndon G. Van Deusen, *The Life of Henry Clay* (Boston: Little, Brown, 1937): 358–378.

12. Clay's view of the Constitution's role with regard to slavery rigorously separated its authority from the moral issue: "The Constitution neither verified, nor does it continue, slavery. Slavery existed independent of the Constitution, and antecedent to the Constitution; and it is dependent in the States, not upon the will of Congress, but upon the law of the respective States. The Constitution is silent and passive upon the subject of the institution of slavery, or rather it deals with a fact as a fact that exists, without having created, continued, or being responsible for it, in the slightest degree, within the States" (Clay, 6.552).

13. Clay, 6.151.

14. Clay, 5.158.

15. Clay, 6.157.

16. *Hamlet*, 3.1.60–64.

17. For a revealing analysis of the 1850 votes on this measure, see Roger L. Ransom, *Conflict and Compromise* (Cambridge: Cambridge University Press, 1989), 121–171.

18. Quoted in John B. Nicolay and John Hay, *Abraham Lincoln: A History*, 10 vols. (New York: Century, 1909): 1.335.

Chapter 6. The Kansas-Nebraska Speech

1. See Lincoln's confirmation of this fact in his letter to James O. Putnam, September 13, 1860 (4.115).

2. William Herndon and Jesse Weik, *Herndon's Lincoln* (New York: Albert and Charles Boni, 1930), 313.

3. Stephen Douglas, speech in the U. S. Senate, January 30, 1854, reprinted in Douglas, *The Nebraska Question* (New York: Redfield, 1854), 43, 45.

4. Thomas Hart Benton, speech in the U.S. House of Representatives, April 25, 1854, in *Congressional Globe Appendix,* 559.

5. Basler includes the editorial in the collected works, 2.229–230. He reports that Lincoln's speech in Springfield lasted "above three hours," indicating that the Springfield newspaper's version of the speech (just over seven pages in the collected works) is much too short to contain Lincoln's entire presentation. The more authoritative Peoria version is thirty-six pages long in Basler's edition. (The other preliminary versions, in two Bloomington newspapers, are three and seven pages long.)

6. Theodore Parker, *The Nebraska Question* (Boston: Benjamin and Mussey, 1854), 71–72.

7. Herndon and Weik, 292–293.

8. Charles Sumner, *The Works of Charles Sumner,* 15 vols. (Boston: Lee and Shephard, 1870–1883), 3.293.

9. Sumner, 3.343.

10. Sumner, 3.344.

11. William Seward, Senate speech of February 17, 1854, *Congressional Globe, Appendix,* 150–155.

12. Henry Clay, speech on the compromise bills, July 22, 1850, in *Life, Correspondence, and Speeches of Henry Clay,* ed. Calvin Colton, 6 vols. (New York: A. S. Barnes, 1857), especially 6.550–554.

13. "[At the time the Constitution was written,] there was no diversity of opinion between the North and the South upon the subject of slavery. It will be found that both parts of the country found it equally an evil, a moral and political evil. It will not be found that, either at the North or at the South, there was much, though there was some, invective against slavery as inhumane or cruel. The great ground of objection to it was political; that it weakened the social fabric; that, taking the place of free labor, society became less strong and labor less productive; and therefore we find from all the eminent men of the time the clearest expression of their opinion that slavery is an evil." Daniel Webster, "The Constitution and the Union," in *The Papers of Daniel Webster: Speeches and Formal Writings,* Charles M. Wiltse, 2 vols. (Hanover, N.H.: University Press of New England, 1988), 2.552. See also 2.534.

14. Webster, especially 2.534.

15. Douglas, 42.

16. Douglas, 40.

17. Douglas, 41.

18. Douglas, 46.

19. Douglas, 46.

20. See Salmon Chase's January 30, 1854 speech in the Senate, in the *Congressional Globe,* 280–282.

21. *Congressional Globe,* 282.

22. *1 Henry IV* 2.4.470–480.

23. *Hamlet* 3.3.93.

24. *Richard III* 1.1.10, 1.2..25, 1.3.335.

Chapter 7. The "House Divided" Speech

1. William Herndon and Jesse Weik, *Herndon's Lincoln* (New York: Albert and Charles Boni, 1930), 325. Herndon's recollection is supported by Leonard Swett quoting J. L. Dickey; see Douglas L. Wilson and Rodney O. Davis, eds. *Herndon's Informants* (Urbana: University of Illinois Press, 1998), 163.

2. Herndon and Weik, 325.

3. Wilson and Davis, 441–442.

4. Herndon and Weik, 326.

5. Douglas L. Wilson, *Honor's Voice: The Transformation of Abraham Lincoln* (New York: Alfred A. Knopf, 1998).

6. See Wilson and Davis, 575.

7. Daniel Webster, *Papers of Daniel Webster, 1800–1833,* ed. Charles M. Wiltse (Hanover, N.H.: University Press of New England, 1986), 347.

8. Webster, 120.

9. *New York Herald,* June 8, 1858.

10. Herndon and Weik, 327.

11. William Henry Seward, "The Irrepressible Conflict," in *New York Tribune* (Rochester), October 25, 1858, 2–7.

12. Henry Clay Whitney, *Life on the Circuit with Lincoln* (Caldwell, Idaho: Caxton Printers, 1940), 121.

13. Here I agree with Don E. Fehrenbacher's argument that Lincoln bases his appeal on a carefully focused antislavery principle, which he sets against Douglas's effort to create public indifference to the moral status of slavery. On the other hand, I see Lincoln's argument as more problematic and daringly persuasive than it is in the historian's analysis. See Fehrenbacher's helpful analysis of the "House Divided" Speech in *Prelude to Greatness: Lincoln in the 1850's* (Stanford: Stanford University Press, 1962), 70–95.

14. Ecclesiastes 9.3–4.

15. David Donald, *Lincoln* (London: Random House, 1995), 208.

Chapter 8. Lecture on Discoveries and Inventions

1. Lawrence Buell, *New England Literary Culture: From Revolution through Renaissance* (Cambridge: Cambridge University Press, 1886), 153.

2. Donald M. Scott, "The Popular Lecture and the Creation of a Public in Mid-

Nineteenth-Century America," *Journal of American History* 66 (December 1979), especially 791, 800.

3. *Illinois State Register,* March 22, January 18, February 3 and 7, 1859.

4. Orville Hickman Browning, *The Diary of Orville Hickman Browning,* ed. Theodore C. Pease and James G. Randall, 2 vols. (Springfield: Illinois State Historical Library, 1925), 1.357.

5. Browning, 1.357.

6. Browning, 1.359–360.

7. Browning, 1.361.

8. Browning, 1.371.

9. Browning, 1.35. In March the next year, Lincoln's partner W. H. Herndon lectured at Cook's Hall, and a month later Lincoln delivered the discoveries lecture there for the library association. The eclectic fare available to Springfield audiences was in ample supply that season, when the notorious libertine Lola Montez drew a much larger crowd to Cook's Hall than Herndon could gather for his learned sorties the night following. See the *Illinois State Journal,* March 19, 1860.

10. Thomas Paine, *The Age of Reason,* ed. William M. Van der Weyde (New Rochelle, N.Y.: T. Paine National Historical Association, 1925), 281.

11. See Basler's note in the collected works, 2.11.

12. David Donald, *Lincoln's Herndon* (New York: Alfred A. Knopf, 1948), 128.

13. For a detailed discussion of these dates, see Wayne C. Temple, "Lincoln as a Lecturer on 'Discoveries, Inventions, and Improvements,'" *Jacksonville Journal Courier,* May 23, 1982, 1– 12. Among his many findings, Temple develops evidence to resolve the long-standing confusion over the date of the Jacksonville speech, which Basler and other scholars have assigned to February 11, 1859 (see p. 6.) The novel claim that there was a Pontiac lecture is based on a single, highly detailed letter from Augustus W. Cowan. Since Pontiac, Illinois, is approximately halfway between Springfield and Chicago, Lincoln could have reached it by train in half a day. *Lincoln Day by Day: A Chronology, 1809–1865,* ed. Earl Schenck Miers (Dayton, Ohio: Morningside, 1991), says nothing about the trip, and indicates that Lincoln was probably engaged in legal business in Springfield on January 27. But the lack of more definite evidence to that effect, joined with availability of transportation to Pontiac that would have allowed a quick return, lends weight to Temple's case. Unfortunately, the local newspaper archive is not available. Temple reports that it was destroyed by fire in 1867.

14. Temple, 10.

15. Temple, 4.

16. *Bloomington Daily Pantagraph,* April 19, 1858.

17. On the basis of this evidence I differ from Temple, who insists on the integrity of both texts and does not allow for the possibility of revision. See Temple, 4.

18. John G. Nicolay, Lincoln's Literary Experiments," *Century Magazine* 47 (1894), 831. Nicolay is correct that Lincoln delivered the address in Springfield, but he either misremembers the date or exposes an uncharacteristic lapse in the *Illinois State Journal*'s coverage of this sort of local event. Nicolay recollects that the date was February 22, 1860, saying truly that Lincoln departed a week later for New York to deliver the Cooper Union Address. But there is no newspaper mention of the speech. The *Illinois State Journal* records that Lincoln gave the Lecture on Discoveries and Inventions at Cook's Hall April 26, 1860, upon his return from New York and one week before the state Republican convention in Chicago. The latter occasion was sponsored by the library society, just as Nicolay claims. He probably mixed up the two somewhat similar occasions. At any rate, the Springfield paper notes that the speech reached a large audience: "A large and intelligent audience listened to Hon. Abraham Lincoln's lecture, 'Inventions and Discoveries,' on Thursday evening. The lecture was a first class production, and gave much pleasure to the audience. It was of the most instructive and entertaining character, and we doubt not that it cost its talented author much time and labor" (*Illinois State Journal*, April 28, 1860).

19. Nicolay, 831.

20. William H. Herndon and Jesse W. Weik, *Herndon's Lincoln* (New York: Albert and Charles Boni, 1930), 362.

21. *Bloomington Daily Pantagraph*, April 9, 1858. The so-called 1859 version elaborates much of the argument and tragicomic spirit of Lincoln's so-called 1858 remarks.

22. Nicolay, 831.

23. Roy P. Basler, *A Touchstone for Greatness* (Westport, Conn.: Greenwood Press, 1973), 82.

24. Garry Wills, *Lincoln at Gettysburg* (New York: Simon and Schuster, 1992), 153–155.

25. Herndon and Weik, 362.

26. Lincoln did not like to repeat entire political speeches verbatim, given his audiences' likely familiarity with their printed versions. He may have refrained from repeating the Cooper Union Address in Springfield largely for that reason. (By his own testimony, he composed new speeches in the East after delivering the Cooper Union Address.) But it remains a curious fact that in Springfield he returned to the discoveries lecture rather than make a political speech. The reason for the switch may lie in the fact that he conceived of both speeches as lectures, one more political than the other. (See chapter 11.) The discoveries lecture would have provided him with an opportunity to address his Springfield audience in a nonpartisan yet highly allusive, flexible mode of speech conducive to making implicit political arguments.

27. Herndon and Weik, 367.

28. Quoted by Donald in *Lincoln's Herndon*, 63.

29. Letter of February 21, 1891, in *The Hidden Lincoln,* ed. Emanuel Hertz (New York: Blue Ribbon Books, 1940), 262.

30. Ward Hill Lamon, *The Life of Abraham Lincoln* (Boston: John R. Osgood, 1872), 421.

31. Henry Clay Whitney, *Life on the Circuit with Lincoln* (Caldwell, Idaho: Caxton Printers, 1940), 436.

32. See Donald, *Lincoln's Herndon,* 61–63.

33. Donald, *Lincoln's Herndon,* 197–217.

34. Douglas L. Wilson, *Honor's Voice: The Transformation of Abraham Lincoln* (New York: Alfred A. Knopf, 1998).

35. Disappointment there would have carried a double sting: Herndon's admiration for his mentor could easily have clashed with his pride in his own educational accomplishments and relatively radical political views. His judgment ran on two tracks not always in tandem. On the one hand, Herndon considered Lincoln to be suited for higher things. On the other, he did not believe that his great partner was beyond criticism. Looking back years later, convinced that Lincoln was without peer in the political world, he might have remembered his friend's imperfect lecture as just one more confirmation of the discrepancy between Lincoln's political greatness and his roughhewn background.

36. Noah Brooks, *Washington in Lincoln's Time* (New York: Century, 1895), 306.

37. Temple, 4–6.

38. See Temple, 1–12.

39. Whitney, 499.

40. Brooks, 306.

41. Edward T. Channing, *Lectures Read to Seniors at Harvard College,* ed. E. J. Anderson and W. W. Braden (1856; Carbondale: Southern Illinois University Press, 1978), 67–68.

42. J. G. Holland, "The Popular Lecture," *Atlantic Monthly* 15 (1865), 367–368.

43. Waldo W. Braden, "The Lecture Movement: 1840–1860," *Quarterly Journal of Speech* 34 (1948), 210. Braden is quoting from *Putnam's Monthly* 9 (1857), 319.

44. M. E. Curti, "Young America," *American Historical Review* 32 (1926), 54–55.

45. Lincoln was, of course, heavily involved in party affairs and had been an avid reader of the *Congressional Globe* for almost twenty years. See David Donald, *Lincoln* (London: Random House, 1995), 78–79.

46. 37th Congress, 2d sess., chap. 130 (1862), 504. The 1862 legislation focused on language as well as material technology. It called for "liberal and practical education" and emphasized agricultural and mechanical arts "without excluding other scientific and classical studies."

47. The general approach to antebellum American oratory as a layering of rhetorical and literary modes is admirably set out in Lawrence Buell's *New England Literary Culture: From Revolution through Renaissance* (London: Cambridge University Press, 1986), 137–165. This portion of my argument is indebted to Buell's discussion of antebellum orators even though he does not discuss Lincoln.

48. Whitney, 499.

49. Whitney, 121.

50. George Bancroft, *Literary and Historical Miscellanies* (New York: Harper and Brothers, 1855), 481–517.

51. Whitney, 209.

52. From a letter to William Herndon dated December 8, 1866, cited by Douglas L. Wilson in *Lincoln before Washington: New Perspective on the Illinois Years* (Urbana : University of Illinois Press, 1997), 177. See the complete letter in Douglas L. Wilson and Rodney O. Davis, ed., *Herndon's Informants* (Urbana: University of Illinois Press, 1998). Lincoln had a practical as well as a philosophical interest in understanding technology's role in the development of civilization. From the beginning of his political career, he had promoted public works. The 1832 pamphlet he used to promote his first political campaign for the Illinois legislature was an attempt to convince Sangamon County's voters to endorse an ingenious method of deepening and straightening the local river so that local farms would have access to markets. In 1849, he patented a device that would have enabled barges to navigate shallow frontier waters (2.32–36). His familiarity with the technology of frontier riverboating, strengthened by his experience in Sangamon waters and his two rafting trips down the big river to New Orleans, contributed to his proposal and helped his legal career. His legal career included effective defenses of the railroads. In 1857 his summation of the famous Rock Island Bridge Case meticulously analyzed the behavior of river waters and the operation of paddle-wheel boats in order to convince the jury that the owners of a railroad bridge were not responsible for the wreck of a steamboat on one of its piers.

53. Bancroft, 484.

54. Bancroft, 484.

55. Bancroft, 487–491.

56. Bancroft, 502–505, 509.

57. Bancroft, 509–514.

58. Bancroft, 503, 507.

59. Bancroft, 515.

60. Henry Ward Beecher, *Lectures and Orations,* ed. Newell Dwight Hillis (New York and Chicago: Flemming H. Revell, Co., 1913).

61. Bancroft, 517.

62. Bancroft, 196.

63. Carl Bode, *The American Lyceum: Town Meeting of the Mind* (New York: Oxford University Press, 1956), 206.

64. One estimate, $250,000, is perhaps excessive. See John L. Lucaites's essay in *American Orators before 1900, ed.* Bernard K. Duffy and Halford R. Ryan (New York: Greenwood Press, 1987), 320. But in an era in which Henry Ward Beecher could command $100 or more for each performance on a circuit packed with eager audiences, two thousand performances (the number that Phillips's publisher claims for "The Lost Arts") could have netted almost as much as Lucaites claims. The more common fee ranged between ten and twenty-five dollars. (See Bode, 31–32.)

65. In the 1850s, Lincoln's partner Herndon had developed a correspondence with Phillips and his fellow abolitionists, Parker and Garrison, though Lincoln kept radical abolitionism at a distance. See Duffy and Ryan, especially 321 and 316–324.

66. Wendell Phillips, *The Lost Arts* (New York: T. Dillingham, 1884), 5–6.

67. Phillips, 21.

68. Phillips, 23.

69. Phillips, 23.

70. Phillips, 22.

71. Phillips, 19.

72. David Hume, *Essays, Literary, Moral, and Political* (London: Ward, Lock, and Tyler, 1870), 65–79.

73. *Bloomington Pantagraph,* April 9, 1858.

74. J. G. Holland, "The Popular Lecture," *Atlantic Monthly* 15 (1865), 367.

75. Bancroft, 494; Lincoln, in Basler, 3.356–357.

76. Joseph Addison, *Cato* (1713; London: Everyman's Library, 1964), 5.1.1–3. See the entire speech for a passage that would have been likely to catch Lincoln's eye.

77. See M. E. Curti, "'Young America,'" *American Historical Review* 32 (1926), 35–55.

78. Curti, 40.

79. Compare Lincoln's subtle and humorous opening paragraphs with Edwin de Leon's explicit expression of radically mixed feelings: "The condition of our country at the present time, is such as to awaken at once the pride and anxiety of every patriot. . . . There is nothing permanently fixed and settled, either in opinion or in action. . . . There is a feverish restlessness, a morbid craving after change, pervading every relation of our social system; an impatience of reaping the rewards of regular and steady industry . . ., and speculation, in its Protean forms, is the idol before which 'Young America' bows down in worship." Edwin de Leon, *The Position and Duties of Young America* (Charleston, 1845), 14.

80. Contrast Lincoln's complex humor with Edwin de Leon's humorless academic treatment of a similar subject: "Let one example of popular ignorance suffice

us. Of the thousands who are daily whirled on the rapid wings of steam, in rail car or steamboat, over the busy thoroughfares of our country, how many, think you, have ever troubled themselves to comprehend the principles which regulate that simple, but wondrous machinery? . . . All this is radically wrong; and it never will be corrected, until our citizens shall learn to appreciate education" (de Leon, 14).

81. Lincoln, as far as I can tell, does not use this hyperbolic phrase in any other extant writing or speech.

82. *Bloomington Pantagraph,* April 9, 1859. In Catholic Bibles, "Miriam" is a version of "Mary."

83. *Encyclopedia Americana,* 13 vols. (Philadelphia: Carey and Lea, 1831), 12.12.

84. Here we have an account of unrecorded paragraphs lost to Lincoln scholarship. If the reporter's memory is not entirely reliable, the particularity of his reference at least indicates the range and detail of Lincoln's lost elaborations.

85. Hugh Blair, *Lectures on Rhetoric and Belles Lettres,* ed. E. Harold F. Harding, 2 vols. (Carbondale: Illinois University Press, 1965), 97–136, especially 136.

86. *Encyclopedia Americana,* 13.271.

87. Donald, *Lincoln,* 164. Herndon makes this assertion in a letter written February 21, 1891.

88. *Encyclopedia Americana,* 7.48.

89. De Leon, 12.

90. Don E. Fehrenbacher, ed., *Lincoln: Speeches, Letters, and Miscellaneous Writings,* 2 vols. (New York: Library of America, 1989), 2.713.

91. Wilson, 177.

Chapter 9. The Milwaukee Address

1. *Illinois State Journal,* October 5, 1859.

2. Don E. Fehrenbacher, ed., *Lincoln: Speeches, Letters, and Miscellaneous Writings,* 2 vols. (New York: Library of America, 1989), 2.710.

3. Alexander Pope, *An Essay on Man,* in *The Poems of Alexander Pope,* ed. John Butt (New Haven: Yale University Press, 1963), 536, 547, Epistle 4, lines 1, 396.

4. Horace Greeley, *What I Know of Farming* (New York: G. W. Carleton, 1871), 94–95.

5. Francis Wayland, *The Elements of Political Economy* (Boston: Gould and Lincoln, 1859), 304. The book was registered for copyright in 1837. The 1859 edition represents its "fortieth thousand."

6. George Fitzhugh, *Sociology for the South* (New York: Burt Franklin, 1854), 94.

7. *Daily Illinois State Journal,* March 2, 1859. The column is reprinted from the *Illinois Farmer,* March 1859.

8. William Henry Seward, "The Irrepressible Conflict," published in pamphlet form by the *New York Tribune,* Rochester, New York. The speech was delivered on October 25, 1858.

9. 3.459. See Basler's note.

10. For an illuminating analysis of Republican and Democratic attitudes toward free labor and its relation to slavery, see Eric Foner, *Free Soil, Free Labor, Free Men: The Ideology of the Republican Party before the Civil War* (Oxford: Oxford University Press, 1995), especially pages 11–72.

11. Pope, *Essay on Man,* 4.363–364.

Chapter 10. The Cooper Union Address

1. Emanuel Hertz, *The Hidden Lincoln* (New York: Viking Press, 1938), 78.

2. *New York Tribune,* February 25, 1860. Cited in Andrew A. Freeman, *Abraham Lincoln Goes to New York* (New York: Coward-McCann, 1960), 16.

3. David Mearns, *Lincoln Papers,* 1.229–30. Cited in Freeman, 52.

4. William Herndon and Jesse Weik, *Herndon's Lincoln* (New York: Albert and Charles Boni, 1930), 367–368.

5. Stephen Douglas, speech at Columbus, Ohio, September 7, 1859, in *In the Name of the People,* ed. Harry Jaffa and Robert Johannsen (Columbus: Ohio State University Press, 1959), 135.

6. Herndon and Weik, 368.

7. Douglas, in Jaffa and Johannsen, *In the Name of the People,* 529.

8. Douglas, in Jaffa and Johannsen, *In the Name of the People,* 528.

9. *New York Daily Tribune,* February 28, 1860, 6.

10. The Cooper Union was also used for more explicitly scholarly events. Two days after Lincoln's triumph, The Reverend Spalding was slated to lecture in the same hall on civilization in the Middle Ages (*New York Daily Tribune,* February 29, 1860).

11. *New York Daily Tribune,* February 28, 1860. Cited in Freeman, 16.

12. *New York Daily Tribune,* February 28, 1860. Cited in Freeman, 9.

13. *New York Herald,* May 19, 1860. Cited by Freeman, 91. I am indebted to Freeman for the newspaper references in the following paragraphs.

Chapter 11. Presidential Eloquence and Political Religion

1. Orville Browning's *Diary,* entry for April 3, 1864 (cited in a note by Basler, 7.283). A published version of the diary is available: *The Diary of Orville Hickman Browning,* ed. Theodore C. Pease and James G. Randall, 2 vols. (Springfield: Illinois State Historical Society, 1925–1933).

2. Basler found this textual information in the Robert Todd Lincoln Collection in the Library of Congress, and placed it in his notes to the December 30, 1862, draft of the Emancipation Proclamation. It is not noted by Chase himself in his diary. See David Donald's *Inside Lincoln's Cabinet* (New York: Longmans Green, 1954). George Anastaplo contributes a rich and concise discussion of the sentence's highly suggestive, almost inchoate syntax in *Abraham Lincoln: A Constitutional Biography* (New York: Rowman and Littlefield, 1999), 222.

3. For an extensive discussion of the relation between love, morality, and politics in this phase of Lincoln's life, see Douglas L. Wilson, *Honor's Voice: The Transformation of Abraham Lincoln* (New York: Alfred A. Knopf, 1998).

4. Matthew 18.7–8.

5. Alexis de Tocqueville, *Democracy in America,* trans. Harvey C. Mansfield and Delba Winthrop (Chicago: University of Chicago Press, 2000), 676; Alexander Hamilton, James, Madison, and John Jay, *The Federalist Papers,* ed. Robert Scigliano (New York: Modern Library, 2000), 9.

6. John Milton, *Paradise Lost,* in *Complete Poems and Major Prose,* ed. Merritt Hughes (New York: Macmillan, 1957), 5.19. Satan's pledge to rule in Hell is only part of an effort to make the universe his domain by ruining all that is good: "To me shall be the glorie sole among / The infernal Powers, in one day to have marr'd / What the *Almightie* styl'd, six Nights and Days / Continued making" (5.135–138).

7. Douglas L. Wilson and Rodney O. Davies, eds., *Herndon's Informants* (Urbana: University of Illinois Press, 1998), 498–499.

8. *Paradise Lost,* 3.114–132.

9. The basic data for these comparisons come from the online concordance of the Abraham Lincoln Association: http:www.hti.umich.edu/l/Lincoln/.

10. William Pitt, *The Speeches of the Right Honorable William Pitt in the House of Commons,* 4 vols. (London: Longman, Hurst, Rees, and Orme, 1806), 1.90–91. Delivered November 18, 1783.

11. Milton, *Paradise Lost* 1.393.

12. Ivan Roots, ed., *Speeches of Oliver Cromwell* (London: J. M. Dent and Sons, 1989), 54. Delivered September 12, 1654.

13. *As You Like It* 2.1.12, and *Richard II* 1.3.275.

14. *King Lear* 1.2.118–133.

15. Oliver Cromwell, *The Letters and Speeches of Oliver Cromwell with Elucidations by Thomas Carlyle,* ed. S. C. Lomis, 3 vols. (London: Methuen, 1904), 54.

Chapter 12. The Farewell Address

1. "B" Verson: "He never would have succeeded except for the aid of Divine Providence, upon which he at all times relied" (4.190). "C" Version: "But if the

same omniscient mind, and Almighty arm that directed and protected him, shall guide and support me, I shall not fail" (4.191).

2. The "C" version appeared in the *Illinois Journal,* February 12, the day after Lincoln departed. It seems highly unlikely that he would have been able to edit it for accuracy. See Basler, 4.191.

3. For an appreciation of Lincoln's frequent resort to *instrumentality* and *instrument* to articulate this relationship, see the concordance of the Abraham Lincoln Association at its website.

4. [David] Elton Trueblood, *Abraham Lincoln: Theologian of American Anguish* (New York: Harper and Row, 1973), 78–79.

5. James F. Wilson, "Some Memories of Lincoln," *North American Review* 163 (December 1896), 667–675.

6. Horace Bushnell, *Reverses Needed, A discourse delivered on the Sunday after the disaster at Bull Run,* reprinted in *Nationalism and Religion in America,* ed. Winthrop S. Hudson (New York: Harper and Row, 1970), 83.

7. *Hamlet* 5.2.10–11.

8. *Hamlet* 5.2.7.

9. *Hamlet* 5.2.10–11.

10. *Hamlet* 5. 2.219–222.

11. *Hamlet* 5.2.360.

Chapter 13. The First Inaugural, the Gettysburg Address, and the Second Inaugural

1. For examples of Lincoln's self-limiting rhetoric before and immediately after the election, see 4.91–92 and 142–144. The passage he wrote for anonymous insertion into Lyman Trumbull's postelection speech, in an attempt to assure the South that the Republican pledge to honor the constitutional protections of slavery was real, was by his own estimate counterproductive. (For the text of insertion, see 4.141–142. The analysis of its negative effect is in the letter to Henry J. Raymond, 4.145–146.)

2. For Basler's explanation of the authorship of this complicated draft, see 4.249 and the notes throughout.

3. For the sake of focusing this commentary on the most important points of comparison, I have omitted Basler's notation of several deletions on Seward draft.

4. John Milton, *Lycidas,* line 163.

5. Here "of" seems to have both a partitive and substantive function: the chorus is of the Union in the sense of belonging to it, and of the Union in the sense of consisting of and constituting it.

6. It is more than likely that Shakespeare's sonnets are the primary source for Lincoln's reference. The poet's "better angel is a man right fair" (Sonnet 3), an animating presence paired with a "bad angel" (Sonnets 2, 6, 12, 14), and is capable of turning into his opposite if the bad angel should succeed in tempting him (Sonnet 6).

7. Richard Weaver, *The Ethics of Rhetoric* (Davis: Hermagorus Press, 1985), 164–185.

8. David Donald, *Lincoln* (London: Random House, 1995), 15.

9. From the letter to Woodhouse, October 27, 1818. See also the letter to George and Tom Keats, December 1817. *The Letters of John Keats*, ed. Robert Gittings (London: Oxford Press, 1970), 158 and 43.

10. John G. Nicolay and John Hay, *Abraham Lincoln: A History*, 10 vols. (New York: Century, 1909), 8.190.

11. See Garry Wills, *Lincoln at Gettysburg* (New York: Simon and Schuster, 1992), 191–203.

12. This rhetorical gesture was not unique in Lincoln's political career. In his 1839 Speech on the Sub-treasury, he had used a dramatic vow to demonstrate his willingness to risk self-sacrifice for the sake of principle and the public good. Like the vow in the Gettysburg Address, the sub-treasury speech is about standing firm, not attacking. It draws much of its authority from the self-effacing confinement of its expression of resolve. But the strident tenor of the 1839 pledge sets it apart from Lincoln's presidential eloquence:

> If I ever feel the soul within me elevate and expand to those dimensions not wholly unworthy of its Almighty Architect, it is when I contemplate the cause of my country, deserted by all the world beside, and I standing up boldly and alone and hurling defiance at her victorious oppressors. Here, without contemplating consequences, before High Heaven and in the face of the world, I swear eternal fidelity to the just cause, as I deem it, of the land of my life, my liberty, and my love. And who, that thinks with me, will not fearlessly adopt the oath that I take. Let none falter, who thinks he is right, and we may succeed. But, if after all, we shall fail, be it so. We still shall have the proud consolation of saying to our consciences, and to the departed shade of our country's freedom, that the cause approved of our judgment, and adored of our hearts, in disaster, in chains, in torture, in death, we NEVER faltered in defending. (1.178–179)

13. For an extensive and probing discussion of these themes, see Eva Brann, "A Reading of the Gettysburg Address," in *Abraham Lincoln, the Gettysburg Address, and American Constitutionalism*, ed. Leo Paul S. Alvarez (Dallas: University of Dallas Press, 1976), 21–52.

14. Farewell Address, September 17, 1796, in *A Compilation of the Messages and Papers of the Presidents, 1789–1908,* ed. James D. Richardson, 11 vols. (Washington: Bureau of National Literature and Art, 1909), 1.216.

15. Nicolay and Hay, 8.190.

16. The syntactical alteration is the shift from the conjunctive function of *that* (the truths "*that* all men are created equal . . . that they are endowed by their Creator . . . that among these are . . . ") to its operative function: *so that.* This is indeed what Lincoln tries to do in the substance of the address by giving—and drawing others to give—enduring life to Jefferson's proposition.

17. Edward Everett, *Orations and Speeches on Various Occasions,* vol. 4 (Little, Brown, 1868); Wills's text of Everett's speech in *Lincoln at Gettysburg,* 229 (paragraph 33).

18. Wills's text of Everett's speech in *Lincoln at Gettysburg,* 246 (paragraph 57).

19. For an extensive and probing discussion of this phenomenon, see Glen E. Thurow, *Abraham Lincoln and American Political Religion* (Albany, N.Y.: SUNY Press, 1976), 63–87.

20. Nicolay and Hay, 8.202.

21. The newspaper quotations are from Donald, 465–466.

22. To appreciate the traditional fusion of religion and moral philosophy in the phrase "moral sentiment," it is worth returning to key texts from the Scottish Enlightenment tradition that made the phrase resonate in eighteenth- and nineteenth-century America—for example, the works of Thomas Reid, Adam Smith, and John Witherspoon. The "moral sentiment" tradition, of course, had a significant influence on Thomas Jefferson.

23. See David Donald's account of the 1864 election in *Lincoln,* 528–545.

24. See the manuscript facsimile in Ronald C. White Jr., *Lincoln's Greatest Speech: The Second Inaugural* (New York: Simon and Schuster, 2002), 13–16. White makes a similar argument on p. 88.

25. White, 88–89.

26. My point here is indebted to White's suggestive discussion of *somehow* on his page 90.

27. Michael Leff, "Dimensions of Temporality in Lincoln's Second Inaugural," in *Readings in Rhetorical Criticism,* ed. Carl R. Burgchardt (State College, Pa.: Strata Publishing, 1995), 526–531.

28. Garry Wills, "Lincoln's Greatest Speech?" *Atlantic Monthly* (September 1999), 60–70; Donald, 546–656.

Postscript. The Letter to Mrs. Bixby

1. A spectacular example is Lincoln's letter of August 17, 1863, to the ambitious Shakespearean James H. Hackett, which was turned into a broadside. It came into the hands of Lincoln's political rivals and was printed in the newspapers. (See Basler, 6.392–393.) Lincoln's response to Hackett made a point of assuming the let-

ter had been confidential while conceding that its publication, and the exposure to public censure that followed, did not surprise him: "My note to you I certainly did not expect to see in print; yet I have not been much shocked by the newspaper comments upon it. Those comments constitute a fair specimen of what has occurred to me through life. I have endured a great deal of ridicule without much malice; and have received a great deal of kindness, not quite free from ridicule. I am used to it" (6.558–559).

2. These words were alleged to have been spoken by Tyler Dennet to Edward C. Stone, who quoted them in a letter to William H. Townsend. These and many other archival sources have been assembled and analyzed by Michael Burlingame in the appendix to his edition of John Hay's writings: *At Lincoln's Side: John Hay's Civil War Correspondence and Selected Writings* (Carbondale: Southern Illinois University Press, 2000), 169–184. The two quotations in this passage are from Burlingame, 175–176.

3. Burlingame, 171–172.

4. Burlingame, 174–178.

5. Burlingame, 178.

6. *Richard III* 2.4.72 and *Hamlet* 1.3.107, 4.3.41.

7. Cited in Burlingame, 171.

8. Letter to William H. Herndon, September 5, 1866. Printed in Burlingame, 110.

9. David Donald, *Lincoln* (London: Random House, 1995), 528.

10. Burlingame, 171.

INDEX